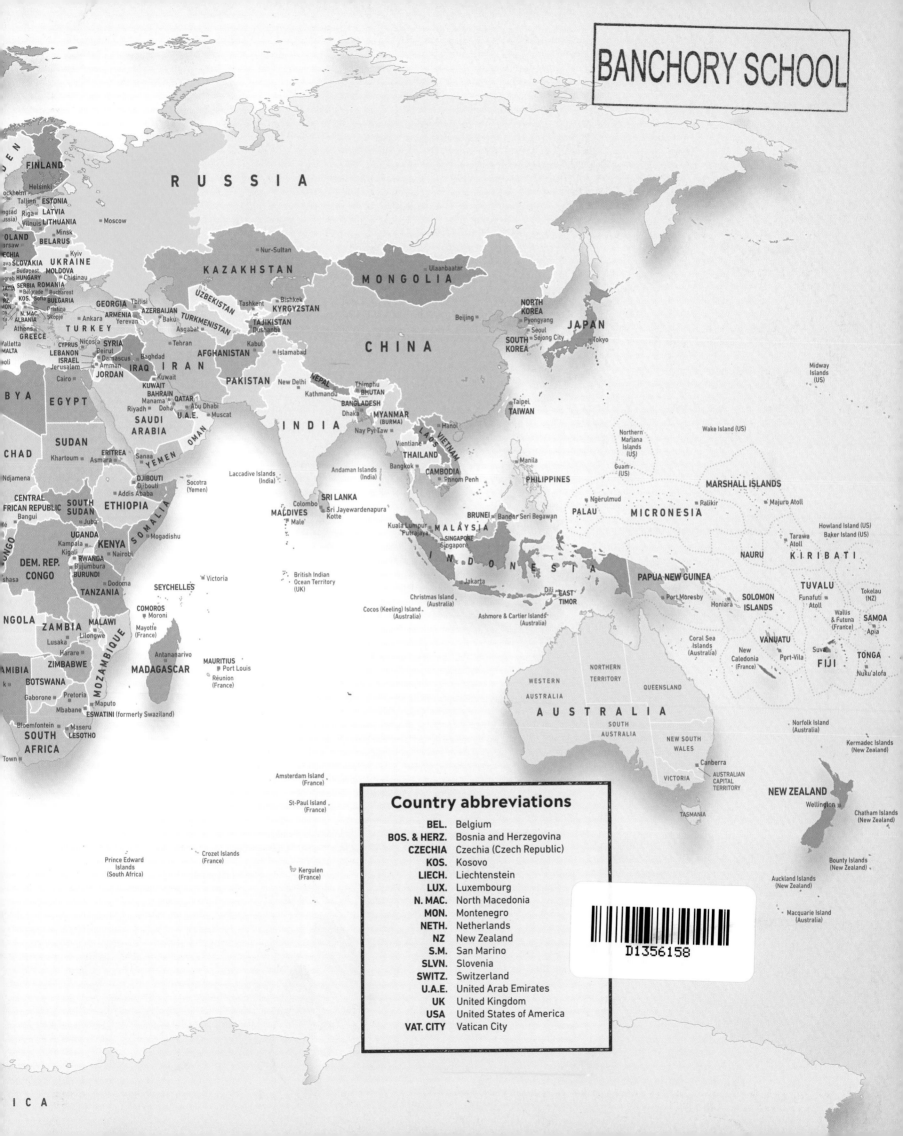

WHAT'S WHERE ON
EARTH

SECOND EDITION
Senior editor Rachel Thompson
Senior art editor Rachael Grady
Senior cartographic editor Simon Mumford
Designers Chrissy Barnard, Kit Lane
Managing editor Francesca Baines
Managing art editor Philip Letsu
Production editor Gillian Reid
Production controller Samantha Cross
Jacket designer Juthi Seth

FIRST EDITION
Senior editor Rob Houston
Senior art editor Philip Letsu
Senior cartographic editor Simon Mumford
Editors Helen Abramson, Steve Setford, Rona Skene
Designers David Ball, Carol Davis, Mik Gates
Researchers Helen Saunders, Suneha Dutta, Kaiya Shang
Cartography Encompass Graphics, Ed Merritt
Illustrators Adam Benton, Stuart Jackson-Carter
Creative retouching Steve Willis

Picture research Taiyaba Khatoon,
Ashwin Adimari, Martin Copeland
Jacket design Laura Brim, Natasha Rees
Jacket design development manager
Sophia M Tampakopoulos Turner
Pre-production producer Rebekah Parsons-King
Production controller Mandy Innes
Publisher Andrew Macintyre
Art director Phil Ormerod
Associate publishing director Liz Wheeler
Publishing director Jonathan Metcalf

This edition published in 2021
First published in Great Britain in 2013
by Dorling Kindersley Limited
DK, One Embassy Gardens, 8 Viaduct Gardens,
London, SW11 7BW

The authorised representative in the EEA is
Dorling Kindersley Verlag GmbH. Arnulfstr. 124,
80636 Munich, Germany

A CIP catalogue record for this book
is available from the British Library.
ISBN: 978-0-2414-9037-2

Printed and bound in the UAE

For the curious
www.dk.com

This book was made with Forest Stewardship Council™
certified paper – one small step in DK's commitment
to a sustainable future.
For more information go to
www.dk.com/our-green-pledge

CONTENTS

Land, sea, and air

Living world

People and planet

Engineering and technology

History

Culture

Land, sea, and air

Skeleton Coast, Namibia
The Atlantic Ocean meets the edge of Africa's Namib Desert at the Skeleton Coast. Rainfall here rarely exceeds 10 mm (0.39 in) per year.

Introduction

Earth is a planet in motion, spinning on its axis as it hurtles through space around the Sun. Warmed by the Sun's rays, Earth's atmosphere and oceans are always on the move, while heat from the planet's core keeps the hot rock of the interior constantly churning. All this enables Earth's surface to teem with life.

Churning interior

The rocks in the mantle flow in currents that rise, flow sideways, cool, and then sink. These currents can force the plates of Earth's crust apart or pull sections of the crust back down into the mantle.

Ocean floor splits, while mantle rock rises and creates new crust in the gap

Continent is dragged along by the mantle moving beneath

Mantle moves in slow circles, driven by the core's heat below

Crust is destroyed as it is dragged into the mantle by the sinking current

Water cycle

The Sun's heat evaporates sea water, causing it to become water vapour in the air. As it rises and cools, the water vapour condenses into clouds of droplets or ice crystals. As the droplets or crystals grow, they fall as snow or rain. If it falls on land, some runs off the surface to form rivers and lakes, which return water to the oceans. A lot of rain seeps through gaps in the soil and rock. It is called groundwater, and it may stay underground or trickle to the sea. This continuous circulation of water is known as the water cycle.

Earth's structure

If we could take a slice out of Earth, we would see that the planet is made up of layers. At its heart lies a solid inner core, surrounded by a liquid outer core. Both are made mainly of heavy iron. The outer core is enclosed by a deep layer of heavy, very hot, yet solid rock called the mantle. Heat from the core drives currents rising through the mantle that keep the rock moving extremely slowly. The crust – the mantle's cool, hard shell – is made up of a number of rocky plates.

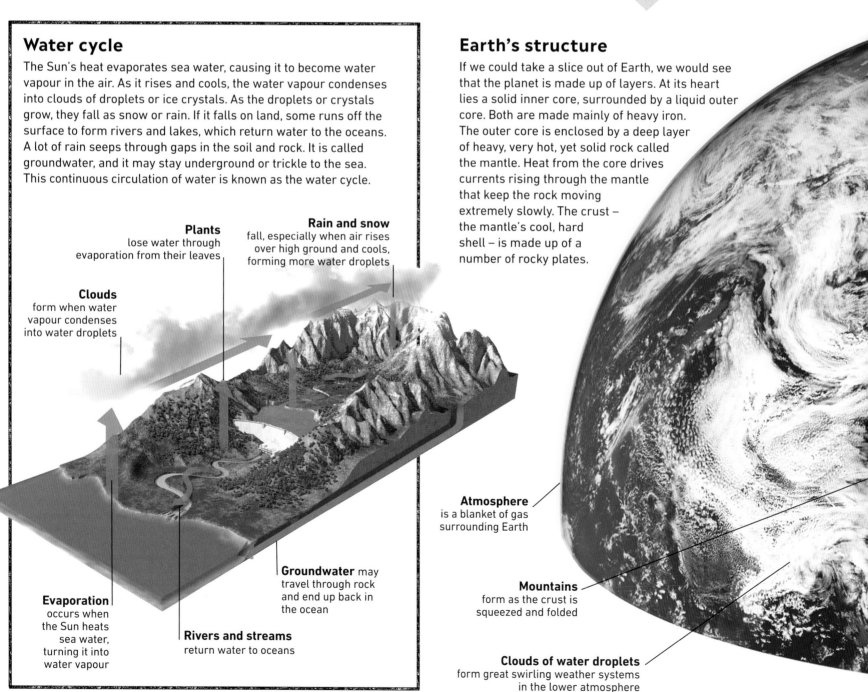

Plants lose water through evaporation from their leaves

Rain and snow fall, especially when air rises over high ground and cools, forming more water droplets

Clouds form when water vapour condenses into water droplets

Evaporation occurs when the Sun heats sea water, turning it into water vapour

Rivers and streams return water to oceans

Groundwater may travel through rock and end up back in the ocean

Atmosphere is a blanket of gas surrounding Earth

Mountains form as the crust is squeezed and folded

Clouds of water droplets form great swirling weather systems in the lower atmosphere

AN AVERAGE WATER MOLECULE SPENDS ABOUT 3,200 YEARS IN THE

The Sun's energy

In the Tropics, near the equator, the Sun's rays strike Earth at a steep angle, so the energy is very concentrated. But near the poles, sunlight hits the surface at a narrow angle. This spreads the Sun's energy, giving a weak heating effect. The result is that polar regions are much colder than tropical zones, allowing ice to form in the Arctic and Antarctic. The difference in the solar heating at different latitudes sets bodies of air and sea water in motion, driving winds and ocean currents.

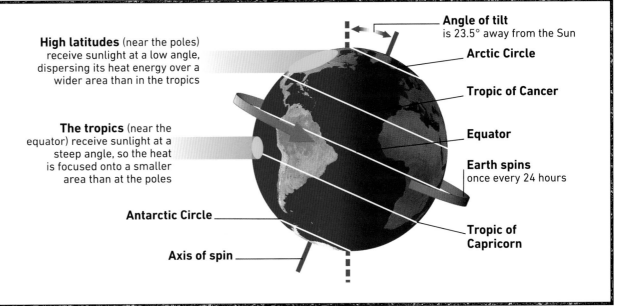

High latitudes (near the poles) receive sunlight at a low angle, dispersing its heat energy over a wider area than in the tropics

The tropics (near the equator) receive sunlight at a steep angle, so the heat is focused onto a smaller area than at the poles

Antarctic Circle

Axis of spin

Angle of tilt is 23.5° away from the Sun

Arctic Circle

Tropic of Cancer

Equator

Earth spins once every 24 hours

Tropic of Capricorn

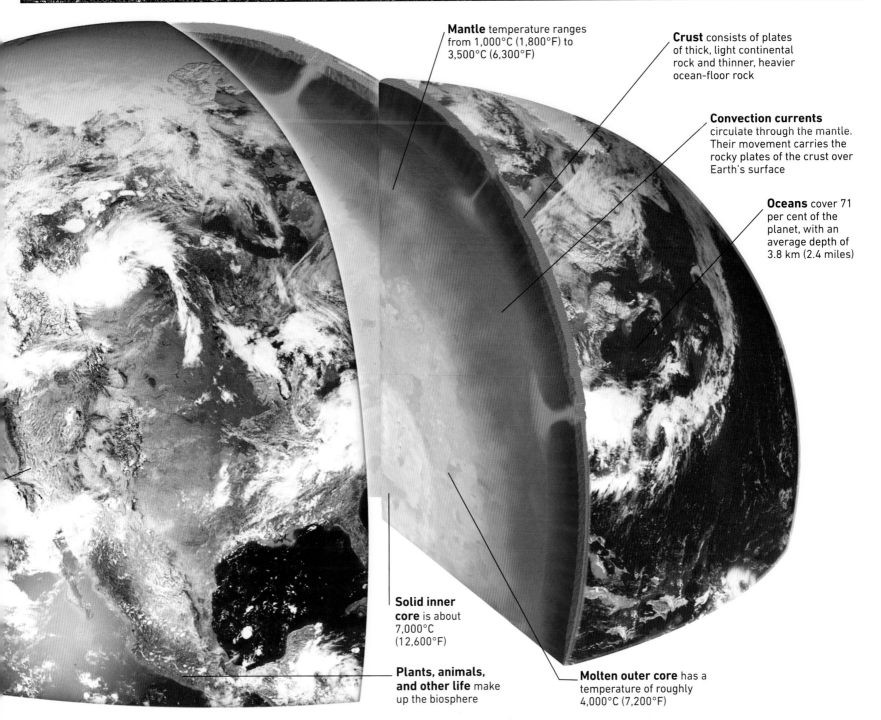

Mantle temperature ranges from 1,000°C (1,800°F) to 3,500°C (6,300°F)

Crust consists of plates of thick, light continental rock and thinner, heavier ocean-floor rock

Convection currents circulate through the mantle. Their movement carries the rocky plates of the crust over Earth's surface

Oceans cover 71 per cent of the planet, with an average depth of 3.8 km (2.4 miles)

Solid inner core is about 7,000°C (12,600°F)

Plants, animals, and other life make up the biosphere

Molten outer core has a temperature of roughly 4,000°C (7,200°F)

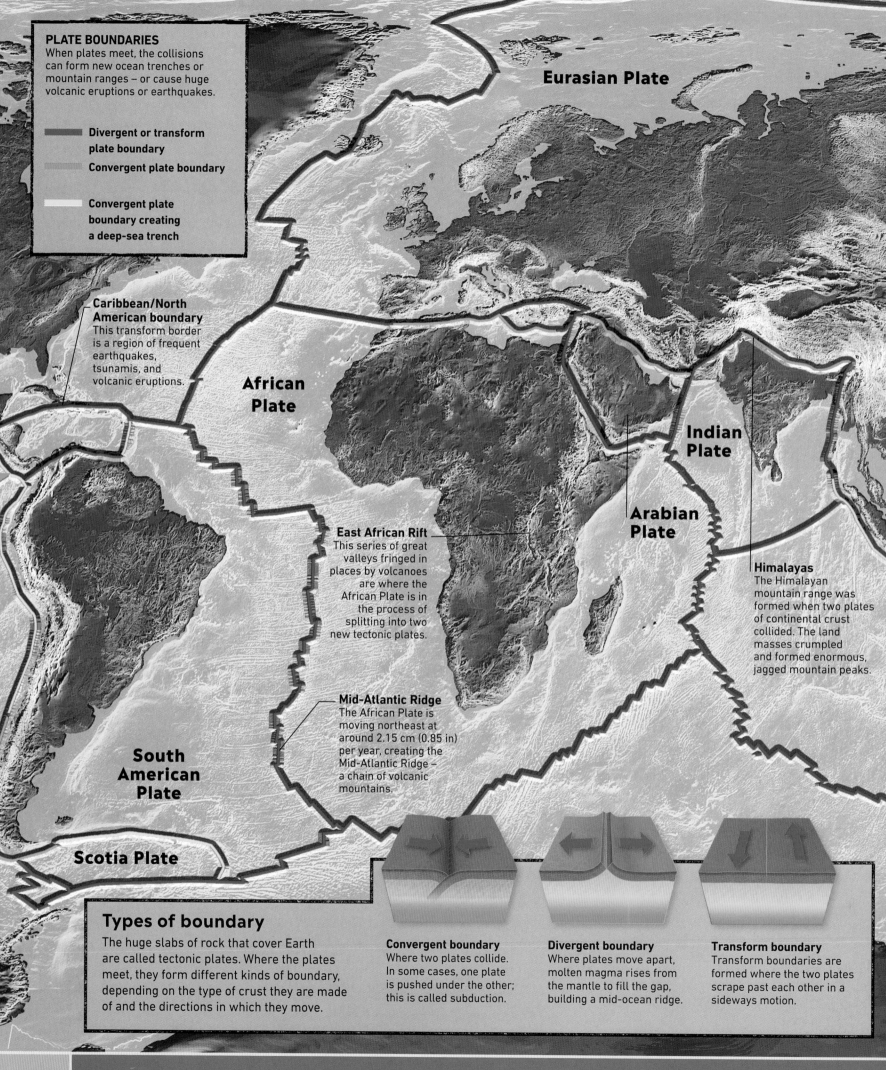

Eurasian Plate

Caribbean/North American boundary
This transform border is a region of frequent earthquakes, tsunamis, and volcanic eruptions.

African Plate

Indian Plate

Arabian Plate

East African Rift
This series of great valleys fringed in places by volcanoes are where the African Plate is in the process of splitting into two new tectonic plates.

Himalayas
The Himalayan mountain range was formed when two plates of continental crust collided. The land masses crumpled and formed enormous, jagged mountain peaks.

Mid-Atlantic Ridge
The African Plate is moving northeast at around 2.15 cm (0.85 in) per year, creating the Mid-Atlantic Ridge – a chain of volcanic mountains.

South American Plate

Scotia Plate

Types of boundary

The huge slabs of rock that cover Earth are called tectonic plates. Where the plates meet, they form different kinds of boundary, depending on the type of crust they are made of and the directions in which they move.

Convergent boundary
Where two plates collide. In some cases, one plate is pushed under the other; this is called subduction.

Divergent boundary
Where plates move apart, molten magma rises from the mantle to fill the gap, building a mid-ocean ridge.

Transform boundary
Transform boundaries are formed where the two plates scrape past each other in a sideways motion.

RELATIVE TO ITS SIZE, THE EARTH'S CRUST IS THINNER THAN THE

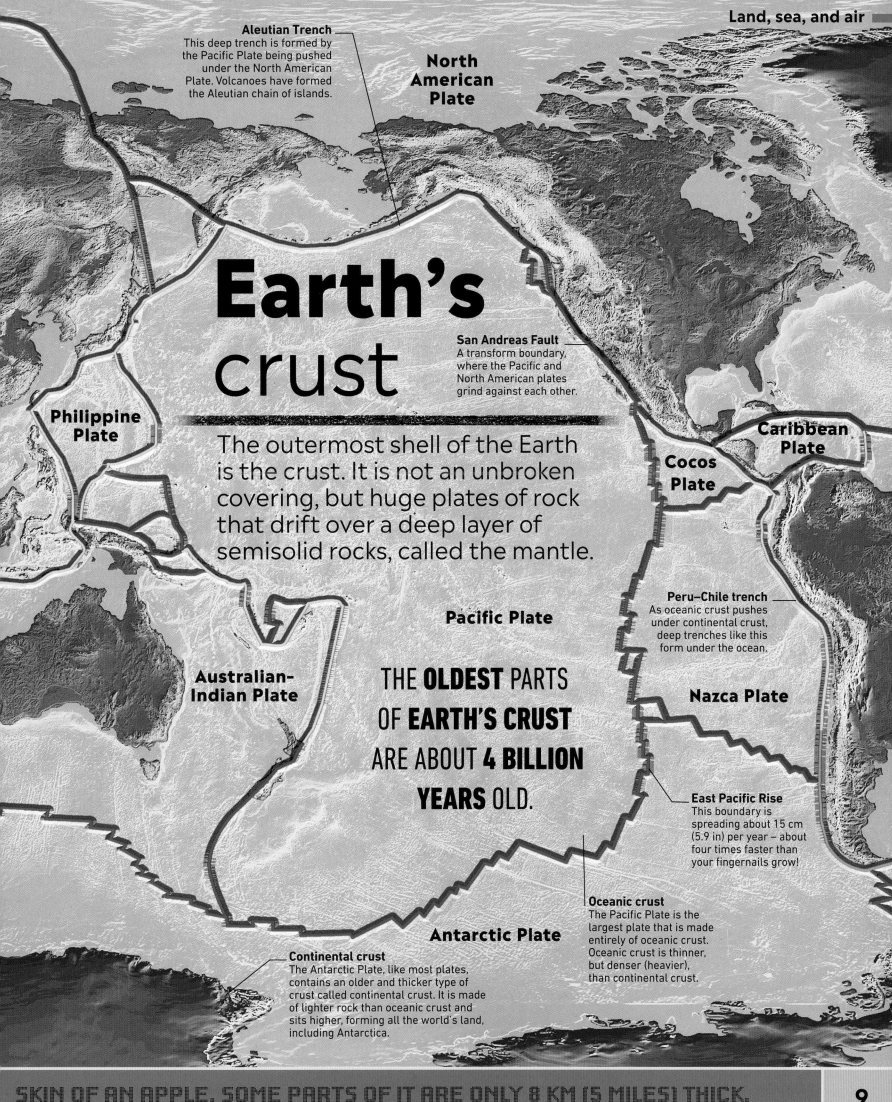

Aleutian Trench
This deep trench is formed by the Pacific Plate being pushed under the North American Plate. Volcanoes have formed the Aleutian chain of islands.

North American Plate

Earth's crust

San Andreas Fault
A transform boundary, where the Pacific and North American plates grind against each other.

Philippine Plate

Caribbean Plate

Cocos Plate

The outermost shell of the Earth is the crust. It is not an unbroken covering, but huge plates of rock that drift over a deep layer of semisolid rocks, called the mantle.

Peru–Chile trench
As oceanic crust pushes under continental crust, deep trenches like this form under the ocean.

Pacific Plate

Australian-Indian Plate

Nazca Plate

THE **OLDEST** PARTS OF **EARTH'S CRUST** ARE ABOUT **4 BILLION YEARS** OLD.

East Pacific Rise
This boundary is spreading about 15 cm (5.9 in) per year – about four times faster than your fingernails grow!

Oceanic crust
The Pacific Plate is the largest plate that is made entirely of oceanic crust. Oceanic crust is thinner, but denser (heavier), than continental crust.

Antarctic Plate

Continental crust
The Antarctic Plate, like most plates, contains an older and thicker type of crust called continental crust. It is made of lighter rock than oceanic crust and sits higher, forming all the world's land, including Antarctica.

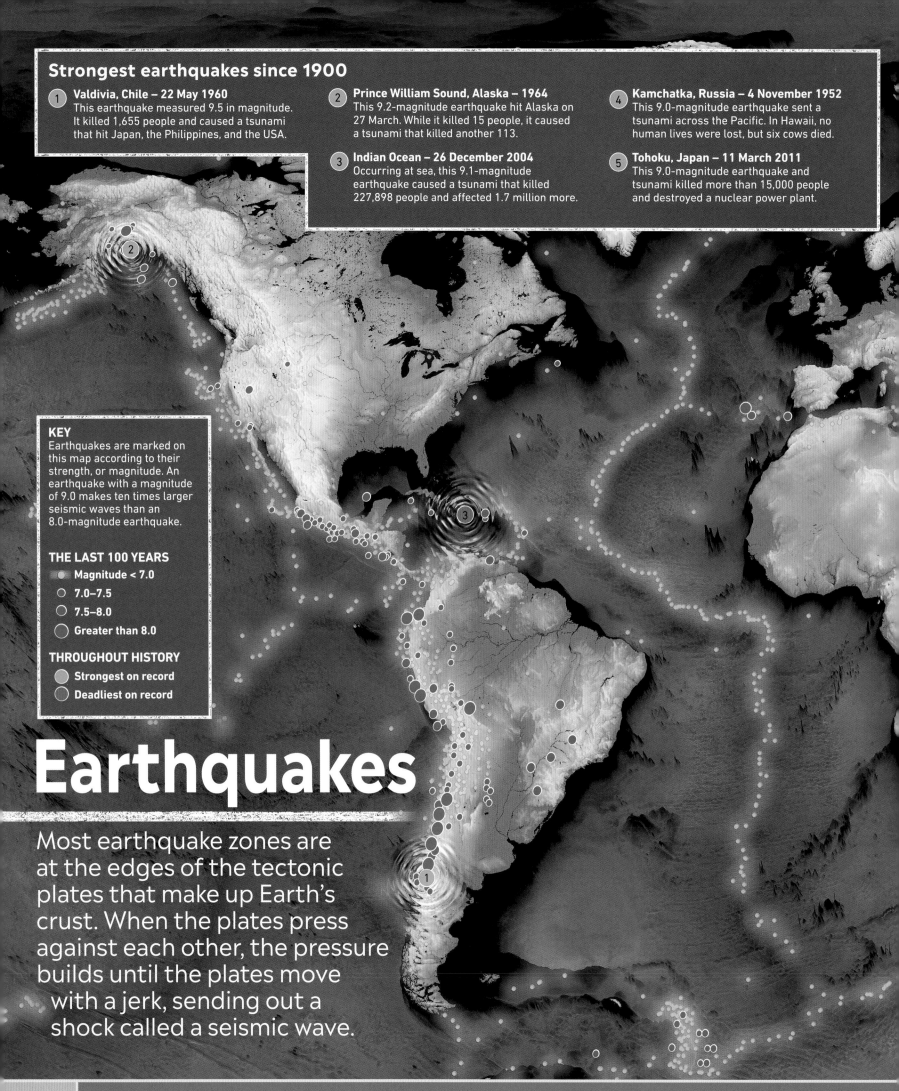

① **Valdivia, Chile – 22 May 1960**
This earthquake measured 9.5 in magnitude. It killed 1,655 people and caused a tsunami that hit Japan, the Philippines, and the USA.

② **Prince William Sound, Alaska – 1964**
This 9.2-magnitude earthquake hit Alaska on 27 March. While it killed 15 people, it caused a tsunami that killed another 113.

④ **Kamchatka, Russia – 4 November 1952**
This 9.0-magnitude earthquake sent a tsunami across the Pacific. In Hawaii, no human lives were lost, but six cows died.

③ **Indian Ocean – 26 December 2004**
Occurring at sea, this 9.1-magnitude earthquake caused a tsunami that killed 227,898 people and affected 1.7 million more.

⑤ **Tohoku, Japan – 11 March 2011**
This 9.0-magnitude earthquake and tsunami killed more than 15,000 people and destroyed a nuclear power plant.

KEY
Earthquakes are marked on this map according to their strength, or magnitude. An earthquake with a magnitude of 9.0 makes ten times larger seismic waves than an 8.0-magnitude earthquake.

THE LAST 100 YEARS
○ Magnitude < 7.0
○ 7.0–7.5
○ 7.5–8.0
○ Greater than 8.0

THROUGHOUT HISTORY
○ Strongest on record
○ Deadliest on record

Earthquakes

Most earthquake zones are at the edges of the tectonic plates that make up Earth's crust. When the plates press against each other, the pressure builds until the plates move with a jerk, sending out a shock called a seismic wave.

THE ASTEROID IMPACT THAT WIPED OUT THE DINOSAURS 65 MILLION YEARS

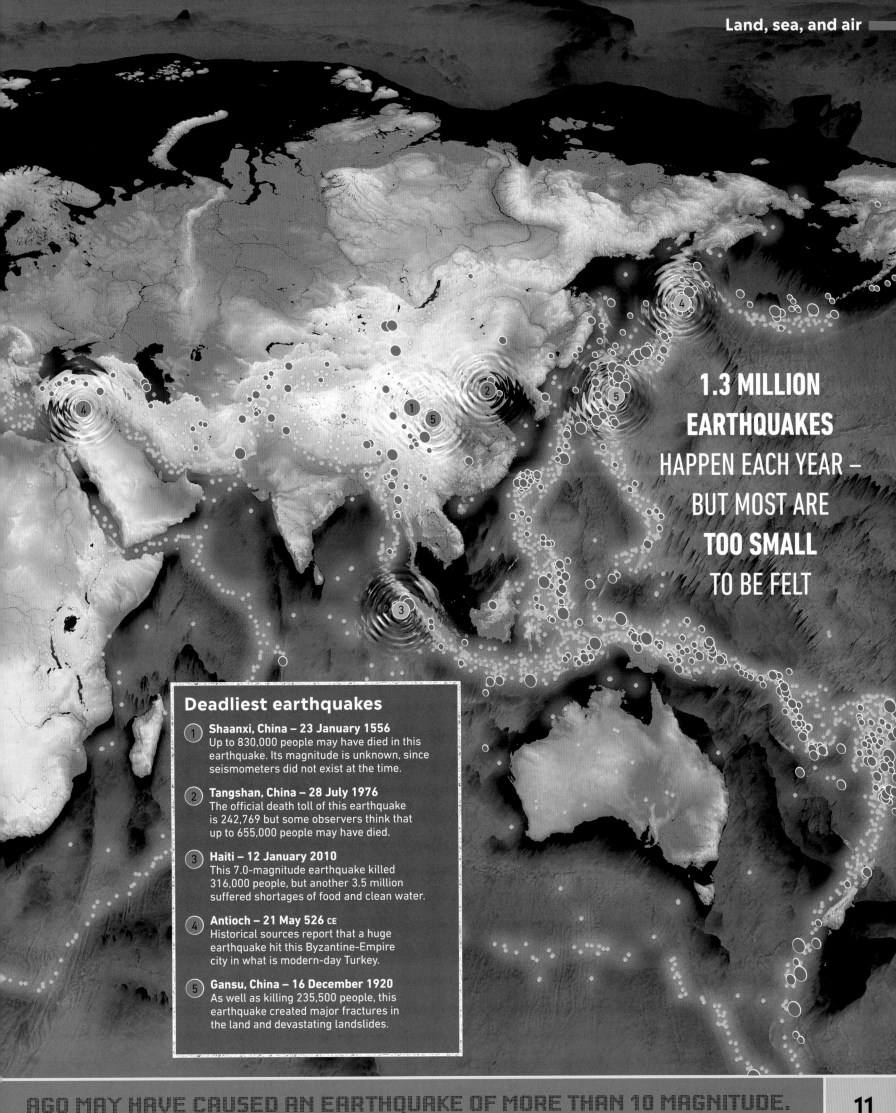

1.3 MILLION EARTHQUAKES HAPPEN EACH YEAR – BUT MOST ARE **TOO SMALL** TO BE FELT

Deadliest earthquakes

1. **Shaanxi, China – 23 January 1556**
Up to 830,000 people may have died in this earthquake. Its magnitude is unknown, since seismometers did not exist at the time.

2. **Tangshan, China – 28 July 1976**
The official death toll of this earthquake is 242,769 but some observers think that up to 655,000 people may have died.

3. **Haiti – 12 January 2010**
This 7.0-magnitude earthquake killed 316,000 people, but another 3.5 million suffered shortages of food and clean water.

4. **Antioch – 21 May 526 CE**
Historical sources report that a huge earthquake hit this Byzantine-Empire city in what is modern-day Turkey.

5. **Gansu, China – 16 December 1920**
As well as killing 235,500 people, this earthquake created major fractures in the land and devastating landslides.

AGO MAY HAVE CAUSED AN EARTHQUAKE OF MORE THAN 10 MAGNITUDE.

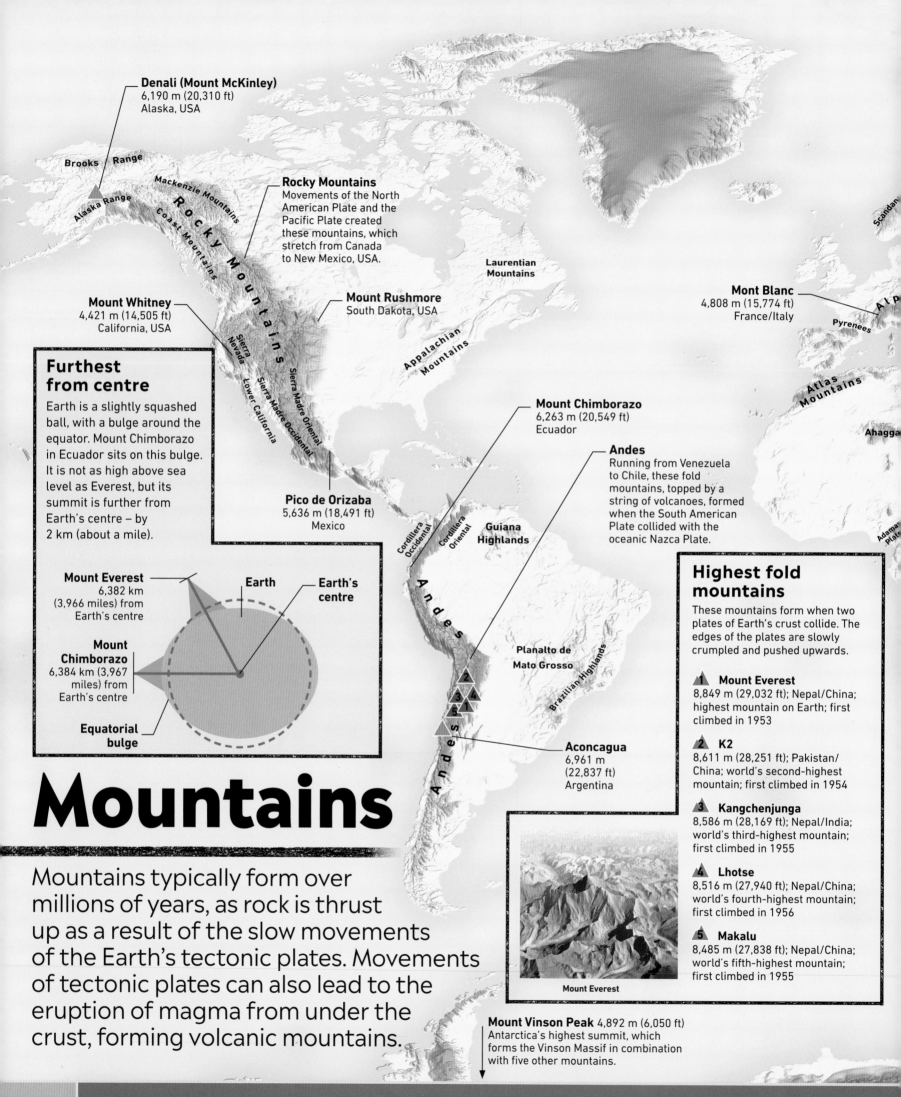

Denali (Mount McKinley)
6,190 m (20,310 ft)
Alaska, USA

Brooks Range

Mackenzie Mountains

Alaska Range

Coast Mountains

Rocky Mountains

Rocky Mountains
Movements of the North
American Plate and the
Pacific Plate created
these mountains, which
stretch from Canada
to New Mexico, USA.

Mount Whitney
4,421 m (14,505 ft)
California, USA

Sierra Nevada

Lower California

Sierra Madre Occidental

Sierra Madre Oriental

Mount Rushmore
South Dakota, USA

Appalachian Mountains

Laurentian Mountains

Mont Blanc
4,808 m (15,774 ft)
France/Italy

Alp[s]

Pyrenees

Atlas Mountains

Ahagga[r]

Adama[n] Plate

Mount Chimborazo
6,263 m (20,549 ft)
Ecuador

Andes
Running from Venezuela
to Chile, these fold
mountains, topped by a
string of volcanoes, formed
when the South American
Plate collided with the
oceanic Nazca Plate.

Pico de Orizaba
5,636 m (18,491 ft)
Mexico

Cordillera Occidental

Cordillera Oriental

Guiana Highlands

Andes

Planalto de Mato Grosso

Brazilian Highlands

Aconcagua
6,961 m
(22,837 ft)
Argentina

Furthest from centre

Earth is a slightly squashed
ball, with a bulge around the
equator. Mount Chimborazo
in Ecuador sits on this bulge.
It is not as high above sea
level as Everest, but its
summit is further from
Earth's centre – by
2 km (about a mile).

Mount Everest
6,382 km
(3,966 miles) from
Earth's centre

Earth

Earth's centre

Mount Chimborazo
6,384 km (3,967
miles) from
Earth's centre

Equatorial bulge

Mountains

Mountains typically form over
millions of years, as rock is thrust
up as a result of the slow movements
of the Earth's tectonic plates. Movements
of tectonic plates can also lead to the
eruption of magma from under the
crust, forming volcanic mountains.

Highest fold mountains

These mountains form when two
plates of Earth's crust collide. The
edges of the plates are slowly
crumpled and pushed upwards.

1 Mount Everest
8,849 m (29,032 ft); Nepal/China;
highest mountain on Earth; first
climbed in 1953

2 K2
8,611 m (28,251 ft); Pakistan/
China; world's second-highest
mountain; first climbed in 1954

3 Kangchenjunga
8,586 m (28,169 ft); Nepal/India;
world's third-highest mountain;
first climbed in 1955

4 Lhotse
8,516 m (27,940 ft); Nepal/China;
world's fourth-highest mountain;
first climbed in 1956

5 Makalu
8,485 m (27,838 ft); Nepal/China;
world's fifth-highest mountain;
first climbed in 1955

Mount Everest

Mount Vinson Peak 4,892 m (6,050 ft)
Antarctica's highest summit, which
forms the Vinson Massif in combination
with five other mountains.

THE TALLEST KNOWN MOUNTAIN ANYWHERE IS OLYMPUS MONS,

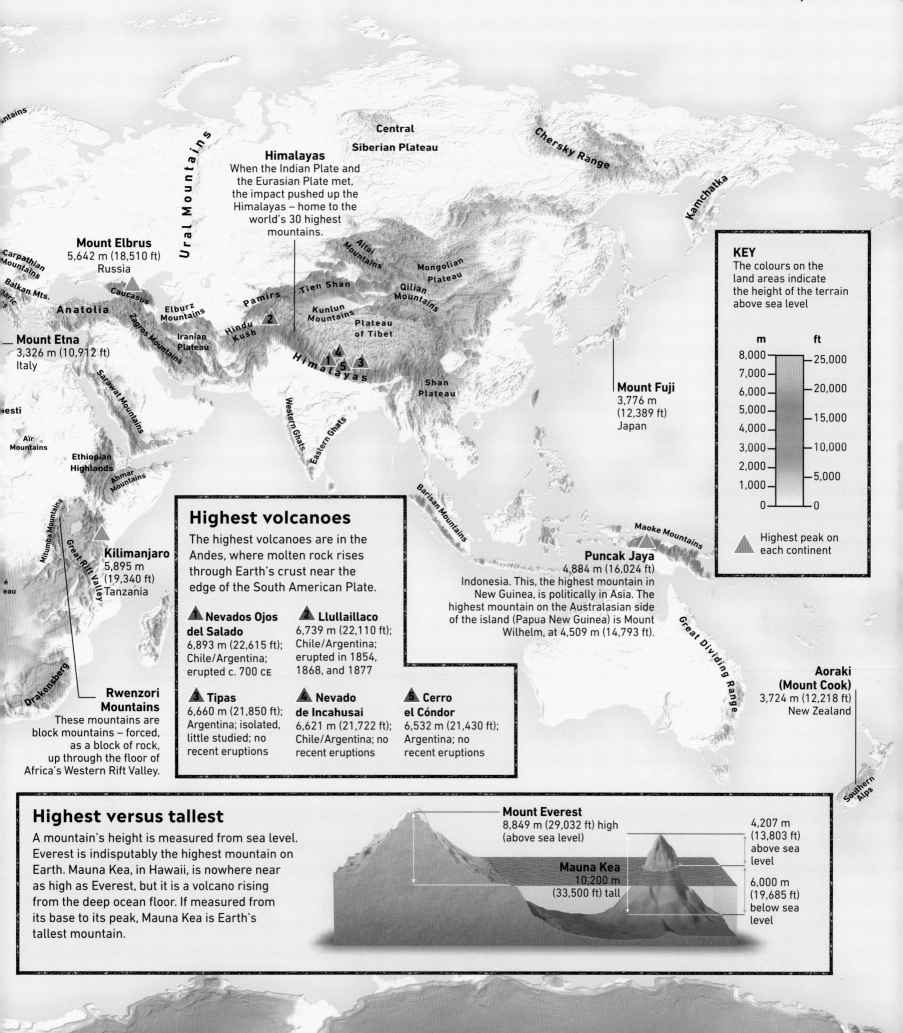

Central
Siberian Plateau

Chersky Range

Kamchatka

Ural Mountains

Himalayas
When the Indian Plate and the Eurasian Plate met, the impact pushed up the Himalayas – home to the world's 30 highest mountains.

Mount Elbrus
5,642 m (18,510 ft)
Russia

Carpathian Mountains

Balkan Mts.

Caucasus

Anatolia

Elburz Mountains

Zagros Mountains

Iranian Plateau

Hindu Kush

Pamirs

Tien Shan

Kunlun Mountains

Altai Mountains

Mongolian Plateau

Qilian Mountains

Plateau of Tibet

Mount Etna
3,326 m (10,912 ft)
Italy

Sarawat Mountains

2

4
1 5 3

Himalayas

Shan Plateau

Western Ghats

Eastern Ghats

Mount Fuji
3,776 m
(12,389 ft)
Japan

Aïr Mountains

Ethiopian Highlands

Ahmar Mountains

Mitumba Mountains

Great Rift Valley

Kilimanjaro
5,895 m
(19,340 ft)
Tanzania

Barisan Mountains

Maoke Mountains

Puncak Jaya
4,884 m (16,024 ft)
Indonesia. This, the highest mountain in New Guinea, is politically in Asia. The highest mountain on the Australasian side of the island (Papua New Guinea) is Mount Wilhelm, at 4,509 m (14,793 ft).

Drakensberg

Rwenzori Mountains
These mountains are block mountains – forced, as a block of rock, up through the floor of Africa's Western Rift Valley.

KEY
The colours on the land areas indicate the height of the terrain above sea level

m	ft
8,000	25,000
7,000	
6,000	20,000
5,000	15,000
4,000	
3,000	10,000
2,000	
1,000	5,000
0	0

▲ Highest peak on each continent

Great Dividing Range

Aoraki (Mount Cook)
3,724 m (12,218 ft)
New Zealand

Southern Alps

Highest volcanoes

The highest volcanoes are in the Andes, where molten rock rises through Earth's crust near the edge of the South American Plate.

1 Nevados Ojos del Salado
6,893 m (22,615 ft);
Chile/Argentina;
erupted c. 700 CE

2 Llullaillaco
6,739 m (22,110 ft);
Chile/Argentina;
erupted in 1854, 1868, and 1877

3 Tipas
6,660 m (21,850 ft);
Argentina; isolated, little studied; no recent eruptions

4 Nevado de Incahusai
6,621 m (21,722 ft);
Chile/Argentina; no recent eruptions

5 Cerro el Cóndor
6,532 m (21,430 ft);
Argentina; no recent eruptions

Highest versus tallest

A mountain's height is measured from sea level. Everest is indisputably the highest mountain on Earth. Mauna Kea, in Hawaii, is nowhere near as high as Everest, but it is a volcano rising from the deep ocean floor. If measured from its base to its peak, Mauna Kea is Earth's tallest mountain.

Mount Everest
8,849 m (29,032 ft) high
(above sea level)

Mauna Kea
10,200 m
(33,500 ft) tall

4,207 m (13,803 ft) above sea level

6,000 m (19,685 ft) below sea level

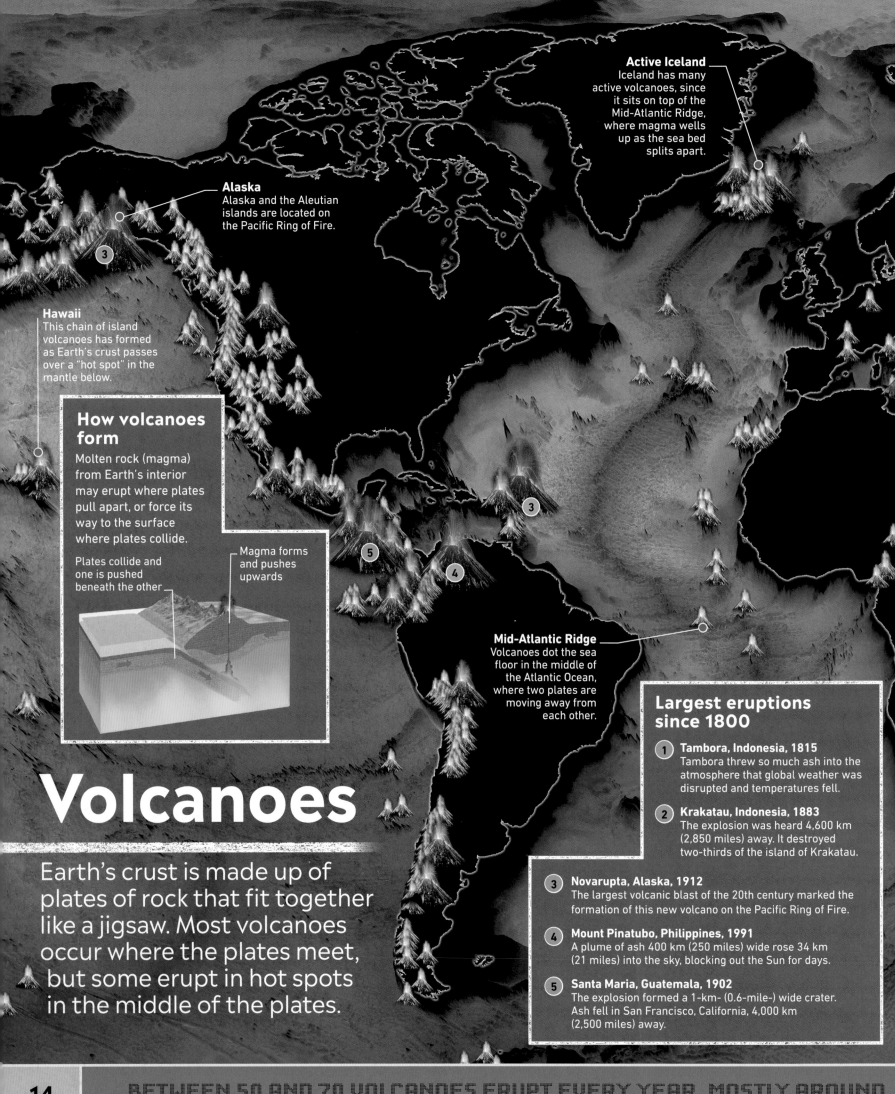

Active Iceland
Iceland has many active volcanoes, since it sits on top of the Mid-Atlantic Ridge, where magma wells up as the sea bed splits apart.

Alaska
Alaska and the Aleutian islands are located on the Pacific Ring of Fire.

Hawaii
This chain of island volcanoes has formed as Earth's crust passes over a "hot spot" in the mantle below.

How volcanoes form

Molten rock (magma) from Earth's interior may erupt where plates pull apart, or force its way to the surface where plates collide.

Plates collide and one is pushed beneath the other

Magma forms and pushes upwards

Mid-Atlantic Ridge
Volcanoes dot the sea floor in the middle of the Atlantic Ocean, where two plates are moving away from each other.

Volcanoes

Earth's crust is made up of plates of rock that fit together like a jigsaw. Most volcanoes occur where the plates meet, but some erupt in hot spots in the middle of the plates.

Largest eruptions since 1800

1 Tambora, Indonesia, 1815
Tambora threw so much ash into the atmosphere that global weather was disrupted and temperatures fell.

2 Krakatau, Indonesia, 1883
The explosion was heard 4,600 km (2,850 miles) away. It destroyed two-thirds of the island of Krakatau.

3 Novarupta, Alaska, 1912
The largest volcanic blast of the 20th century marked the formation of this new volcano on the Pacific Ring of Fire.

4 Mount Pinatubo, Philippines, 1991
A plume of ash 400 km (250 miles) wide rose 34 km (21 miles) into the sky, blocking out the Sun for days.

5 Santa Maria, Guatemala, 1902
The explosion formed a 1-km- (0.6-mile-) wide crater. Ash fell in San Francisco, California, 4,000 km (2,500 miles) away.

KEY
The map shows volcanoes above sea level. Many more volcanoes erupt on the sea bed.

Most lethal

Largest since 1800

Recent volcano active since 2006

Other volcanoes, either single or in a cluster of up to six

Japan
Part of the Pacific Ring of Fire, Japan has more than 70 active volcanoes.

Europe
There are few volcanoes in Europe, which is on the Eurasian Plate.

East African Rift
Volcanoes occur here because the African Plate is slowly splitting in two.

Pacific Ring of Fire
Volcanoes are common along the edges of the plates forming the floor of the Pacific Ocean.

Inactive Australia
Australia lies in the middle of a plate and has no active volcanoes.

THERE ARE AROUND **1,500** KNOWN **ACTIVE VOLCANOES** ON EARTH

Most lethal volcanoes

1 Mount Tambora, Indonesia, 1815
Falling volcanic ash destroyed plants and crops leading to famine. More than 71,000 Indonesians died, the majority from starvation.

2 Krakatau, Indonesia, 1883
The official death toll was 36,417, most of whom died when tsunamis (tidal waves) created by the explosion swept through the region.

3 Mont Pelée, Martinique, 1902
A rapidly moving cloud of glowing gas, ash, and

dust engulfed the town of St Pierre on the Caribbean island of Martinique, killing all but two of its inhabitants. In all, nearly 30,000 people lost their lives.

4 Nevado Del Ruiz, Colombia, 1985
The eruption melted snow and ice on the volcano, creating mudflows that killed around 25,000 people in surrounding valleys.

5 Mount Unzen, Japan, 1792
Some 14,300 people died when, about a month after lava stopped erupting, part of the volcano collapsed in a landslide, triggering a tsunami.

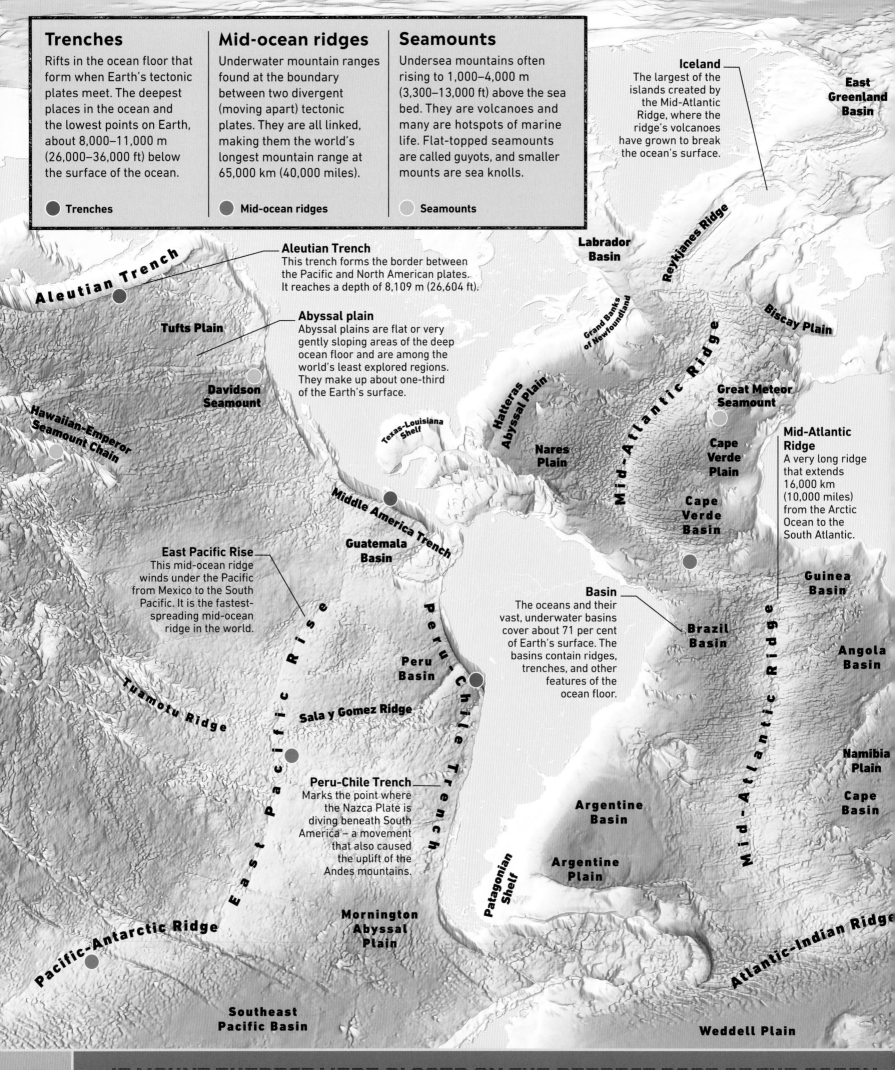

Trenches

Rifts in the ocean floor that form when Earth's tectonic plates meet. The deepest places in the ocean and the lowest points on Earth, about 8,000–11,000 m (26,000–36,000 ft) below the surface of the ocean.

● Trenches

Mid-ocean ridges

Underwater mountain ranges found at the boundary between two divergent (moving apart) tectonic plates. They are all linked, making them the world's longest mountain range at 65,000 km (40,000 miles).

● Mid-ocean ridges

Seamounts

Undersea mountains often rising to 1,000–4,000 m (3,300–13,000 ft) above the sea bed. They are volcanoes and many are hotspots of marine life. Flat-topped seamounts are called guyots, and smaller mounts are sea knolls.

● Seamounts

Iceland
The largest of the islands created by the Mid-Atlantic Ridge, where the ridge's volcanoes have grown to break the ocean's surface.

East Greenland Basin

Aleutian Trench

Aleutian Trench
This trench forms the border between the Pacific and North American plates. It reaches a depth of 8,109 m (26,604 ft).

Tufts Plain

Abyssal plain
Abyssal plains are flat or very gently sloping areas of the deep ocean floor and are among the world's least explored regions. They make up about one-third of the Earth's surface.

Labrador Basin

Reykjanes Ridge

Biscay Plain

Grand Banks of Newfoundland

Davidson Seamount

Hawaiian-Emperor Seamount Chain

Hatteras Abyssal Plain

Texas-Louisiana Shelf

Nares Plain

Great Meteor Seamount

Mid-Atlantic Ridge

Cape Verde Plain

Middle America Trench

Cape Verde Basin

Mid-Atlantic Ridge
A very long ridge that extends 16,000 km (10,000 miles) from the Arctic Ocean to the South Atlantic.

Guatemala Basin

East Pacific Rise
This mid-ocean ridge winds under the Pacific from Mexico to the South Pacific. It is the fastest-spreading mid-ocean ridge in the world.

Basin
The oceans and their vast, underwater basins cover about 71 per cent of Earth's surface. The basins contain ridges, trenches, and other features of the ocean floor.

Guinea Basin

Peru Basin

Brazil Basin

Angola Basin

East Pacific Rise

Peru-Chile Trench

Tuamotu Ridge

Sala y Gomez Ridge

Namibia Plain

Peru-Chile Trench
Marks the point where the Nazca Plate is diving beneath South America – a movement that also caused the uplift of the Andes mountains.

Cape Basin

Argentine Basin

Argentine Plain

Patagonian Shelf

Mornington Abyssal Plain

Pacific-Antarctic Ridge

Mid-Atlantic Ridge

Atlantic-Indian Ridge

Southeast Pacific Basin

Weddell Plain

IF MOUNT EVEREST WERE PLACED ON THE DEEPEST PART OF THE OCEAN

Fram Basin

G a k k e l   R i d g e

Nansen Basin

Continental shelf
A continental shelf is the edge of a
land mass that lies under the ocean.
It slopes gently from the shore
towards the continental slope,
where the deep ocean truly begins.

Kara Shelf

Mendelev Ridge

Canada
Basin

Barents
Shelf

Laptev Shelf

East Siberian
Shelf

Chukchi
Shelf

Ocean floor

The enormous mountain ranges, vast plains,
and deep trenches of the ocean floor were
created by the constant shifting and
colliding of the plates that make
up Earth's crust.

Aleutian
Basin

Kuril Trench

Northwest
Pacific
Basin

Emperor Seamounts
A chain of undersea
volcanoes stretching from
the seamounts at the end
of the Hawaiian chain all the
way to the Aleutian Islands.

Great
Yangtze
Bank

Makarov
Seamount

Mid-Pacific Seamounts

Hawaiian Ridge

Philippine
Basin

Arabian
Basin

Mariana
Trench

Central
Pacific
Basin

Somali
Basin

Mid-Indian Ridge

Ninetyeast Ridge

Mid-Indian
Basin

Muirfield
Seamount

Christmas
Island
Seamounts

Arafura Shelf

Mariana Trench
The deepest part of the
world's oceans. Its lowest
point, the Challenger
Deep valley, is 10,994 m
(36,070 ft) below the surface.

Tonga Trench

Southwest Indian Ridge

Crozet
Basin

S o u t h e a s t   I n d i a n   R i d g e

Kerguelen Plateau

Campbell
Plateau

Enderby Plain

South
Indian Basin

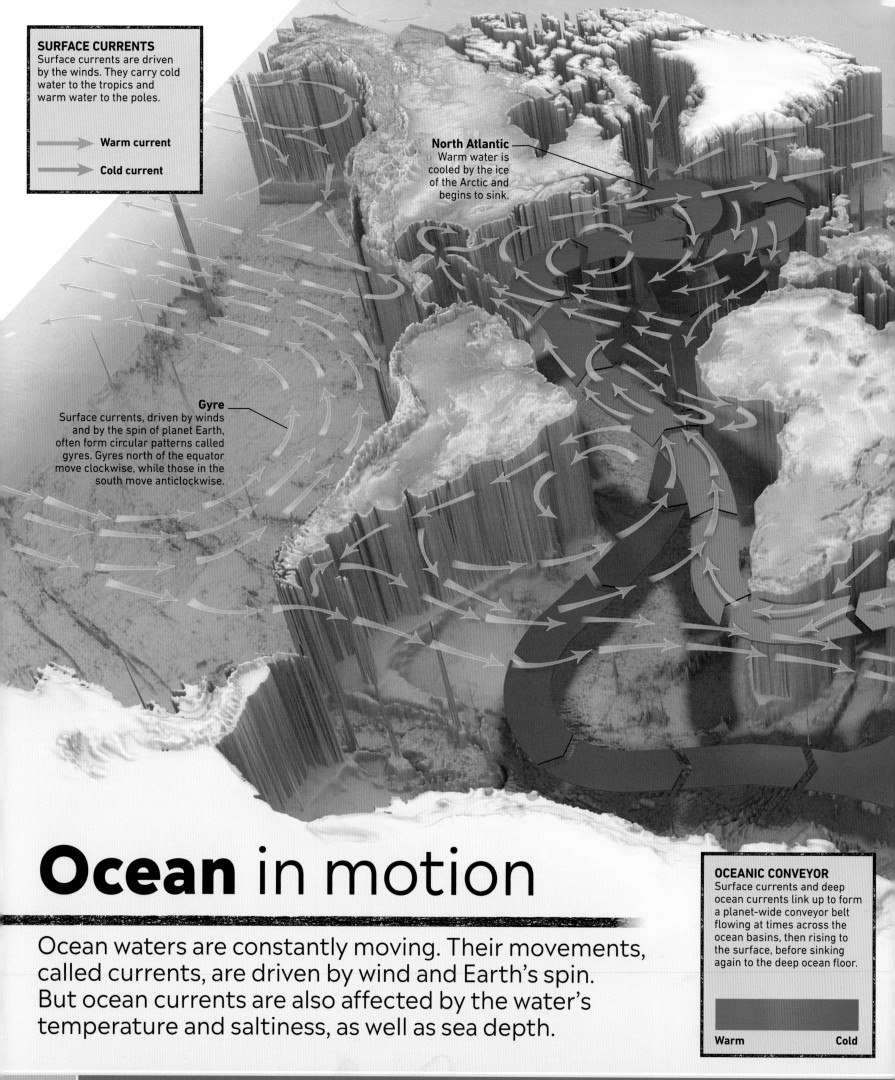

SURFACE CURRENTS
Surface currents are driven by the winds. They carry cold water to the tropics and warm water to the poles.

→ **Warm current**

→ **Cold current**

North Atlantic
Warm water is cooled by the ice of the Arctic and begins to sink.

Gyre
Surface currents, driven by winds and by the spin of planet Earth, often form circular patterns called gyres. Gyres north of the equator move clockwise, while those in the south move anticlockwise.

Ocean in motion

Ocean waters are constantly moving. Their movements, called currents, are driven by wind and Earth's spin. But ocean currents are also affected by the water's temperature and saltiness, as well as sea depth.

OCEANIC CONVEYOR
Surface currents and deep ocean currents link up to form a planet-wide conveyor belt flowing at times across the ocean basins, then rising to the surface, before sinking again to the deep ocean floor.

Warm ———— Cold

IT CAN TAKE UP TO 1,000 YEARS FOR OCEAN CURRENTS TO

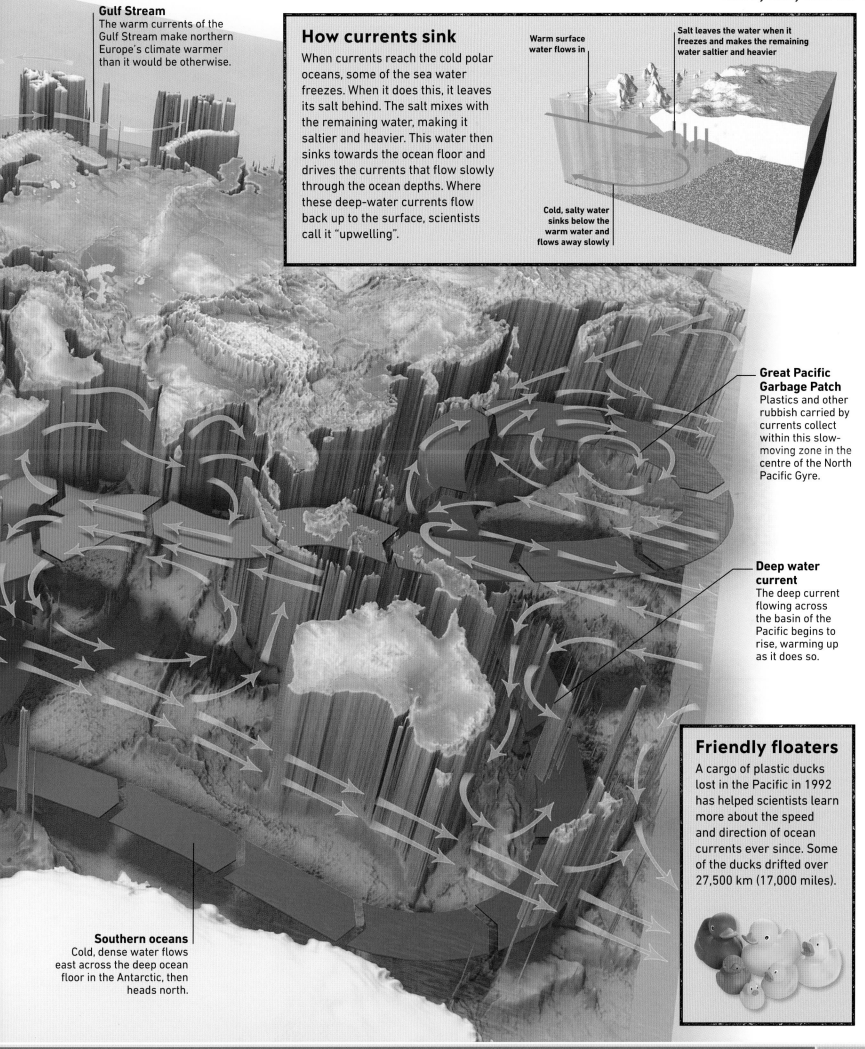

Gulf Stream
The warm currents of the Gulf Stream make northern Europe's climate warmer than it would be otherwise.

How currents sink

When currents reach the cold polar oceans, some of the sea water freezes. When it does this, it leaves its salt behind. The salt mixes with the remaining water, making it saltier and heavier. This water then sinks towards the ocean floor and drives the currents that flow slowly through the ocean depths. Where these deep-water currents flow back up to the surface, scientists call it "upwelling".

Warm surface water flows in

Salt leaves the water when it freezes and makes the remaining water saltier and heavier

Cold, salty water sinks below the warm water and flows away slowly

Great Pacific Garbage Patch
Plastics and other rubbish carried by currents collect within this slow-moving zone in the centre of the North Pacific Gyre.

Deep water current
The deep current flowing across the basin of the Pacific begins to rise, warming up as it does so.

Friendly floaters
A cargo of plastic ducks lost in the Pacific in 1992 has helped scientists learn more about the speed and direction of ocean currents ever since. Some of the ducks drifted over 27,500 km (17,000 miles).

Southern oceans
Cold, dense water flows east across the deep ocean floor in the Antarctic, then heads north.

Rivers

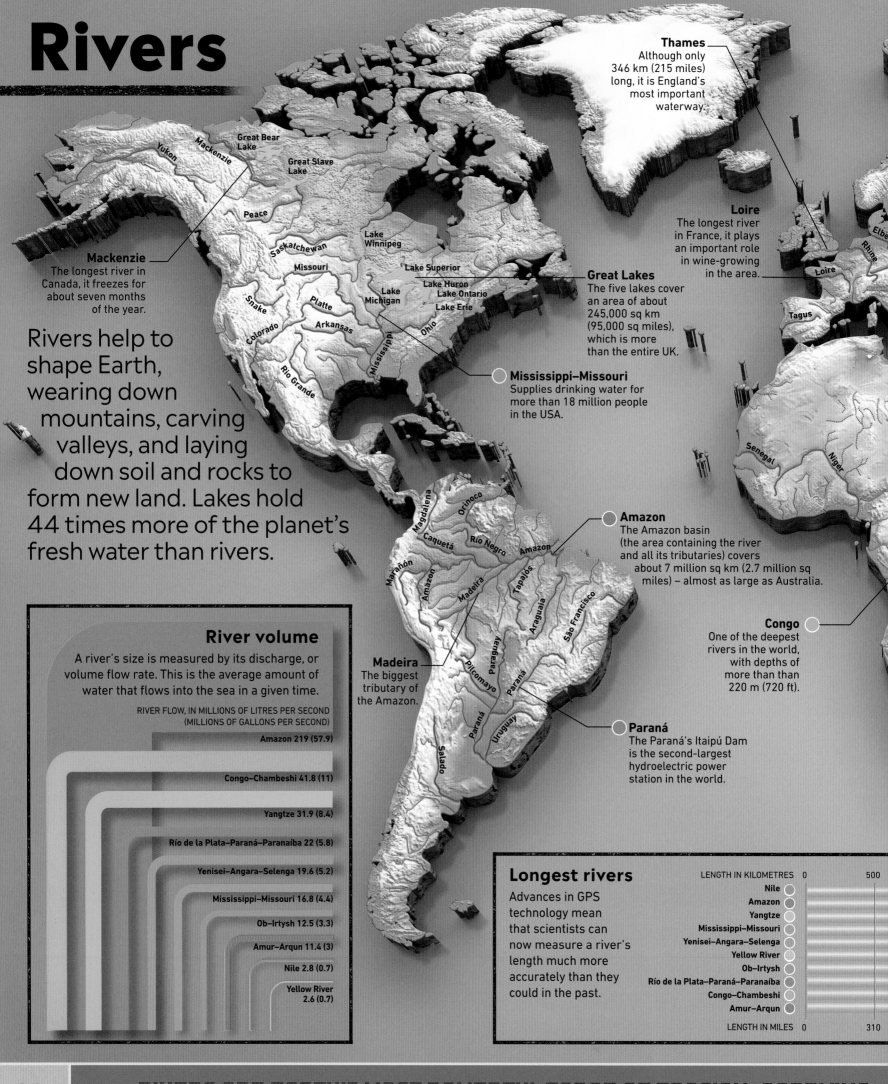

Rivers help to shape Earth, wearing down mountains, carving valleys, and laying down soil and rocks to form new land. Lakes hold 44 times more of the planet's fresh water than rivers.

Mackenzie
The longest river in Canada, it freezes for about seven months of the year.

Thames
Although only 346 km (215 miles) long, it is England's most important waterway.

Loire
The longest river in France, it plays an important role in wine-growing in the area.

Great Lakes
The five lakes cover an area of about 245,000 sq km (95,000 sq miles), which is more than the entire UK.

Mississippi–Missouri
Supplies drinking water for more than 18 million people in the USA.

Amazon
The Amazon basin (the area containing the river and all its tributaries) covers about 7 million sq km (2.7 million sq miles) – almost as large as Australia.

Congo
One of the deepest rivers in the world, with depths of more than 220 m (720 ft).

Madeira
The biggest tributary of the Amazon.

Paraná
The Paraná's Itaipú Dam is the second-largest hydroelectric power station in the world.

River volume

A river's size is measured by its discharge, or volume flow rate. This is the average amount of water that flows into the sea in a given time.

RIVER FLOW, IN MILLIONS OF LITRES PER SECOND
(MILLIONS OF GALLONS PER SECOND)

- Amazon 219 (57.9)
- Congo–Chambeshi 41.8 (11)
- Yangtze 31.9 (8.4)
- Río de la Plata–Paraná–Paranaíba 22 (5.8)
- Yenisei–Angara–Selenga 19.6 (5.2)
- Mississippi–Missouri 16.8 (4.4)
- Ob–Irtysh 12.5 (3.3)
- Amur–Arqun 11.4 (3)
- Nile 2.8 (0.7)
- Yellow River 2.6 (0.7)

Longest rivers

Advances in GPS technology mean that scientists can now measure a river's length much more accurately than they could in the past.

LENGTH IN KILOMETRES 0 — 500

- Nile
- Amazon
- Yangtze
- Mississippi–Missouri
- Yenisei–Angara–Selenga
- Yellow River
- Ob–Irtysh
- Río de la Plata–Paraná–Paranaíba
- Congo–Chambeshi
- Amur–Arqun

LENGTH IN MILES 0 — 310

RIVERS ARE EARTH'S MOST POWERFUL FORCE OF EROSION, CARRYING

Ob' Ends in the Arctic Ocean.

Yenisey
Freezes along its whole
length by mid-November
each year.

Danube
Flows through 10
countries on its way
to the Black Sea.

Pechora

Northern
Dvina

Lake
Onega

Lake
Ladoga

Oder

Danube

Volga

Dnieper

Don

Volga

Aral
Sea

Syr Darya

Amu Darya

Tigris

Euphrates

Nile

Ob'

Ob'

Irtysh

Lake
Balkash

Lower Tunguska

Olenëk

Vilyuy

Angara

Lake
Baikal

Lena

Aldan

Lena

Kolyma

Amur

Lake Baikal
At around 25 million
years old, by far the
oldest lake on Earth.

Indus

Brahmaputra

Ganges

Irrawaddy

Salween

Mekong

Yellow River

Yangtze

Amur
Part of the Amur provides a natural
boundary between Russia and the
People's Republic of China.

Yellow River (Huang He)
So-called because of the huge
amounts of mineral-rich silt
it carries downstream.

Yangtze (Chang Jiang)
One of the world's busiest rivers,
it flows through the major Chinese
cities of Shanghai and Nanjing.

Nile
About 90 per cent
of the people of Egypt
live close to the banks
of the Nile.

Ubangi

Congo

Nile

Nile

Lake
Victoria

Lake
Tanganyika

Lake
Nyasa

asai

Zambezi

Orange River

Lake Victoria
The world's second-
largest freshwater lake
by area (after Lake
Superior), it provides
water for the Nile.

Ganges
Holy river to
the world's
1.2 billion Hindus.

Seasonal rivers
Some rivers, shown in
brown, flow only in the
wet season. Some of
these flow only in
particularly wet years.

Darling

Murray

Murray–Darling
Makes up a large
river basin in
south-east
Australia,
connecting the
Snowy Mountains to
the Indian Ocean.

THE AMAZON CARRIES ONE-FIFTH OF ALL THE FRESH WATER EMPTIED INTO THE OCEANS

1,000	1,500	2,000	2,500	3,000	3,500	4,000	4,500	5,000	5,500	6,000	6,500
620	930	1,240	1,550	1,860	2,170	2,480	2,790	3,100	3,410	3,720	4,030

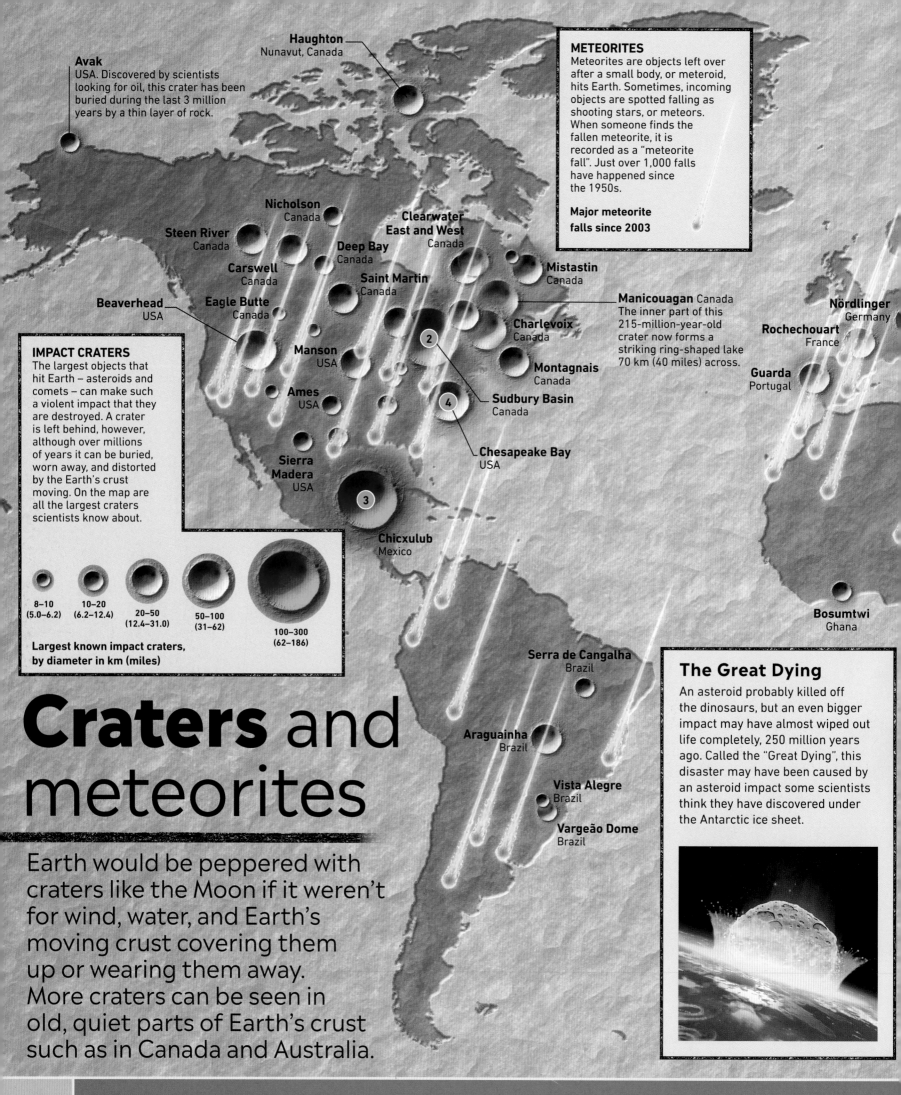

Avak
USA. Discovered by scientists looking for oil, this crater has been buried during the last 3 million years by a thin layer of rock.

Haughton
Nunavut, Canada

METEORITES
Meteorites are objects left over after a small body, or meteroid, hits Earth. Sometimes, incoming objects are spotted falling as shooting stars, or meteors. When someone finds the fallen meteorite, it is recorded as a "meteorite fall". Just over 1,000 falls have happened since the 1950s.

Major meteorite falls since 2003

Nicholson
Canada

Steen River
Canada

Deep Bay
Canada

Clearwater East and West
Canada

Carswell
Canada

Saint Martin
Canada

Mistastin
Canada

Beaverhead
USA

Eagle Butte
Canada

Manicouagan Canada
The inner part of this 215-million-year-old crater now forms a striking ring-shaped lake 70 km (40 miles) across.

Nördlinger
Germany

Rochechouart
France

Manson
USA

Charlevoix
Canada

Guarda
Portugal

IMPACT CRATERS
The largest objects that hit Earth – asteroids and comets – can make such a violent impact that they are destroyed. A crater is left behind, however, although over millions of years it can be buried, worn away, and distorted by the Earth's crust moving. On the map are all the largest craters scientists know about.

Montagnais
Canada

Ames
USA

Sudbury Basin
Canada

Sierra Madera
USA

Chesapeake Bay
USA

| 8–10 (5.0–6.2) | 10–20 (6.2–12.4) | 20–50 (12.4–31.0) | 50–100 (31–62) | 100–300 (62–186) |

Largest known impact craters, by diameter in km (miles)

Chicxulub
Mexico

Bosumtwi
Ghana

Serra de Cangalha
Brazil

The Great Dying
An asteroid probably killed off the dinosaurs, but an even bigger impact may have almost wiped out life completely, 250 million years ago. Called the "Great Dying", this disaster may have been caused by an asteroid impact some scientists think they have discovered under the Antarctic ice sheet.

Araguainha
Brazil

Craters and meteorites

Vista Alegre
Brazil

Vargeão Dome
Brazil

Earth would be peppered with craters like the Moon if it weren't for wind, water, and Earth's moving crust covering them up or wearing them away. More craters can be seen in old, quiet parts of Earth's crust such as in Canada and Australia.

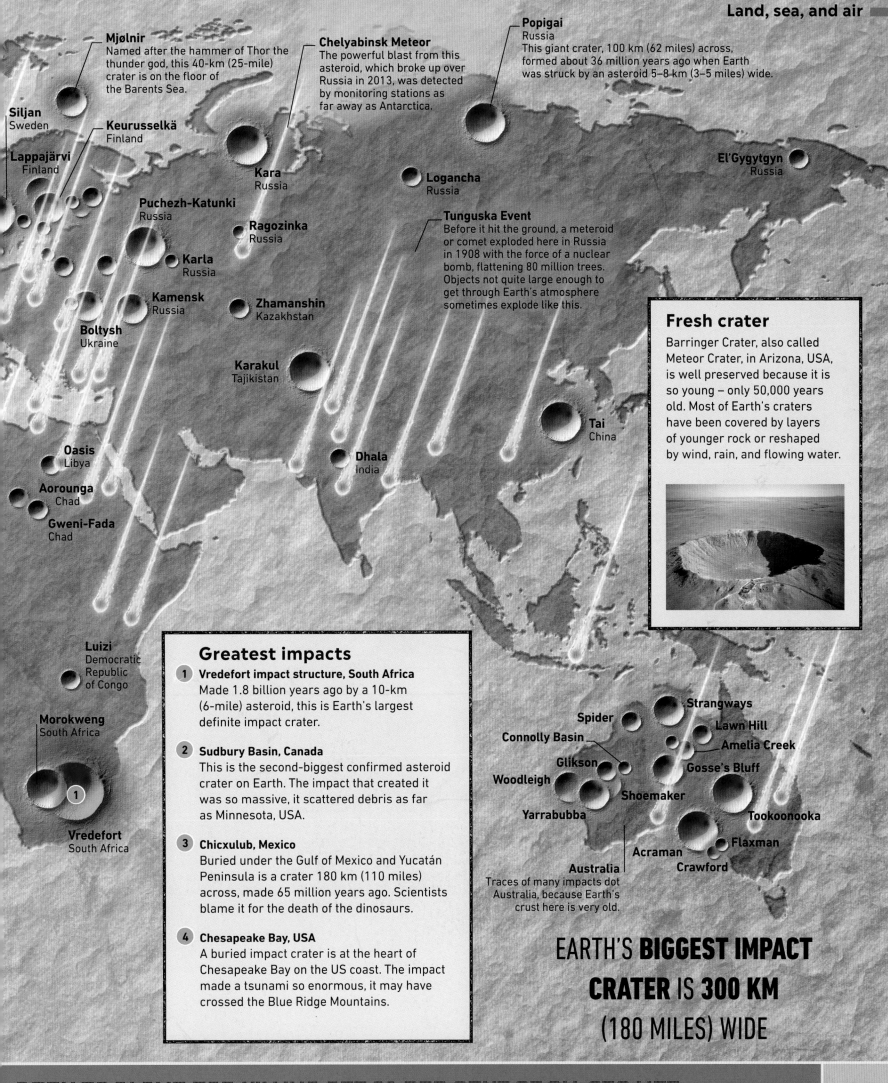

Mjølnir
Named after the hammer of Thor the thunder god, this 40-km (25-mile) crater is on the floor of the Barents Sea.

Chelyabinsk Meteor
The powerful blast from this asteroid, which broke up over Russia in 2013, was detected by monitoring stations as far away as Antarctica.

Popigai
Russia
This giant crater, 100 km (62 miles) across, formed about 36 million years ago when Earth was struck by an asteroid 5–8 km (3–5 miles) wide.

Siljan
Sweden

Keurusselkä
Finland

Lappajärvi
Finland

El'Gygytgyn
Russia

Kara
Russia

Logancha
Russia

Puchezh-Katunki
Russia

Ragozinka
Russia

Tunguska Event
Before it hit the ground, a meteroid or comet exploded here in Russia in 1908 with the force of a nuclear bomb, flattening 80 million trees. Objects not quite large enough to get through Earth's atmosphere sometimes explode like this.

Karla
Russia

Kamensk
Russia

Zhamanshin
Kazakhstan

Boltysh
Ukraine

Karakul
Tajikistan

Tai
China

Fresh crater
Barringer Crater, also called Meteor Crater, in Arizona, USA, is well preserved because it is so young – only 50,000 years old. Most of Earth's craters have been covered by layers of younger rock or reshaped by wind, rain, and flowing water.

Oasis
Libya

Dhala
India

Aorounga
Chad

Gweni-Fada
Chad

Luizi
Democratic Republic of Congo

Greatest impacts

1 Vredefort impact structure, South Africa
Made 1.8 billion years ago by a 10-km (6-mile) asteroid, this is Earth's largest definite impact crater.

2 Sudbury Basin, Canada
This is the second-biggest confirmed asteroid crater on Earth. The impact that created it was so massive, it scattered debris as far as Minnesota, USA.

3 Chicxulub, Mexico
Buried under the Gulf of Mexico and Yucatán Peninsula is a crater 180 km (110 miles) across, made 65 million years ago. Scientists blame it for the death of the dinosaurs.

4 Chesapeake Bay, USA
A buried impact crater is at the heart of Chesapeake Bay on the US coast. The impact made a tsunami so enormous, it may have crossed the Blue Ridge Mountains.

Morokweng
South Africa

Vredefort
South Africa

Strangways

Spider

Lawn Hill

Connolly Basin

Amelia Creek

Glikson

Gosse's Bluff

Woodleigh

Shoemaker

Yarrabubba

Tookoonooka

Flaxman

Acraman

Crawford

Australia
Traces of many impacts dot Australia, because Earth's crust here is very old.

EARTH'S **BIGGEST IMPACT** CRATER IS 300 KM
(180 MILES) WIDE

Prospect Creek, USA
At −62.2°C (−80°F), this is the seventh-coldest place on the planet.

Malgovik, Sweden
The coldest spot in Sweden, with a record of −53°C (−63.4°F).

Snag, Canada
Recorded temperature of −63°C (−81°F), to make it the coldest site in North America.

Klinck Automated Weather Station, Greenland
Fourth-coldest spot on Earth, at −69.6°C. (−93.3°F).

Kebili, Tunisia
Recorded temperature of 55°C (131°F) in 1931, tying for the third-hottest place ever.

Furnace Creek, USA
The world's highest ever air temperature, 56.7°C (134°F), was recorded here in 1913.

Mexicali area, Mexico
A 1995 record of 52.0°C (125.6 °F).

Daily differences

Many deserts are hot during the day but drastically cooler at night. With no clouds or mist in the way of the Sun, the ground warms up fast during the day. With no blanketing cloud at night, the heat escapes quickly. In humid climates, daily temperatures vary a lot less.

① Luxor, Egypt
Luxor has a dry, desert climate. In June, the daily temperature varies hugely, from an average maximum of 41°C (105.8°F) down to 22°C (71.6°F) at night.

② Singapore
Singapore's climate is very warm and humid all year round. In June, the daily temperature varies from 31.3°C (88.3°F) to a sticky 24.7°C (76.5°F) at night.

Cold mountains
The higher up you are, the lower the air pressure – and the temperature. The Andes mountain range is much colder than the land that surrounds it.

Al 'Aziziyah, Libya
Lost its title as world's hottest place in 2012, when weather scientists found its 1922 record measurement was probably wrong.

Blazing summers, freezing winters

In the middle of large continents, it is often hot in summer and very cold in winter. In coastal areas, warm or cool winds and currents carried by the sea moderate temperatures. Without this balance, inland areas can become extremely hot or cold.

① Verkhoyansk, Russia
The world's biggest seasonal temperature differences are found in Verkhoyansk. The highest temperature ever recorded was 39.9°C (103.8°F) and the lowest was -67.8°C (−90°F).

② Regina, Canada
Regina's highest-ever temperature was 43.3°C (109.9°F) and the lowest was -50°C (-58°F).

IN **1924**, THE AUSTRALIAN TOWN OF **MARBLE BAR** REACHED 37.8°C (100°F) OR ABOVE FOR **160 DAYS** IN A ROW

Amundsen–Scott Station, South Pole
The second-coldest point on Earth, at −82.8°C (−117°F).

THE "GULF STREAM" OCEAN CURRENT FROM THE GULF OF MEXICO GIVES

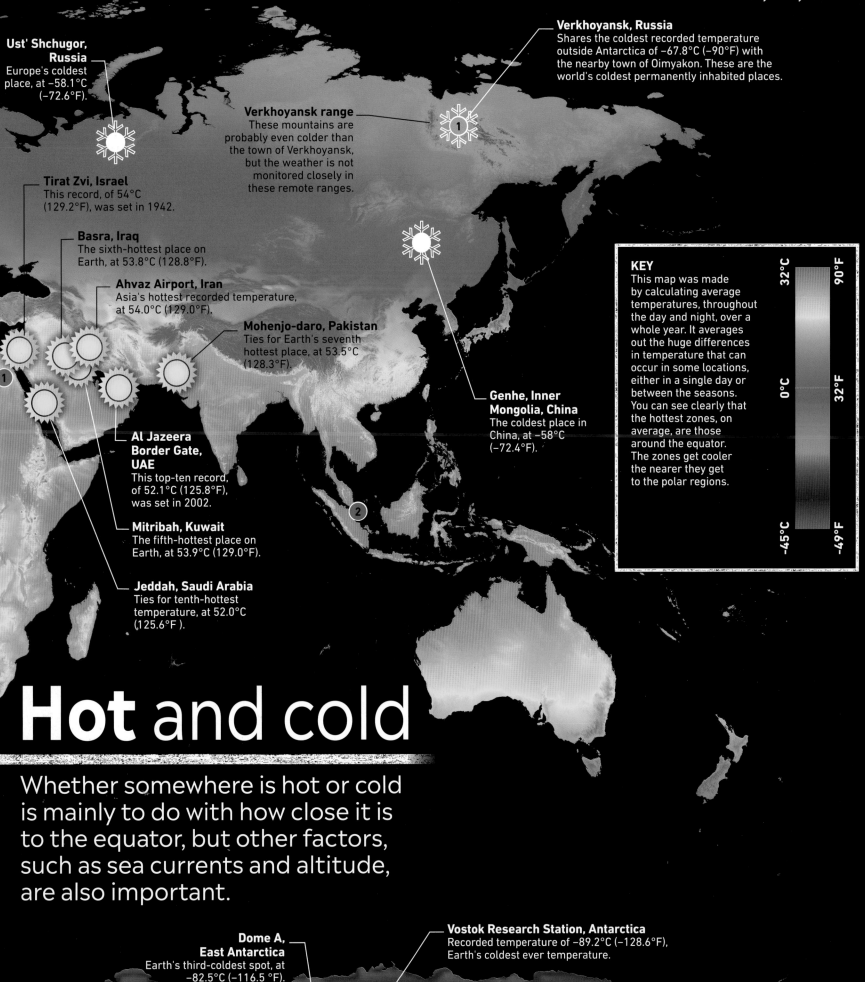

Verkhoyansk, Russia
Shares the coldest recorded temperature outside Antarctica of −67.8°C (−90°F) with the nearby town of Oimyakon. These are the world's coldest permanently inhabited places.

Ust' Shchugor, Russia
Europe's coldest place, at −58.1°C (−72.6°F).

Verkhoyansk range
These mountains are probably even colder than the town of Verkhoyansk, but the weather is not monitored closely in these remote ranges.

Tirat Zvi, Israel
This record, of 54°C (129.2°F), was set in 1942.

Basra, Iraq
The sixth-hottest place on Earth, at 53.8°C (128.8°F).

Ahvaz Airport, Iran
Asia's hottest recorded temperature, at 54.0°C (129.0°F).

Mohenjo-daro, Pakistan
Ties for Earth's seventh hottest place, at 53.5°C (128.3°F).

Genhe, Inner Mongolia, China
The coldest place in China, at −58°C (−72.4°F).

Al Jazeera Border Gate, UAE
This top-ten record, of 52.1°C (125.8°F), was set in 2002.

Mitribah, Kuwait
The fifth-hottest place on Earth, at 53.9°C (129.0°F).

Jeddah, Saudi Arabia
Ties for tenth-hottest temperature, at 52.0°C (125.6°F).

KEY
This map was made by calculating average temperatures, throughout the day and night, over a whole year. It averages out the huge differences in temperature that can occur in some locations, either in a single day or between the seasons. You can see clearly that the hottest zones, on average, are those around the equator. The zones get cooler the nearer they get to the polar regions.

32°C | 90°F
0°C | 32°F
−45°C | −49°F

Hot and cold

Whether somewhere is hot or cold is mainly to do with how close it is to the equator, but other factors, such as sea currents and altitude, are also important.

Dome A, East Antarctica
Earth's third-coldest spot, at −82.5°C (−116.5 °F).

Vostok Research Station, Antarctica
Recorded temperature of −89.2°C (−128.6°F), Earth's coldest ever temperature.

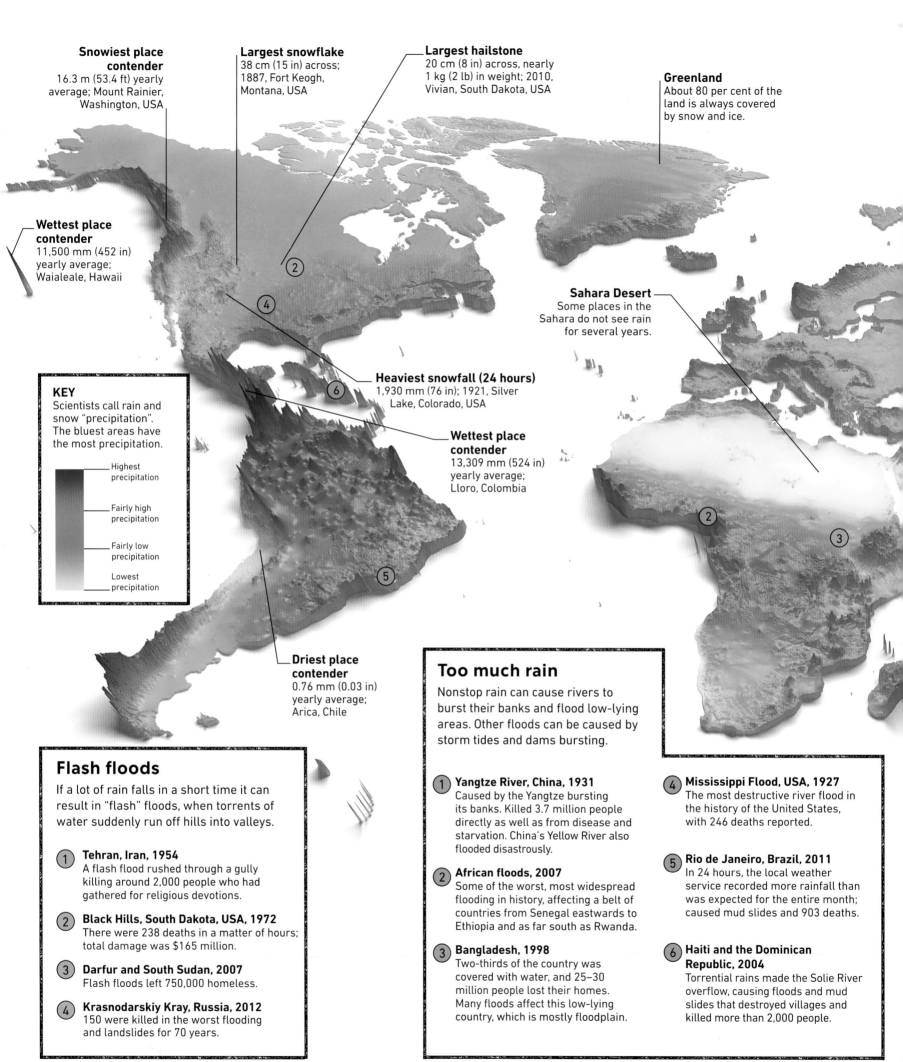

Snowiest place contender
16.3 m (53.4 ft) yearly average; Mount Rainier, Washington, USA

Largest snowflake
38 cm (15 in) across; 1887, Fort Keogh, Montana, USA

Largest hailstone
20 cm (8 in) across, nearly 1 kg (2 lb) in weight; 2010, Vivian, South Dakota, USA

Greenland
About 80 per cent of the land is always covered by snow and ice.

Wettest place contender
11,500 mm (452 in) yearly average; Waialeale, Hawaii

Sahara Desert
Some places in the Sahara do not see rain for several years.

Heaviest snowfall (24 hours)
1,930 mm (76 in); 1921, Silver Lake, Colorado, USA

Wettest place contender
13,309 mm (524 in) yearly average; Lloro, Colombia

KEY
Scientists call rain and snow "precipitation". The bluest areas have the most precipitation.

- Highest precipitation
- Fairly high precipitation
- Fairly low precipitation
- Lowest precipitation

Driest place contender
0.76 mm (0.03 in) yearly average; Arica, Chile

Too much rain

Nonstop rain can cause rivers to burst their banks and flood low-lying areas. Other floods can be caused by storm tides and dams bursting.

1. **Yangtze River, China, 1931**
Caused by the Yangtze bursting its banks. Killed 3.7 million people directly as well as from disease and starvation. China's Yellow River also flooded disastrously.

2. **African floods, 2007**
Some of the worst, most widespread flooding in history, affecting a belt of countries from Senegal eastwards to Ethiopia and as far south as Rwanda.

3. **Bangladesh, 1998**
Two-thirds of the country was covered with water, and 25–30 million people lost their homes. Many floods affect this low-lying country, which is mostly floodplain.

4. **Mississippi Flood, USA, 1927**
The most destructive river flood in the history of the United States, with 246 deaths reported.

5. **Rio de Janeiro, Brazil, 2011**
In 24 hours, the local weather service recorded more rainfall than was expected for the entire month; caused mud slides and 903 deaths.

6. **Haiti and the Dominican Republic, 2004**
Torrential rains made the Solie River overflow, causing floods and mud slides that destroyed villages and killed more than 2,000 people.

Flash floods

If a lot of rain falls in a short time it can result in "flash" floods, when torrents of water suddenly run off hills into valleys.

1. **Tehran, Iran, 1954**
A flash flood rushed through a gully killing around 2,000 people who had gathered for religious devotions.

2. **Black Hills, South Dakota, USA, 1972**
There were 238 deaths in a matter of hours; total damage was $165 million.

3. **Darfur and South Sudan, 2007**
Flash floods left 750,000 homeless.

4. **Krasnodarskiy Kray, Russia, 2012**
150 were killed in the worst flooding and landslides for 70 years.

Rain and snow

5,000 MM (197 IN) OF RAIN MAY FALL IN ONE PLACE DURING INDIA'S MONSOON SEASON

Rainfall varies dramatically with place. Torrential rain drenches southern Asia during the monsoon season, yet some desert regions have virtually no rain at all. Near the poles, very little snow falls, but the snow rarely melts, so some land is permanently under a layer of ice.

Heaviest rainfall (1 month, and 1 year)
9,300 mm (370 in) and 22,987 mm (905 in); both 1860–61, Cherrapunji, India

Arabian Peninsula
As in the Sahara, there is very little rain in this largely desert region.

Heaviest rainfall (24 hours)
1,825 mm (71.9 in); 1966, Foc-Foc, Réunion, during Tropical Cyclone Denise

Snowiest place contender
15 m (49.5 ft) yearly average; Niseko, Japan

Borneo
Many equatorial rainforests, such as those in Borneo, have no dry season, and it rains every day.

Monsoon extremes

Chittagong, in Bangladesh, has almost no rain in the dry season, but its monsoon rains are torrential. Paris, in France, has much more even monthly rainfall.

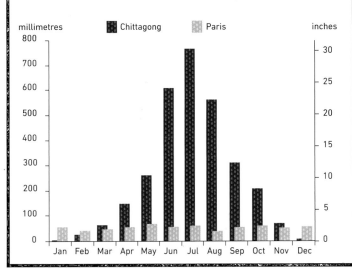

millimetres / inches — ▇ Chittagong ▨ Paris

Australia
This is the driest inhabited continent.

New Zealand
Rainfall is fairly high and is spread evenly throughout the year.

Driest place on Earth
0 mm (0 in) yearly average; Antarctica's Dry Valleys, which are free of snow and ice.

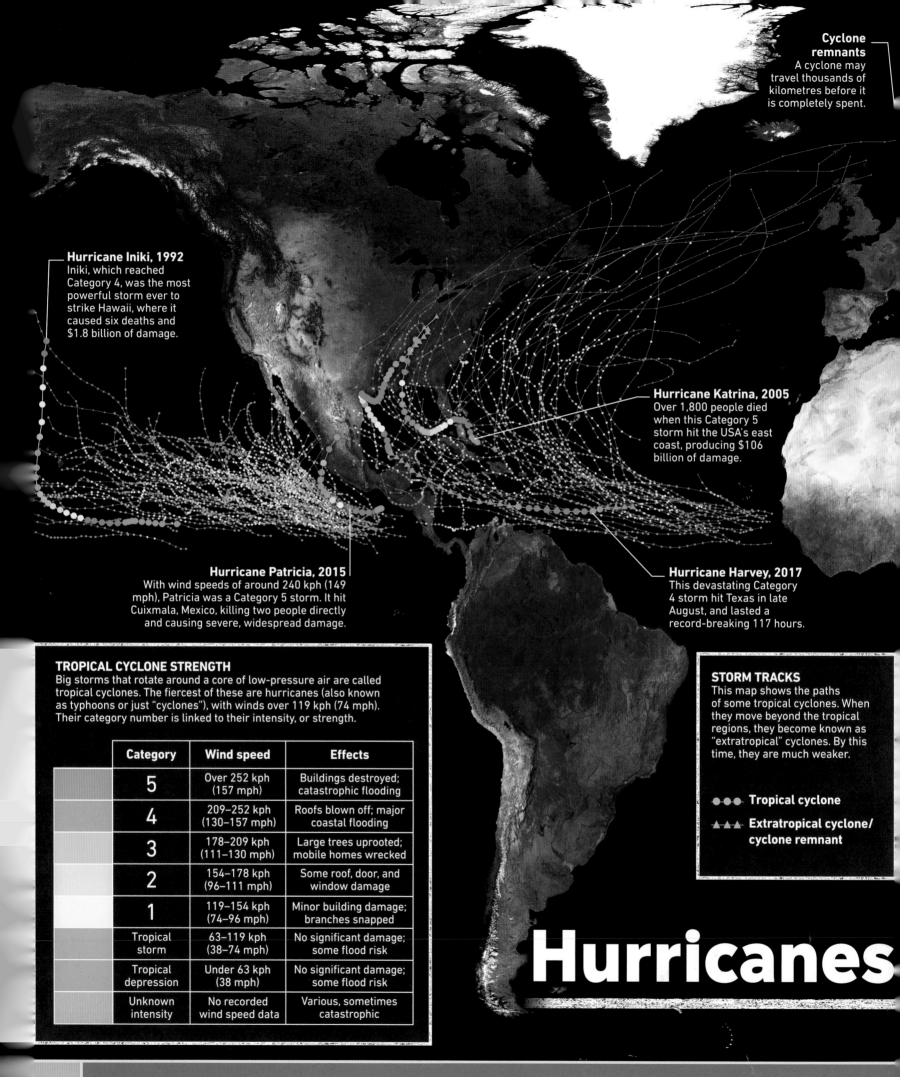

Cyclone remnants
A cyclone may travel thousands of kilometres before it is completely spent.

Hurricane Iniki, 1992
Iniki, which reached Category 4, was the most powerful storm ever to strike Hawaii, where it caused six deaths and $1.8 billion of damage.

Hurricane Katrina, 2005
Over 1,800 people died when this Category 5 storm hit the USA's east coast, producing $106 billion of damage.

Hurricane Patricia, 2015
With wind speeds of around 240 kph (149 mph), Patricia was a Category 5 storm. It hit Cuixmala, Mexico, killing two people directly and causing severe, widespread damage.

Hurricane Harvey, 2017
This devastating Category 4 storm hit Texas in late August, and lasted a record-breaking 117 hours.

TROPICAL CYCLONE STRENGTH

Big storms that rotate around a core of low-pressure air are called tropical cyclones. The fiercest of these are hurricanes (also known as typhoons or just "cyclones"), with winds over 119 kph (74 mph). Their category number is linked to their intensity, or strength.

Category	Wind speed	Effects
5	Over 252 kph (157 mph)	Buildings destroyed; catastrophic flooding
4	209–252 kph (130–157 mph)	Roofs blown off; major coastal flooding
3	178–209 kph (111–130 mph)	Large trees uprooted; mobile homes wrecked
2	154–178 kph (96–111 mph)	Some roof, door, and window damage
1	119–154 kph (74–96 mph)	Minor building damage; branches snapped
Tropical storm	63–119 kph (38–74 mph)	No significant damage; some flood risk
Tropical depression	Under 63 kph (38 mph)	No significant damage; some flood risk
Unknown intensity	No recorded wind speed data	Various, sometimes catastrophic

STORM TRACKS

This map shows the paths of some tropical cyclones. When they move beyond the tropical regions, they become known as "extratropical" cyclones. By this time, they are much weaker.

●●● **Tropical cyclone**

▲▲▲ **Extratropical cyclone/ cyclone remnant**

Hurricanes

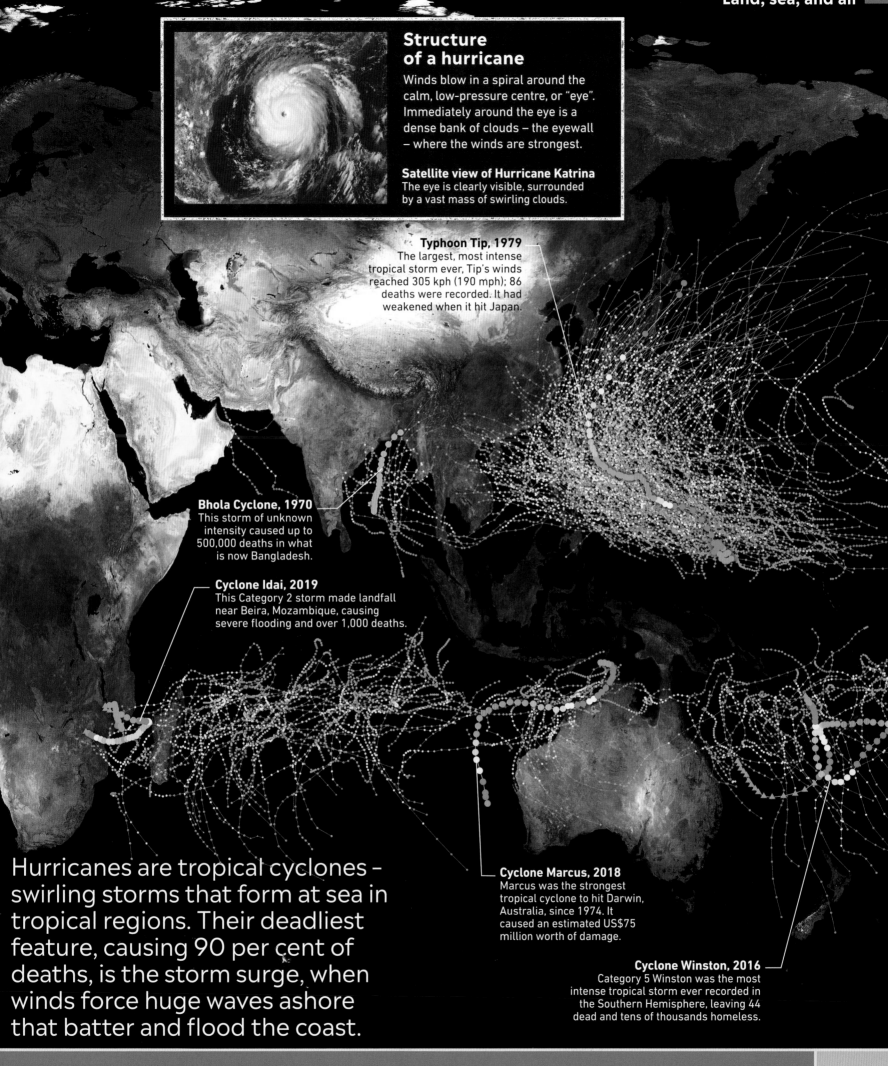

Structure of a hurricane

Winds blow in a spiral around the calm, low-pressure centre, or "eye". Immediately around the eye is a dense bank of clouds – the eyewall – where the winds are strongest.

Satellite view of Hurricane Katrina
The eye is clearly visible, surrounded by a vast mass of swirling clouds.

Typhoon Tip, 1979
The largest, most intense tropical storm ever, Tip's winds reached 305 kph (190 mph); 86 deaths were recorded. It had weakened when it hit Japan.

Bhola Cyclone, 1970
This storm of unknown intensity caused up to 500,000 deaths in what is now Bangladesh.

Cyclone Idai, 2019
This Category 2 storm made landfall near Beira, Mozambique, causing severe flooding and over 1,000 deaths.

Cyclone Marcus, 2018
Marcus was the strongest tropical cyclone to hit Darwin, Australia, since 1974. It caused an estimated US$75 million worth of damage.

Cyclone Winston, 2016
Category 5 Winston was the most intense tropical storm ever recorded in the Southern Hemisphere, leaving 44 dead and tens of thousands homeless.

Hurricanes are tropical cyclones – swirling storms that form at sea in tropical regions. Their deadliest feature, causing 90 per cent of deaths, is the storm surge, when winds force huge waves ashore that batter and flood the coast.

Tropical broadleaf moist forest
Also known as rainforest, these warm, wet woods support a huge variety of animal and plant life.

Tropical dry broadleaf forest
These areas are warm all year round but have a long dry season, and many trees lose their leaves.

Tropical coniferous forest
Many migrating birds and butterflies spend the winter in these warm, dense conifer forests.

Temperate broadleaf forest
The most common habitat of northern Europe and home to trees that lose their leaves in winter.

Temperate coniferous forest
Giant trees, such as the California redwood, thrive in these regions of warm summers and cool winters.

Boreal forest
Also called taiga, this is the largest land biome on Earth. It is dominated by just a few types of coniferous tree.

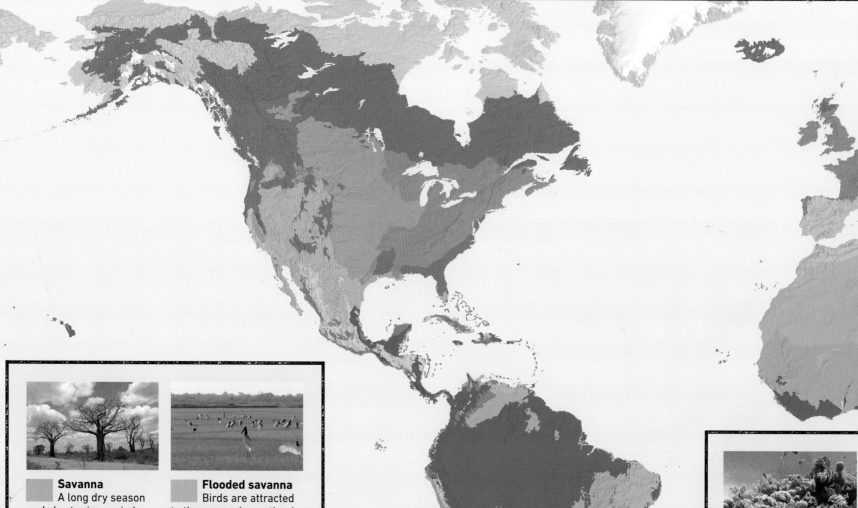

Savanna
A long dry season and short rainy periods results in a grassland studded with trees and herds of grazing animals.

Flooded savanna
Birds are attracted to these marshy, wetland areas that are flooded in the wet season but grassland at other times.

Temperate grassland
Also known as prairie, steppe, or pampas, many of these vast, fertile plains are now farmland.

Mountain grassland
The inhabitants of these remote, high habitats must adapt to the cold and the intense sunlight.

Coral reef
The warm, shallow waters of a reef support a huge variety of life, from sharks to tiny sea horses.

Marine Biomes

Sea biomes are as varied as those on land. From beaches to the darkest ocean depths, living things find ways to survive and thrive.

Mangrove
On the shore, the mangroves' thick, tangled roots slow the water's flow and create a swamp.

TROPICAL RAINFORESTS COVER AROUND 6 PER CENT OF THE LAND,

Mediterranean shrubland
Hot, dry summers can lead to fires that actually help the biome's typical shrubby plants sprout.

Desert and dry shrubland
Desert inhabitants have to be able to survive on less than 250 mm (10 in) of rainfall per year.

Arctic Tundra
A cold, dry biome where the soil stays frozen at depth. This permafrost stops trees from growing.

Polar desert
Too cold and dry for almost all plants. Only animals dependent on the sea, such as penguins, can live here.

A **BIOME'S PLANTS** AND **ANIMALS** FORM A **COMPLEX** AND **INTERCONNECTED** COMMUNITY

Biomes

A biome is an area that we define according to the animals and plants that live there. They have to adapt to the biome's specific conditions such as temperature, type of soil, and the amount of light and water.

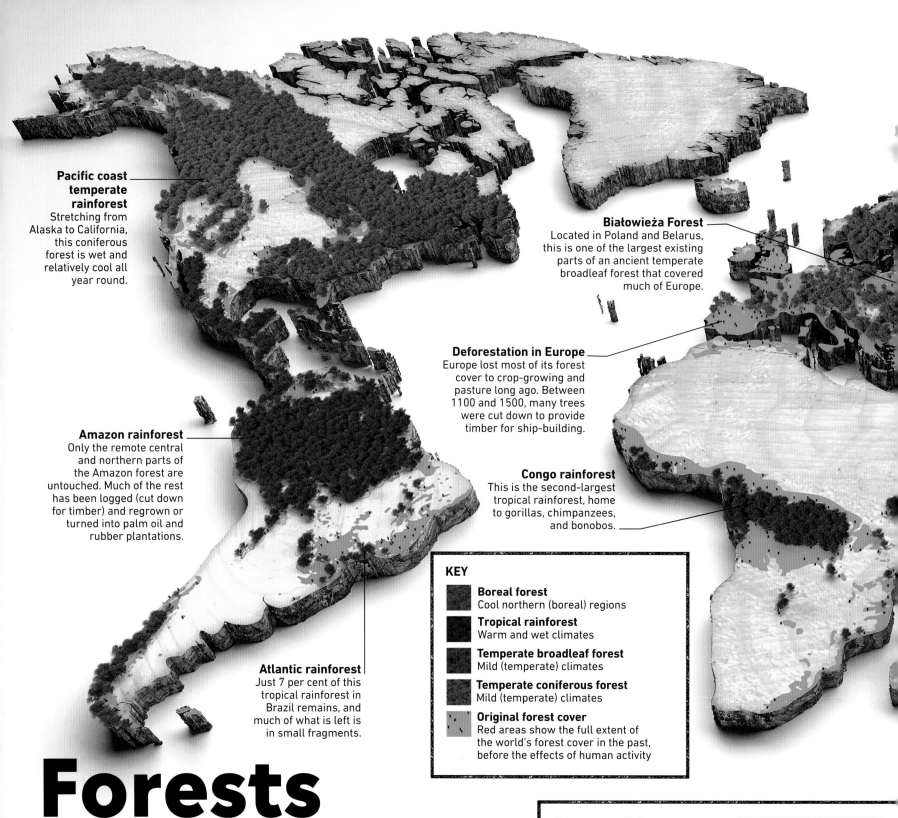

Pacific coast temperate rainforest
Stretching from Alaska to California, this coniferous forest is wet and relatively cool all year round.

Białowieża Forest
Located in Poland and Belarus, this is one of the largest existing parts of an ancient temperate broadleaf forest that covered much of Europe.

Deforestation in Europe
Europe lost most of its forest cover to crop-growing and pasture long ago. Between 1100 and 1500, many trees were cut down to provide timber for ship-building.

Amazon rainforest
Only the remote central and northern parts of the Amazon forest are untouched. Much of the rest has been logged (cut down for timber) and regrown or turned into palm oil and rubber plantations.

Congo rainforest
This is the second-largest tropical rainforest, home to gorillas, chimpanzees, and bonobos.

Atlantic rainforest
Just 7 per cent of this tropical rainforest in Brazil remains, and much of what is left is in small fragments.

KEY

Boreal forest
Cool northern (boreal) regions

Tropical rainforest
Warm and wet climates

Temperate broadleaf forest
Mild (temperate) climates

Temperate coniferous forest
Mild (temperate) climates

Original forest cover
Red areas show the full extent of the world's forest cover in the past, before the effects of human activity

Forests

Forests are vital to life on Earth. They make the air breathable, protect the soil, and preserve fresh water supplies. But they are disappearing – and while efforts are being made to slow deforestation, around 10 million hectares are still lost each year.

Types of forest

Forests differ according to climate. Each type of forest has its own distinct collection of trees, forest-floor plants, and animal life. Tropical rainforests are the most diverse – 30 per cent all plant and animal species live in the Amazon alone. Some tropical forests are evergreen, while in others the trees lose their leaves in the dry season.

Temperate broadleaf
Deciduous trees, such as oak and beech. Herbs, ferns, and shrubs on the forest floor.

Taiga
This vast belt of boreal forest stretches right across northern Europe and Asia. In the east, it is wilderness, but much in the west is working forest, managed for timber and paper production.

Disappearing forests
With the world's population growing, demand for timber and land for farming and towns has increased the rate of forest clearance. Here you can see the decline in Borneo's forests from 1950 to 2010.

Borneo, 1950   **1985**   **2010**

Japan
Japan retains a lot of its original woodland and is the most thickly forested industrialized country.

Borneo
Home of most of the world's orangutans, Borneo's rainforest has declined by more than 50 per cent since the mid-20th century (see above).

New Guinea
Two-thirds of New Guinea is largely unspoiled rainforest, with many unique species. It is at risk from logging, mining, and agriculture.

AT CURRENT RATES OF **LOGGING**, IN **100 YEARS** WE WILL **NO LONGER** HAVE ANY **RAINFORESTS**

New Zealand
The remote southwest of New Zealand is home to unique temperate rainforests full of lush tree ferns.

Australia
About 38 per cent of Australia's forests have been lost since European settlers arrived around 200 years ago.

Tropical rainforest
As many as 300 tree species per hectare (2.5 acres). Often rich in forest-floor plants.

Boreal forest
Hardy conifers, such as larch, spruce, fir, and pine. Mosses dominate the forest floor.

Desert tortoise
Has shovel-shaped forefeet that help it dig burrows, where it shelters from the extreme heat of the day and the cold of the night.

Mesquite
Tree with a long taproot that can grow up to 60 m (190 ft) long, as it searches for water deep underground.

Caribou
A deer specialized in living in the cold, high Arctic. Although it experiences the low rainfall of a desert, there is rarely a water shortage, because water collects in pools above the deeply frozen soil. There is no hot Sun to dry it up.

Greenland ice sheet
This region experiences the coldest and driest conditions in the Arctic. Nothing can live on top of the ice.

Great Basin
USA

Chihuahuan Desert
Northern Mexico

Almería, Spain
Europe's driest region is true desert in parts.

Syrian Desert

Negev Desert

Mojave Desert
USA

Spadefoot toad
Digs a burrow with spadelike ridges on its back feet. It then makes a watertight cocoon of shed skin and waits – sometimes for months – for the next rains to fall.

Sonoran Desert
USA and Mexico

Sahara

Saguaro cactus
Tall, treelike cactus that grows in the Sonoran Desert. Survives by storing water in its fleshy trunk and stems when it rains. It lives off this water until the rains come again.

Sechura Desert
Peru

Dromedary camel
Native to Arabia but lives throughout deserts of north Africa. Can live on fat stored in its hump and survives for 2 weeks without a drink.

Sahel
A belt of semidesert, also known as arid savanna, or dry grassland.

Atacama Desert, Chile
Like the Namib, this is a coastal desert, kept dry by a cold ocean current nearby.

Tsamma watermelon
Wild ancestor of the watermelon. Grows in the Kalahari Desert and stores water in its big, round fruits.

Patagonian Desert, Argentina
Some experts call this a dry grassland rather than a desert.

Lithops, or "living stones"
Plants also known as pebble plants, because their single pair of round leaves looks like stones, camouflaging them against grazers. The leaves also help the plants to save and store water.

Namib Desert
Namibia

Namib desert beetle
Collects minute droplets of water from early-morning fog on its legs and hard wing cases. When enough water forms, a droplet rolls down the beetle's body into its mouth.

Kalahari Desert
Botswana and South Africa

Deserts

Deserts are found from the icy poles to the tropics. So while all deserts have low rainfall – less than 250 mm (10 in) a year, and often much less – they are not always hot. Even in hot deserts, the nights are often cold.

Antarctica
One of the most arid parts of Earth's largest desert is its Dry Valleys region (right), the only area of Antarctica not covered in thick ice, and where there is almost no snowfall. Cold, dry winds blast down from mountain peaks and turn all moisture to water vapour.

Desert terrain

Deserts range widely in how they look. Soil forms only very slowly and the land is often bare rock or gravel. Any loose sandy soil may be blown into dunes. Sometimes, though, tough grasses or fleshy plants bind the soil together.

Dunes, or "sand seas"
Shifting mountains of sand can prevent plant growth.

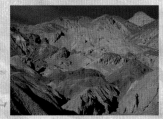

Rock and gravel
Where no plants grow, the bedrock is often visible.

Dry grassland
Desert grasses can form soil and provide food for grazers.

Fleshy plants
Fleshy, water-storing plants may form thick vegetation.

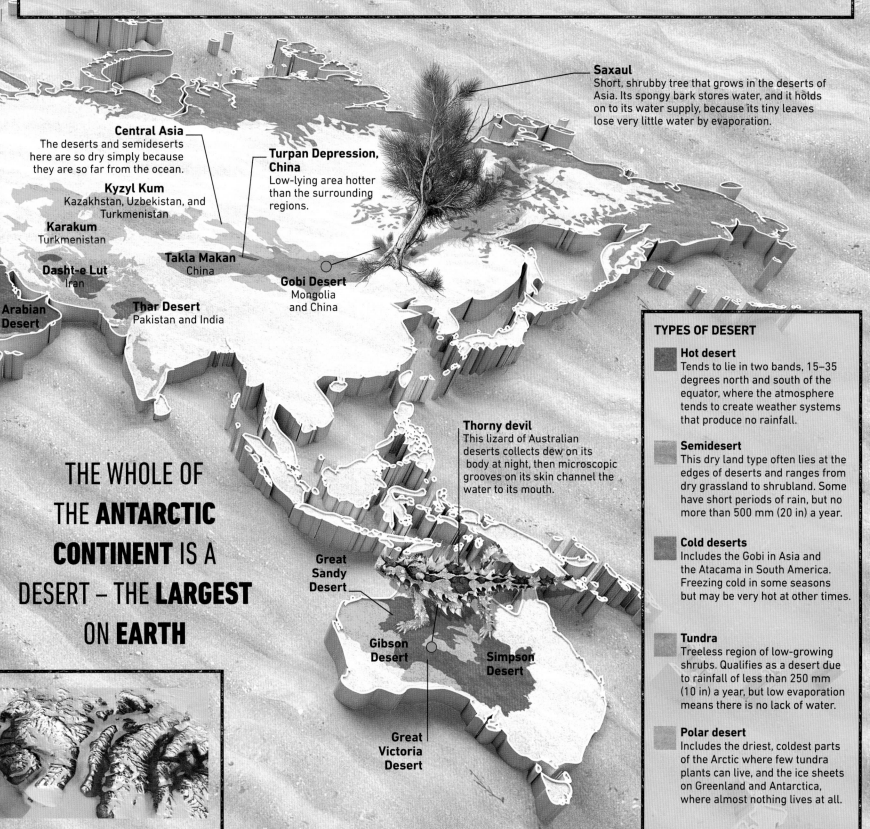

Saxaul
Short, shrubby tree that grows in the deserts of Asia. Its spongy bark stores water, and it holds on to its water supply, because its tiny leaves lose very little water by evaporation.

Central Asia
The deserts and semideserts here are so dry simply because they are so far from the ocean.

Kyzyl Kum
Kazakhstan, Uzbekistan, and Turkmenistan

Karakum
Turkmenistan

Dasht-e Lut
Iran

Arabian Desert

Thar Desert
Pakistan and India

Takla Makan
China

Turpan Depression, China
Low-lying area hotter than the surrounding regions.

Gobi Desert
Mongolia and China

Thorny devil
This lizard of Australian deserts collects dew on its body at night, then microscopic grooves on its skin channel the water to its mouth.

THE WHOLE OF THE **ANTARCTIC CONTINENT** IS A DESERT – THE **LARGEST** ON **EARTH**

Great Sandy Desert

Gibson Desert

Simpson Desert

Great Victoria Desert

TYPES OF DESERT

Hot desert
Tends to lie in two bands, 15–35 degrees north and south of the equator, where the atmosphere tends to create weather systems that produce no rainfall.

Semidesert
This dry land type often lies at the edges of deserts and ranges from dry grassland to shrubland. Some have short periods of rain, but no more than 500 mm (20 in) a year.

Cold deserts
Includes the Gobi in Asia and the Atacama in South America. Freezing cold in some seasons but may be very hot at other times.

Tundra
Treeless region of low-growing shrubs. Qualifies as a desert due to rainfall of less than 250 mm (10 in) a year, but low evaporation means there is no lack of water.

Polar desert
Includes the driest, coldest parts of the Arctic where few tundra plants can live, and the ice sheets on Greenland and Antarctica, where almost nothing lives at all.

Ice

Ice covers one-tenth of Earth's land surface, mostly in the polar regions. At earlier times in Earth's history, when the climate was much cooler, ice covered an area up to three times larger than it does today.

Sea ice

Sea ice is frozen sea. It forms when the ocean's surface freezes in winter. Where it lasts year round, it may be 6 m (20 ft) thick – elsewhere it is thinner. "Pancake ice" (right) is discs of sea ice up to 10 cm (4 in) thick.

Summer ice
The polar sea ice cover shrinks in summer, but some sea always remains under a layer of ice.

Winter ice As the weather gets colder, the polar sea ice spreads far beyond its summer limits.

SOUTH AMERICA

Sea of Okhotsk

ASIA

New Siberian Islands

Laptev Sea

East Siberian Sea

AVERAGE EDGE OF SUMMER SEA ICE, 1981-2010

Severnaya Zemlya

Kara Sea

Novaya Zemlya

Franz Josef Land

Barents Sea

EUROPE

Wrangel Island

PACIFIC OCEAN

Chukchi Sea

Bering Strait

North Pole

Svalbard

ARCTIC OCEAN

Greenland Sea

Norwegian Sea

Wandel Sea

Queen Elizabeth Islands

Amundsen Gulf

Greenland

Iceland

Davis Strait

Baffin Island

Baffin Bay

Labrador Sea

Hudson Bay

AVERAGE EDGE OF WINTER SEA ICE 1981-2010

NORTH AMERICA

Land ice

Thick ice gradually builds up on land as old, unmelted snow is compacted by layers of fresh snow and turned into ice. Antarctica's ice sheet is up to 4.8 km (3 miles) thick.

Ice sheet A vast layer of land ice that has formed over thousands or even millions of years.

Ice shelf A floating extension of an ice sheet or glacier, usually hundreds of metres thick.

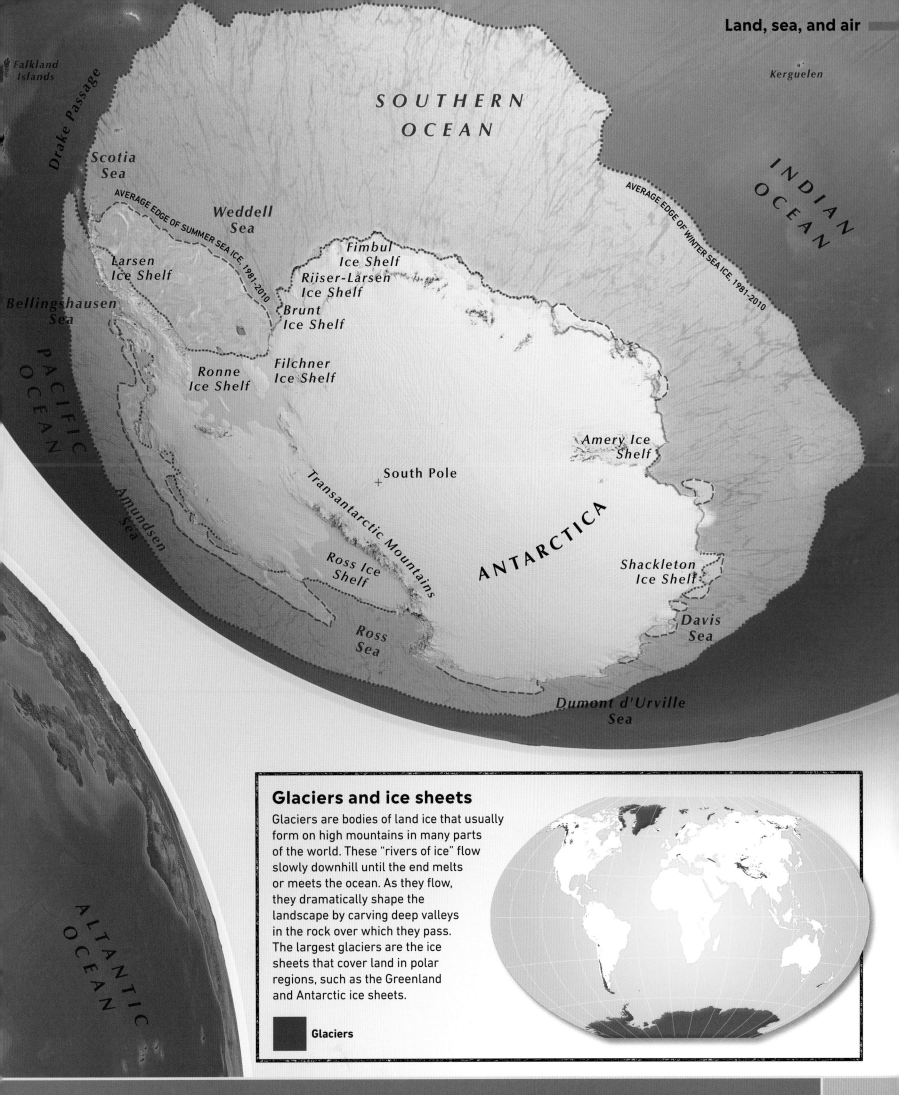

Falkland
Islands

Kerguelen

Drake Passage

S O U T H E R N
O C E A N

*Scotia
Sea*

I N D I A N
O C E A N

AVERAGE EDGE OF SUMMER SEA ICE, 1981–2010

AVERAGE EDGE OF WINTER SEA ICE, 1981–2010

*Weddell
Sea*

*Fimbul
Ice Shelf*

*Larsen
Ice Shelf*

*Riiser-Larsen
Ice Shelf*

*Bellingshausen
Sea*

*Brunt
Ice Shelf*

P A C I F I C   O C E A N

*Ronne
Ice Shelf*

*Filchner
Ice Shelf*

*Amery Ice
Shelf*

+ South Pole

*Amundsen
Sea*

Transantarctic Mountains

A N T A R C T I C A

*Shackleton
Ice Shelf*

*Ross Ice
Shelf*

*Davis
Sea*

*Ross
Sea*

*Dumont d'Urville
Sea*

A T L A N T I C   O C E A N

Glaciers and ice sheets

Glaciers are bodies of land ice that usually
form on high mountains in many parts
of the world. These "rivers of ice" flow
slowly downhill until the end melts
or meets the ocean. As they flow,
they dramatically shape the
landscape by carving deep valleys
in the rock over which they pass.
The largest glaciers are the ice
sheets that cover land in polar
regions, such as the Greenland
and Antarctic ice sheets.

■ **Glaciers**

(551 FT) ABOVE SEA LEVEL - HIGHER THAN A 55-STOREY BUILDING!

37

Time zones map

The map shows the time of day at 12 noon Coordinated Universal Time (UTC), the base from which all times are set. The columns are time zones labelled with the number of hours they are ahead or behind UTC. If you stood halfway between the boundaries of a time zone with your watch set to the correct time, at 12 noon the Sun would be at its highest point.

Time zones

As Earth rotates, some of it faces the Sun and the rest is in darkness. Since the Sun is high in the sky at noon, noon is at different times in different places. We adjust by splitting Earth into time zones.

Day and night

On the globe of Earth, we can see day and night divided by a straight line from north to south. When Earth is laid flat as on the map here, the light and dark areas form a bell shape.

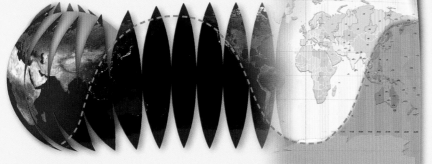

Northern summer
Earth is tilted. When the North Pole tilts towards the Sun and the South Pole leans away, it is summer in the northern hemisphere (northern half of the world) and winter in the southern hemisphere, as on the main map.

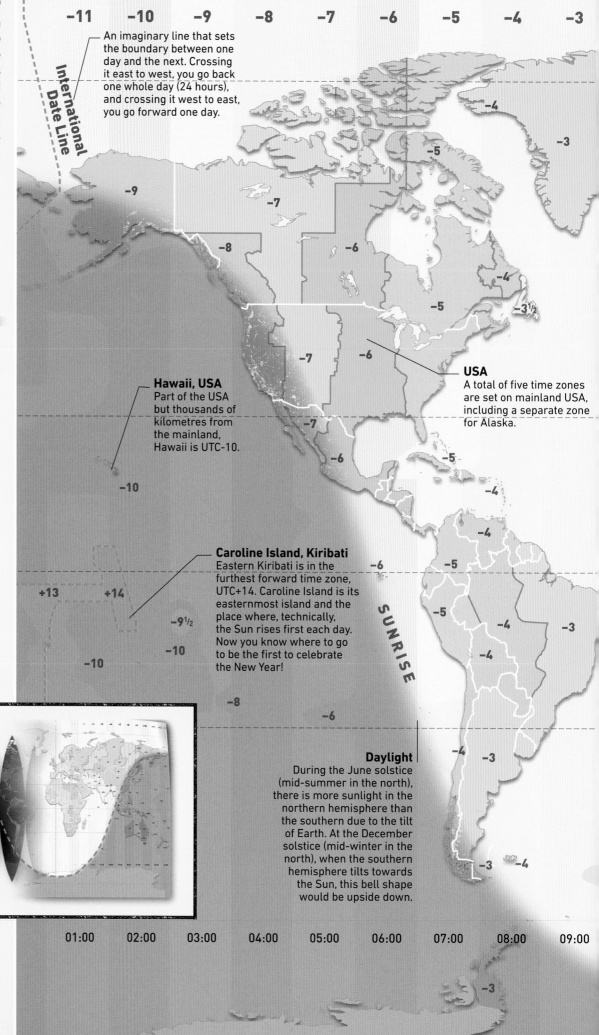

International Date Line
An imaginary line that sets the boundary between one day and the next. Crossing it east to west, you go back one whole day (24 hours), and crossing it west to east, you go forward one day.

Hawaii, USA
Part of the USA but thousands of kilometres from the mainland, Hawaii is UTC-10.

USA
A total of five time zones are set on mainland USA, including a separate zone for Alaska.

Caroline Island, Kiribati
Eastern Kiribati is in the furthest forward time zone, UTC+14. Caroline Island is its easternmost island and the place where, technically, the Sun rises first each day. Now you know where to go to be the first to celebrate the New Year!

Daylight
During the June solstice (mid-summer in the north), there is more sunlight in the northern hemisphere than the southern due to the tilt of Earth. At the December solstice (mid-winter in the north), when the southern hemisphere tilts towards the Sun, this bell shape would be upside down.

SUNRISE

-11 -10 -9 -8 -7 -6 -5 -4 -3

+13 +14 -9½ -10

01:00 02:00 03:00 04:00 05:00 06:00 07:00 08:00 09:00

BEFORE TIME ZONES, LOCAL TIME WAS DECIDED BY THE TOWN TIME-

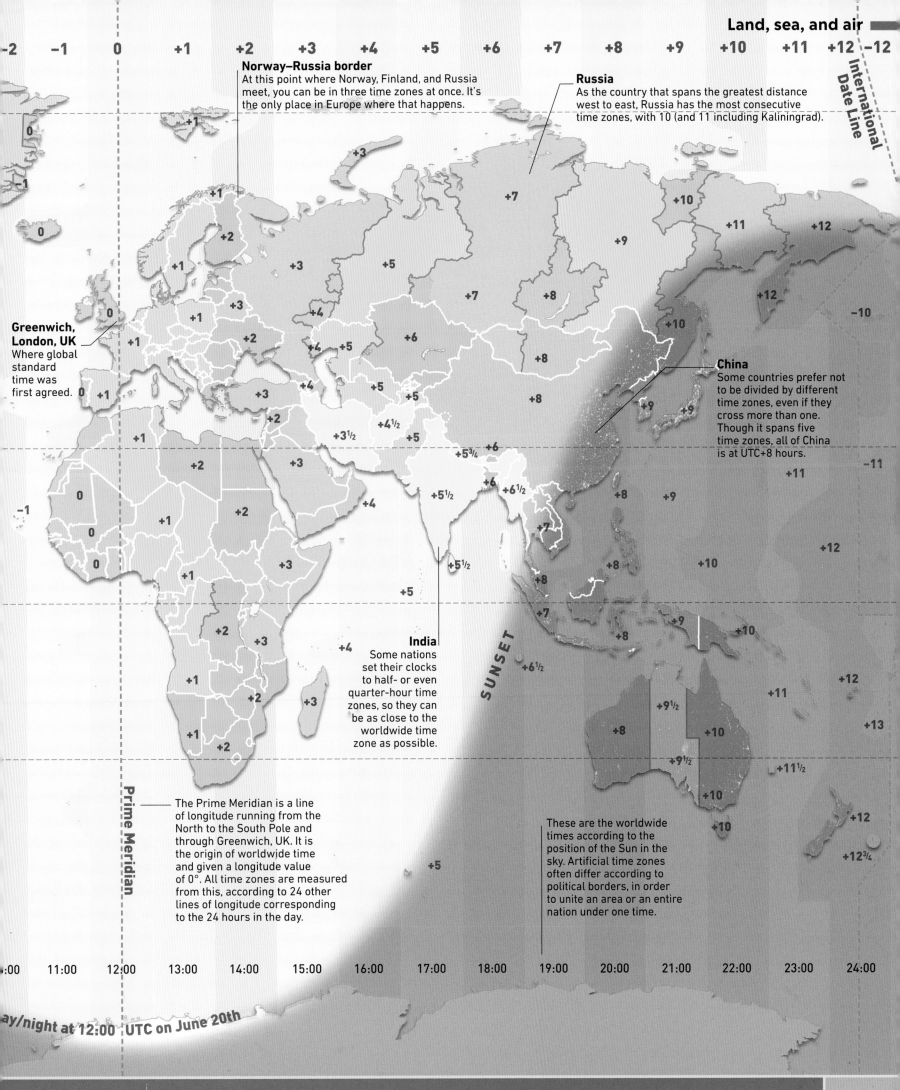

-2 -1 0 +1 +2 +3 +4 +5 +6 +7 +8 +9 +10 +11 +12 -12

International Date Line

Norway–Russia border
At this point where Norway, Finland, and Russia meet, you can be in three time zones at once. It's the only place in Europe where that happens.

Russia
As the country that spans the greatest distance west to east, Russia has the most consecutive time zones, with 10 (and 11 including Kaliningrad).

Greenwich, London, UK
Where global standard time was first agreed.

China
Some countries prefer not to be divided by different time zones, even if they cross more than one. Though it spans five time zones, all of China is at UTC+8 hours.

India
Some nations set their clocks to half- or even quarter-hour time zones, so they can be as close to the worldwide time zone as possible.

SUNSET

Prime Meridian

The Prime Meridian is a line of longitude running from the North to the South Pole and through Greenwich, UK. It is the origin of worldwide time and given a longitude value of 0°. All time zones are measured from this, according to 24 other lines of longitude corresponding to the 24 hours in the day.

These are the worldwide times according to the position of the Sun in the sky. Artificial time zones often differ according to political borders, in order to unite an area or an entire nation under one time.

:00 11:00 12:00 13:00 14:00 15:00 16:00 17:00 18:00 19:00 20:00 21:00 22:00 23:00 24:00

ay/night at 12:00 UTC on June 20th

Living world

Humpback whales
Two humpbacks "breach" (leap out of the water) off the coast of Alaska, USA. During winter, humpbacks move south to warmer waters.

Introduction

Life exists in every corner of the planet – from high mountains to deep oceans, and from blazing deserts to the freezing polar regions. Each animal's body, life cycle, and behaviour is adapted to its particular habitat, because this maximizes its chances of survival. Plant species, too, have their own adaptations that help them thrive.

Bald eagle
A North American bird of prey, the bald eagle snatches fish from lakes.

Birds

The power of flight allows birds to reach the remotest islands, and some to live in different parts of the world in summer and winter, migrating between the two. There is almost nowhere on Earth that lacks birdlife. Here are their secrets.

- **Lightweight bones**
  Most bird bones are hollow, reinforced by bony struts.

- **Flight feathers**
  Wing and tail feathers provide lift and steer the bird in fight.

- **Warming feathers**
  Two layers of body feathers keep the bird's skin warm.

- **Efficient lungs**
  Bird lungs are far more efficient than mammals', giving them the oxygen they need for energetic flight.

Marine animals

Living in water gives more support than living on land, so many sea creatures survive without strong skeletons. Sea water carries clouds of microscopic life-forms and dead matter, and many sea animals can afford to give up moving from place to place, fix themselves to the sea bed, and "filter feed" by grabbing these passing pieces of food.

Coral
Tropical coral reefs are giant growths of filter-feeding life forms on the sea bed.

- **Gills**
  Sea mammals must surface to breathe, but fish take oxygen directly from the water using their gills.

- **Smooth shape**
  Fast-moving marine animals have a streamlined body, which helps them move through the water easily.

- **Buoyancy aid**
  Some fish have an air-filled "swim bladder" to help control buoyancy.

- **Bioluminescence**
  It is dark in the ocean depths. Many deep-sea animals produce light by chemical reactions in their bodies.

Desert cacti
The waxy, fleshy bodies of these desert plants store water. The leaves are reduced to spines, which lose less water to the air. The roots of a cactus may spread out over a wide area, to absorb as much water as possible.

Spineless cactus
A spineless variety of the prickly pear.

THERE ARE PROBABLY AT LEAST 1 MILLION UNDISCOVERED SPECIES IN

Polar regions

The sea in the Arctic and Antarctic is so cold, fish are in danger of freezing. Above the water it is even colder, and no large, cold-blooded animals exist. Warm-blooded animals – those able to retain body heat – predominate. Polar mammals often have two layers of fur: an underlayer of soft hairs that trap air warmed by the animal's body close to the skin, and an outer coat of coarse hairs that keeps out the fiercest gales.

Polar bear
This Arctic mammal has a bulky, rounded body surrounded by fat and fur that keep it warm.

- **Natural antifreeze**
  Most polar fish have a chemical in their blood that prevents ice crystals forming in the body.

- **Small extremities**
  Polar bears and Arctic foxes have small, rounded ears and muzzles that reduce heat loss.

- **Legs and feet**
  Some animals have long legs that wade through snow or broad feet that act like snowshoes.

Western brown snake
A venomous Australian desert species.

Desert regions

The driest parts of the world challenge plants and animals, and desert wildlife is not as abundant as in wetter regions. Desert life-forms must get enough water – and keep what they have. Some desert animals get all the water they need from their food.

- **Nocturnal lifestyle**
  Many animals are active only at night. Gerbils and jerboas retreat into daytime burrows to stay cool.

- **Large extremities**
  Fennec foxes have huge ears that radiate heat away from the body.

- **Drinking dew**
  Insects and lizards drink dewdrops. Larger desert animals that feed at dawn take in dew as they eat plants.

Plant adaptations

In rainforests, plants are in strong competition to reach sunlight. They all grow as fast as possible whenever there is an opening allowing in the Sun. In deserts, plants get plenty of light, but they struggle to get enough water from the soil.

Bo tree leaves
This fig tree with drip-tip leaves grows in the rainforests of southern Asia.

Rainforest plants
To reach the Sun, many rainforest plants are specialist climbers, and others are epiphytes, which grow on top of other plants. Many rainforest leaves taper to a long point, a "drip tip", to help excess rainwater run off.

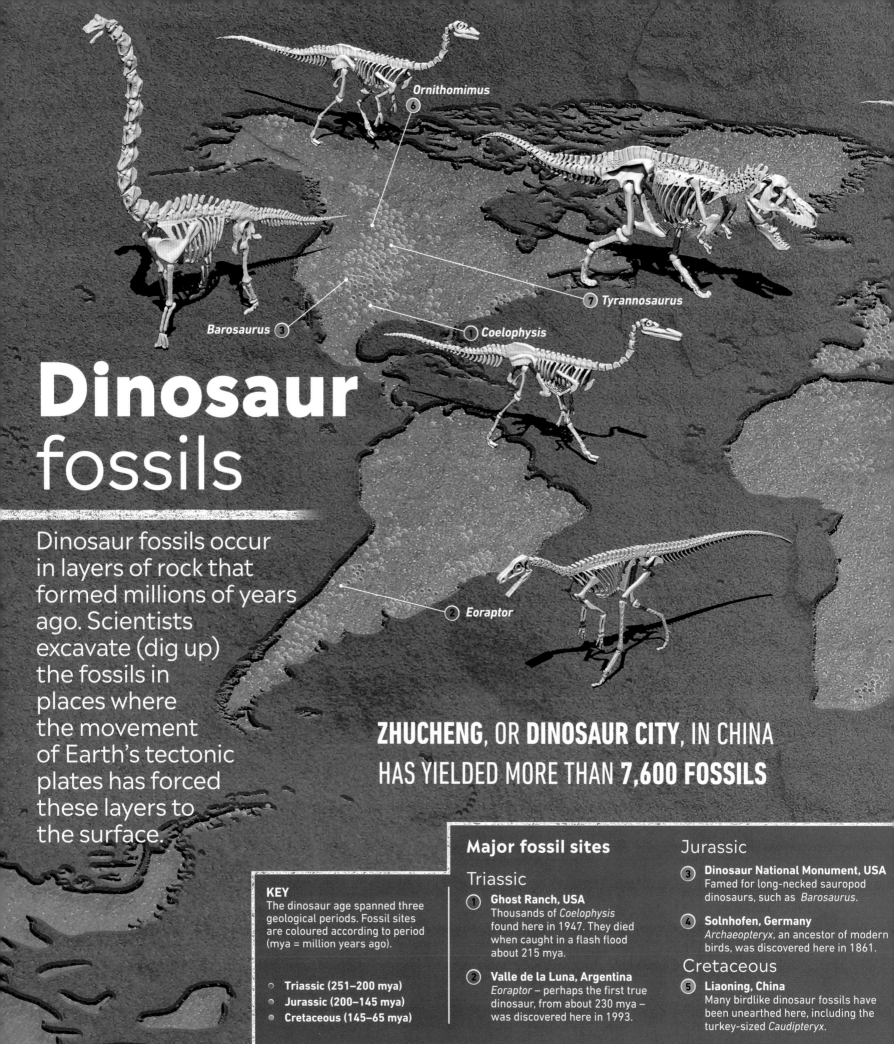

Dinosaur fossils

Dinosaur fossils occur in layers of rock that formed millions of years ago. Scientists excavate (dig up) the fossils in places where the movement of Earth's tectonic plates has forced these layers to the surface.

Ornithomimus ⑥

Barosaurus ③

⑦ *Tyrannosaurus*

① *Coelophysis*

② *Eoraptor*

ZHUCHENG, OR **DINOSAUR CITY**, IN CHINA HAS YIELDED MORE THAN **7,600 FOSSILS**

KEY
The dinosaur age spanned three geological periods. Fossil sites are coloured according to period (mya = million years ago).

- ○ Triassic (251–200 mya)
- ● Jurassic (200–145 mya)
- ● Cretaceous (145–65 mya)

Major fossil sites

Triassic

① **Ghost Ranch, USA**
Thousands of *Coelophysis* found here in 1947. They died when caught in a flash flood about 215 mya.

② **Valle de la Luna, Argentina**
Eoraptor – perhaps the first true dinosaur, from about 230 mya – was discovered here in 1993.

Jurassic

③ **Dinosaur National Monument, USA**
Famed for long-necked sauropod dinosaurs, such as *Barosaurus*.

④ **Solnhofen, Germany**
Archaeopteryx, an ancestor of modern birds, was discovered here in 1861.

Cretaceous

⑤ **Liaoning, China**
Many birdlike dinosaur fossils have been unearthed here, including the turkey-sized *Caudipteryx*.

AS WELL AS BONES, NESTS, EGGS, AND TRACKS, FOSSILS INCLUDE

Dinosaur footprints

Fossil-hunters have found tracks preserved in mud and sand that later turned into rock. These tracks can tell us how dinosaurs walked, and whether they lived alone or in groups. The sites shown here are all in the USA.

Dinosaur Ridge
Colorado. Hundreds of prints unearthed when building a road.

Dinosaur State Park
Connecticut. One of the largest track sites in North America.

Purgatoire River site
Colorado. Giant sauropod prints left on a lake shore.

4 *Archaeopteryx*

5 *Caudipteryx*

9 *Hadrosaurus*

8 *Protoceratops*

10 *Leaellynasaura*

6 **Dinosaur Provincial Park, Canada**
An entire *Ornithomimus*, from 75 mya, was discovered here in 1995.

7 **Hell Creek, USA**
Ancient rocks here have yielded a range of dinosaur fossils – among them, *Tyrannosaurus*.

8 **Flaming Cliffs, Mongolia**
The first *Protoceratops* fossils and dinosaur nest were found here.

9 **Zhucheng, China**
Since the 1960s, over 50 tonnes of fossils have been found here. Rich in remains of "duck-billed" dinosaurs such as *Hadrosaurus*.

10 **Dinosaur Cove, Australia**
About 105 mya this was near the South Pole. Until the discovery of *Leaellynasaura* here in 1989, no one knew dinosaurs could live through cold, long, dark winters.

TRACES OF SKIN AND FEATHERS, AND EVEN DINOSAUR POO!

Americas

1. Bald eagle
Stabs its sharp talons into prey and rips open the body with its hooked bill.

2. Wolverine
Preys on rodents, other small mammals, and even weakened reindeer.

3. Coyote
Eats almost anything, from insects and frogs to calves and lambs.

4. Boa constrictor
A large snake, the boa coils around its prey and squeezes until the victim suffocates.

5. Jaguar
Unable to run fast for very long, the jaguar relies on stealth to creep up on prey.

6. Piranha
Using razor-sharp teeth, a shoal can reduce a deer to bones in minutes.

Africa

7. African rock python
Growing up to 8.5 m (28 ft) long, pythons prey on monkeys, pigs, and birds.

8. African lion
The females do most of the hunting. The male defends the pride's territory.

9. African wild dog
Can chase down prey at 40 kph (25 mph) for 5 km (3 miles) or more.

Eurasia

10. Polar bear
Can kill with a single swipe from one of its 18-kg (40-lb) front paws.

11. Golden eagle
With its amazing eyesight, can spot prey 2 km (1.25 miles) away.

12. Grey wolf
Packs can bring down animals as large as reindeer or musk ox.

---

10. Polar bear
On land and sea ice within the Arctic Circle

11. Golden eagle
Europe, North America, northern Asia, and Africa

1. Bald eagle
Throughout North America

2. Wolverine
Canada and northern USA; Scandinavia and Siberia

3. Coyote
From Alaska to Central America

19. Killer whale (orca)
Oceans worldwide

4. Boa constrictor
From Mexico to Argentina

20. Common dolphin
Cool and warm oceans worldwide

21. Sperm whale
Worldwide, to the edge of the polar ice

7. African rock python
Africa, south of the Sahara

18. California sea lion
Pacific coast of North America and the Galápagos Islands

5. Jaguar
Southwestern USA to northern Argentina

22. Tuna
Cool and warm oceans worldwide

6. Piranha
North, central, and eastern South America

23. Great white shark
Cool and warm oceans worldwide

3,000–4,000:
THE NUMBER OF **TIGERS** LEFT IN THE WILD

Predators

Found on every continent and in every ocean, predators are animals that kill and eat other creatures. With their incredible array of hunting strategies and body parts adapted for killing, they include some of the most fascinating species on the planet.

WHEN A PEREGRINE FALCON DIVES ON A PIGEON AT FULL SPEED,

13. Eurasian lynx
Furry ear tufts gather prey noises in the dense forest, where sounds are muffled.

14. Peregrine falcon
Dives onto prey at 320 kph (200 mph), making it the fastest animal on Earth.

15. Eurasian badger
Eats worms, insects, birds, frogs, lizards, and small mammals, plus plants.

16. Tiger
Camouflaged by its stripes, a tiger stalks its prey and kills with a bite to the neck.

17. Sunda clouded leopard
For its size, this shy forest-dweller has longer canine teeth than any other cat.

Oceans

18. California sea lion
May hunt nonstop for 30 hours, diving for up to 5 minutes at a time.

19. Killer whale (orca)
Many hunt sea lions, dolphins, and even whales. Can snatch seals off the ice.

20. Common dolphin
Together, dolphins can herd fish to the surface, where they are easier to catch.

21. Sperm whale
May dive to 3,000 m (9,843 ft) deep in search of giant squid.

22. Tuna
Able to swim at 80 kph (50 mph); hunts fish and squid near surface.

23. Great white shark
Kills dolphins, seals, and big fish, including other sharks, with its jagged teeth.

12. Grey wolf
Much of Asia, parts of Europe, and northern North America

13. Eurasian lynx
Europe (mainly northern and eastern parts) to northern and central Asia

14. Peregrine falcon
Lives on every continent except Antarctica

16. Tiger
Parts of India, China, Siberia, and southeast Asia

15. Eurasian badger
Europe and Asia below the Arctic Circle

Australasia

24. Saltwater crocodile
Preys on water buffalo and cattle on land. Spends much of its life at sea, catching fish.

25. Tasmanian devil
This marsupial's strong jaws can crush the bones of birds, fish, and small mammals.

8. African lion
Africa, south of the Sahara

17. Sunda clouded leopard
Sumatra and Borneo in southeast Asia

9. African wild dog
Africa, south of the Sahara

Food chains

A food chain shows how food energy passes from one living thing to the next. Food chains start with plants, which use sunlight to make their own food. Plants are eaten by herbivores. Predators eat herbivores and smaller predators.

Martial eagle (top predator)

Meerkat (predator)

Imperial scorpion (predator)

Grasshopper (herbivore)

Grass

A FOOD CHAIN IN THE AFRICAN SAVANNA

24. Saltwater crocodile
Southeast Asia and Northern Australia

25. Tasmanian devil
Tasmania, an island off the southeastern tip of Australia

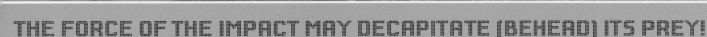

THE FORCE OF THE IMPACT MAY DECAPITATE (BEHEAD) ITS PREY!

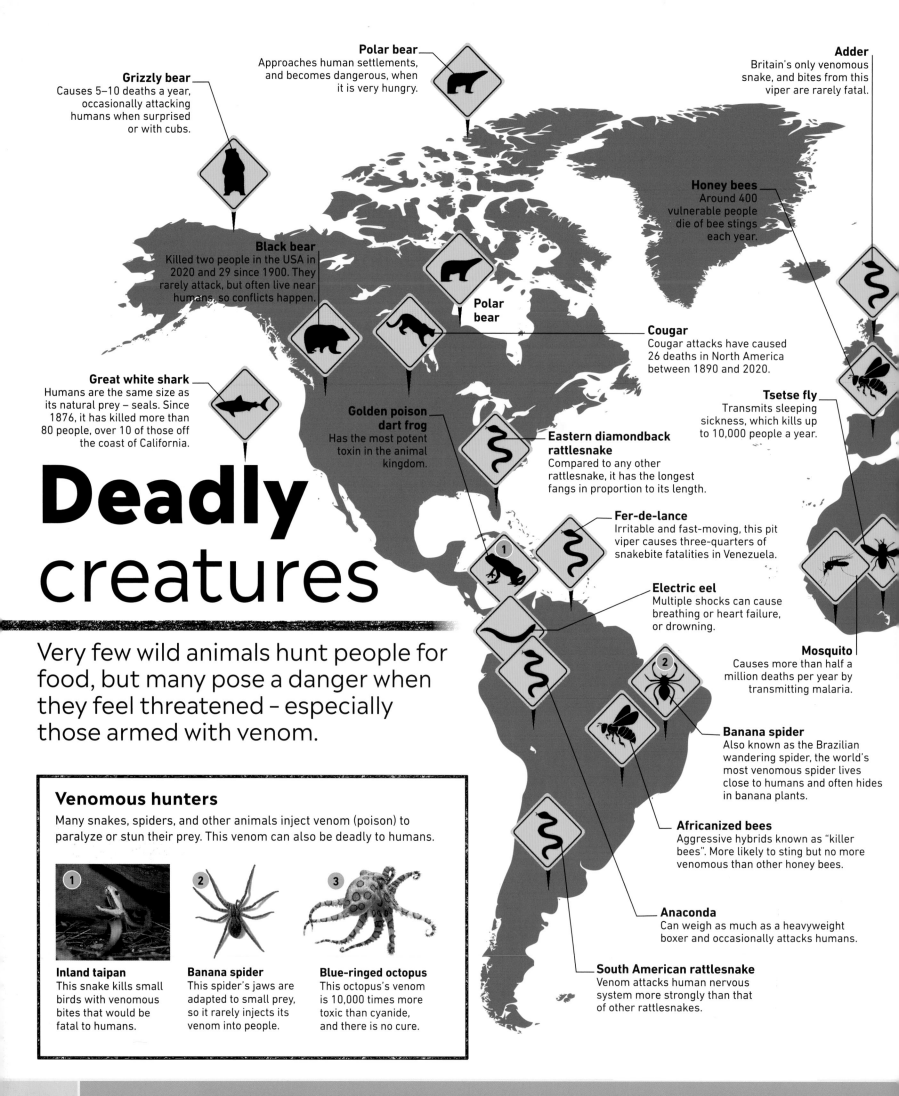

Deadly creatures

Very few wild animals hunt people for food, but many pose a danger when they feel threatened – especially those armed with venom.

Grizzly bear
Causes 5–10 deaths a year, occasionally attacking humans when surprised or with cubs.

Polar bear
Approaches human settlements, and becomes dangerous, when it is very hungry.

Adder
Britain's only venomous snake, and bites from this viper are rarely fatal.

Black bear
Killed two people in the USA in 2020 and 29 since 1900. They rarely attack, but often live near humans, so conflicts happen.

Honey bees
Around 400 vulnerable people die of bee stings each year.

Polar bear

Cougar
Cougar attacks have caused 26 deaths in North America between 1890 and 2020.

Great white shark
Humans are the same size as its natural prey – seals. Since 1876, it has killed more than 80 people, over 10 of those off the coast of California.

Tsetse fly
Transmits sleeping sickness, which kills up to 10,000 people a year.

Golden poison dart frog
Has the most potent toxin in the animal kingdom.

Eastern diamondback rattlesnake
Compared to any other rattlesnake, it has the longest fangs in proportion to its length.

Fer-de-lance
Irritable and fast-moving, this pit viper causes three-quarters of snakebite fatalities in Venezuela.

Electric eel
Multiple shocks can cause breathing or heart failure, or drowning.

Mosquito
Causes more than half a million deaths per year by transmitting malaria.

Banana spider
Also known as the Brazilian wandering spider, the world's most venomous spider lives close to humans and often hides in banana plants.

Africanized bees
Aggressive hybrids known as "killer bees". More likely to sting but no more venomous than other honey bees.

Anaconda
Can weigh as much as a heavyweight boxer and occasionally attacks humans.

South American rattlesnake
Venom attacks human nervous system more strongly than that of other rattlesnakes.

Venomous hunters

Many snakes, spiders, and other animals inject venom (poison) to paralyze or stun their prey. This venom can also be deadly to humans.

Inland taipan
This snake kills small birds with venomous bites that would be fatal to humans.

Banana spider
This spider's jaws are adapted to small prey, so it rarely injects its venom into people.

Blue-ringed octopus
This octopus's venom is 10,000 times more toxic than cyanide, and there is no cure.

ANIMAL TOXINS ARE USEFUL. SCIENTISTS HAVE ADAPTED THE

SOME VICTIMS OF **STONEFISH VENOM** SAY IT'S GOOD FOR THEIR ARTHRITIS

Defensive poisons

Many animals use toxins (poisons) against predators. The poisons may be in spines or stings, or they may ooze from the skin.

Golden poison dart frog
The skin has enough toxin to kill 10 people. It is effective against its snake predators.

Pufferfish
The poison in puffers' skin and liver could kill a human, but these fish make a prized dish in Japan.

Stonefish
This fish's spines stop predators, but also endanger humans who are pricked by accident.

Asp viper
Causes about 90 per cent of all snake bites in Italy, but only 4 per cent of bites are fatal.

Pallas's viper
0.1 gram (0.004 oz) of venom can kill a human, but only strikes if threatened.

European black widow spider
Venom is 15 times stronger than a rattlesnake's.

Fat-tailed scorpion
Most dangerous scorpion in North Africa and the Middle East.

Tiger
Until recent improvements in tiger management, hunted and killed around 50 people every year in the Sundarbans mangroves of India.

Common krait
Most venomous land snake in Asia.

Pufferfish
Eaten as *fugu* in Japan and *bok-uh* in Korea, but some parts highly poisonous. Accidents happen when untrained people catch and eat the fish.

Malayan pit viper
Responsible for 700 snakebites annually in Malaysia.

Box jellyfish
Has enough toxin to kill 60 humans, and in the Philippines 20–40 people die each year from stings.

Puff adder
Lives in heavily populated areas and is the most dangerous snake in Africa.

Lionfish
Its venomous spines can cause severe injuries, breathing difficulties, and temporary paralysis.

Saltwater crocodile
Makes frequent fatal attacks on humans in New Guinea, the Solomon Islands, and Indonesia.

Elephant
Attacks people when threatened and kills nearly 300 people a year.

African lion
Kills 70 people a year in Tanzania, either by hunting them for food, or in defence.

Asian cobra
Responsible for more human deaths than any other snake.

Stonefish
Venom injected by spines causes unbearable pain and death in a few hours if not treated.

Hippopotamus
Causes more than 300 deaths a year, sometimes by upturning boats.

Komodo dragon
Giant lizard that grows up to 3 m (10 ft) long and may, very rarely, attack and eat humans.

Cape buffalo
Attacks when defending itself and kills more than 200 people a year.

Blue-ringed octopus
Enough toxin in its body to kill 26 adult humans. It can cause respiratory failure.

Tiger snake
In humans, 60 per cent of untreated bites result in serious poisoning or death.

Black mamba
Fastest snake on Earth and kills any human it bites unless the victim takes antivenom.

Redback spider
Also known as the Australian black widow. Deaths are rare, but bites can result in fatal complications.

Six-eyed sand spider
There is no antivenom for its bite but (luckily) it is shy and has little contact with people.

Inland taipan
Deadliest venom of any land snake, but snake scientists are almost the only known victims. They recovered after treatment with antivenom.

Funnel-web spider
Its extremely toxic venom could kill a small child in 15 minutes.

TOXIN FROM POISON DART FROGS TO PRODUCE A POTENT PAINKILLER.

49

How the aliens invade

Stowaways
Fleas and other parasites can hitch a ride via animal or human hosts. Rats, mice, and insects can travel hidden in ships' cargo. Some species sneak in when empty cargo ships take on local sea water as ballast, then pump it out at their destination. Every day, large numbers of marine organisms are transported around the globe in this way.

Black rat

Introduced by humans
Some species are deliberately introduced by humans. This can be by hunters, for meat, fur, or sport; by farmers; or for biological control, where a new species is introduced to control native pests. Some invaders are escaped pets, or plants washed out of home aquariums. A few have even been released by immigrants who introduce familiar wildlife to remind them of home!

Cane toad

Racoon
Since its introduction, has devastated the seabird population of Canada's Scott Islands.

Zebra mussel
Travelled from the Caspian Sea to the Great Lakes of North America in the ballast water of ships.

Common starling
European native bird released in New York City in 1890 by homesick English settler Eugene Schieffelin.

Stoat
Introduced to islands off Denmark and the Netherlands, it eradicated the native water voles.

Grey squirrel
This US import to Britain competes for habitat with the native red squirrel.

Rainbow trout
In California, this fish has endangered the Sierra Nevada yellow-legged frog.

Gypsy moth
This European native costs about $870 million each year in damage to US trees.

Japanese knotweed
Dense thickets of this weed crowd out native plant life on riverbanks and roadsides in Europe.

Velvet tree
Known as the "purple plague of Hawaii", it threatens native rainforest plant species.

Flowerpot snake
Emigrated to the USA from Africa and Asia by stowing away in the soil of exported pot plants.

Chinese mitten crab
A burrowing species that threatens the US fishery industry by eating bait and trapped fish.

Feral pig
In Mexico's Revillagigedo Islands, this former farm animal preys on the endangered Townsend's shearwater bird.

American bullfrog
Native to North America, it is now a resident of more than 40 countries.

Fire ant
Threatens tortoises on the Galápagos Islands by eating hatchlings and attacking adults.

Red-vented bulbul
A major agricultural pest in Tahiti, it feeds on fruit and vegetable crops.

Feral goat
Has caused serious damage to native vegetation on the Galápagos Islands.

Africanized honey bee
Specially bred for survival in the tropics, this "killer bee" turned out to be too aggressive and unpredictable for beekeepers.

ABOUT
90 PER CENT
OF THE WORLD'S **ISLANDS**
HAVE NOW BEEN
INVADED BY RATS

Red Deer
Introduced from Europe to provide sportspeople with game.

House mouse
With no predators on Gough Island, non-native mice have grown to three times their usual size.

INVASIVE SPECIES HAVE PLAYED A PART IN ALMOST HALF OF THE

Alien invasion

Invasive species are animals or plants that enter and thrive in an environment where they are not native. Native species (plants and animals already living there) usually have no defence. The invading aliens can wipe out native species by preying on them or out-competing them.

Signal crayfish
Introduced from North America to Scandinavia for food, but carries "crayfish plague" which hits native crayfish.

"Warty" comb jellyfish
A recent arrival via tankers from the USA, it peaked at more than 95 per cent of the weight of all living things in the Black Sea.

Chinese creeper vine
Introduced to India in World War II to camouflage airfields, it is now a rampant weed.

African land snail
Brought to Taiwan as human food, it carries diseases, including meningitis.

Small Indian mongoose
Has destroyed seven native animal species on Japan's Amami Ōshima Island since 1979.

Arctic fox
Its introduction to the Aleutian Islands by fur-hunters has been disastrous for ground-nesting birds.

Brown tree snake
Accidentally introduced, it has caused the extinction of most of Guam's native birds and lizards.

Water hyacinth
Kills fish and turtles in Papua New Guinea by blocking sunlight and starving the water of oxygen.

Cane toad
Australians are trying to control their 200 million cane toads (which were themselves introduced to control beetle crop pests) by culling and genetic engineering.

Brown rat
A threat to island-nesting seabirds everywhere, it was eradicated from seven islands in Fiji in 2010.

Polynesian rat (kiore)
Stowed away with Māori settlers. Eats nesting seabirds.

Nile perch
This fish has contributed to the extinction of more than 200 fish species in Lake Victoria.

Giant sensitive plant
A serious weed in Thailand, it clogs irrigation systems and lowers crop yields.

Yellow crazy ants
On Christmas Island, millions of red land crabs have been killed by these invaders.

European rabbit
More than 200 million rabbits overran Australia, from an original 24 released by an English immigrant for hunting.

Common brushtail possum
First brought to New Zealand to establish a fur trade.

Prickly pear
South Africa is looking at biological methods of controlling this invasive weed – for instance, by introducing the cactus moth, whose caterpillars eat it.

Feral cat
On the Kerguelen Islands, cats kill 1.2 million nesting seabirds every year.

Dromedary camel
Originally brought in for transport, there are now 1.1 million feral ("gone wild") camels in Australia.

Northern Pacific seastar
In Tasmania, volunteers organize "hunting days" to try to eradicate this Japanese starfish.

Black swan
Introduced in 1864 to New Zealand from Australia as an ornamental bird.

Wasps
Have reached plague proportions in the beech forests of the South Island.

ANIMAL EXTINCTIONS THAT HAVE OCCURRED IN THE LAST 400 YEARS.

51

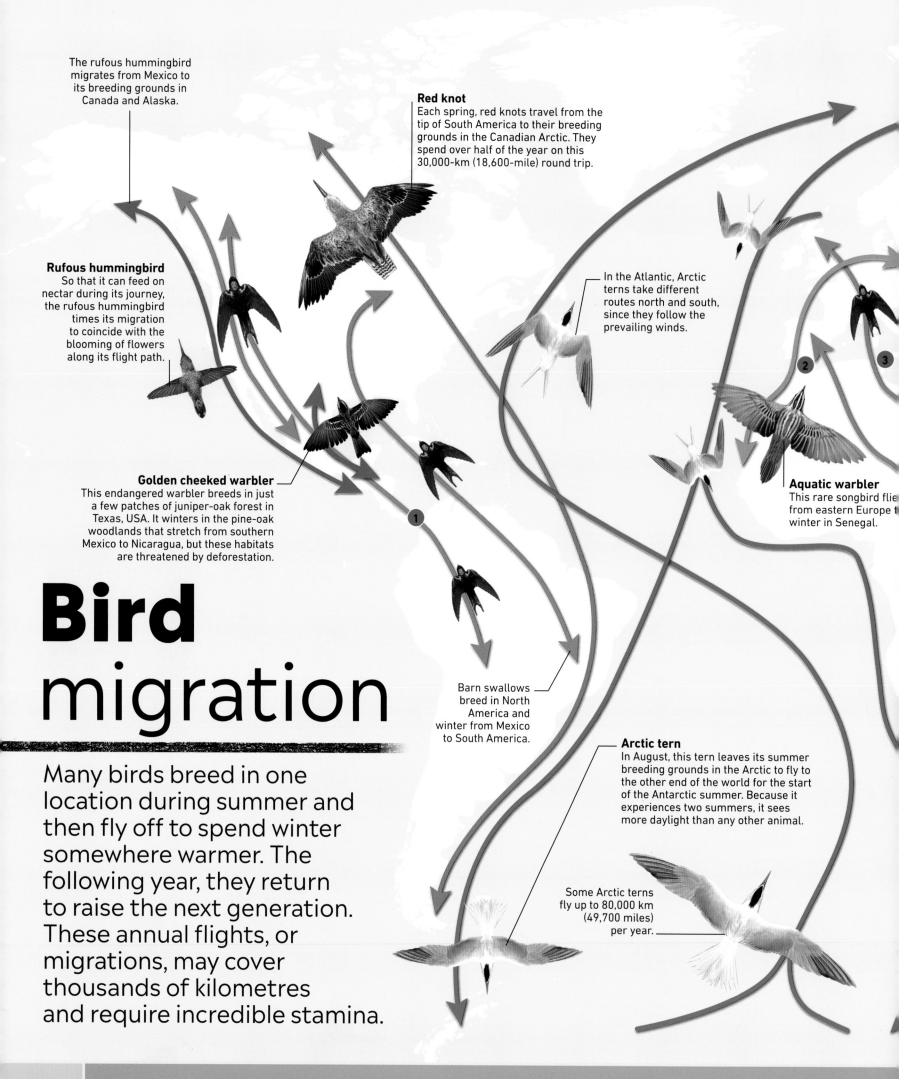

The rufous hummingbird migrates from Mexico to its breeding grounds in Canada and Alaska.

Red knot
Each spring, red knots travel from the tip of South America to their breeding grounds in the Canadian Arctic. They spend over half of the year on this 30,000-km (18,600-mile) round trip.

Rufous hummingbird
So that it can feed on nectar during its journey, the rufous hummingbird times its migration to coincide with the blooming of flowers along its flight path.

In the Atlantic, Arctic terns take different routes north and south, since they follow the prevailing winds.

Golden cheeked warbler
This endangered warbler breeds in just a few patches of juniper-oak forest in Texas, USA. It winters in the pine-oak woodlands that stretch from southern Mexico to Nicaragua, but these habitats are threatened by deforestation.

Aquatic warbler
This rare songbird flie[s] from eastern Europe t[o] winter in Senegal.

Bird
migration

Barn swallows breed in North America and winter from Mexico to South America.

Arctic tern
In August, this tern leaves its summer breeding grounds in the Arctic to fly to the other end of the world for the start of the Antarctic summer. Because it experiences two summers, it sees more daylight than any other animal.

Many birds breed in one location during summer and then fly off to spend winter somewhere warmer. The following year, they return to raise the next generation. These annual flights, or migrations, may cover thousands of kilometres and require incredible stamina.

Some Arctic terns fly up to 80,000 km (49,700 miles) per year.

Red-breasted goose
After wintering on the Black Sea coast, the red-breasted goose heads north to raise chicks on the Russian tundra.

Barn swallows that spend winter in India fly north to nest in northern Asia.

Barn swallows of southern Africa fly to Europe to breed.

Ferruginous duck
This widespread duck breeds on marshes and lakes and makes relatively short migrations. Ferruginous ducks that breed in western China and Mongolia winter in India and Pakistan.

A bar-tailed godwit may travel up to 460,000 km (286,000 miles) during the course of its life.

Sociable lapwing
In 2007, the sociable lapwing's migration route from east Africa to Kazakhstan and Russia was revealed for the first time by satellite-tracking.

Barn swallow
Each year, huge flocks migrate between northern Australia and eastern Russia. These birds can catch insects on the wing and drink by scooping water from lakes.

ARCTIC TERNS FLY FROM THE **ANTARCTIC** TO **GREENLAND** IN **40 DAYS**

Aided by strong tailwinds at high altitude, the godwits can make the return journey to New Zealand in just over eight days.

Migration bottlenecks
Places that lie on the flight paths of many birds are known as migration bottlenecks. They are especially important for soaring birds such as storks and birds of prey. These birds can't fly far over water, so they rely on routes with the shortest sea crossings. Millions of birds may pass at these favourite spots.

1 **Panama**
About 3 million birds of prey use this land bridge between North and South America.

2 **Strait of Gibraltar**
Soaring birds fly to Europe from Africa on this sea crossing of only 14 km (9 miles).

3 **Sicily and Malta**
These islands are "stepping stones" for birds flying from Italy to Tunisia and Libya.

4 **Egypt**
Egypt has several bottlenecks – such as Suez, Hurghada, and Zaranik – for birds flying between Africa and Europe or Asia.

Bar-tailed godwit
Bar-tailed godwits fly from New Zealand to breed in Alaska. On the return trip, one was tracked flying 11,680 km (7,258 miles) nonstop over the Pacific Ocean – the longest continuous journey ever recorded for a bird.

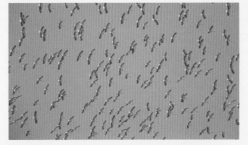

This flock of white storks flying over Spain reached Europe via the Strait of Gibraltar.

1. Gulf of Alaska
Humpbacks make "bubblenets". They blow a curtain of bubbles around a shoal of fish. This causes the fish to cluster tightly, making them easier to catch.

2. Sea of Cortez
Humpback whales in the Sea of Cortez can often be seen breaching (launching out of the water) and slapping their fins and tails on the surface. Whales are social animals, and this behaviour may be a form of communication.

4. Western North Atlantic
There are only about 450 North Atlantic right whales left. Most spend the summer feeding in the waters from New York to Nova Scotia. They head south in winter to breed in the warmer waters off Georgia and Florida.

3. Baja California, Mexico
The gray whales here are exceptionally friendly, approaching boats to let whale-watchers touch them and even scratch their tongues. The whales migrate between Baja California and Alaska.

5. Brazil
From June to November each year, more than 300 southern right whales gather off the state of Santa Catarina to mate, calve, and nurse their young.

Whales

Graceful swimmers, superb divers, and powerful predators, whales and orcas (killer whales) are among the most impressive ocean creatures. They were once hunted near to extinction. Today, thousands of people take whale-watching trips to see these majestic marine mammals in the wild.

7. South Africa
Each June, southern right whales arrive off the coast of South Africa from their Antarctic breeding grounds, giving whale-watchers a chance to enjoy their spectacular acrobatic displays.

6. Patagonia, Argentina
Orcas snatch elephant seals and sea lions from their colonies. They surge ashore on the surf and grab prey in their jaws as they land on the beach, before manoeuvring back into the water with the next wave. If they misjudged the attack, they would become fatally stranded on the beach.

THE BLUE WHALE IS THE LARGEST ANIMAL EVER TO HAVE LIVED

1 MILLION SPERM WHALES WERE KILLED BEFORE HUNTING THEM WAS BANNED IN 1981

Migration

Whales travel to cold waters near the poles to feed, then move to warmer waters closer to the equator to breed. Few species migrate across the equator, so there can be separate populations in the northern and southern hemispheres.

KEY

Breeding areas Warmer waters for giving birth

Feeding areas Cooler waters that are rich in food

Migration routes Breeding-to-feeding areas and back

Site of spectacular whale behaviour

10. Northwest Pacific
In winter, the humpbacks of the western Pacific mate and calve in warm, subtropical waters from the Philippines to Japan. Summer sees them travelling to feed in the extreme north of the Pacific, around the Aleutian Islands.

8. Sri Lanka
Between December and April, Dondra Point, on Sri Lanka's southern tip, is the best place to see blue whales. Unlike most populations of blue whales, this one does not migrate to polar waters to feed. These northern Indian Ocean blue whales both breed and feed year round in tropical waters.

9. Antarctica
Antarctic orcas often hunt in teams, herding their prey together before attacking from different angles. They will also tip over ice floes to knock penguins and seals into the water.

11. Kaikoura, New Zealand
This one of few places in the world where sperm whales can be seen year round. They are attracted by an underwater canyon close to the shore that has abundant marine life, including the giant squid that the whales hunt.

ON EARTH. ITS TONGUE ALONE CAN WEIGH AS MUCH AS AN ELEPHANT!

SOME **SHARKS** GROW UP TO **30,000 TEETH** IN THEIR **LIFETIME**

Freshwater sharks

Some shark species are found in freshwater habitats. The bull shark, for example, lives in warm coastal waters worldwide, but it sometimes swims up larger rivers and into lakes. Bull sharks are very territorial, so if they find humans swimming in their river, they may attack them.

Mississippi River
One bull shark reached Alton, Illinois, 1,850 km (1,150 miles) upstream.

Potomac River
Bull sharks up to 2.4 m (8 ft) long have been caught in the Potomac.

Lake Nicaragua
Bull sharks reach the lake via the San Juan River.

Amazon River
There have been sightings of bull sharks 2,000 km (1,200 miles) from the sea.

Nicole

In 2003–04, a female great white shark, nicknamed Nicole, made the longest known migration by a shark. Nicole swam from Africa to Australia and back – more than 20,000 km (12,400 miles) – in 9 months. She mostly swam at the surface, but at times she reached depths of up to 980 m (3,200 ft).

- - - - - - - ->

Nicole's route was tracked using an electronic tag fitted to her fin.

DISTRIBUTION OF SHARKS WORLDWIDE

Some shark species cruise almost all the world's oceans, while others have a more limited range, preferring either cooler or warmer seas.

Whale shark
The largest fish in the sea, reaching lengths of 12 m (40 ft) or more, the whale shark prefers warm waters. It feeds mainly on plankton.

Basking shark
At 10 m (30 ft) long, this is the second-largest fish. Found in temperate seas, it swims open-mouthed, filtering plankton from the water.

Great white shark
Found in the majority of the world's seas, the great white has made the most recorded attacks on humans. It can swim at over 40 kph (25 mph).

Great hammerhead shark
Often found near tropical reefs, the great hammerhead preys on stingrays, using its hammer to pin down the fish before biting them.

Port Jackson shark
A reef-dweller from around southern Australia, this shark has wide, flat teeth that crush hard-shelled prey such as oysters, snails, and crabs.

Pygmy shark
At 20–25 cm (8–10 in) long, this is one of the smallest sharks. It hunts squid at depths of up to 1,800 m (6,000 ft) in subtropical and temperate seas.

Sharks

Fast, powerful, and armed with razor-sharp teeth, sharks are superb predators. They are much feared, but attacks on people are relatively rare. Humans, in contrast, kill 100 million sharks per year.

Subarctic species
Piked dogfish inhabit temperate and cool seas, venturing as far north as the edge of the Arctic Circle.

Ganges River
In the Ganges and Brahmaputra, the bull shark is often mistaken for the rare Ganges shark.

Zambezi River
Bull sharks are known to attack young hippos.

Wide distribution
The great white shark has one of the greatest ranges of any shark species. However, it is not found in polar waters.

Nicole's route
The trip from South Africa to Australia took Nicole the great white shark 99 days. After about 3 months, she set off again on the return journey.

Pacific angel shark
This shark of the eastern Pacific lies on the sea bed and ambushes passing fish. It is superbly camouflaged by its mottled, sandy back.

Ornate wobbegong
Elaborately patterned and with fleshy projections around its jaws, this shark inhabits tropical waters, mainly around the Australian coast.

Frilled shark
With its flat head and eel-like body, this frilled shark looks very different to other sharks. It lives near the sea bed in deep water.

Longnose sawshark
The longnose lives off southern Australia. Its snout is a long, sawlike projection edged with rows of large, sharp teeth.

Bull shark
This shark is one of the most dangerous to humans. It preys on sharks, rays, and other fish, as well as squid, turtles, and crustaceans.

Piked dogfish
Once among the most abundant sharks, the piked dogfish is now threatened as a result of overfishing. It gathers in shoals by the thousand.

DROPS OF BLOOD IN THE WATER FROM 5 KM (3 MILES) AWAY.

Americas

1. North American white sturgeon
Similar to sturgeons living 100 million years ago, this fish depends heavily on its sense of smell.

2. American paddlefish
Takes its name from its long, paddle-shaped snout.

3. Alligator gar
Hides in aquatic plants to ambush its prey.

4. Electric eel
Generates huge electric shocks to stun prey and ward off attackers.

5. Redtail catfish
Stops feeding to shed its skin like a snake.

6. Spectacled caiman
Named after the bony ridge between its eyes.

7. Arapaima
The adult fish relies on air-breathing, not gills, to get oxygen. But its need to come to the surface makes it vulnerable to hunters.

8. Amazon river dolphin
Hunts in the murky water by sonar and uses its long snout to catch prey hiding in underwater plants. Females are normally larger than males.

Eurasia

9. Wels catfish
Uses its fins to capture prey before swallowing its catch whole.

10. Beluga sturgeon
The world's largest river fish, it spends some of its life in salt water. Extra-large beluga no longer exist due to persistent overfishing and poaching of the species.

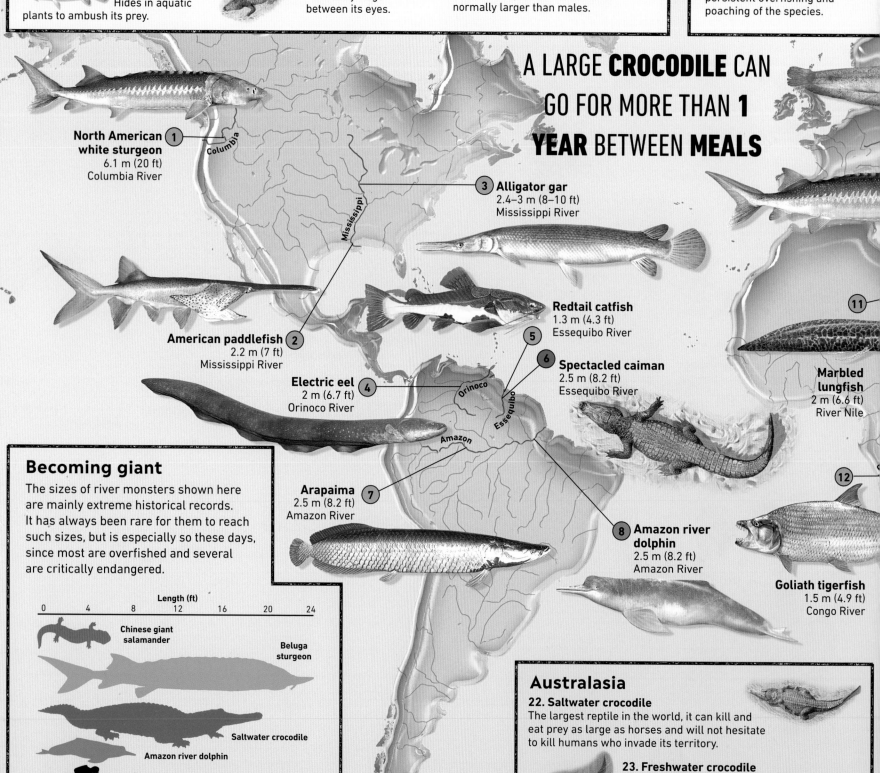

A LARGE **CROCODILE** CAN GO FOR MORE THAN **1** **YEAR** BETWEEN **MEALS**

North American white sturgeon
6.1 m (20 ft)
Columbia River

Alligator gar
2.4–3 m (8–10 ft)
Mississippi River

American paddlefish
2.2 m (7 ft)
Mississippi River

Redtail catfish
1.3 m (4.3 ft)
Essequibo River

Electric eel
2 m (6.7 ft)
Orinoco River

Spectacled caiman
2.5 m (8.2 ft)
Essequibo River

Marbled lungfish
2 m (6.6 ft)
River Nile

Arapaima
2.5 m (8.2 ft)
Amazon River

Amazon river dolphin
2.5 m (8.2 ft)
Amazon River

Goliath tigerfish
1.5 m (4.9 ft)
Congo River

Becoming giant

The sizes of river monsters shown here are mainly extreme historical records. It has always been rare for them to reach such sizes, but is especially so these days, since most are overfished and several are critically endangered.

Length (ft)
0 4 8 12 16 20 24

Chinese giant salamander
Beluga sturgeon
Saltwater crocodile
Amazon river dolphin
Human

0 1 2 3 4 5 6 7
Length (m)

Australasia

22. Saltwater crocodile
The largest reptile in the world, it can kill and eat prey as large as horses and will not hesitate to kill humans who invade its territory.

23. Freshwater crocodile
Much smaller than its saltwater relative, will not attack humans unless provoked.

IN ANCIENT JAPANESE FOLKLORE, A GIANT CATFISH, NAMAZU,

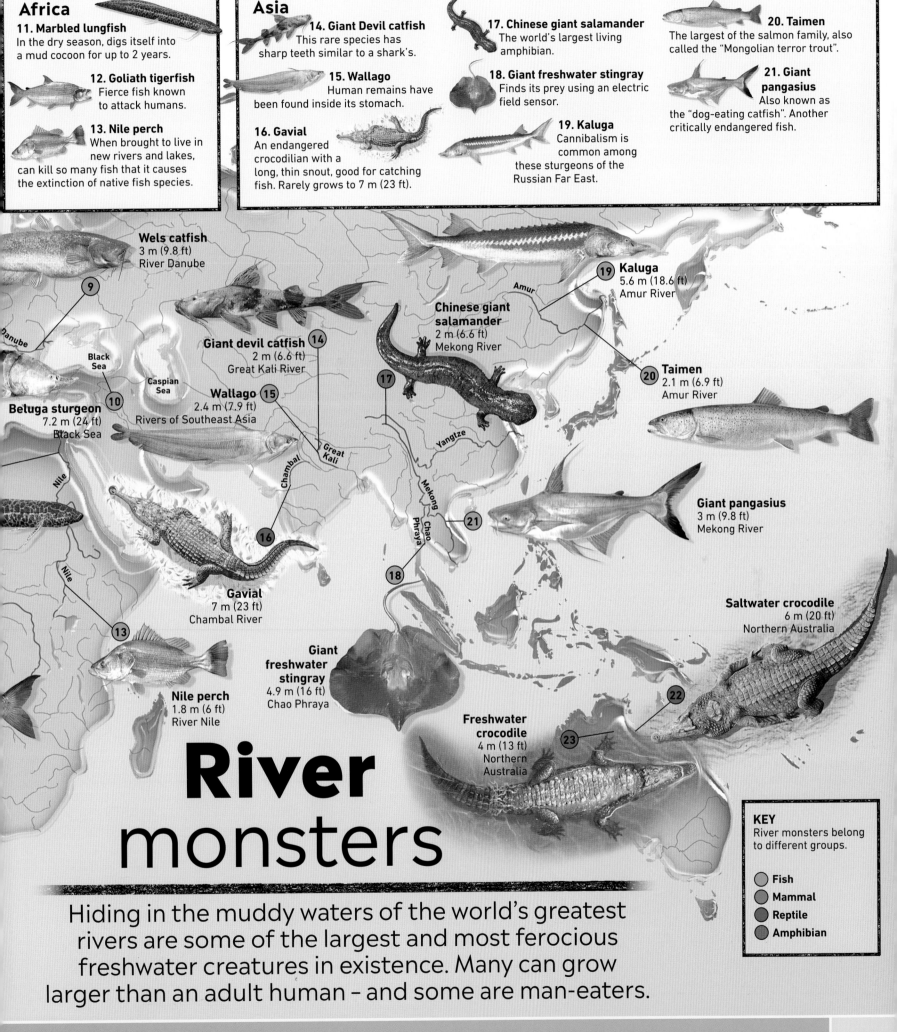

Africa

11. Marbled lungfish
In the dry season, digs itself into a mud cocoon for up to 2 years.

12. Goliath tigerfish
Fierce fish known to attack humans.

13. Nile perch
When brought to live in new rivers and lakes, can kill so many fish that it causes the extinction of native fish species.

Asia

14. Giant Devil catfish
This rare species has sharp teeth similar to a shark's.

15. Wallago
Human remains have been found inside its stomach.

16. Gavial
An endangered crocodilian with a long, thin snout, good for catching fish. Rarely grows to 7 m (23 ft).

17. Chinese giant salamander
The world's largest living amphibian.

18. Giant freshwater stingray
Finds its prey using an electric field sensor.

19. Kaluga
Cannibalism is common among these sturgeons of the Russian Far East.

20. Taimen
The largest of the salmon family, also called the "Mongolian terror trout".

21. Giant pangasius
Also known as the "dog-eating catfish". Another critically endangered fish.

Wels catfish
3 m (9.8 ft)
River Danube

Beluga sturgeon
7.2 m (24 ft)
Black Sea

Giant devil catfish
2 m (6.6 ft)
Great Kali River

Wallago
2.4 m (7.9 ft)
Rivers of Southeast Asia

Chinese giant salamander
2 m (6.6 ft)
Mekong River

Kaluga
5.6 m (18.6 ft)
Amur River

Taimen
2.1 m (6.9 ft)
Amur River

Gavial
7 m (23 ft)
Chambal River

Nile perch
1.8 m (6 ft)
River Nile

Giant freshwater stingray
4.9 m (16 ft)
Chao Phraya

Giant pangasius
3 m (9.8 ft)
Mekong River

Saltwater crocodile
6 m (20 ft)
Northern Australia

Freshwater crocodile
4 m (13 ft)
Northern Australia

Danube, Black Sea, Caspian Sea, Nile, Chambal, Great Kali, Yangtze, Mekong, Chao Phraya, Amur

River monsters

Hiding in the muddy waters of the world's greatest rivers are some of the largest and most ferocious freshwater creatures in existence. Many can grow larger than an adult human – and some are man-eaters.

KEY
River monsters belong to different groups.

- Fish
- Mammal
- Reptile
- Amphibian

LIVES IN THE MUD UNDER THE SEA AND CAUSES EARTHQUAKES.

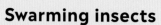
Types of swarms
When insects form a large group that moves as a single unit, it is called a swarm. Insects sometimes migrate in swarms, or they swarm when looking for a new home, a mate, or for food.

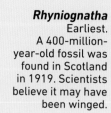

Maricopa harvester ant
Most venomous.
12 stings can kill a rat.

Rhyniognatha
Earliest.
A 400-million-year-old fossil was found in Scotland in 1919. Scientists believe it may have been winged.

Mayflies
Shortest adult life.
Mayflies spend most of their lives as water-living nymphs. They transform into winged adults that live just long enough to mate and lay eggs. The most extreme example is the American sand-burrowing mayfly whose adult life lasts just a few minutes.

Fairy wasp
Smallest.
0.14 mm (0.006 in) long. Only visible under a powerful microscope.

Termite queen
Longest life.
Can live up to 45 years.

Goliath Beetle
Heaviest larva.
Weighs up to 100 g (3.5 oz).

Swarming insects

1 Asian ladybird
Swarm through Oregon, USA, in autumn looking for somewhere to hibernate for the winter.

2 Army cutworm moths
Six- to eight-week migration from eastern plains of Colorado, USA, to the mountains.

3 Monarch butterfly
The long migration from the northern USA to Mexico lasts generations – no one butterfly makes the whole journey.

4 Termites
In New Orleans, Louisiana, USA, termites build colonies by invading people's homes.

5 Cicadas
In the eastern states of the USA, cicada swarms have 13- or 17-year cycles. Young cicadas, known as nymphs, mature, mate, and then die.

6 Mayflies
Annual mass hatching from Lake Erie, Ohio, USA. They mate, reproduce, then die.

7 Army ants
Found in Central and South America, swarms are called "raids" made up of 100,000–2,000,000 adults.

8 Africanized bees
Aggressive hybrid first released in São Paulo, Brazil. Swarm in thousands when forming new colonies.

9 Dragonflies
A single swarm in Argentina in 1991 was estimated to contain 4–6 billion migrating dragonflies.

10 Flying ants
Swarm annually in Britain as part of a mating ritual.

11 Driver ants
Found in central and east Africa, vast swarms kill animals in their path. People who cannot move out of the way, such as the sick or injured, can be killed.

12 Mosquito swarms
In May 2012, immense swarms of mosquitoes hatched from a lake near Mikoltsy, Belarus.

13 Locusts
The largest swarm recorded was in Kenya in 1954. It covered 200 sq km (77 sq miles) and involved an estimated 10 billion locusts.

14 Midges
The midges that form mating swarms start out as underwater larvae in lakes. Once they can fly, they take off and try to find a mate.

Honey bees
Bees swarm when they leave their hive to find a new home. Once a small number of special "scouts" have agreed on the most suitable site, the queen and the main cluster of bees fly to the new location.

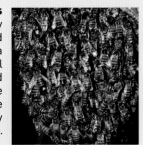

Monarch migration
Every year, by instinct alone, millions of monarch butterflies travel up to 4,000 km (2,500 miles) from northern parts of America to warmer climates as far south as Mexico, before they return north in spring.

Midges
Huge swarms appear over Lake Victoria in Africa during the annual mating season, as thousands of dancing male midges try to attract females. Swarms are so big, they look like giant brown clouds.

Froghopper
Highest jumper.
Jumps 71 cm (28 in) – 150 times its own height, which is comparable to a human jumping over a 60-storey building!

12

Himalayan cicada
Loudest.
Calls at up to 120 decibels – as loud as an ambulance siren.

Stink bug
Smelliest.
Toxic odour can be smelled by humans about 1–1.5 m (3.3–5 ft) away.

Flea
Longest jumper.
Can jump over 200 times its body length.

SCIENTISTS ESTIMATE **4–20 MILLION** TYPES OF **INSECT** HAVE YET TO BE **DISCOVERED**

13

14

Dung beetle
Strongest.
Can pull 1,141 times its own body weight – the equivalent to an average human pulling six double-decker buses full of people.

Chan's megastick
Longest.
56.7 cm (22.3 in).
Only six specimens have ever been found, all on the island of Borneo.

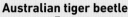

Australian tiger beetle
Fastest runner.
9 kph (5.6 mph). Equivalent to a human running at 770 kph (480 mph).

Giant weta
Heaviest.
Weighs up to 70 g (2.5 oz) – heavier than a sparrow.

Insects

We know of more than 1 million different types of insect, and more are identified every year. They have fascinating habits, and their strange appearances can be seen with the help of microscopes and special cameras.

Horse fly
Fastest flyer.
Maximum speed recorded briefly on take-off at 145 kph (90 mph). The next fastest are dragonflies and hawk moths, at around 50–55 kph (30–35 mph).

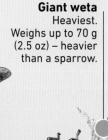

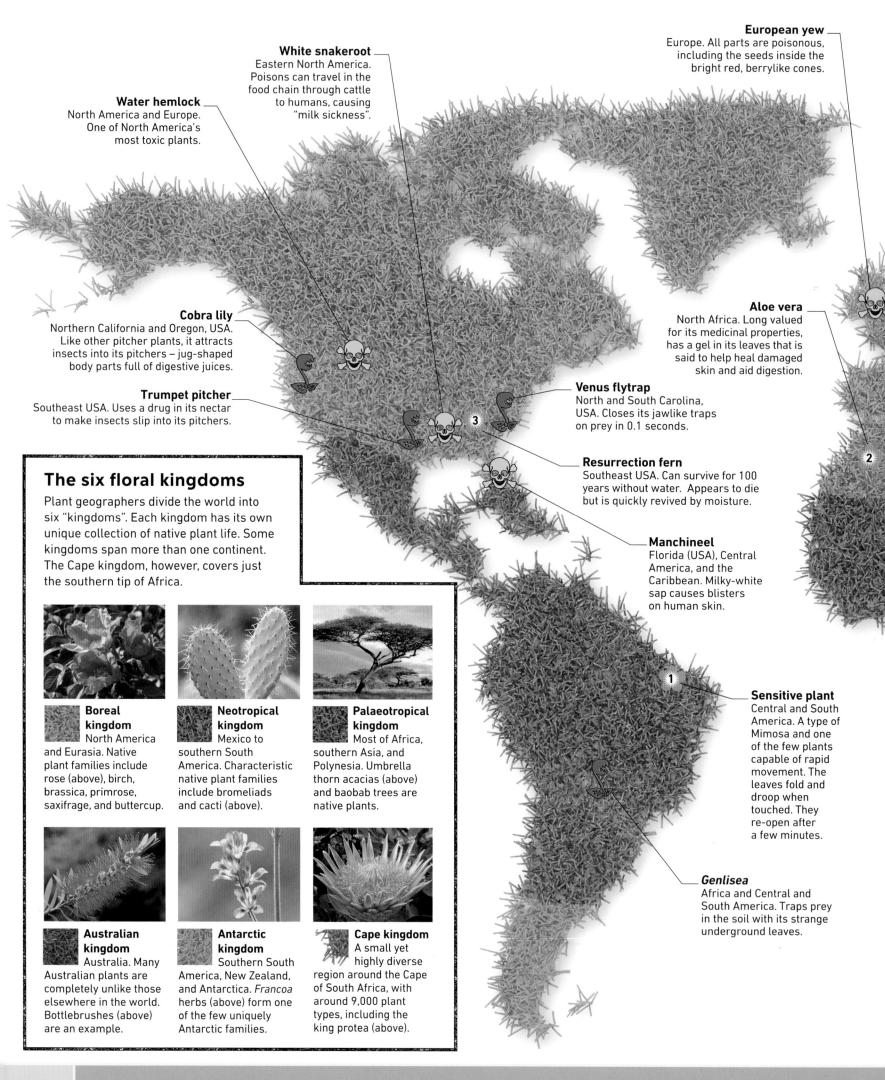

European yew
Europe. All parts are poisonous, including the seeds inside the bright red, berrylike cones.

White snakeroot
Eastern North America. Poisons can travel in the food chain through cattle to humans, causing "milk sickness".

Water hemlock
North America and Europe. One of North America's most toxic plants.

Cobra lily
Northern California and Oregon, USA. Like other pitcher plants, it attracts insects into its pitchers – jug-shaped body parts full of digestive juices.

Trumpet pitcher
Southeast USA. Uses a drug in its nectar to make insects slip into its pitchers.

Aloe vera
North Africa. Long valued for its medicinal properties, has a gel in its leaves that is said to help heal damaged skin and aid digestion.

Venus flytrap
North and South Carolina, USA. Closes its jawlike traps on prey in 0.1 seconds.

Resurrection fern
Southeast USA. Can survive for 100 years without water. Appears to die but is quickly revived by moisture.

Manchineel
Florida (USA), Central America, and the Caribbean. Milky-white sap causes blisters on human skin.

The six floral kingdoms

Plant geographers divide the world into six "kingdoms". Each kingdom has its own unique collection of native plant life. Some kingdoms span more than one continent. The Cape kingdom, however, covers just the southern tip of Africa.

Boreal kingdom
North America and Eurasia. Native plant families include rose (above), birch, brassica, primrose, saxifrage, and buttercup.

Neotropical kingdom
Mexico to southern South America. Characteristic native plant families include bromeliads and cacti (above).

Palaeotropical kingdom
Most of Africa, southern Asia, and Polynesia. Umbrella thorn acacias (above) and baobab trees are native plants.

Australian kingdom
Australia. Many Australian plants are completely unlike those elsewhere in the world. Bottlebrushes (above) are an example.

Antarctic kingdom
Southern South America, New Zealand, and Antarctica. *Francoa* herbs (above) form one of the few uniquely Antarctic families.

Cape kingdom
A small yet highly diverse region around the Cape of South Africa, with around 9,000 plant types, including the king protea (above).

Sensitive plant
Central and South America. A type of Mimosa and one of the few plants capable of rapid movement. The leaves fold and droop when touched. They re-open after a few minutes.

Genlisea
Africa and Central and South America. Traps prey in the soil with its strange underground leaves.

Butterwort
Boggy parts of Europe, North and South America, and Asia. Sticky hairs on its leaves trap insects.

Monkshood
Mountains of the northern hemisphere. Also known as aconite, it is a source of a deadly poison contained in the seeds.

KEY

 Poisonous plants
Some plants contain toxic chemicals. The map shows eight of the most poisonous.

 Carnivorous plants
These plants trap and consume insects and other small creatures.

 Incredible plants
Four amazing plants are highlighted on the map, but there are many thousands more worldwide.

Sundew
Worldwide in boggy places. Traps insects with droplets of glue coating its leaves.

Waterwheel plant
Africa, Asia, Australia, and Europe. Freshwater plant a little like an underwater Venus flytrap.

Deadly nightshade
Europe, north Africa, and west Asia

Castor oil plant
East Africa, Mediterranean, and India. Origin of the poison ricin.

Welwitschia
Namib Desert. Has just two strap-like leaves. They can grow up to 6.2 m (20 ft) long over several centuries.

Nepenthes rajah
Borneo. This giant pitcher plant may sometimes catch rats or lizards to eat.

Rosary pea
Indonesia. Toxins are used in herbal medicines of southern India.

World of plants

Terrestrial bladderwort
Worldwide. Grows on wet, rocky surfaces and catches tiny prey in bladderlike traps.

Rainbow plant
Australia. Catches insects on its sticky leaves.

Scientists estimate there are at least 400,000 species of plants on Earth – and possibly many thousands more. Some parts of the world have a rich diversity of plant life; in others, such as Antarctica, plants are scarce.

Total number of life-forms

There are many thousands of species of vertebrate animals, such as birds and reptiles. But these numbers are dwarfed by the amazing number of other life-forms, particularly insects.

NUMBER OF KNOWN SPECIES IN EACH GROUP	
13,000	Algae
74,000	Fungi
17,000	Lichens
320,000	Plants
85,000	Molluscs (squid, clams, snails, and relatives)
47,000	Crustaceans (crabs, shrimps, and relatives)
102,000	Arachnids (spiders, scorpions, and relatives)
1,000,000	Insects
71,000	Other invertebrates (without backbones)
62,000	Vertebrates (animals with backbones)

70,000 weevils

Weevils form only one family of beetles, yet there are more different types than all the world's vertebrates.

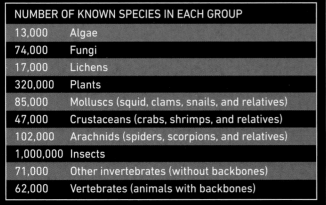

Giraffe-necked weevil

Cratosomus roddami, a weevil

Eupholus linnei, a weevil

Biodiversity

Richness of different life-forms, or species, is called biodiversity. Places such as tropical rainforests are naturally high in biodiversity. Harsh environments have fewer species, but those species might be unique and equally precious.

Barren Arctic

Plants grow very slowly in the cold Canadian Arctic, so there is not a lot of food to go round. Vegetation is ground-hugging, with little variety of homes for small animals – unlike forests. Biodiversity is low.

Rich Amazon

The Amazon is the largest and most diverse tropical forest on Earth. In general, large, continuous areas of habitat support the greatest diversity of species.

Deserted Sahara

There are hardly any amphibians in this dry environment, but the few that survive here are uniquely adapted to the conditions. Preserving areas of pristine Sahara would ensure the survival of some rare creatures.

Unique Atlantic Forest

What remains of the rainforest region in Brazil is not only rich in species. Because it is isolated from other rainforests, many of its species are also found nowhere else.

KEY

This map shows the pattern of biodiversity across the world's land, combining measures of 5,700 mammal species, 7,000 amphibians, and 10,000 species of bird. This gives an overall measure, because the variety of these three groups usually mirrors the total biodiversity, including the numbers of different insects and plants. Scientists know biodiversity in the oceans is lower than on land, but it is not shown on the map.

Lowest | Highest

BIODIVERSITY (SPECIES RICHNESS)

SCIENTISTS ESTIMATE THAT GLOBAL BIODIVERSITY HAS FALLEN TO 84.6

A few tough species
Only a few animal species have what it takes to survive in cold habitats such as the Russian Arctic.

Diverse tropical Asian forests
Tropical rainforest is the most biodiverse habitat. It has abundant water and no shortage of food. The trees provide a multitude of animal homes, from their roots up to their crowns. The climate changes little. All these things allow plants and animals to diversify by evolution into thousands of species.

Borneo
Scientists found an amazing 1,200 tree species here within a tiny plot of rainforest.

Himalayas and Hundu Kush
This mountainous region is home to 25,000 plant species, or nearly 10 per cent of the world's total.

Varied African highlands
Mountains are diverse places because they contain a range of different conditions at different heights. At each height lives a different community of plants and animals adapted to those conditions.

LIFE ON LAND IS AS MUCH AS **25 TIMES** AS VARIED AS **LIFE IN THE SEA**

POISON-DART FROGS
There are 175 species in the poison-dart frog family, which lives in the tropical rainforests of Central and South America. They are all related, but each has evolved slightly differently.

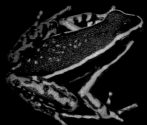

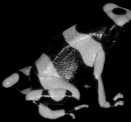

| Mimic poison-dart frog | Granular poison-dart frog | Three-striped poison-dart frog | Yellow-banded poison-dart frog | Brazil-nut poison-dart frog | Golden poison-dart frog |

PER CENT OF ITS LEVEL BEFORE PEOPLE CHANGED THE LANDSCAPE.

Unique wildlife

Some parts of the world are home to animals and plants that live nowhere else. These places are often remote islands, where life is cut off. In other cases, they are patches of unusual habitat, complete with the unique wildlife that depends on it.

California
A Mediterranean-type climate results in some unique forests featuring the world's largest living organism – the giant sequoia, a gigantic species of coniferous tree.

Mexican pine-oak forests
These forests on Mexican mountain ridges are patches of habitat not found anywhere else nearby. There are nearly 4,000 endemic plants and unique birds such as the Montezuma quail.

Hawaii and Polynesia
Only certain life-forms have reached these remote islands. Hawaii has no ants, but has 500 species of unique fruit fly, all evolved from a single species blown ashore 8 million years ago. Some of them are flightless and have taken up antlike lifestyles. Hawaii also has many unique plants, including the strange Hawaiian silversword, endemic to its mountain tops.

Galápagos Islands
These islands were made famous by Charles Darwin for their unique wildlife, including their giant tortoises.

Tropical Andes
Perhaps the richest region on Earth, these mountains are home to 664 species of amphibian, 450 of which are in danger of dying out. Of 1,700 bird species, 600 – including this fiery-throated fruiteater – are found nowhere else.

Western Mediterranean
Europe's hot spot of unique wildlife. One species of midwife toad lives only on Majorca, and Barbary macaques live only on Gibraltar and in patches of habitat in Morocco and Algeria.

Canary Islands
Rich in endemic plants, the Canary Islands off Africa gave their name to the bird that lives only here and on nearby Atlantic islands – the canary.

Caribbean Islands
Each island has its own versions of many plants and animals. This Cuban knight anole lives only on Cuba.

Atlantic Forest
This thin strip of rainforest is cut off from the Amazon rainforest, so it has its own set of wildlife, including the endangered golden lion tamarin.

75 PER CENT OF THE UNIQUE PLANTS OF THE CANARY ISLANDS ARE ENDANGERED

NEARLY 7 PER CENT OF THE WORLD'S PLANTS ARE UNIQUE TO THE

ENDEMIC HOT SPOTS
Scientists have shown that these regions have the greatest number of plant species living only within a small area. They call these species "endemic" to that area. In these hot spots of unique plants, scientists tend to find lots of endemic animals, too.

▨ **Region rich in endemic species**

BIOMES

▨ **Tropical dry broadleaf forest**

▨ **Tropical coniferous forest**

▨ **Temperate broadleaf forest**

▨ **Temperate coniferous forest**

▨ **Tropical moist broadleaf forest**

▨ **Boreal forest**

▨ **Savanna**

▨ **Flooded savanna**

▨ **Steppe**

▨ **Mountain grasslands and shrublands**

▨ **Mediterranean shrublands**

▨ **Desert and dry shrublands**

▨ **Arctic tundra**

▨ **Polar desert**

▨ **Mangroves**

Mountains of southwest China
Each ridge of mountains has its own distinct wildlife. Endangered species, such as the Yunnan snub-nosed monkey, live only here.

Eastern Mediterranean
The Cedar of Lebanon lives only in a small area, including Lebanon, Israel, Palestine, and parts of Syria, Jordan, and Turkey.

Philippines
Of this country's 1,000 types of orchid, 70 per cent grow nowhere else.

Wallacea
This region is named after 19th-century naturalist Alfred Russel Wallace, who noticed its unique wildlife such as the piglike babirusa.

New Guinea
This large island is home to many unique birds of paradise and several endemic tree kangaroos, including this species, the ursine tree kangaroo.

Ethiopian Highlands
These highlands are home to 30 endemic bird species and the endangered Ethiopian wolf.

East Melanesia
This string of islands has 3,000 endemic plant species and spectacular birdwing and swallowtail butterflies. This is a Ulysses swallowtail.

Sri lanka and Western Ghats
This hot spot is home to 5,000 species of flowering plant, 139 mammal species, 508 birds, and 179 amphibian species.

Madagascar
Ninety-eight per cent of Madagascar's land mammals, 92 per cent of its reptiles, 68 per cent of its plants, and 41 per cent of its breeding bird species exist nowhere else on Earth. All 16 mantella frogs are also endemic to the island.

East African Highlands
These islands of high ground in a sea of savanna support unusual plants such as this giant lobelia that grows on the slopes of Mount Kenya and Kilimanjaro.

Sundaland
Naturalists outline this region because its wildlife is distinct from next-door regions. One bizarre plant unique to Sundaland is *Rafflesia*, the stinking corpse lily.

Cape region
This is a small area of amazingly distinctive plantlife, including 6,000 endemic species such as this pincushion protea.

Western Australia
Like the South African Cape region, this is a "habitat island" of Mediterranean-type shrubland, full of plants found nowhere else, including the odd "kangaroo paw".

New Caledonia
Nothing like the strange, flightless kagu bird is found anywhere else in the world.

TROPICAL ANDES, WHICH COVER ONLY 0.8 PER CENT OF THE LAND AREA.

Kittlitz's murrelet
Alaska and Russian Far East

Maui parrotbill
Hawaii, USA

Vaquita
Gulf of California

Hawaiian monk seal
Hawaii, USA

Iberian lynx
Spain

Blue iguana
Grand Cayman Island, Caribbean

Lamotte's roundleaf bat
Mount Nimba (border area of Guinea, Liberia, and Côte d'Ivoire)

Variable harlequin frog
Costa Rica

Short-tailed chinchilla
Mountains on the Bolivia–Chile border

Maui parrotbill
In danger because of the loss of its forest habitat – only around 500 now survive.

Hawaiian monk seal
Once hunted for its skin and oil, today many become tangled in fishing nets or die because of pollution.

Glaucous macaw
Argentina, Uruguay, Paraguay, and Brazil

Western gorilla
Congo rainforest

MORE THAN 7,000 ANIMAL SPECIES ARE CRITICALLY ENDANGERED

Blue-eyed black lemur
Madagascar

In the red
Animals on the Red List – a list kept by the IUCN (International Union for the Conservation of Nature) – are in varying levels of endangerment. Those that are "critically endangered" may soon die out completely in the wild.

Vaquita This porpoise is the world's most endangered sea mammal; scientists estimate only around 10 are left.

Kittlitz's murrelet
Thousands of these seabirds have been killed by sticky oil, spilled from giant tankers.

Blue iguana
This lizard lives only on Grand Cayman Island. Numbers are increasing due to conservation.

Variable harlequin frog
One of several harlequin frog species critically endangered due to a fungal disease.

Short-tailed chinchilla
Hunted for its soft grey fur, this rock-dwelling rodent is now almost extinct in the wild.

Glaucous macaw
Became rare because so many were caught and sold as pets. Only sighted twice in 100 years.

Iberian lynx
If it dies out, it will be the first big cat species to go extinct for 10,000 years.

Western gorilla
Many of these apes are killed for their meat, or have died from disease.

Lamotte's roundleaf bat
This African mammal has become endangered mainly through the loss of its habitat.

Greater bamboo lemur
Less than 100 have been spotted in 20 years of surveys.

Blue-eyed black lemur
Like many other lemurs, this one could soon die out due to loss of its forest habitat.

Russian sturgeon
This fish has been killed for its roe (eggs), known as caviar.

Indian vulture
Many of these birds died after feeding on cattle that had been given medicine to help them work longer.

Bactrian camel
Fewer than 1,000 survive in the wild.

Irrawaddy river shark
As no one has seen this species for many years, it may be extinct in the wild.

Sumatran orangutan
Just 15,000 of this species are left, since their forest is being cut down.

Endangered animals

Our world has thousands of species, or kinds, of animal. Many are in danger of dying out, mainly because humans are destroying their habitats, or homes. Some animals have not been seen in their habitats for 50 years or more and can be declared "extinct in the wild".

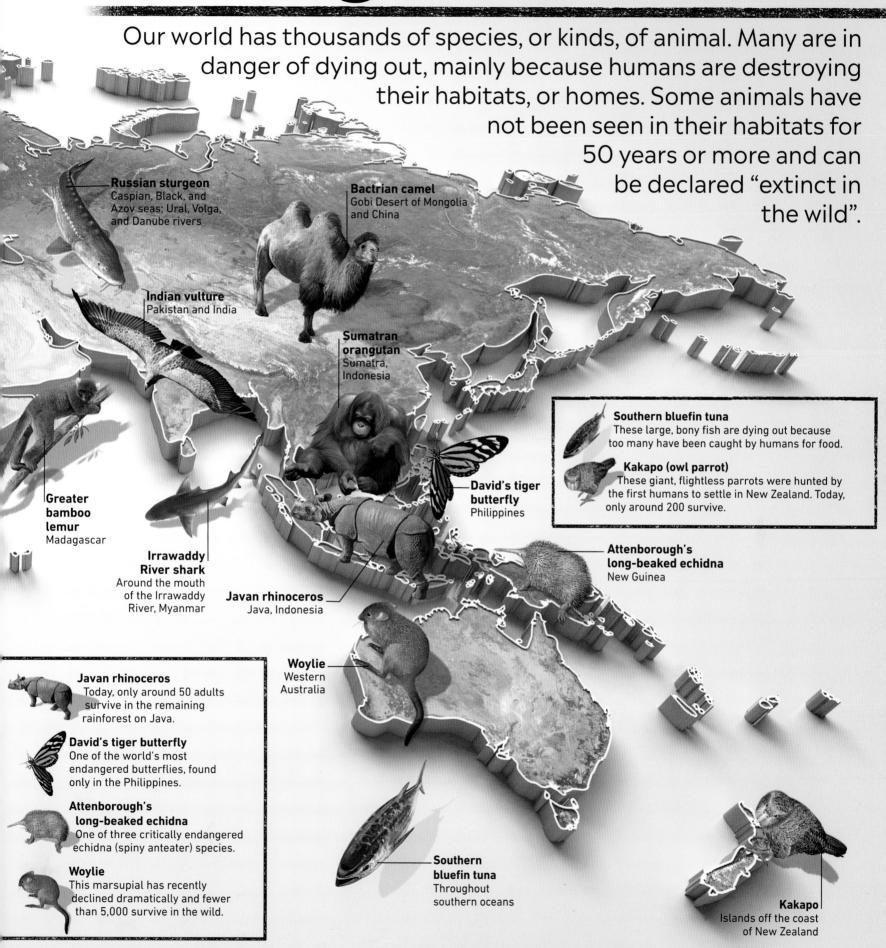

Russian sturgeon
Caspian, Black, and Azov seas; Ural, Volga, and Danube rivers

Bactrian camel
Gobi Desert of Mongolia and China

Indian vulture
Pakistan and India

Sumatran orangutan
Sumatra, Indonesia

Greater bamboo lemur
Madagascar

Irrawaddy River shark
Around the mouth of the Irrawaddy River, Myanmar

Javan rhinoceros
Java, Indonesia

David's tiger butterfly
Philippines

Attenborough's long-beaked echidna
New Guinea

Woylie
Western Australia

Southern bluefin tuna
Throughout southern oceans

Kakapo
Islands off the coast of New Zealand

Southern bluefin tuna
These large, bony fish are dying out because too many have been caught by humans for food.

Kakapo (owl parrot)
These giant, flightless parrots were hunted by the first humans to settle in New Zealand. Today, only around 200 survive.

Javan rhinoceros
Today, only around 50 adults survive in the remaining rainforest on Java.

David's tiger butterfly
One of the world's most endangered butterflies, found only in the Philippines.

Attenborough's long-beaked echidna
One of three critically endangered echidna (spiny anteater) species.

Woylie
This marsupial has recently declined dramatically and fewer than 5,000 survive in the wild.

Americas

Passenger pigeon
A flock of this once-common species could contain 2 million birds.

Laysan rail
This bird's Hawaiian habitat was taken over by non-native rats and rabbits.

Xerces blue butterfly
Its habitat of sand dunes in California was replaced by growing cities.

Golden toad
Its extinction may have been caused by habitat loss or a fungal disease.

Labrador duck
Its extinction was not caused by hunting, as its flesh reportedly tasted horrible!

Pinta Island tortoise
The last tortoise on this Galápagos island, Lonesome George, died in 2012.

Red-bellied gracile opossum
Its Argentinian forest habitat was turned into grazing land for cattle.

Falkland Island wolf
Hunted to extinction by human settlers.

Eurasia

Great auk
Hunted by humans mainly for its meat and feathers.

Eurasian aurochs
Massive cattle species wiped out by overhunting.

Yunnan lake newt
Became extinct due to the introduction of exotic fish and frogs.

Baiji
River dolphin that died out when its habitat was taken over by industry.

Japanese sea lion
Killed by fishermen to prevent them competing for fish.

Woolly mammoth
Lost much of its habitat when the Ice Age ended.

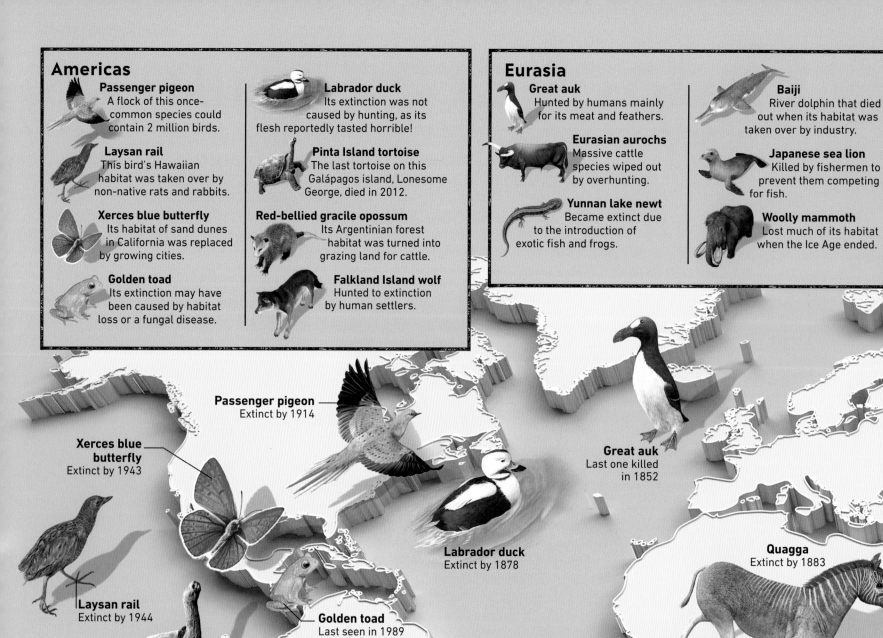

Passenger pigeon
Extinct by 1914

Xerces blue butterfly
Extinct by 1943

Laysan rail
Extinct by 1944

Pinta Island tortoise
Extinct in 2012

Golden toad
Last seen in 1989

Labrador duck
Extinct by 1878

Red-bellied gracile opossum
Last seen in 1962

Great auk
Last one killed in 1852

Quagga
Extinct by 1883

Elephant bird
(Madagascar)
Extinct since 17th century

Falkland Island wolf
Presumed extinct in 1876

Extinct animals

The animal species on this map died out, or became extinct, quite recently and probably as a result of the actions of humans. But extinction has been happening naturally in the animal kingdom for millions of years.

ANIMALS ARE GOING EXTINCT TODAY AT LEAST 1,000

Africa

Quagga
Its very distinctive markings made it an easy target for hunters.

Aldabra banded snail
A sudden decrease in rainfall, possibly caused by climate change, spelled extinction for this species.

Large sloth lemur
Gorilla-sized species that died out in Madagascar around 400 years ago.

Elephant bird
Huge flightless bird that was wiped out by hunting.

Dodo
This flightless bird became extinct within only 100 years of humans and their domestic animals arriving on the island of Mauritius.

Australasia

Lesser bilby
Probably wiped out by cats and foxes.

Eastern hare wallaby
Extinction was partly due to the introduction of cats, which hunted them.

Desert-rat kangaroo
Thought extinct, recovered, then declared extinct again in 1994.

King Island emu
Wiped out by sealers and their hunting dogs.

Tasmanian wolf
Hunted and trapped by human settlers in Tasmania – its last hiding place.

Moa
Victims of overhunting and loss of habitat.

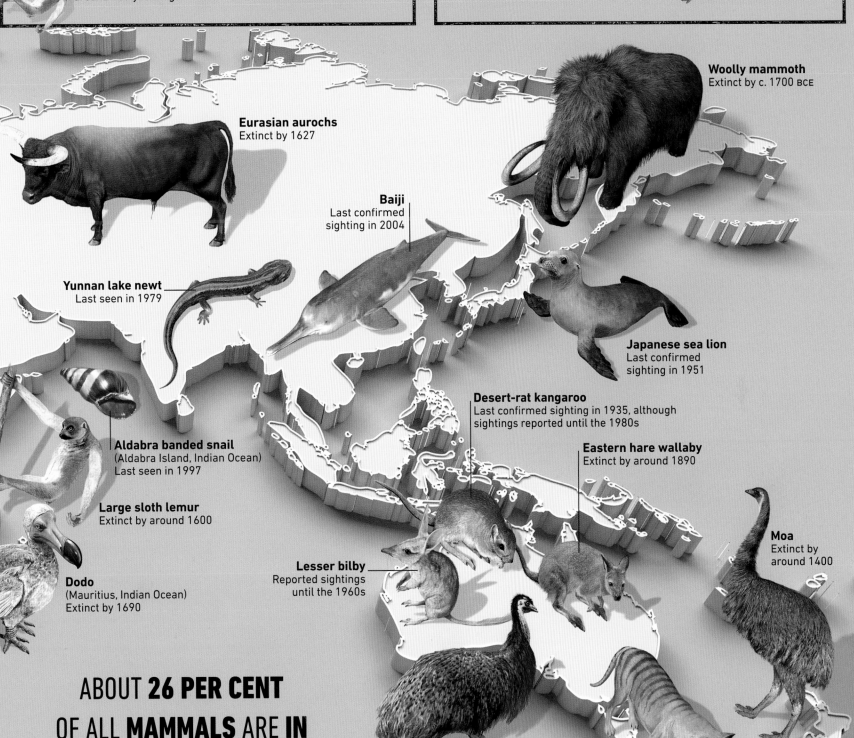

Woolly mammoth
Extinct by c. 1700 BCE

Eurasian aurochs
Extinct by 1627

Baiji
Last confirmed sighting in 2004

Yunnan lake newt
Last seen in 1979

Japanese sea lion
Last confirmed sighting in 1951

Desert-rat kangaroo
Last confirmed sighting in 1935, although sightings reported until the 1980s

Eastern hare wallaby
Extinct by around 1890

Aldabra banded snail
(Aldabra Island, Indian Ocean)
Last seen in 1997

Large sloth lemur
Extinct by around 1600

Lesser bilby
Reported sightings until the 1960s

Dodo
(Mauritius, Indian Ocean)
Extinct by 1690

Moa
Extinct by around 1400

ABOUT **26 PER CENT** OF ALL **MAMMALS** ARE **IN DANGER** OF **EXTINCTION**

King Island emu
Extinct by around 1802

Tasmanian wolf
Presumed extinct in 1936

TIMES FASTER THAN THE NATURAL EXTINCTION RATE.

People and planet

Sprawling city
Los Angeles, California, USA, stretches as far as the horizon in this photo taken from Mount Hollywood. The skyscrapers of downtown LA can be seen on the left.

Introduction

Humans, together with animals and other living things, form what is called the biosphere – the living part of the world. Since modern humans first appeared in Africa about 200,000 years ago, we have colonized virtually the entire world – even hot deserts and the ice-cold Arctic. As we have done so, our impact on the biosphere has been far-reaching.

Human impact

The human "footprint" on planet Earth is deep and broad. We have transformed the landscape – clearing forests to produce food, digging minerals and ores from the ground, and channelling and storing water to meet our needs. Our living space is concentrated into larger and larger cities, but these cities are hungry for food and energy taken from the surrounding land.

Renewable energy
New ways of harnessing the energy of sunlight and wind are reducing our use of fossil fuels. Unlike fossil fuels, these energy sources will never run out.

Natural resources

Buried within Earth's crust there are limited supplies of minerals, metal ores, and fossil fuels (coal, oil, and gas). Once these reserves are exhausted, they cannot be replaced. Burning these fuels also damages Earth's atmosphere and is contributing to global warming.

Population

For most of humanity's existence, the human population grew relatively slowly. In 10,000 BCE, there were only 1–5 million people on Earth. By 1000 BCE, after farming was invented, the population had increased to about 50 million. Since reaching the 1 billion mark in 1804, during the early Industrial Revolution, the population has expanded much more quickly than ever before.

Growing bigger, fast
The period since the late 1950s has seen the human population more than double.

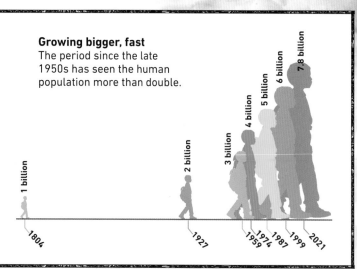

1 billion — 1804
2 billion — 1927
3 billion — 1959
4 billion — 1974
5 billion — 1987
6 billion — 1999
7.8 billion — 2021

Agriculture
In 1700 CE, about 7 per cent of Earth's land area was used for growing crops and raising farm animals. Today, that figure has risen to around 50 per cent.

Pollution
Vehicle exhaust gases, smoke and waste chemicals from factories, and oil spills all poison the environment, threatening plant and animal life.

Conservation
To protect the plant and animal life of unique habitats, many countries set up conservation areas, where no farming, industry, or new settlement can occur.

Using water
We build dams and reservoirs to store water. We need it for drinking, for use in industrial processes, and to irrigate crops and generate electricity.

Successful species

Part of the success of humans is down to our ability to use the materials around us to give us protection and shelter. This ability opens up nearly every part of the globe for human living space, no matter how harsh the environment. Even thousands of years ago, the Inuit of the North American Arctic made coats from the fur of caribou (reindeer) and waterproof boots from seal skin. They found a way to live on the meagre resources of the high Arctic.

Inuit boat
The *umiak* is a type of traditional open boat used by Inuit people. The frame is made of driftwood or whalebone, with a walrus- or seal-skin covering. These boats are still used, since the law allows whale hunting only with traditional Inuit tools.

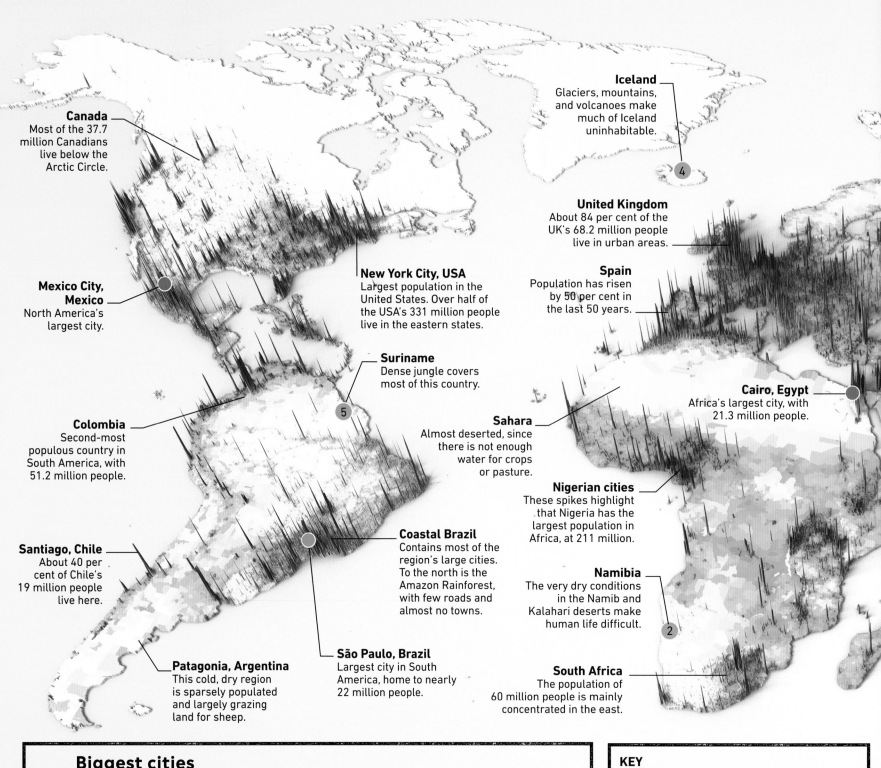

Canada
Most of the 37.7 million Canadians live below the Arctic Circle.

Mexico City, Mexico
North America's largest city.

Colombia
Second-most populous country in South America, with 51.2 million people.

Santiago, Chile
About 40 per cent of Chile's 19 million people live here.

Patagonia, Argentina
This cold, dry region is sparsely populated and largely grazing land for sheep.

New York City, USA
Largest population in the United States. Over half of the USA's 331 million people live in the eastern states.

Suriname
Dense jungle covers most of this country.

5

Coastal Brazil
Contains most of the region's large cities. To the north is the Amazon Rainforest, with few roads and almost no towns.

São Paulo, Brazil
Largest city in South America, home to nearly 22 million people.

Iceland
Glaciers, mountains, and volcanoes make much of Iceland uninhabitable.

4

United Kingdom
About 84 per cent of the UK's 68.2 million people live in urban areas.

Spain
Population has risen by 50 per cent in the last 50 years.

Sahara
Almost deserted, since there is not enough water for crops or pasture.

Nigerian cities
These spikes highlight that Nigeria has the largest population in Africa, at 211 million.

Cairo, Egypt
Africa's largest city, with 21.3 million people.

Namibia
The very dry conditions in the Namib and Kalahari deserts make human life difficult.

2

South Africa
The population of 60 million people is mainly concentrated in the east.

Biggest cities

More than half the world's people now live in towns and cities, rather than in the countryside. Many cities have grown quickly and have been dubbed "megacities", with more than 10 million people in a metropolitan area. Below are the 10 largest.

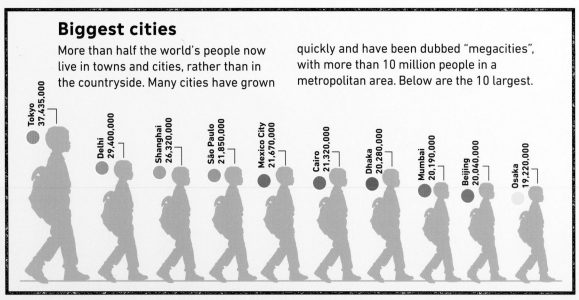

Tokyo 37,435,000
Delhi 29,400,000
Shanghai 26,320,000
São Paulo 21,850,000
Mexico City 21,670,000
Cairo 21,320,000
Dhaka 20,280,000
Mumbai 20,190,000
Beijing 20,040,000
Osaka 19,220,000

KEY
The map shows population density, or how closely people are packed together. Denser places, such as cities, appear as red mountains.

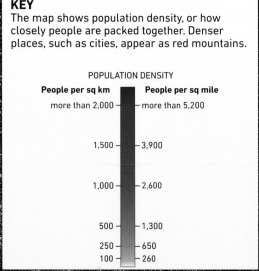

POPULATION DENSITY

People per sq km	People per sq mile
more than 2,000	more than 5,200
1,500	3,900
1,000	2,600
500	1,300
250	650
100	260

IN 1800, THE WORLD'S POPULATION WAS LESS THAN 1 BILLION PEOPLE.

Where people live

The world's 7.8 billion people are not spread evenly across the globe: most live where there are natural resources and fertile land for farming. Some places are too hostile for humans to thrive in.

Siberia, Russia
Few people live here, since the climate is too cold to grow crops. Some spikes show the location of cities based around extracting oil and gas from under the frozen tundra.

Moscow, Russia
Home to 12.5 million people.

Kolkata, India
Centre of eastern India.

Mongolia
Little of the land is good for growing crops and many people are scattered in small communities of nomadic herdspeople.

Shanghai, China
China's largest city.

Beijing
The capital of China.

Tokyo, Japan
The largest city in the world since the 1960s.

Osaka, Japan
The second-largest city in Japan.

Delhi, India
India's capital sits in the densely populated Ganges River basin, home to 650 million people packed in at nearly 400 per sq km (1,000 per sq mile).

Eastern China
Most of China's 1.4 billion people live here.

Manila, Philippines
Discounting its outlying districts, this is the world's most densely populated city.

Dhaka, Bangladesh
The world's most densely populated, continuously built-up area.

Mumbai, India
Fast-growing entertainment hub of India.

IN **MANILA**, PHILIPPINES, ON AVERAGE **296 PEOPLE** **LIVE** IN AN AREA THE SIZE OF A **FOOTBALL PITCH**

Jakarta, Indonesia
Of all Indonesia's islands, Java is by far the most crowded and contains the booming capital, Jakarta.

Australia
Australia's centre is too dry to support farming and very few people live here.

Auckland, New Zealand
Around one in three New Zealanders live here.

Melbourne, Australia
Most of Australia's population lives on the southeastern coast, in cities including Melbourne.

Most sparsely populated countries

		total population	people per sq km	people per sq mile
1	Mongolia	3,278,000	2.1	5.5
2	Namibia	2,541,000	3.1	8.0
3	Australia	25,500,000	3.3	8.6
4	Iceland	341,000	3.4	8.8
5	Suriname	587,000	3.8	9.7

Inuit
Arctic parts of Alaska, Canada, and Greenland, beyond the northernmost trees.

Sami
Northern Scandinavia and Finland

Pavee
Ireland

Beja
Sudan, Eritrea, and Egypt

Awá
Rainforests of northern Ecuador and southern Colombia

Tuareg
Sahara Desert

Fulani
West Africa

Nukak-Maku
Tropical forests of the Amazon Basin

Ayoreo
Dry lowlands of Bolivia and Paraguay

Toubou
Tibesti mountains, Chad

Karamojong
Northern Uganda

San
Kalahari Desert – Botswana, Namibia, and South Africa

THERE ARE UP TO 40 MILLION NOMADS AROUND THE WORLD

Americas

Inuit
For 4,000 years, the Inuit have roamed the region they call Nunavut, "our land".

Awá
The Awá speak their own ancient language called Awa Pit.

Nukak-Maku
The Nukak people are expert hunters who were entirely isolated until 1988.

Ayoreo
The Ayoreo mix a hunter-gatherer lifestyle with agriculture.

Europe

Pavee, or Irish Travellers
The Pavee have strict moral beliefs laid out in "The Travellers' Code".

Sami
The Sami reindeer herders and fur trappers have existed for over 5,000 years.

Roma
There are 2–5 million Roma worldwide, mostly in Europe.

Nenets
Every year, Nenets move huge herds of reindeer up to 1,000 km (620 miles).

Africa

Beja
Only some Beja clans are nomadic.

Tuareg
In Tuareg culture, men rather than women wear the veil.

Toubou
The Toubou are divided into two peoples: the Teda and the Daza.

Fulani
The Fulani traditionally herd goats, sheep, and cattle across large areas of west Africa.

Gabra
These herders make their dome-shaped houses out of acacia roots and cloth.

Afar
The Afar live by rivers in the dry season and head for higher ground in the wet season.

Karamojong
This name means "the old men can walk no further".

San
The San are famous for being excellent trackers and hunters.

MOST NOMADS LIVE IN DESERT, STEPPE, OR TUNDRA – DRY PLACES THAT

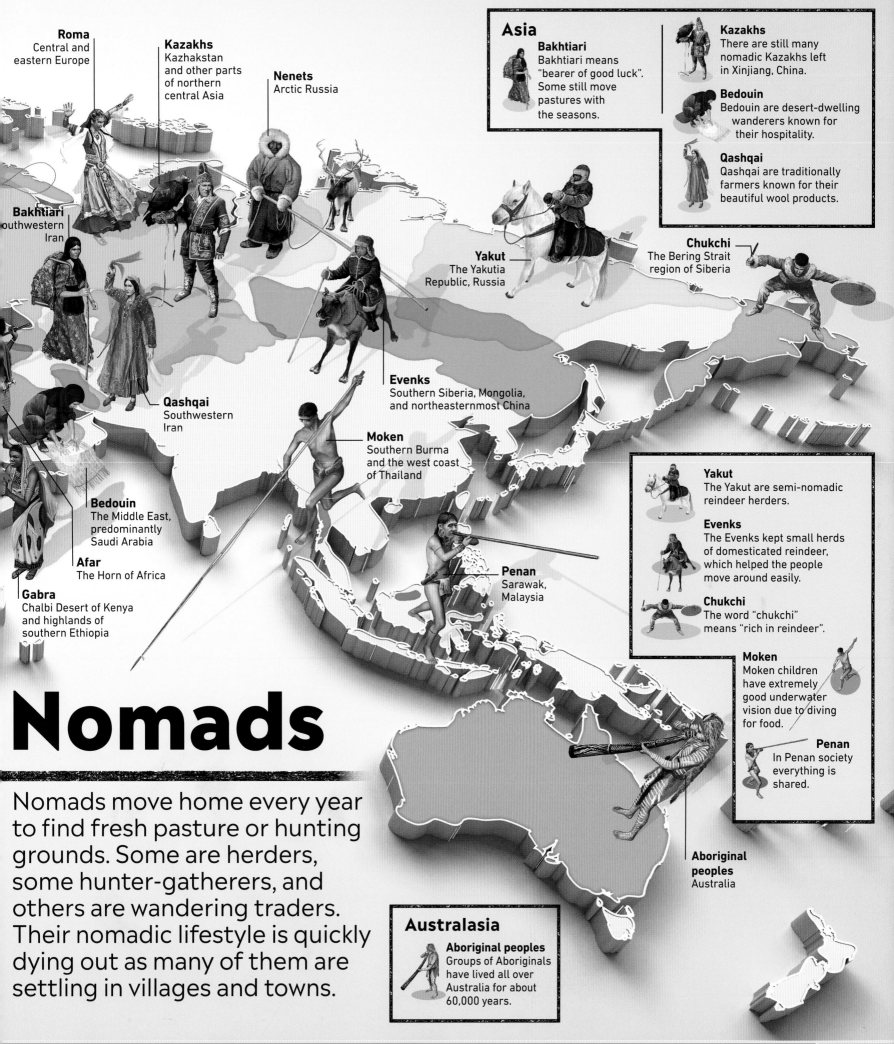

Roma
Central and eastern Europe

Kazakhs
Kazhakstan and other parts of northern central Asia

Nenets
Arctic Russia

Bakhtiari
Southwestern Iran

Qashqai
Southwestern Iran

Bedouin
The Middle East, predominantly Saudi Arabia

Afar
The Horn of Africa

Gabra
Chalbi Desert of Kenya and highlands of southern Ethiopia

Yakut
The Yakutia Republic, Russia

Chukchi
The Bering Strait region of Siberia

Evenks
Southern Siberia, Mongolia, and northeasternmost China

Moken
Southern Burma and the west coast of Thailand

Penan
Sarawak, Malaysia

Aboriginal peoples
Australia

Asia

Bakhtiari
Bakhtiari means "bearer of good luck". Some still move pastures with the seasons.

Kazakhs
There are still many nomadic Kazakhs left in Xinjiang, China.

Bedouin
Bedouin are desert-dwelling wanderers known for their hospitality.

Qashqai
Qashqai are traditionally farmers known for their beautiful wool products.

Yakut
The Yakut are semi-nomadic reindeer herders.

Evenks
The Evenks kept small herds of domesticated reindeer, which helped the people move around easily.

Chukchi
The word "chukchi" means "rich in reindeer".

Moken
Moken children have extremely good underwater vision due to diving for food.

Penan
In Penan society everything is shared.

Nomads

Nomads move home every year to find fresh pasture or hunting grounds. Some are herders, some hunter-gatherers, and others are wandering traders. Their nomadic lifestyle is quickly dying out as many of them are settling in villages and towns.

Australasia

Aboriginal peoples
Groups of Aboriginals have lived all over Australia for about 60,000 years.

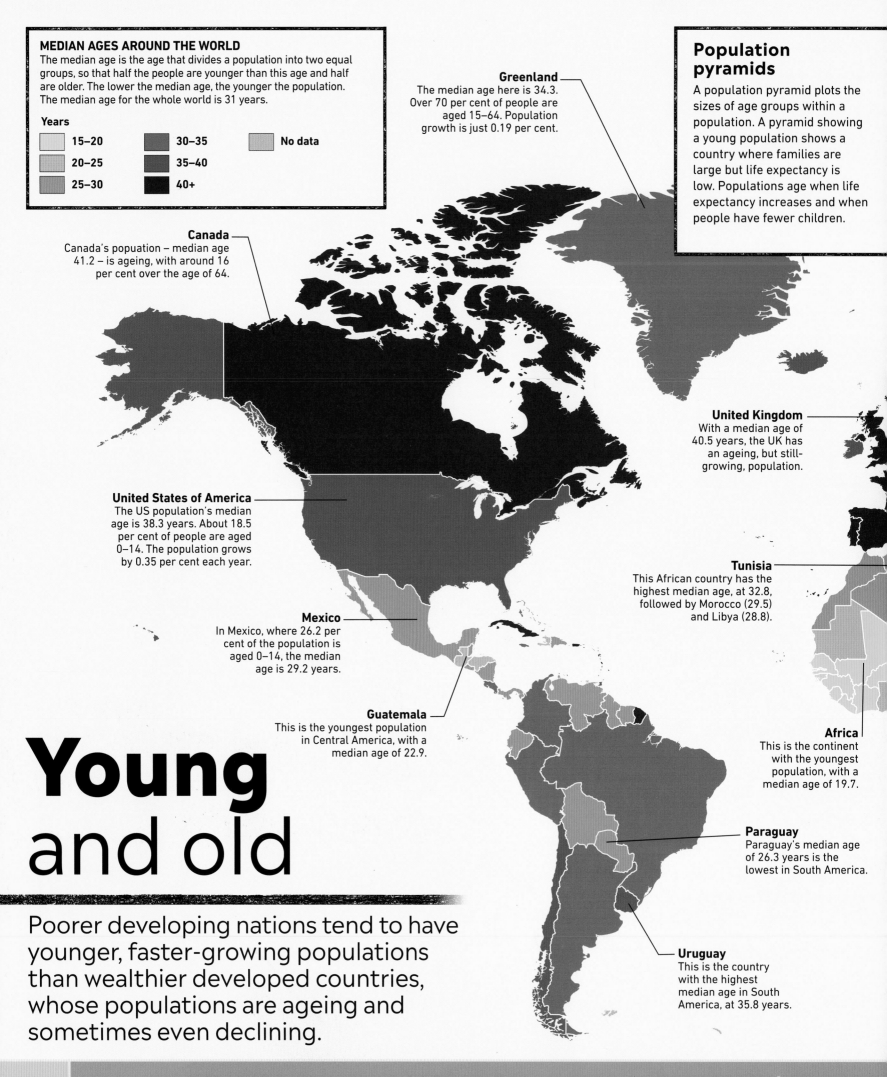

MEDIAN AGES AROUND THE WORLD

The median age is the age that divides a population into two equal groups, so that half the people are younger than this age and half are older. The lower the median age, the younger the population. The median age for the whole world is 31 years.

Years

15–20	30–35
20–25	35–40
25–30	40+
No data	

Population pyramids

A population pyramid plots the sizes of age groups within a population. A pyramid showing a young population shows a country where families are large but life expectancy is low. Populations age when life expectancy increases and when people have fewer children.

Greenland
The median age here is 34.3. Over 70 per cent of people are aged 15–64. Population growth is just 0.19 per cent.

Canada
Canada's popuation – median age 41.2 – is ageing, with around 16 per cent over the age of 64.

United Kingdom
With a median age of 40.5 years, the UK has an ageing, but still-growing, population.

United States of America
The US population's median age is 38.3 years. About 18.5 per cent of people are aged 0–14. The population grows by 0.35 per cent each year.

Tunisia
This African country has the highest median age, at 32.8, followed by Morocco (29.5) and Libya (28.8).

Mexico
In Mexico, where 26.2 per cent of the population is aged 0–14, the median age is 29.2 years.

Guatemala
This is the youngest population in Central America, with a median age of 22.9.

Africa
This is the continent with the youngest population, with a median age of 19.7.

Paraguay
Paraguay's median age of 26.3 years is the lowest in South America.

Uruguay
This is the country with the highest median age in South America, at 35.8 years.

Young
and old

Poorer developing nations tend to have younger, faster-growing populations than wealthier developed countries, whose populations are ageing and sometimes even declining.

BY 2050, ABOUT 16 PER CENT OF THE WORLD'S POPULATION WILL

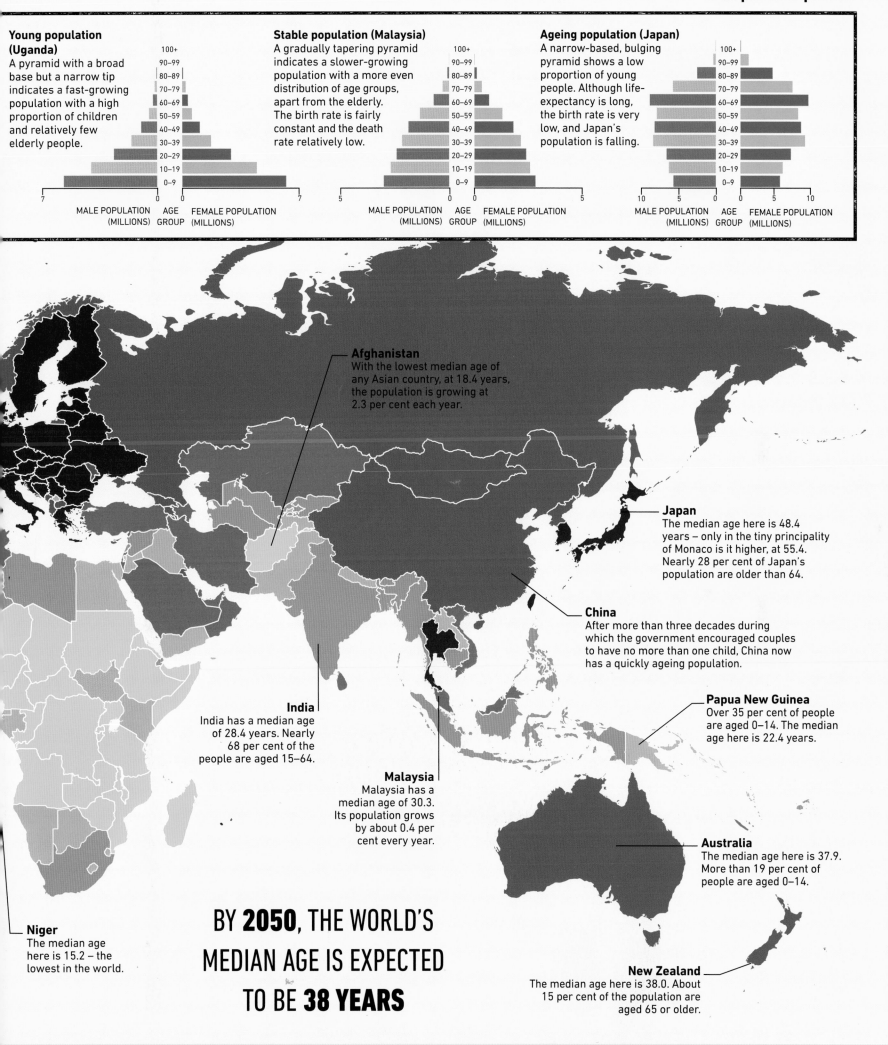

Young population (Uganda)
A pyramid with a broad base but a narrow tip indicates a fast-growing population with a high proportion of children and relatively few elderly people.

100+
90–99
80–89
70–79
60–69
50–59
40–49
30–39
20–29
10–19
0–9

7   0   0   7
MALE POPULATION (MILLIONS)   AGE GROUP   FEMALE POPULATION (MILLIONS)

Stable population (Malaysia)
A gradually tapering pyramid indicates a slower-growing population with a more even distribution of age groups, apart from the elderly. The birth rate is fairly constant and the death rate relatively low.

100+
90–99
80–89
70–79
60–69
50–59
40–49
30–39
20–29
10–19
0–9

5   0   0   5
MALE POPULATION (MILLIONS)   AGE GROUP   FEMALE POPULATION (MILLIONS)

Ageing population (Japan)
A narrow-based, bulging pyramid shows a low proportion of young people. Although life-expectancy is long, the birth rate is very low, and Japan's population is falling.

100+
90–99
80–89
70–79
60–69
50–59
40–49
30–39
20–29
10–19
0–9

10   5   0   0   5   10
MALE POPULATION (MILLIONS)   AGE GROUP   FEMALE POPULATION (MILLIONS)

Afghanistan
With the lowest median age of any Asian country, at 18.4 years, the population is growing at 2.3 per cent each year.

Japan
The median age here is 48.4 years – only in the tiny principality of Monaco is it higher, at 55.4. Nearly 28 per cent of Japan's population are older than 64.

China
After more than three decades during which the government encouraged couples to have no more than one child, China now has a quickly ageing population.

India
India has a median age of 28.4 years. Nearly 68 per cent of the people are aged 15–64.

Malaysia
Malaysia has a median age of 30.3. Its population grows by about 0.4 per cent every year.

Papua New Guinea
Over 35 per cent of people are aged 0–14. The median age here is 22.4 years.

Australia
The median age here is 37.9. More than 19 per cent of people are aged 0–14.

Niger
The median age here is 15.2 – the lowest in the world.

BY **2050**, THE WORLD'S MEDIAN AGE IS EXPECTED TO BE **38 YEARS**

New Zealand
The median age here is 38.0. About 15 per cent of the population are aged 65 or older.

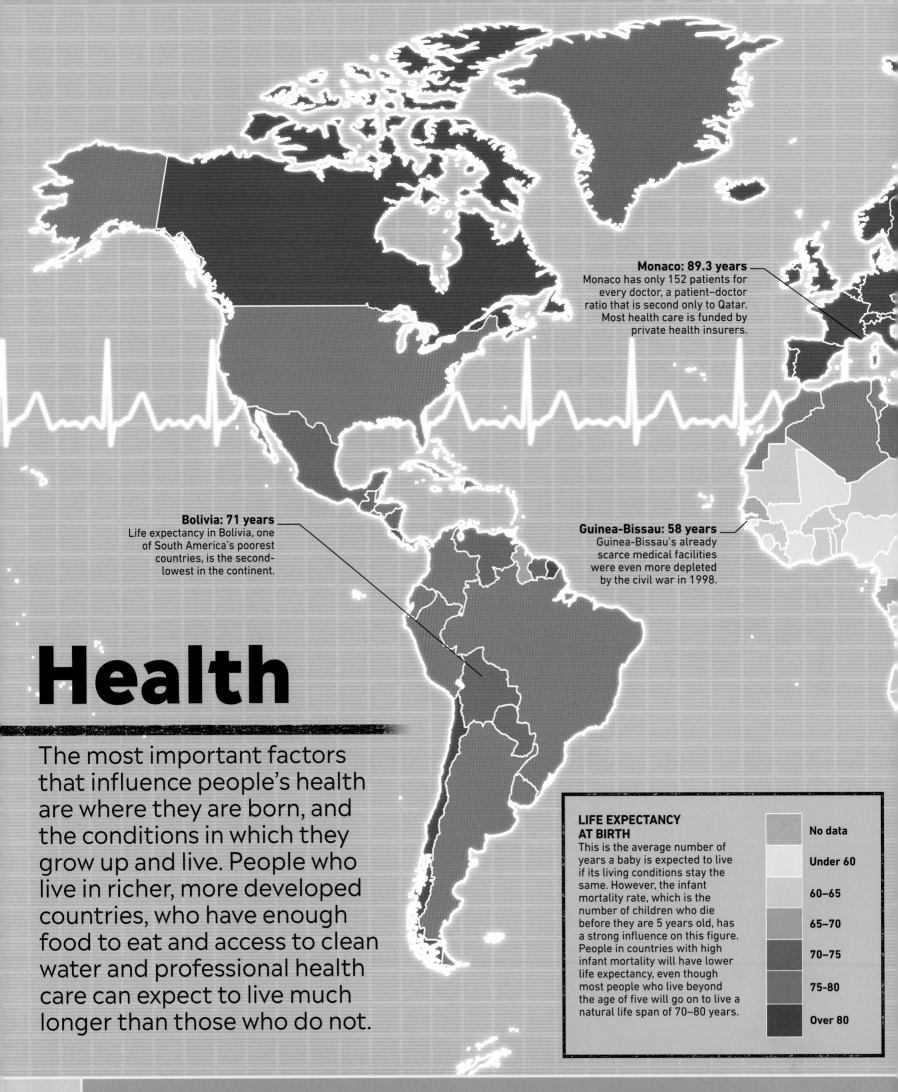

Health

The most important factors that influence people's health are where they are born, and the conditions in which they grow up and live. People who live in richer, more developed countries, who have enough food to eat and access to clean water and professional health care can expect to live much longer than those who do not.

Monaco: 89.3 years
Monaco has only 152 patients for every doctor, a patient–doctor ratio that is second only to Qatar. Most health care is funded by private health insurers.

Bolivia: 71 years
Life expectancy in Bolivia, one of South America's poorest countries, is the second-lowest in the continent.

Guinea-Bissau: 58 years
Guinea-Bissau's already scarce medical facilities were even more depleted by the civil war in 1998.

LIFE EXPECTANCY AT BIRTH
This is the average number of years a baby is expected to live if its living conditions stay the same. However, the infant mortality rate, which is the number of children who die before they are 5 years old, has a strong influence on this figure. People in countries with high infant mortality will have lower life expectancy, even though most people who live beyond the age of five will go on to live a natural life span of 70–80 years.

	No data
	Under 60
	60–65
	65–70
	70–75
	75–80
	Over 80

A CHILD BORN IN ESWATINI IS NEARLY 30 TIMES MORE LIKELY

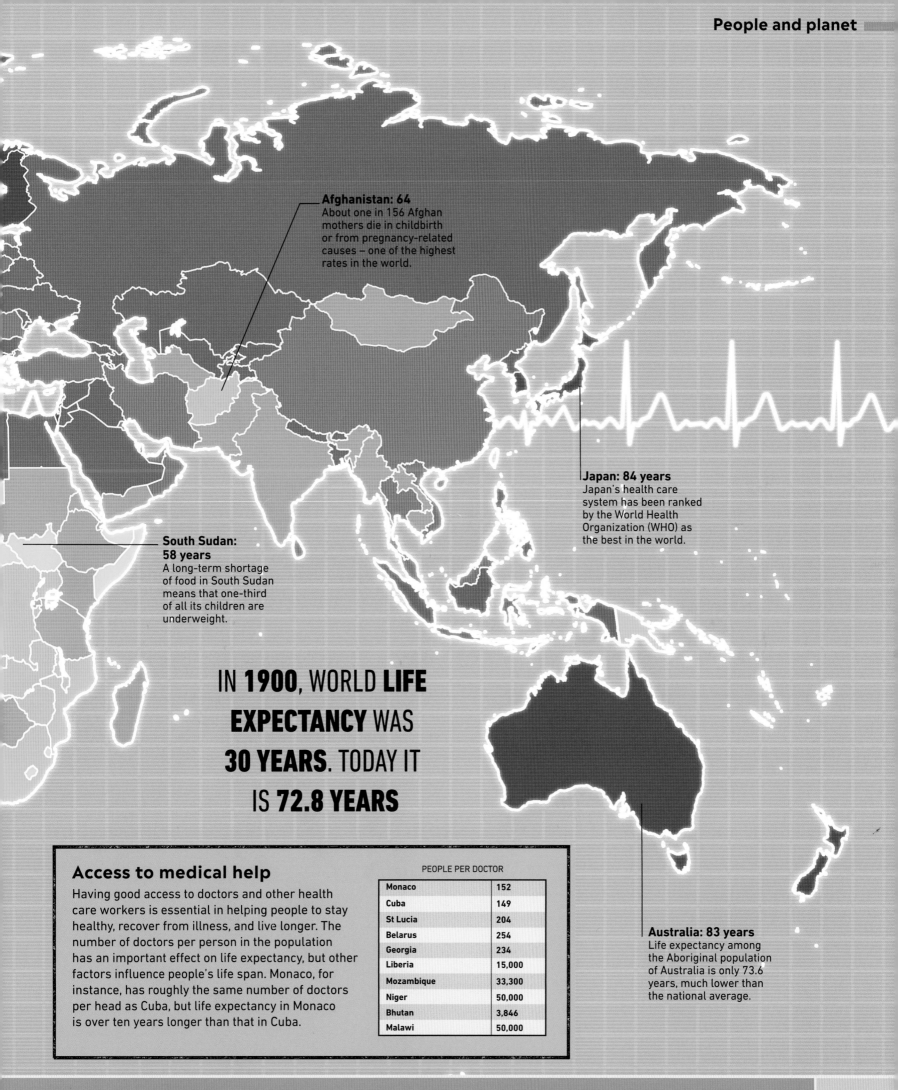

Afghanistan: 64
About one in 156 Afghan mothers die in childbirth or from pregnancy-related causes – one of the highest rates in the world.

Japan: 84 years
Japan's health care system has been ranked by the World Health Organization (WHO) as the best in the world.

South Sudan: 58 years
A long-term shortage of food in South Sudan means that one-third of all its children are underweight.

IN **1900**, WORLD **LIFE EXPECTANCY** WAS **30 YEARS**. TODAY IT IS **72.8 YEARS**

Australia: 83 years
Life expectancy among the Aboriginal population of Australia is only 73.6 years, much lower than the national average.

Access to medical help

Having good access to doctors and other health care workers is essential in helping people to stay healthy, recover from illness, and live longer. The number of doctors per person in the population has an important effect on life expectancy, but other factors influence people's life span. Monaco, for instance, has roughly the same number of doctors per head as Cuba, but life expectancy in Monaco is over ten years longer than that in Cuba.

PEOPLE PER DOCTOR	
Monaco	152
Cuba	149
St Lucia	204
Belarus	254
Georgia	234
Liberia	15,000
Mozambique	33,300
Niger	50,000
Bhutan	3,846
Malawi	50,000

TO DIE BEFORE THE AGE OF FIVE THAN A CHILD BORN IN SWEDEN.

Infecting germs

Many infectious diseases are caused by microscopic living organisms. They live and multiply inside our bodies and can pass from human to human by touch, through blood or saliva, and through the air.

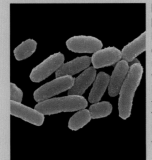

Bubonic plague bacteria

Bacteria are single-celled organisms that multiply by dividing into two again and again. Millions could fit on the head of a pin. Today, many bacterial infections can be treated with antibiotics.

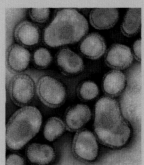

Flu virus

Viruses are very simple organisms far smaller even than bacteria. They spread by invading and taking over cells in the body. Viruses are unharmed by antibiotics, but the body can be fortified against them with a vaccine.

The Black Death ravaged Britain in 1348–50.

Troops returning home from Asia at the end of World War I brought Spanish Flu back with them.

③

In August 1918, a second wave of Spanish Flu crossed the Atlantic and hit the port city of Freetown, Sierra Leone.

④

Spanish Flu

This infection was called "Spanish Flu" because people first thought it began in Spain. However, it actually was first reported at a training camp for American soldiers in the United States. The disease spread quickly when infected soldiers travelled to Europe to fight in World War I. It is estimated to have killed 20–50 million people.

Freetown

According to some studies, HIV began its spread through the human population in Cameroon.

Pandemics

Infectious diseases – illnesses that pass between people – can spread rapidly. Many people become ill, causing a local disaster called an epidemic. When this effect becomes global, we call it a pandemic.

KEY
This map shows the spread of three of history's most lethal pandemics – in ancient times, the Middle Ages, and modern times

 Plague of Justinian
Bubonic plague, 541–42 CE

 Black Death
Bubonic plague, 1346–55 CE

 Spanish Flu
Influenza, 1918–20

SPANISH FLU MAY HAVE KILLED UP TO 50 MILLION PEOPLE.

Superbugs and new viruses

Bacteria and viruses change fast. "Superbug" bacteria become immune to antibiotics, while scientists try to develop vaccines against new viruses. Today, air travel can spread infection worldwide in days, so the fear of a fast-spreading pandemic is greater than ever. Here are five recent cases of new viruses.

1 **Hong Kong Flu, 1968–69**
In 2 years, Hong Kong Flu caused about 1 million deaths. The virus killed around 34,000 people in the United States alone.

2 **Avian (Bird) Flu, Hong Kong, 1997–present**
This virus first appeared in humans in Hong Kong, through contact with infected poultry. It has killed hundreds of people since then.

3 **H1N1 ("Swine Flu"), Mexico City, 2009–10**
This new flu developed from viruses of birds, pigs, and humans. Up to 575,400 people died in the first year of this pandemic.

4 **HIV, west–central Africa, 1981–present**
This virus causes AIDS – an often-fatal disease of the body's defences. It now infects more than 30 million people worldwide.

Black Death
In the 14th century, an outbreak of bubonic plague spread from Asia across Europe, causing devastation along the way. It caused around 50 million deaths – about half in Europe, where 25 per cent of the population was killed.

Constantinople (Istanbul)

Some experts think the Plague of Justinian began not in Ethiopia, but in Central Asia.

The Black Death passed along sea trade routes, since the bacteria that caused the disease lived in fleas, which lived on ships' rats.

Plague of Justinian
At its height, during the rule of the Emperor Justinian (ruler of the Byzantine, or Eastern Roman, Empire), this disease killed at least 25 million people. It may have started in Ethiopia, then spread along trade routes through northern Egypt and Constantinople (modern-day Istanbul) into Europe.

COVID-19

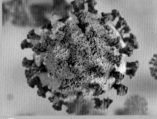

5 **Dec 2019–present**
First identified in Wuhan, China, in late 2019, this fast-spreading virus can cause severe respiratory problems; up to 2.6 million deaths were reported in the first year of the pandemic. Vaccines have now been developed to help protect against the disease.

UP TO **2,000 PEOPLE** STILL SUFFER FROM **PLAGUE** EACH YEAR

Spanish Flu was brought to New Zealand in 1918 by soldiers returning home from fighting in World War I in Europe.

THAT'S MORE THAN THE TOTAL NUMBER OF DEATHS DURING WORLD WAR I.

The poverty line

A poverty line is the minimum level of income thought to be enough for a person to live on. It is the least amount needed to provide basic necessities: food, clothing, health care, and shelter. The cost of living is different around the world, so the poverty line varies from country to country.

PEOPLE ON LESS THAN $1.90 A DAY

The international extreme poverty line of $1.90 income a day is a global measure of absolute poverty. This amount was set by the World Bank in 2015, and will be updated when necessary to reflect the cost of living. The map shows the percentage of each country's people earning less than $1.90 a day.

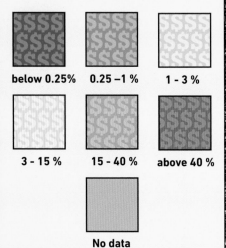

below 0.25%   0.25 –1 %   1 - 3 %

3 - 15 %   15 - 40 %   above 40 %

No data

Morocco
Income inequality here is the highest in North Africa.

USA
The wealth gap is huge in America; the top 1 per cent of US households hold 15 times more wealth than the entirety of the lower 50 per cent.

Haiti
The most cases of extreme poverty in the western hemisphere. Haiti's economy was severely affected by a 2010 earthquake, and is still yet to recover.

Bolivia
One of the poorest countries in South America. Ambitious goals have been set surrounding the country's sanitation services, but currently only a third of Bolivia's rural population has access to proper sewage systems.

Liberia
One of the poorest countries in the world. An estimated 64 per cent of the population lives below the $1.90-a-day line.

Ghana
While the overall poverty rate has gone down sharply over the last 30 years, poverty in the north of the country has changed little.

Argentina
Lower unemployment has helped drastically to reduce poverty in recent years.

Poverty

The COVID-19 pandemic means that global poverty is expected to rise for the first time since 2000. Sub-Saharan Africa has by far the most cases of extreme poverty – half of the countries in this region have a poverty rate higher than 35%.

Inequality

In many countries, the gap between rich and poor is widening. Tax, special benefits for the lowest earners, and free education, among other things, can help reduce this. These charts show how much of a country's overall wealth the richest people own. The countries shown here are those with a very large gap between rich and poor, and those where the gap is less noticeable.

OVER 24% OF THE WORLD'S POPULATION LIVED ON LESS THAN

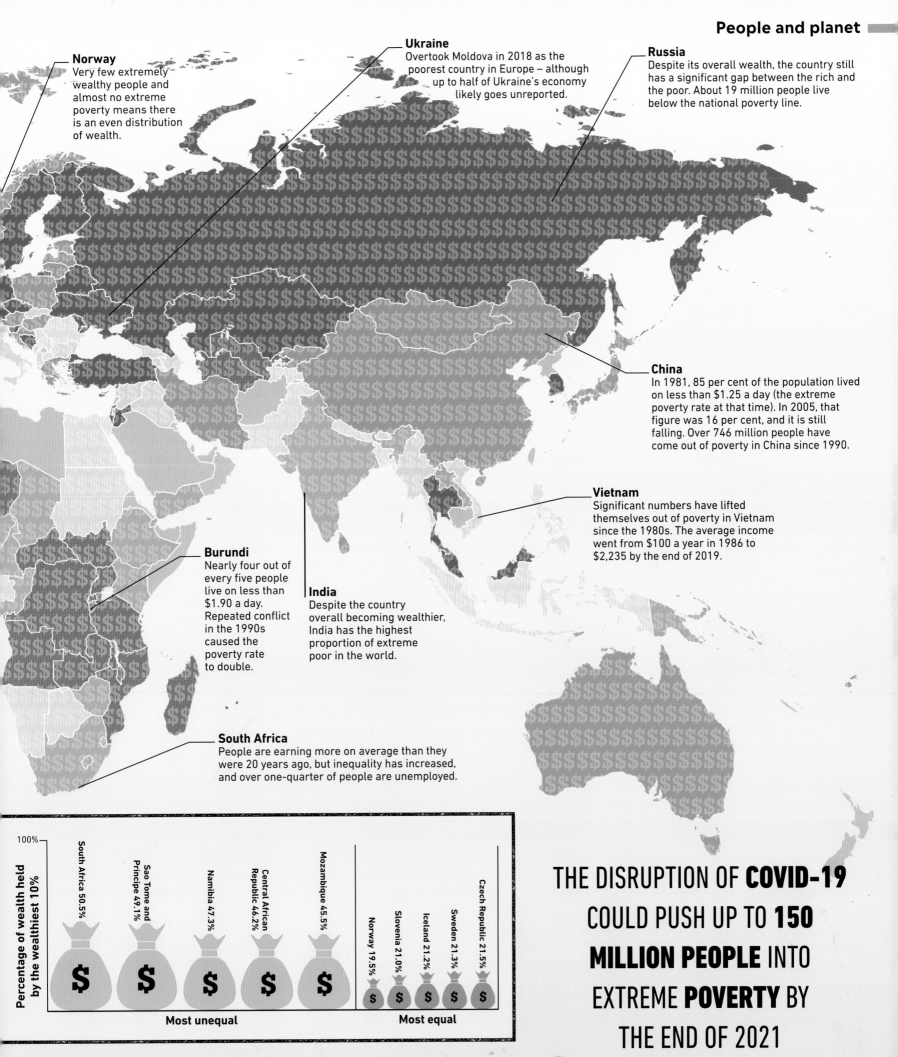

Norway
Very few extremely wealthy people and almost no extreme poverty means there is an even distribution of wealth.

Ukraine
Overtook Moldova in 2018 as the poorest country in Europe – although up to half of Ukraine's economy likely goes unreported.

Russia
Despite its overall wealth, the country still has a significant gap between the rich and the poor. About 19 million people live below the national poverty line.

China
In 1981, 85 per cent of the population lived on less than $1.25 a day (the extreme poverty rate at that time). In 2005, that figure was 16 per cent, and it is still falling. Over 746 million people have come out of poverty in China since 1990.

Vietnam
Significant numbers have lifted themselves out of poverty in Vietnam since the 1980s. The average income went from $100 a year in 1986 to $2,235 by the end of 2019.

Burundi
Nearly four out of every five people live on less than $1.90 a day. Repeated conflict in the 1990s caused the poverty rate to double.

India
Despite the country overall becoming wealthier, India has the highest proportion of extreme poor in the world.

South Africa
People are earning more on average than they were 20 years ago, but inequality has increased, and over one-quarter of people are unemployed.

Percentage of wealth held by the wealthiest 10%

100%

South Africa 50.5%
Sao Tome and Principe 49.1%
Namibia 47.3%
Central African Republic 46.2%
Mozambique 45.5%

Norway 19.5%
Slovenia 21.0%
Iceland 21.2%
Sweden 21.3%
Czech Republic 21.5%

Most unequal

Most equal

THE DISRUPTION OF **COVID-19** COULD PUSH UP TO **150 MILLION PEOPLE** INTO EXTREME **POVERTY** BY THE END OF 2021

$3.20 A DAY IN 2017, AND 43.6% LIVED ON LESS THAN $5.50 A DAY.

The world's gold

Beautiful, rare, and highly prized, gold has been mined since ancient Egyptian times. Sometimes a discovery of gold led to a "gold rush", with thousands of people flocking to the site in the hope of making their fortune.

Klondike gold rush, Canada, 1897–99
100,000 prospectors headed for Klondike. About 4,000 found gold.

California gold rush, USA, 1848–55
300,000 people flocked to California, aiming to strike gold.

Canada
Five per cent of the world's gold comes from Canada.

United States
This is the fourth-largest gold producer, mining 200 tonnes annually (6 per cent of the global total).

Ghana
Ghana is Africa's largest gold producer, snatching this top ranking from South Africa in 2019.

Peru
Peru is the largest gold producer in South America, and the world's sixth largest (4 per cent of all gold).

Top 10 gold mines
Figures show gold mined in 2019.

1. **Muruntau, Uzbekistan** 62.2 tonnes
2. **Olimpiada, Russia** 43.2 tonnes
3. **Carlin, Nevada, USA** 40.9 tonnes
4. **Pueblo Viejo, Dominican Republic** 30.6 tonnes
5. **Cortez, Nevada, USA** 29.9 tonnes
6. **Lihir, Papua New Guinea** 27.4 tonnes
7. **Cadia East, Australia** 27.1 tonnes
8. **Grasberg, Indonesia** 26.8 tonnes
9. **Kibali, Democratic Republic of Congo** 25.3 tonnes
10. **Loulo-Gounkoto, Mali** 22.2 tonnes

ALL THE **GOLD** THAT HAS EVER BEEN **MINED** WOULD MAKE A CUBE **28 M** (92 FT) ALONG EACH SIDE

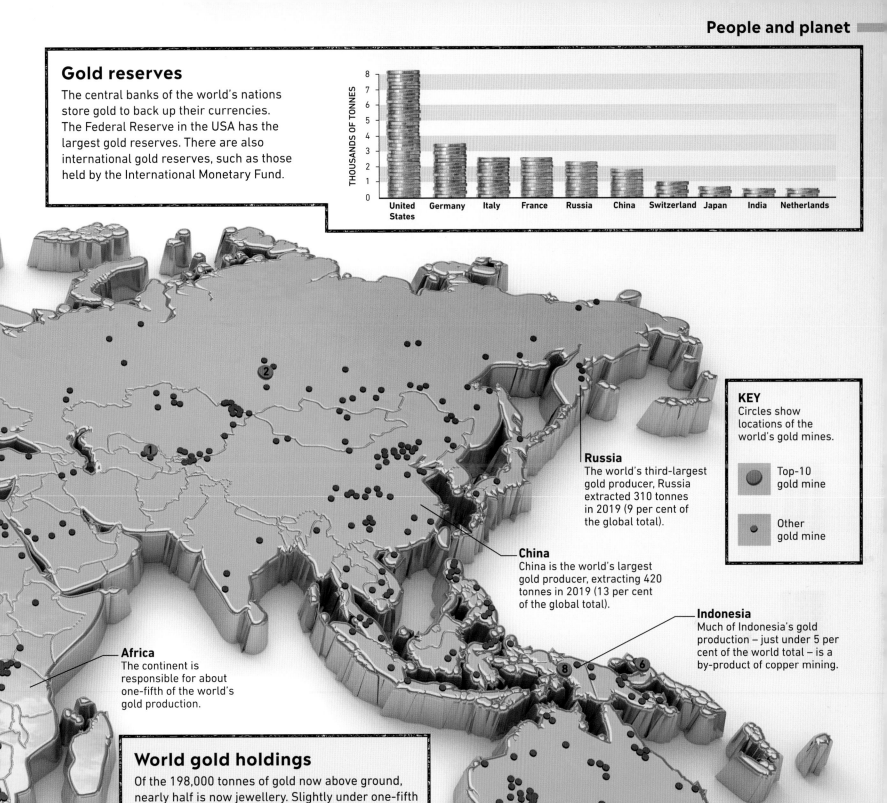

Gold reserves

The central banks of the world's nations store gold to back up their currencies. The Federal Reserve in the USA has the largest gold reserves. There are also international gold reserves, such as those held by the International Monetary Fund.

THOUSANDS OF TONNES

United States | Germany | Italy | France | Russia | China | Switzerland | Japan | India | Netherlands

KEY
Circles show locations of the world's gold mines.

Top-10 gold mine

Other gold mine

Russia
The world's third-largest gold producer, Russia extracted 310 tonnes in 2019 (9 per cent of the global total).

China
China is the world's largest gold producer, extracting 420 tonnes in 2019 (13 per cent of the global total).

Indonesia
Much of Indonesia's gold production – just under 5 per cent of the world total – is a by-product of copper mining.

Africa
The continent is responsible for about one-fifth of the world's gold production.

World gold holdings

Of the 198,000 tonnes of gold now above ground, nearly half is now jewellery. Slightly under one-fifth is stored as reserves in central banks (see above). Some of the rest exists as parts in engineering such as electric cables and protective coatings on spacecraft. Still more is in the hands of investors, waiting for the right time to sell.

Witwatersrand gold rush, South Africa, 1886
Triggered by the discovery of the "Golden Arc" – an ancient lake bed rich in gold deposits that stretches from Johannesburg to Welkom.

Jewellery 47% | Central banks 17% | Investment 22% | Industrial 12% | Other 2%

WORLD'S GOLD HOLDINGS

Australia
With 330 tonnes mined in 2019 (10 per cent of the global total), Australia is the second-largest gold-producing nation.

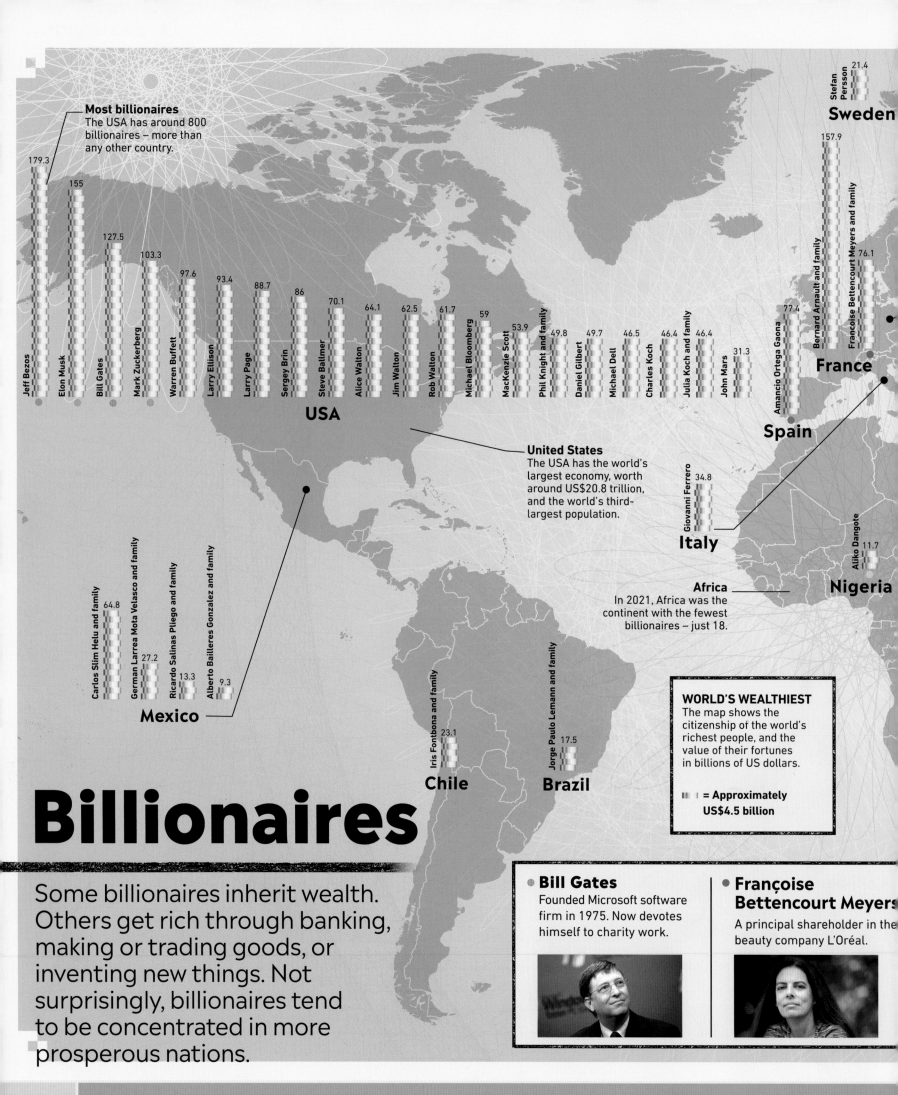

Most billionaires
The USA has around 800 billionaires – more than any other country.

179.3 Jeff Bezos
155 Elon Musk
127.5 Bill Gates
103.3 Mark Zuckerberg
97.6 Warren Buffett
93.4 Larry Ellison
88.7 Larry Page
86 Sergey Brin
70.1 Steve Ballmer
64.1 Alice Walton
62.5 Jim Walton
61.7 Rob Walton
59 Michael Bloomberg
53.9 MacKenzie Scott
49.8 Phil Knight and family
49.7 Daniel Gilbert
46.5 Michael Dell
46.4 Charles Koch
46.4 Julia Koch and family
31.3 John Mars

USA

United States
The USA has the world's largest economy, worth around US$20.8 trillion, and the world's third-largest population.

64.8 Carlos Slim Helu and family
27.2 German Larrea Mota Velasco and family
13.3 Ricardo Salinas Pliego and family
9.3 Alberto Baillères Gonzalez and family

Mexico

21.4 Stefan Persson
Sweden

157.9 Bernard Arnault and family
76.1 Françoise Bettencourt Meyers and family
France

77.4 Amancio Ortega Gaona
Spain

34.8 Giovanni Ferrero
Italy

11.7 Aliko Dangote
Nigeria

Africa
In 2021, Africa was the continent with the fewest billionaires – just 18.

23.1 Iris Fontbona and family
Chile

17.5 Jorge Paulo Lemann and family
Brazil

WORLD'S WEALTHIEST
The map shows the citizenship of the world's richest people, and the value of their fortunes in billions of US dollars.

▌▌ ▌ = Approximately US$4.5 billion

Billionaires

Some billionaires inherit wealth. Others get rich through banking, making or trading goods, or inventing new things. Not surprisingly, billionaires tend to be concentrated in more prosperous nations.

● **Bill Gates**
Founded Microsoft software firm in 1975. Now devotes himself to charity work.

● **Françoise Bettencourt Meyers**
A principal shareholder in the beauty company L'Oréal.

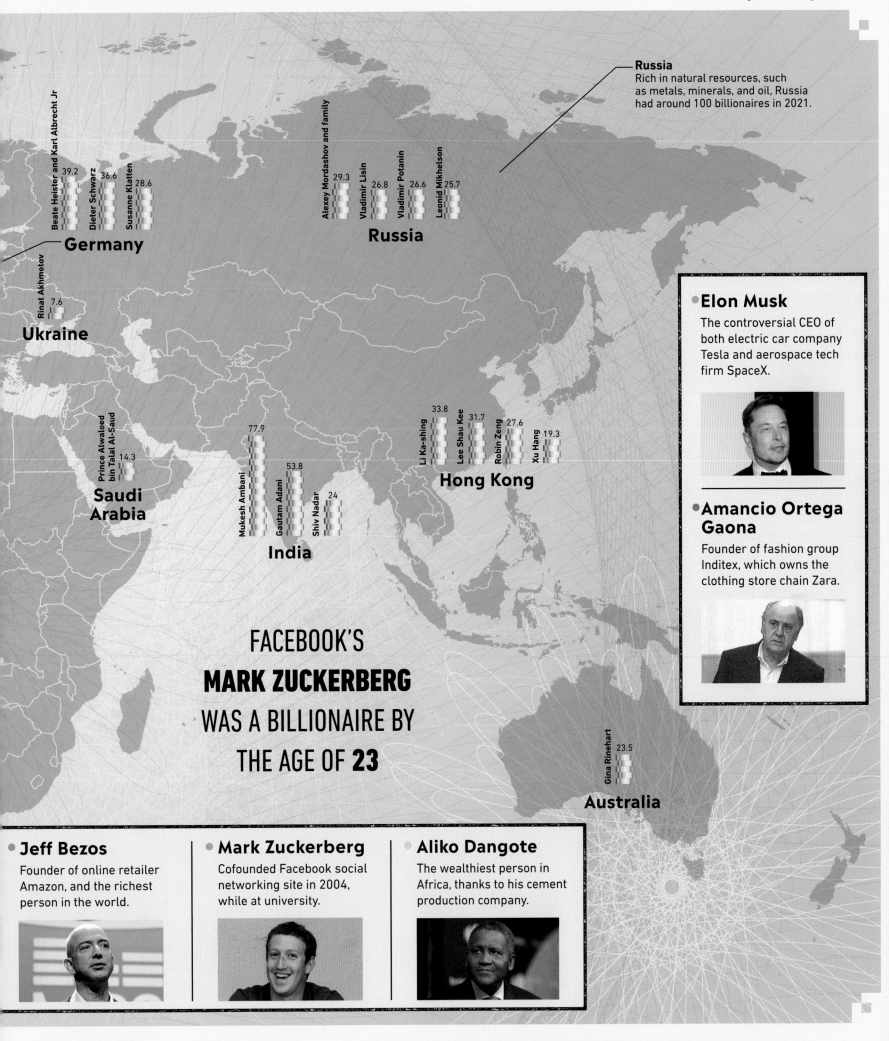

Russia
Rich in natural resources, such as metals, minerals, and oil, Russia had around 100 billionaires in 2021.

Germany
- Beate Heister and Karl Albrecht Jr — 39.2
- Dieter Schwarz — 36.6
- Susanne Klatten — 28.6

Russia
- Alexey Mordashov and family — 29.3
- Vladimir Lisin — 26.8
- Vladimir Potanin — 26.6
- Leonid Mikhelson — 25.7

Ukraine
- Rinat Akhmetov — 7.6

Saudi Arabia
- Prince Alwaleed bin Talal Al-Saud — 14.3

India
- Mukesh Ambani — 77.9
- Gautam Adani — 53.8
- Shiv Nadar — 24

Hong Kong
- Li Ka-shing — 33.8
- Lee Shau Kee — 31.7
- Robin Zeng — 27.6
- Xu Hang — 19.3

Australia
- Gina Rinehart — 23.5

FACEBOOK'S MARK ZUCKERBERG WAS A BILLIONAIRE BY THE AGE OF 23

•Elon Musk
The controversial CEO of both electric car company Tesla and aerospace tech firm SpaceX.

•Amancio Ortega Gaona
Founder of fashion group Inditex, which owns the clothing store chain Zara.

•Jeff Bezos
Founder of online retailer Amazon, and the richest person in the world.

•Mark Zuckerberg
Cofounded Facebook social networking site in 2004, while at university.

•Aliko Dangote
The wealthiest person in Africa, thanks to his cement production company.

MORE THAN 45.5 BILLION US DOLLARS TO CHARITABLE CAUSES.

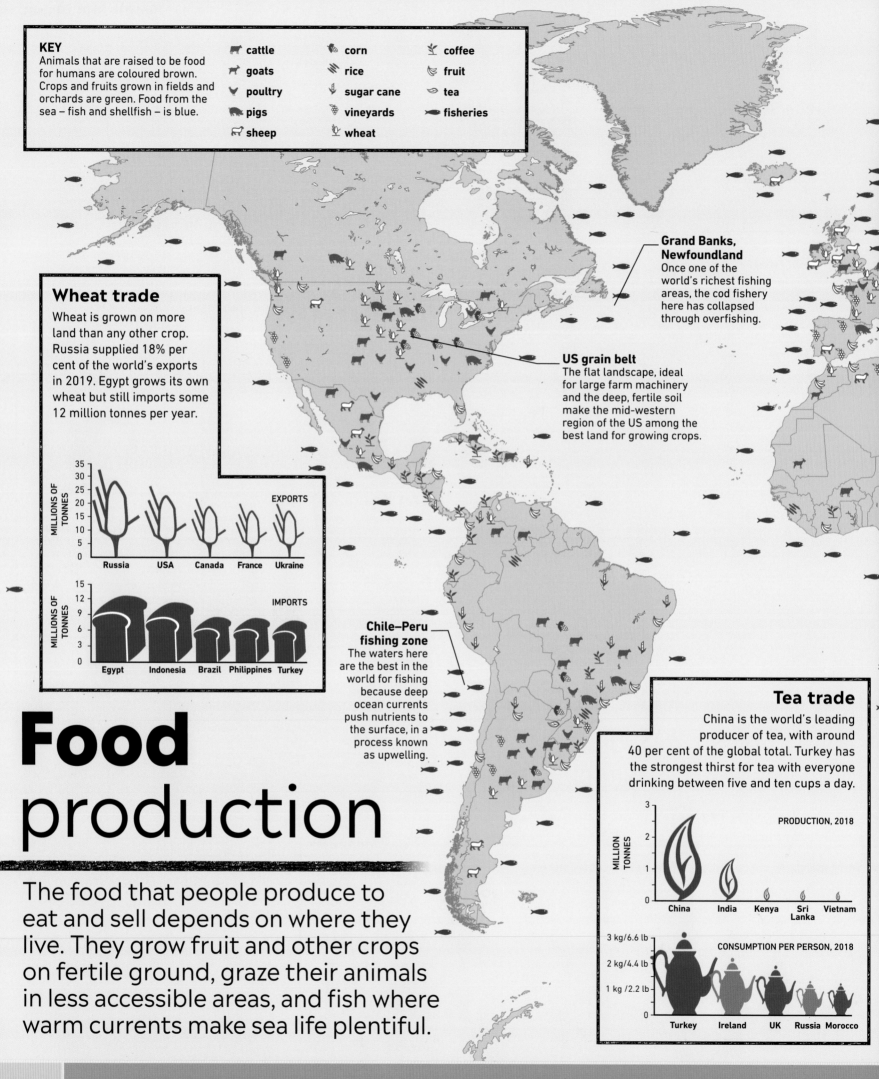

KEY
Animals that are raised to be food for humans are coloured brown. Crops and fruits grown in fields and orchards are green. Food from the sea – fish and shellfish – is blue.

- cattle
- goats
- poultry
- pigs
- sheep
- corn
- rice
- sugar cane
- vineyards
- wheat
- coffee
- fruit
- tea
- fisheries

Wheat trade
Wheat is grown on more land than any other crop. Russia supplied 18% per cent of the world's exports in 2019. Egypt grows its own wheat but still imports some 12 million tonnes per year.

EXPORTS (MILLIONS OF TONNES)
Russia, USA, Canada, France, Ukraine

IMPORTS (MILLIONS OF TONNES)
Egypt, Indonesia, Brazil, Philippines, Turkey

Grand Banks, Newfoundland
Once one of the world's richest fishing areas, the cod fishery here has collapsed through overfishing.

US grain belt
The flat landscape, ideal for large farm machinery and the deep, fertile soil make the mid-western region of the US among the best land for growing crops.

Chile–Peru fishing zone
The waters here are the best in the world for fishing because deep ocean currents push nutrients to the surface, in a process known as upwelling.

Food production

The food that people produce to eat and sell depends on where they live. They grow fruit and other crops on fertile ground, graze their animals in less accessible areas, and fish where warm currents make sea life plentiful.

Tea trade
China is the world's leading producer of tea, with around 40 per cent of the global total. Turkey has the strongest thirst for tea with everyone drinking between five and ten cups a day.

PRODUCTION, 2018 (MILLION TONNES)
China, India, Kenya, Sri Lanka, Vietnam

CONSUMPTION PER PERSON, 2018
3 kg/6.6 lb, 2 kg/4.4 lb, 1 kg /2.2 lb
Turkey, Ireland, UK, Russia, Morocco

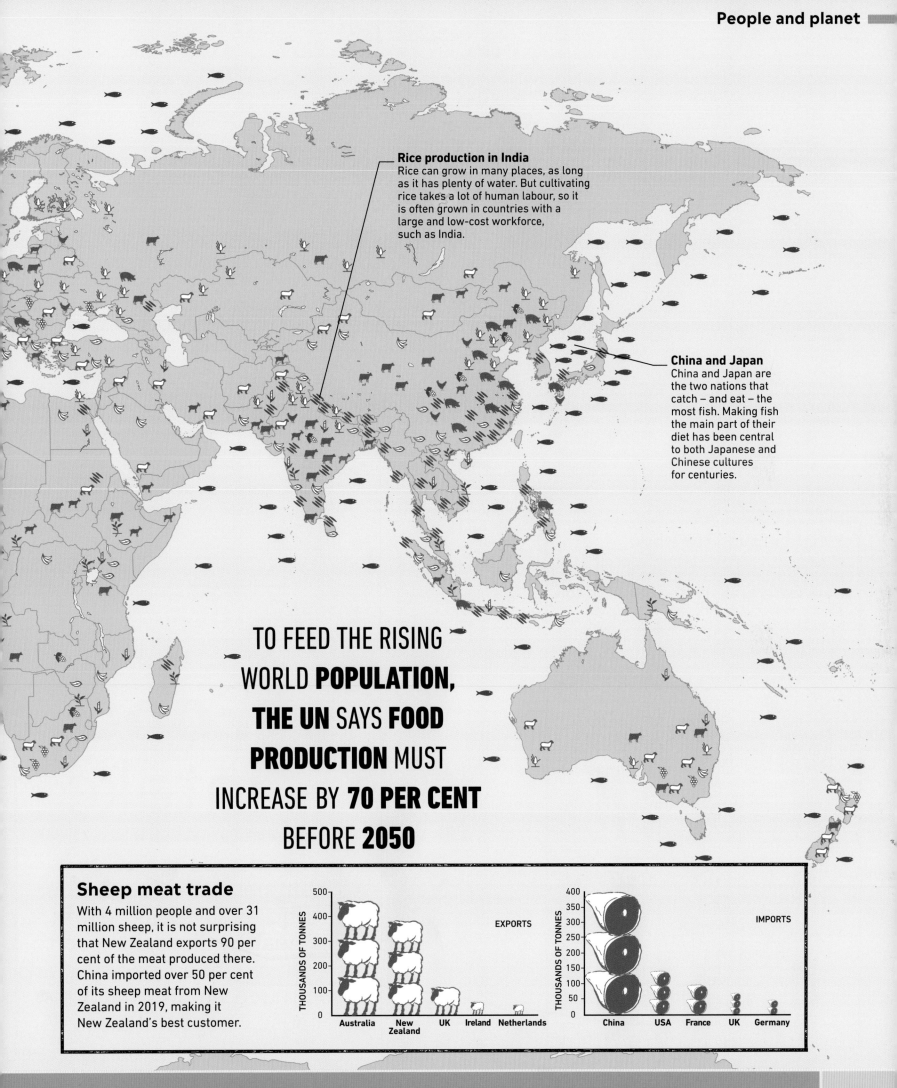

Rice production in India
Rice can grow in many places, as long as it has plenty of water. But cultivating rice takes a lot of human labour, so it is often grown in countries with a large and low-cost workforce, such as India.

China and Japan
China and Japan are the two nations that catch – and eat – the most fish. Making fish the main part of their diet has been central to both Japanese and Chinese cultures for centuries.

TO FEED THE RISING WORLD **POPULATION,** **THE UN** SAYS **FOOD PRODUCTION** MUST INCREASE BY **70 PER CENT** BEFORE **2050**

Sheep meat trade

With 4 million people and over 31 million sheep, it is not surprising that New Zealand exports 90 per cent of the meat produced there. China imported over 50 per cent of its sheep meat from New Zealand in 2019, making it New Zealand's best customer.

THOUSANDS OF TONNES

500
400
300
200
100
0

EXPORTS

Australia | New Zealand | UK | Ireland | Netherlands

THOUSANDS OF TONNES

400
350
300
250
200
150
100
50
0

IMPORTS

China | USA | France | UK | Germany

Canada
Canada has a lower adult obesity rate than the United States, at about 27.7 per cent. Daily calorie intake is around 3,530 kcal.

United Kingdom
Obesity in the UK is estimated to add an extra £6.1 billion each year to the country's national health-care costs.

United States
Larger portions and cheap, high-calorie, high-fat fast foods and ready meals have helped raise average daily intake levels to 3,800 kcal. Adult obesity is now around 39.6 per cent.

Africa
Africa is the continent with the lowest calorie intake, at 2,550 kcal per day. The global average is 2,870 kcal.

Cuba
Although Cuba is not a rich country, its citizens are well fed, with a daily intake of about 3,420 kcal.

Bolivia
Daily calorie intake for the average adult in Bolivia is around 2,100 kcal.

Weight around the world

Pacific island nations such as Nauru, the Cook Islands, and Tonga have among the highest obesity levels. This is partly because the islanders now eat mainly cheap, fatty, imported foods, and partly because plumpness traditionally signifies wealth and fertility.

PERCENTAGE OF THE POPULATION CLASSED AS OBESE

61.0%	55.9%	48.2%
Nauru	**Cook Islands**	**Tonga**

36.2%	35.4%	31.7%
USA	**Saudi Arabia**	**United Arab Emirates**

Food intake

Food and the energy it contains is the fuel for our bodies. Overeating and unhealthy diets can lead to obesity – when a person gains so much weight that it can cause illness and disease.

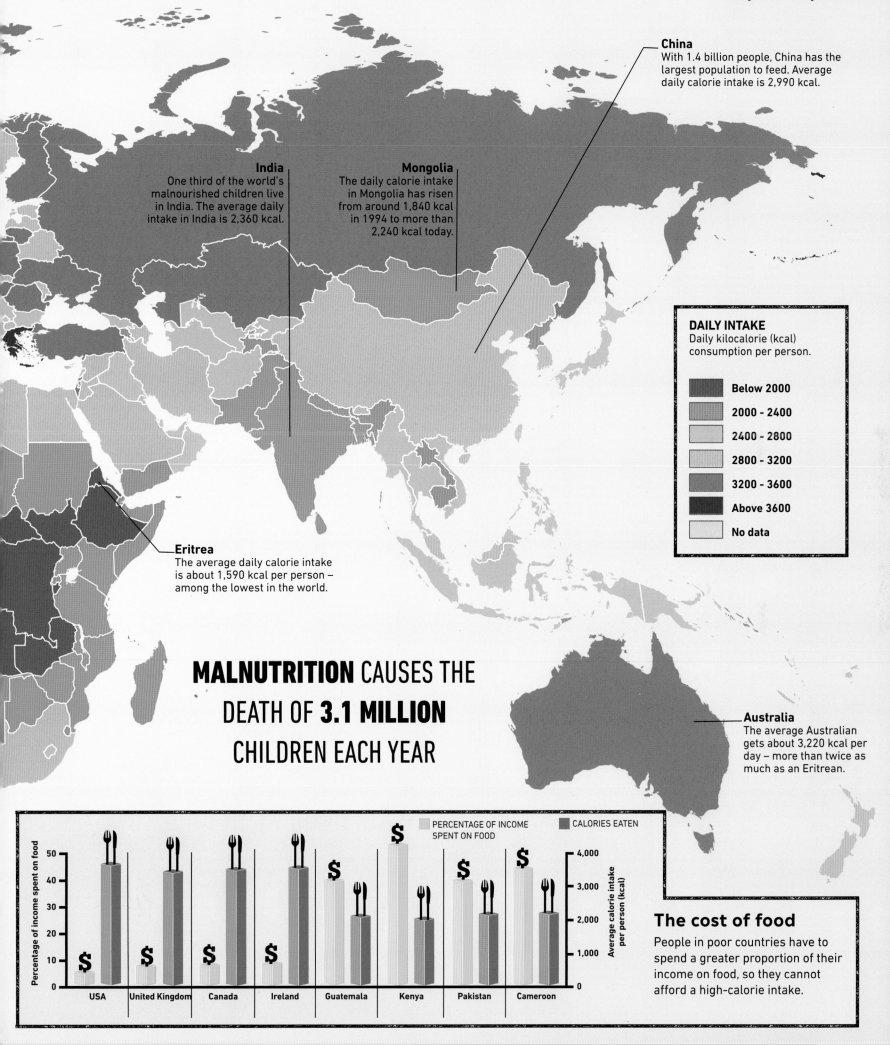

China
With 1.4 billion people, China has the largest population to feed. Average daily calorie intake is 2,990 kcal.

India
One third of the world's malnourished children live in India. The average daily intake in India is 2,360 kcal.

Mongolia
The daily calorie intake in Mongolia has risen from around 1,840 kcal in 1994 to more than 2,240 kcal today.

DAILY INTAKE
Daily kilocalorie (kcal) consumption per person.

Below 2000
2000 – 2400
2400 – 2800
2800 – 3200
3200 – 3600
Above 3600
No data

Eritrea
The average daily calorie intake is about 1,590 kcal per person – among the lowest in the world.

MALNUTRITION CAUSES THE DEATH OF **3.1 MILLION** CHILDREN EACH YEAR

Australia
The average Australian gets about 3,220 kcal per day – more than twice as much as an Eritrean.

PERCENTAGE OF INCOME SPENT ON FOOD   CALORIES EATEN

Percentage of income spent on food

USA   United Kingdom   Canada   Ireland   Guatemala   Kenya   Pakistan   Cameroon

Average calorie intake per person (kcal)

The cost of food

People in poor countries have to spend a greater proportion of their income on food, so they cannot afford a high-calorie intake.

Canada
Around 16 per cent of Canadians struggle to pass basic literary tests.

Europe
Although most countries in Europe have very high literacy rates, over 55 million adults classed as "literate" still lack basic reading and writing skills.

United States
Around 21 per cent of adults in the US are classed as "functionally illiterate".

Mauritania
Little more than half of Mauritania's population – 52.1 per cent – can read and write.

Chad
Just 23.3 per cent of people in Chad are literate – the world's lowest literacy rate.

Brazil
Just over nine out of every ten Brazilians are literate.

Going to secondary school

Wealthy nations can afford to provide secondary education for all children, but governments in poorer countries cannot offer every child a place. This is particularly true in Africa south of the Sahara. In Niger, for example, only 24 per cent of children go to secondary school.

PERCENTAGE OF SECONDARY-SCHOOL-AGE CHILDREN ENROLLED IN SCHOOL

100%
80%
60%
40%
20%
0%

France
Japan
Sweden
New Zeland
Seychelles
Burundi
Burkina Faso
Mozambique
Niger
Central African Republic

Literacy

Literacy – being able to read and write – is an essential life skill. Being literate makes it easier for people to learn, make the most of their abilities, and get better jobs. High levels of illiteracy make it difficult for nations to develop and become wealthier.

IN DEVELOPING COUNTRIES, **200 MILLION** PEOPLE AGED **15–24** HAVE NOT COMPLETED **PRIMARY SCHOOL**

ABOUT 61 MILLION PRIMARY-AGE CHILDREN WORLDWIDE WERE RECEIVING

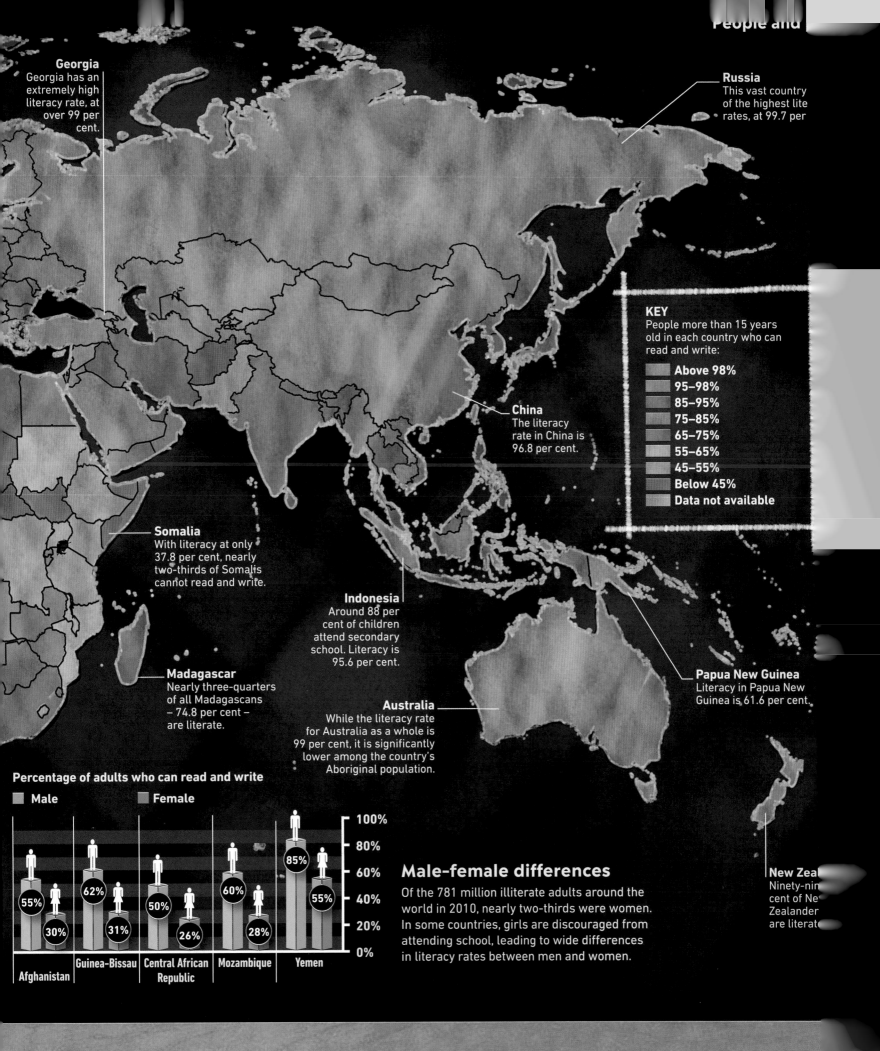

Georgia
Georgia has an extremely high literacy rate, at over 99 per cent.

Russia
This vast country of the highest lite rates, at 99.7 per

KEY
People more than 15 years old in each country who can read and write:

Above 98%
95–98%
85–95%
75–85%
65–75%
55–65%
45–55%
Below 45%
Data not available

China
The literacy rate in China is 96.8 per cent.

Somalia
With literacy at only 37.8 per cent, nearly two-thirds of Somalis cannot read and write.

Indonesia
Around 88 per cent of children attend secondary school. Literacy is 95.6 per cent.

Madagascar
Nearly three-quarters of all Madagascans – 74.8 per cent – are literate.

Australia
While the literacy rate for Australia as a whole is 99 per cent, it is significantly lower among the country's Aboriginal population.

Papua New Guinea
Literacy in Papua New Guinea is 61.6 per cent.

New Zea
Ninety-nin cent of Ne Zealander are literat

Percentage of adults who can read and write

■ Male   ■ Female

	Male	Female
Afghanistan	55%	30%
Guinea-Bissau	62%	31%
Central African Republic	50%	26%
Mozambique	60%	28%
Yemen	85%	55%

100%
80%
60%
40%
20%
0%

Male-female differences

Of the 781 million illiterate adults around the world in 2010, nearly two-thirds were women. In some countries, girls are discouraged from attending school, leading to wide differences in literacy rates between men and women.

Biggest oil spills

Oil spills – when oil escapes into the environment – cause devastation to wildlife and are difficult and costly to clean up.

1 Gulf War oil spill, Persian Gulf, 1991
300,000–1,200,000 tonnes
Iraqi forces opened valves on Kuwaiti oil wells and pipes, causing a 160-km (100-mile) slick.

2 Lakeview gusher, California, USA, 1910-11
1,100,000 tonnes
An oil well erupted like a geyser, spilling out oil for over a year until it naturally died down.

3 Deepwater Horizon, Gulf of Mexico, 2010
671,000 tonnes
A deep-sea oil spill occurred when an explosion destroyed the Deepwater Horizon drillling rig.

4 Ixtoc 1 oil spill, Gulf of Mexico, USA, 1979–80
412,000–435,000 tonnes
The Ixtoc 1 drilling platform collapsed after an explosion. The spill continued for 9 months.

5 *Atlantic Empress*, Trinidad and Tobago, 1979
260,000 tonnes
The largest oil spill from a ship. The tanker *Atlantic Empress* hit another ship, killing 26 crew.

Persistent organic pollutants (POPs): Canadian Arctic
These pollutants include industrial products and pesticides. They travel on the world's oceans and air currents, accumulate in the Arctic regions, and contaminate the foods that Inuit people eat.

Lead: La Oroya, Peru
A metal smelting plant has emitted toxic lead since 1922. This has led to contaminated water supplies, dangerously polluted air, and unsafe levels of lead in the blood of local residents.

Pollution

Oil spills, industrial waste, and radiation leaks from nuclear power stations cause harm to people and the environment. Carbon dioxide gas (CO_2) produced by transport and industry is adding to global warming.

THE 1991 **GULF WAR** OIL SLICK WAS UP TO **13 CM (5 IN)** THICK

Nuclear accidents
Splitting atoms in nuclear reactors produces energy for generating electricity. Accidents at reactors may lead to radioactive material escaping, which can cause illness such as cancer for many years.

 1 Chernobyl, Ukraine 26 April 1986
A reactor explosion released radioactive material. Radiation-related illnesses may have caused thousands of deaths.

Chemical waste: Dzerzhinsk, Russia
Chemical weapons were made here until 1998. The town's water contains extreme levels of toxic chemicals. Average life expectancy for the area in 2007 was 45.

Organic chemicals, Sumgayit, Azerbaijan
A town once home to chemical plants that released 109,000 tonnes of toxic chemicals per year. Cancer rates are up to 51 per cent higher than elsewhere in the country.

Nickel ore: Norilsk, Russia
Few trees grow within 48 km (30 miles) of a massive metal-smelting complex in this industrial town, due to acid rain and smog.

Industrial chemicals: Bhopal, India
In 1984, poisonous gas escaped from a pesticide factory, killing 4,000–15,000 people. Thousands continue to suffer and die from illnesses related to the accident.

Air pollution: Linfen, China
Among the world's most polluted cities, Linfen is at the heart of China's coal industry. Soot and coal dust fill the air, raising the risk of bronchitis, pneumonia, and lung cancer in the people.

Mercury: Central Kalimantan, Indonesia
Toxic mercury is used to extract gold from mines in Kalimantan, with about 45 tonnes of mercury released into the air each year.

Pesticides: Kasaragod, India
Decades of pesticide use on cashew-nut plantations have caused disease and mental illness for a generation of residents.

Tanning wastes: Ranipet, India
Water polluted by waste from a leather-tanning factory stings the skin and causes ulcers.

Lead: Kabwe, Zambia
A once-thriving lead industry has resulted in lead levels in Kabwe's children of 5–10 times the safe limit.

Acid mine drainage: Johannesburg, South Africa
Acidified water flows from old mines into rivers. It contaminates water supplies and crops and harms wildlife.

Carbon dioxide

The map shows how much CO_2 each country produces per person. Wealthy nations tend to produce the most.

Tonnes of CO_2 per person

	Below 1.5
	1.5–3.0
	3.0–5.0
	5.0–10.0
	10.0–15.0
	Above 15.0
	No data

Fukushima, Japan
11 March 2011
A tsunami hit this coastal power plant, triggering explosions. Over 100,000 people had to be evacuated from their homes.

Three Mile Island, USA
28 March 1979
A reactor was damaged when it overheated. The cost of decontaminating the site after the event was US$1 billion.

Idaho Falls, USA
3 January 1961
An explosion at the SL-1 prototype reactor killed three workers – the first in the world to die in a reactor accident.

Lucens reactor, Switzerland
21 January 1969
Built in a cavern, this reactor leaked radiation. None of the workers were contaminated, but the cavern was sealed to contain the radiation.

Pollution hotspots

FOR 240,000 YEARS - LONGER THAN MODERN HUMANS HAVE EXISTED!

KEY
The world's five largest rubbish dumps, or landfills, labelled with the amount of waste dumped in them every day.

Puente Hills – Los Angeles, USA
Approximately 10,300 tonnes per day.

Apex – Las Vegas, USA
Approximately 10,500 tonnes per day.

Greenland
Currently Greenland produces 30% more waste than it can process, though two new rubbish-to-energy incinerators are due to open in 2021 and 2022.

Western Pacific Garbage Patch
A lot of discarded litter ends up in rivers, which take it to the sea, where circular currents called gyres collect it into vast patches in the ocean surface waters. This patch is the largest of these oceanic rubbish dumps.

North Atlantic Garbage Patch
The North Atlantic Garbage Patch measures hundreds of kilometres across. It shifts by as much as 1,600 km (990 miles) north and south with the seasons.

Bordo Poniente Landfill – Nezahualcoyotl, Mexico
Over 12,000 tonnes per day.

Gabon
Less wealthy countries, such as Gabon, produce less rubbish because people buy less overall, they buy proportionally more local produce without plastic packaging, and do more recycling.

Rubbish
and waste

As living standards improve worldwide and cities grow, so does the amount of rubbish that people produce. Most waste goes to rubbish dumps, which are expensive, use up a lot of land, and are harmful to the environment. Recycling is one way of helping to stop the global rubbish heap growing any bigger.

South Pacific Garbage Patch
So far, the South Pacific Gyre appears to contain less plastic waste than other ocean garbage patches.

South Atlantic Garbage Patch
The first evidence of a South Atlantic Garbage Patch was discovered in 2011. Most plastic particles in ocean garbage patches are too small to be seen with the naked eye.

Top of the recycling table
Only a handful of countries currently recycle more than half their waste; Germany tops this list, recycling 56.1% of all waste in 2019. This figure is a rapid increase from 1991, when the country recycled only 3% of its rubbish.

RECYCLING ONE ALUMINIUM CAN SAVES ENOUGH ENERGY TO BURN A

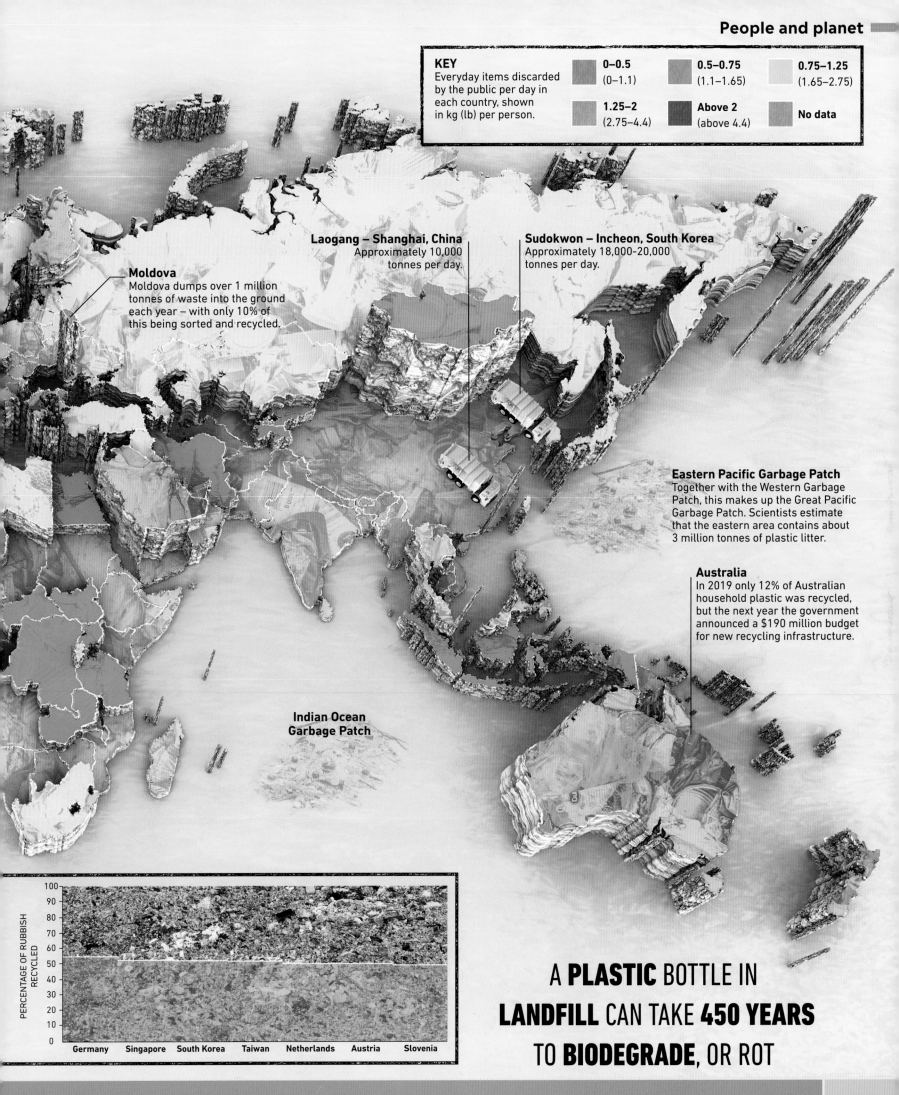

KEY
Everyday items discarded by the public per day in each country, shown in kg (lb) per person.

0–0.5 (0–1.1)	**0.5–0.75** (1.1–1.65)	**0.75–1.25** (1.65–2.75)
1.25–2 (2.75–4.4)	**Above 2** (above 4.4)	**No data**

Laogang – Shanghai, China
Approximately 10,000 tonnes per day.

Sudokwon – Incheon, South Korea
Approximately 18,000–20,000 tonnes per day.

Moldova
Moldova dumps over 1 million tonnes of waste into the ground each year – with only 10% of this being sorted and recycled.

Eastern Pacific Garbage Patch
Together with the Western Garbage Patch, this makes up the Great Pacific Garbage Patch. Scientists estimate that the eastern area contains about 3 million tonnes of plastic litter.

Australia
In 2019 only 12% of Australian household plastic was recycled, but the next year the government announced a $190 million budget for new recycling infrastructure.

Indian Ocean Garbage Patch

PERCENTAGE OF RUBBISH RECYCLED

100 90 80 70 60 50 40 30 20 10 0

Germany   Singapore   South Korea   Taiwan   Netherlands   Austria   Slovenia

A **PLASTIC** BOTTLE IN **LANDFILL** CAN TAKE **450 YEARS** TO **BIODEGRADE**, OR ROT

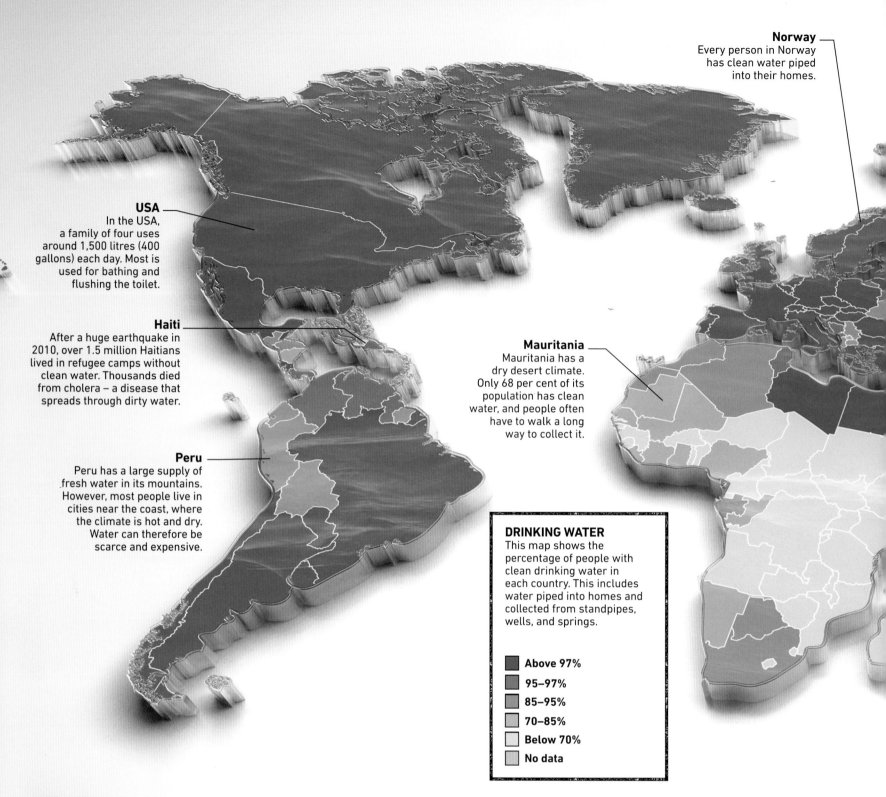

Norway
Every person in Norway has clean water piped into their homes.

USA
In the USA, a family of four uses around 1,500 litres (400 gallons) each day. Most is used for bathing and flushing the toilet.

Haiti
After a huge earthquake in 2010, over 1.5 million Haitians lived in refugee camps without clean water. Thousands died from cholera – a disease that spreads through dirty water.

Mauritania
Mauritania has a dry desert climate. Only 68 per cent of its population has clean water, and people often have to walk a long way to collect it.

Peru
Peru has a large supply of fresh water in its mountains. However, most people live in cities near the coast, where the climate is hot and dry. Water can therefore be scarce and expensive.

DRINKING WATER
This map shows the percentage of people with clean drinking water in each country. This includes water piped into homes and collected from standpipes, wells, and springs.

- Above 97%
- 95–97%
- 85–95%
- 70–85%
- Below 70%
- No data

Clean water

The tap in your home may give you an instant supply of clean drinking water. However, millions of people around the world must fetch their water from a standpipe or a well. For one in three people, their sources of water are contaminated and unsafe to drink.

Thirsty crops

Growing crops in dry climates is by far the thirstiest human activity. It uses much more water than is used in people's homes and dominates water use in many countries. That's why parts of central Asia, where farmers water fields of cotton, top this list of overall water consumers.

IN DEVELOPING COUNTRIES, 70 PER CENT OF INDUSTRIAL WASTE IS

Russia
Russia's rivers and lakes provide plentiful water, but the quality of water supplies is not reliable and most people must buy bottled water to drink.

Water use in the home
These glasses show how many of litres (gallons) of water each person uses a day for such things as drinking, washing, cooking, and cleaning. In Cambodia, each person manages on just 19 litres (5 gallons) of water a day. In the USA, people use 30 times more.

Cambodia
19.6
(5.2)

Kenya
34.4
(9.1)

Brazil
234
(61.9)

Kuwait
501
(133)

USA
593
(157)

India
Nineteen per cent of the world's population without clean water access live in India. Around 850 children here under five die every day from diarrhoea.

Indonesia
Many water supplies are polluted by waste from factories and by sewage. Around 70 per cent of people lack clean water.

THE **UN** SAYS EACH PERSON SHOULD HAVE **50 LITRES (13 GALLONS)** OF **CLEAN WATER** EVERY DAY

Total water use (million litres per person per year)

0   1   2   3   4   5   6

Turkmenistan

Chile

Guyana

Uzbekistan

Tajikistan

Kyrgyzstan

USA

Iran

Estonia

Azerbaijan

Australia
A history of terrible droughts caused Australia rethink its water use. Measures include recycling sewage and encouraging grey water recycling (waste water from baths and washing machines), in an attempt to "drought-proof" the nation.

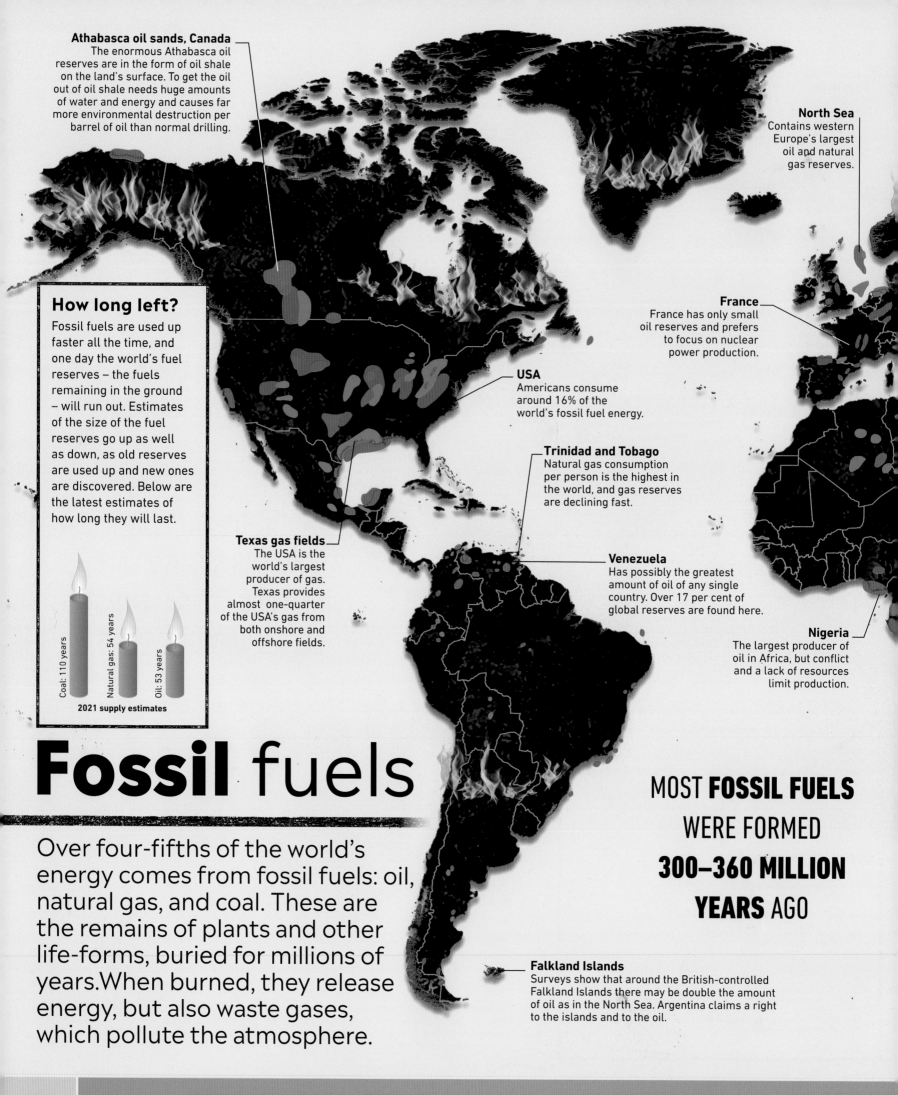

Athabasca oil sands, Canada
The enormous Athabasca oil reserves are in the form of oil shale on the land's surface. To get the oil out of oil shale needs huge amounts of water and energy and causes far more environmental destruction per barrel of oil than normal drilling.

North Sea
Contains western Europe's largest oil and natural gas reserves.

France
France has only small oil reserves and prefers to focus on nuclear power production.

USA
Americans consume around 16% of the world's fossil fuel energy.

Trinidad and Tobago
Natural gas consumption per person is the highest in the world, and gas reserves are declining fast.

Venezuela
Has possibly the greatest amount of oil of any single country. Over 17 per cent of global reserves are found here.

Nigeria
The largest producer of oil in Africa, but conflict and a lack of resources limit production.

Texas gas fields
The USA is the world's largest producer of gas. Texas provides almost one-quarter of the USA's gas from both onshore and offshore fields.

Falkland Islands
Surveys show that around the British-controlled Falkland Islands there may be double the amount of oil as in the North Sea. Argentina claims a right to the islands and to the oil.

How long left?

Fossil fuels are used up faster all the time, and one day the world's fuel reserves – the fuels remaining in the ground – will run out. Estimates of the size of the fuel reserves go up as well as down, as old reserves are used up and new ones are discovered. Below are the latest estimates of how long they will last.

Coal: 110 years

Natural gas: 54 years

Oil: 53 years

2021 supply estimates

Fossil fuels

Over four-fifths of the world's energy comes from fossil fuels: oil, natural gas, and coal. These are the remains of plants and other life-forms, buried for millions of years. When burned, they release energy, but also waste gases, which pollute the atmosphere.

MOST FOSSIL FUELS WERE FORMED 300–360 MILLION YEARS AGO

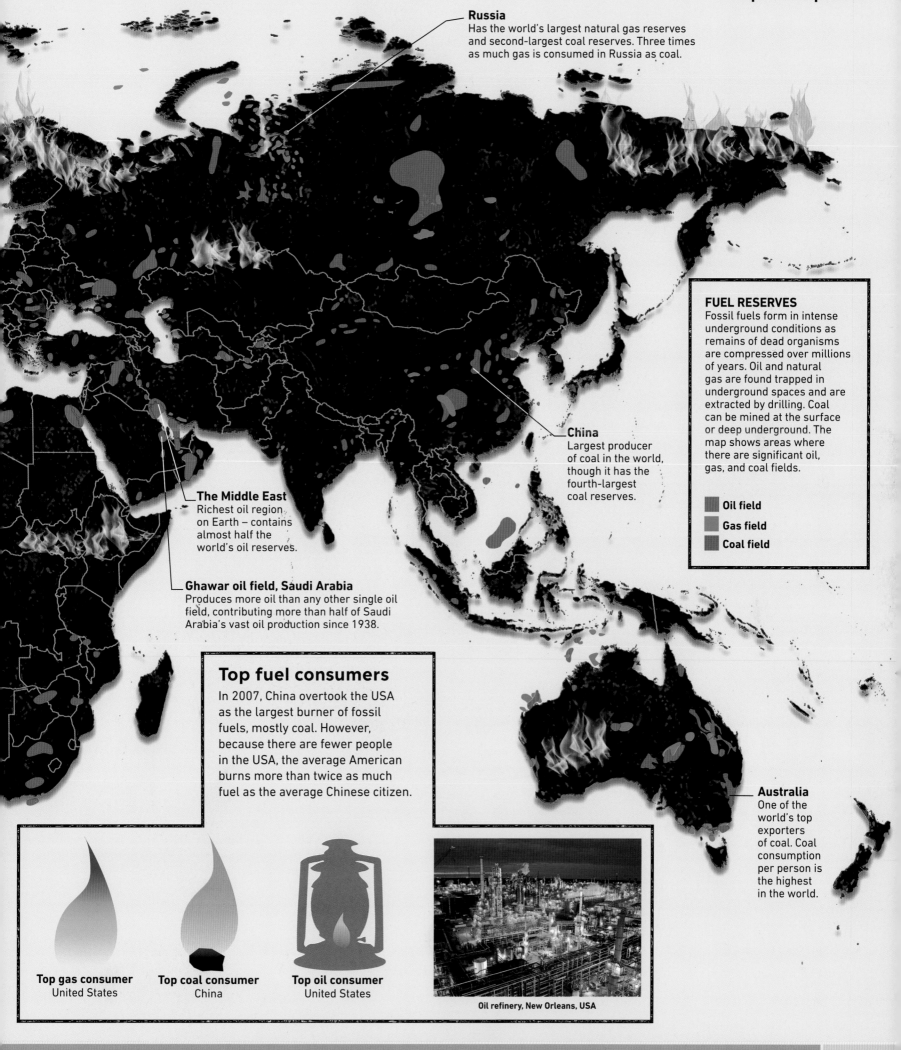

Russia
Has the world's largest natural gas reserves and second-largest coal reserves. Three times as much gas is consumed in Russia as coal.

China
Largest producer of coal in the world, though it has the fourth-largest coal reserves.

The Middle East
Richest oil region on Earth – contains almost half the world's oil reserves.

Ghawar oil field, Saudi Arabia
Produces more oil than any other single oil field, contributing more than half of Saudi Arabia's vast oil production since 1938.

FUEL RESERVES
Fossil fuels form in intense underground conditions as remains of dead organisms are compressed over millions of years. Oil and natural gas are found trapped in underground spaces and are extracted by drilling. Coal can be mined at the surface or deep underground. The map shows areas where there are significant oil, gas, and coal fields.

- Oil field
- Gas field
- Coal field

Top fuel consumers

In 2007, China overtook the USA as the largest burner of fossil fuels, mostly coal. However, because there are fewer people in the USA, the average American burns more than twice as much fuel as the average Chinese citizen.

Australia
One of the world's top exporters of coal. Coal consumption per person is the highest in the world.

Top gas consumer
United States

Top coal consumer
China

Top oil consumer
United States

Oil refinery, New Orleans, USA

COAL ON A LARGE SCALE TO HEAT HOUSES THROUGH UNDERFLOOR PIPES.

Alternative energy

There are several types of alternative energy, some of which are also renewable (see opposite page).

Wind
Mounted on tall masts, huge rotating blades called wind turbines harness the wind's energy and use it to drive electricity generators.

Solar
The Sun's energy can be used to heat water in homes or to produce high temperatures for electricity generation. Photovoltaic panels convert sunlight directly into electricity.

Nuclear
The nuclei (cores) of atoms are split apart in nuclear power plants, releasing vast amounts of energy. However, the process also creates dangerous nuclear waste.

Geothermal
A geothermal power plant taps underground steam or hot water, which it uses to generate electricity or to heat buildings directly.

Hydroelectric
A hydroelectric power plant is a dam with generators built into it. Water builds up behind the dam. When gates in the dam are opened, the force of the falling water drives the generators.

Biofuel, biogas, and biomass
Liquid fuel made from plants, rather than oil, is called biofuel. When farm waste, sewage, and rubbish rot, they release biogas, which can be burned as fuel. Biomass is any plant-based material burned for warmth or to generate electricity.

Canada
Fourth-largest producer of hydroelectricity; sixth for nuclear; ninth for wind

USA
World's top producer of geothermal, biofuel, and nuclear energy; in second place for wind and hydroelectricity; and fifth for solar

Mexico
Sixth for geothermal

El Salvador
Ninth for geothermal

Venezuela
Eighth for hydroelectricity

Brazil
Ranked second for electricity production by biofuel, third for hydroelectricity, and eighth for wind

Argentina
Seventh-largest producer of electricity from biofuel

Iceland
Ninth on the "top 10" list of geothermal producers

Norway
Number six for hydroelectricity

Germany
First in the world for solar, third for wind, fourth for biofuel, and eighth for nuclear

France
Ranked second for nuclear, fifth for biofuel, seventh for wind, and ninth for solar

Spain
Number five for wind and ten for biofuel

Italy
Ranked fourth for solar, seventh for geothermal, and tenth for wind

Alternative energy

Burning fossil fuels – coal, oil, and gas – creates a lot of pollution. People are developing alternative, cleaner energy sources, and some are renewable – they never run out.

HYDROELECTRIC POWER PLANTS SUPPLY 90 PER CENT OF NORWAY'S ENERGY

KEY
Top 10 alternative-energy producing countries in each field

- Wind energy
- Solar energy
- Nuclear energy
- Geothermal energy
- Hydroelectric energy
- Biofuel energy

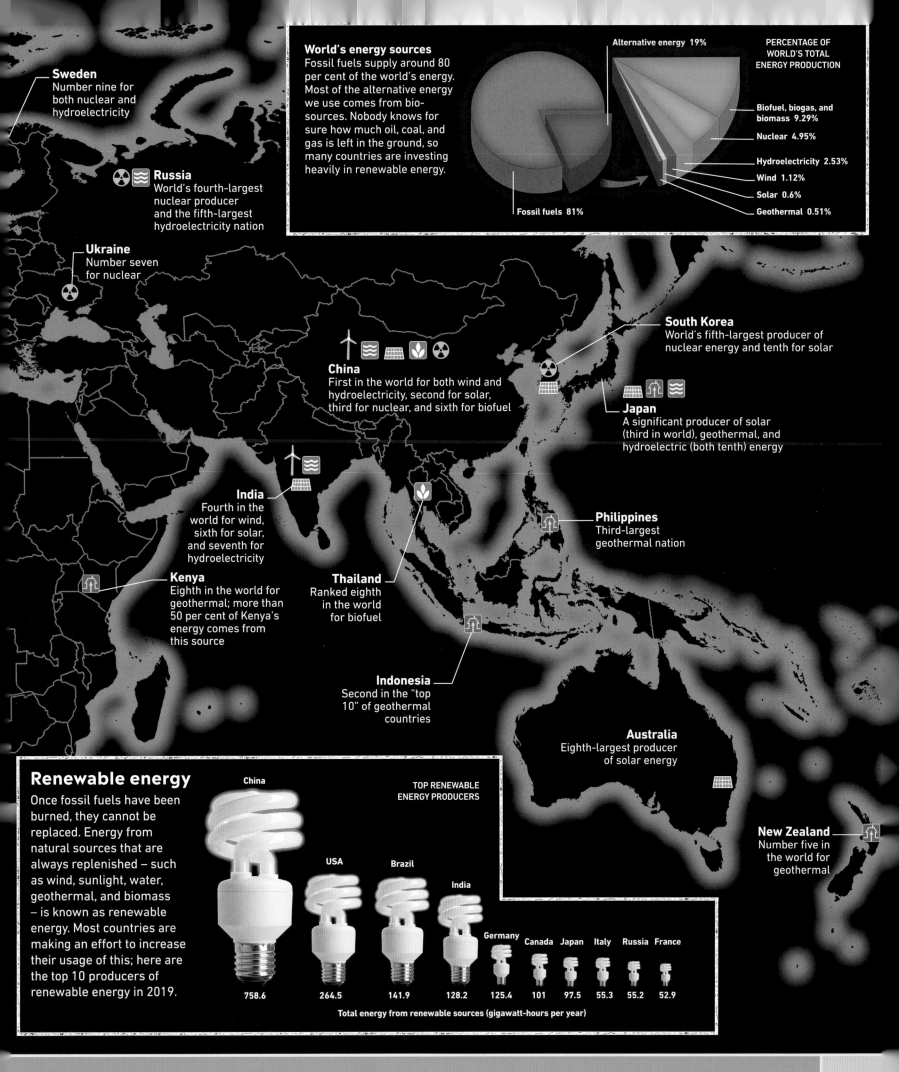

Sweden
Number nine for both nuclear and hydroelectricity

Russia
World's fourth-largest nuclear producer and the fifth-largest hydroelectricity nation

Ukraine
Number seven for nuclear

World's energy sources

Fossil fuels supply around 80 per cent of the world's energy. Most of the alternative energy we use comes from bio-sources. Nobody knows for sure how much oil, coal, and gas is left in the ground, so many countries are investing heavily in renewable energy.

Alternative energy 19%

PERCENTAGE OF WORLD'S TOTAL ENERGY PRODUCTION

Biofuel, biogas, and biomass 9.29%
Nuclear 4.95%
Hydroelectricity 2.53%
Wind 1.12%
Solar 0.6%
Geothermal 0.51%

Fossil fuels 81%

China
First in the world for both wind and hydroelectricity, second for solar, third for nuclear, and sixth for biofuel

South Korea
World's fifth-largest producer of nuclear energy and tenth for solar

Japan
A significant producer of solar (third in world), geothermal, and hydroelectric (both tenth) energy

India
Fourth in the world for wind, sixth for solar, and seventh for hydroelectricity

Philippines
Third-largest geothermal nation

Kenya
Eighth in the world for geothermal; more than 50 per cent of Kenya's energy comes from this source

Thailand
Ranked eighth in the world for biofuel

Indonesia
Second in the "top 10" of geothermal countries

Australia
Eighth-largest producer of solar energy

New Zealand
Number five in the world for geothermal

Renewable energy

Once fossil fuels have been burned, they cannot be replaced. Energy from natural sources that are always replenished – such as wind, sunlight, water, geothermal, and biomass – is known as renewable energy. Most countries are making an effort to increase their usage of this; here are the top 10 producers of renewable energy in 2019.

TOP RENEWABLE ENERGY PRODUCERS

China	USA	Brazil	India	Germany	Canada	Japan	Italy	Russia	France
758.6	264.5	141.9	128.2	125.4	101	97.5	55.3	55.2	52.9

Total energy from renewable sources (gigawatt-hours per year)

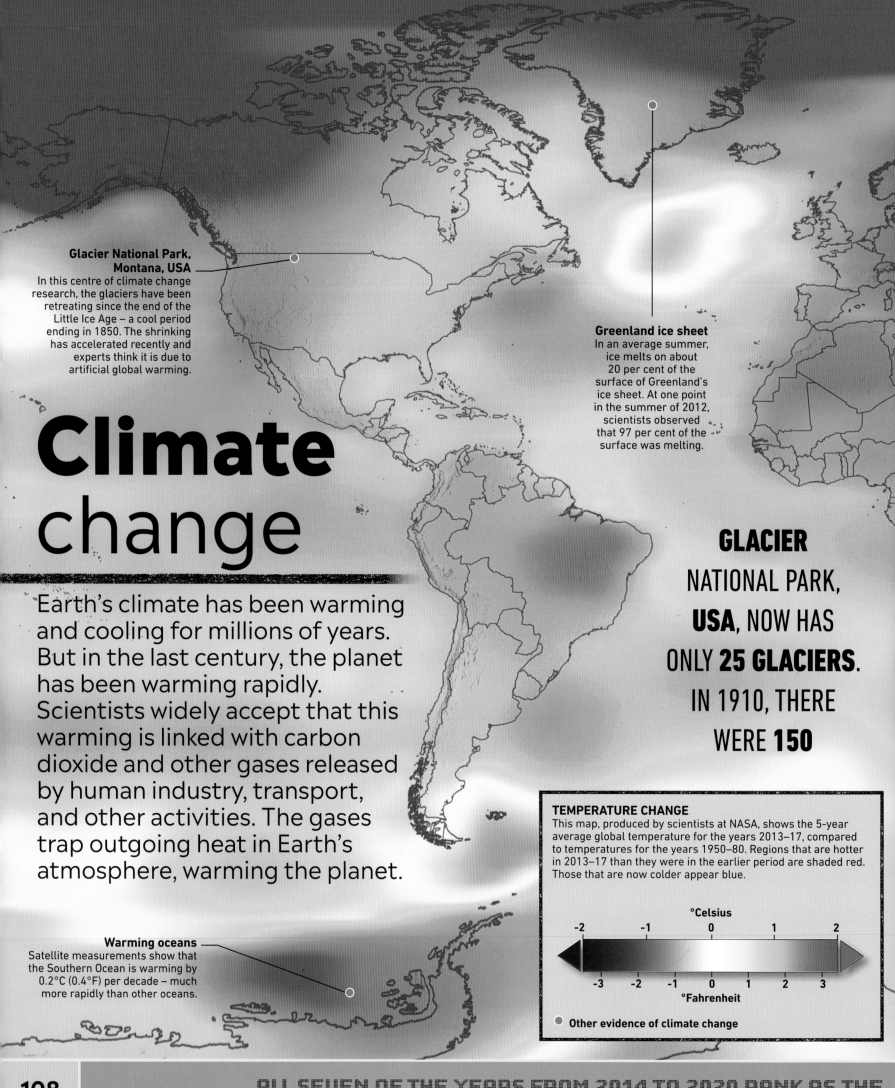

Climate change

Earth's climate has been warming and cooling for millions of years. But in the last century, the planet has been warming rapidly. Scientists widely accept that this warming is linked with carbon dioxide and other gases released by human industry, transport, and other activities. The gases trap outgoing heat in Earth's atmosphere, warming the planet.

Glacier National Park, Montana, USA
In this centre of climate change research, the glaciers have been retreating since the end of the Little Ice Age – a cool period ending in 1850. The shrinking has accelerated recently and experts think it is due to artificial global warming.

Greenland ice sheet
In an average summer, ice melts on about 20 per cent of the surface of Greenland's ice sheet. At one point in the summer of 2012, scientists observed that 97 per cent of the surface was melting.

Warming oceans
Satellite measurements show that the Southern Ocean is warming by 0.2°C (0.4°F) per decade – much more rapidly than other oceans.

GLACIER NATIONAL PARK, USA, NOW HAS ONLY 25 GLACIERS. IN 1910, THERE WERE 150

TEMPERATURE CHANGE
This map, produced by scientists at NASA, shows the 5-year average global temperature for the years 2013–17, compared to temperatures for the years 1950–80. Regions that are hotter in 2013–17 than they were in the earlier period are shaded red. Those that are now colder appear blue.

°Celsius
-2   -1   0   1   2

-3   -2   -1   0   1   2   3
°Fahrenheit

● Other evidence of climate change

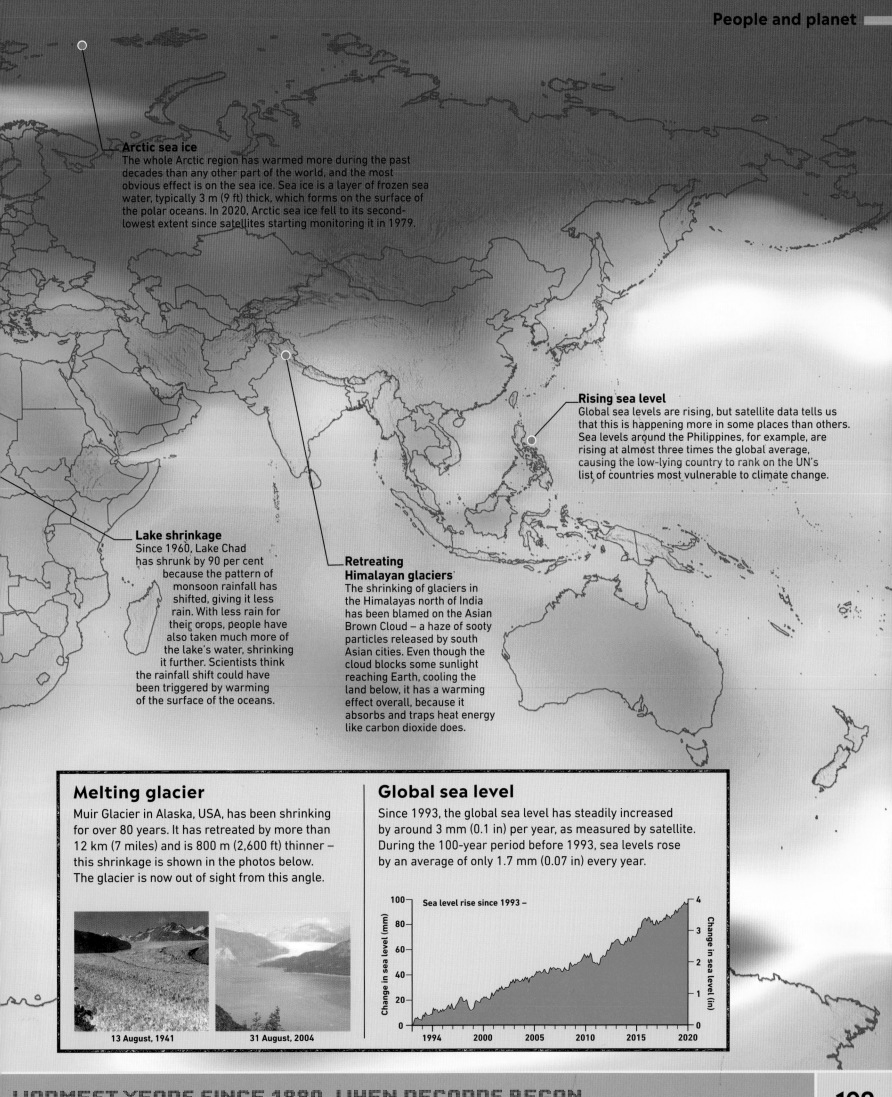

Arctic sea ice
The whole Arctic region has warmed more during the past decades than any other part of the world, and the most obvious effect is on the sea ice. Sea ice is a layer of frozen sea water, typically 3 m (9 ft) thick, which forms on the surface of the polar oceans. In 2020, Arctic sea ice fell to its second-lowest extent since satellites starting monitoring it in 1979.

Rising sea level
Global sea levels are rising, but satellite data tells us that this is happening more in some places than others. Sea levels around the Philippines, for example, are rising at almost three times the global average, causing the low-lying country to rank on the UN's list of countries most vulnerable to climate change.

Lake shrinkage
Since 1960, Lake Chad has shrunk by 90 per cent because the pattern of monsoon rainfall has shifted, giving it less rain. With less rain for their crops, people have also taken much more of the lake's water, shrinking it further. Scientists think the rainfall shift could have been triggered by warming of the surface of the oceans.

Retreating Himalayan glaciers
The shrinking of glaciers in the Himalayas north of India has been blamed on the Asian Brown Cloud – a haze of sooty particles released by south Asian cities. Even though the cloud blocks some sunlight reaching Earth, cooling the land below, it has a warming effect overall, because it absorbs and traps heat energy like carbon dioxide does.

Melting glacier

Muir Glacier in Alaska, USA, has been shrinking for over 80 years. It has retreated by more than 12 km (7 miles) and is 800 m (2,600 ft) thinner – this shrinkage is shown in the photos below. The glacier is now out of sight from this angle.

13 August, 1941   **31 August, 2004**

Global sea level

Since 1993, the global sea level has steadily increased by around 3 mm (0.1 in) per year, as measured by satellite. During the 100-year period before 1993, sea levels rose by an average of only 1.7 mm (0.07 in) every year.

Sea level rise since 1993

Change in sea level (mm)

Change in sea level (in)

100 · 80 · 60 · 40 · 20 · 0

4 · 3 · 2 · 1 · 0

1994 · 2000 · 2005 · 2010 · 2015 · 2020

Kluane/Wrangell-St Elias/ Glacier Bay/Tatshenshini-Alsek, Alaska and British Columbia
Home to some of the world's most spectacular glaciers.

Queen Maud Gulf Migratory Bird Sanctuary, Arctic Canada

Alert, Canada

Northeast Greenland National Park
Once the world's largest protected area, mostly made up of the Greenland Ice Sheet.

Charlie-Gibbs Marine Protected Area, Atlantic Ocean

Yellowstone National Park, Wyoming, USA
The first national park in the world, founded in 1872. The large alpine meadows and grass prairies provide ideal habitat for the large herds of bison living in the park.

Northern Canada
Permafrost (permanently frozen soil) makes this vast region inaccessible to people, preserving the Arctic tundra plains for the wolves and caribou.

Papahānaumokuākea Marine National Monument
Hawaii, 1,508,000 sq km (585,242 sq mi).

Sahara desert
World's largest hot desert. Supports little human life other than in scattered oases.

Pacific Remote Islands Marine National Monument
Central Pacific Ocean, 1,270,500 sq km (490,543 sq mi).

Galápagos Islands

Aïr and Ténéré Natural Reserves, Niger

Marae Moana
Cook Islands, 1,976,000 sq km (762,938 sq mi).

Jaú National Park, Amazonas, Brazil
One of the largest protected rainforest areas in the world and the largest in the Amazon basin. The park includes the entire Jaú River, where the water is black from minerals in dissolved organic matter.

Amazon rainforest
The north and west of this great forest have few or no roads and are far from human impact. Some areas are flooded to great depth every year. Some parts have never been logged and are "pristine".

WILDERNESS AREAS
The map shows the level of human influence across the world. The colours are based on the "wilderness value", which measures how far any one place is from permanent human settlements, roads, and man-made structures. This measure of remoteness from human development shows how much wilderness is left.

Key

High wilderness — Low wilderness

PROTECTED AREAS OF THE WORLD
The blue areas on the map show some of the world's protected areas of wilderness. Damaging activities, such as hunting and mining, are usually banned. The areas include wildlife reserves, national parks, marine parks, and more.

Top 5 largest protected areas

ABOUT **50 PER CENT** OF THE WORLD'S **PEOPLE** LIVE ON JUST **1 PER CENT** OF THE **LAND**

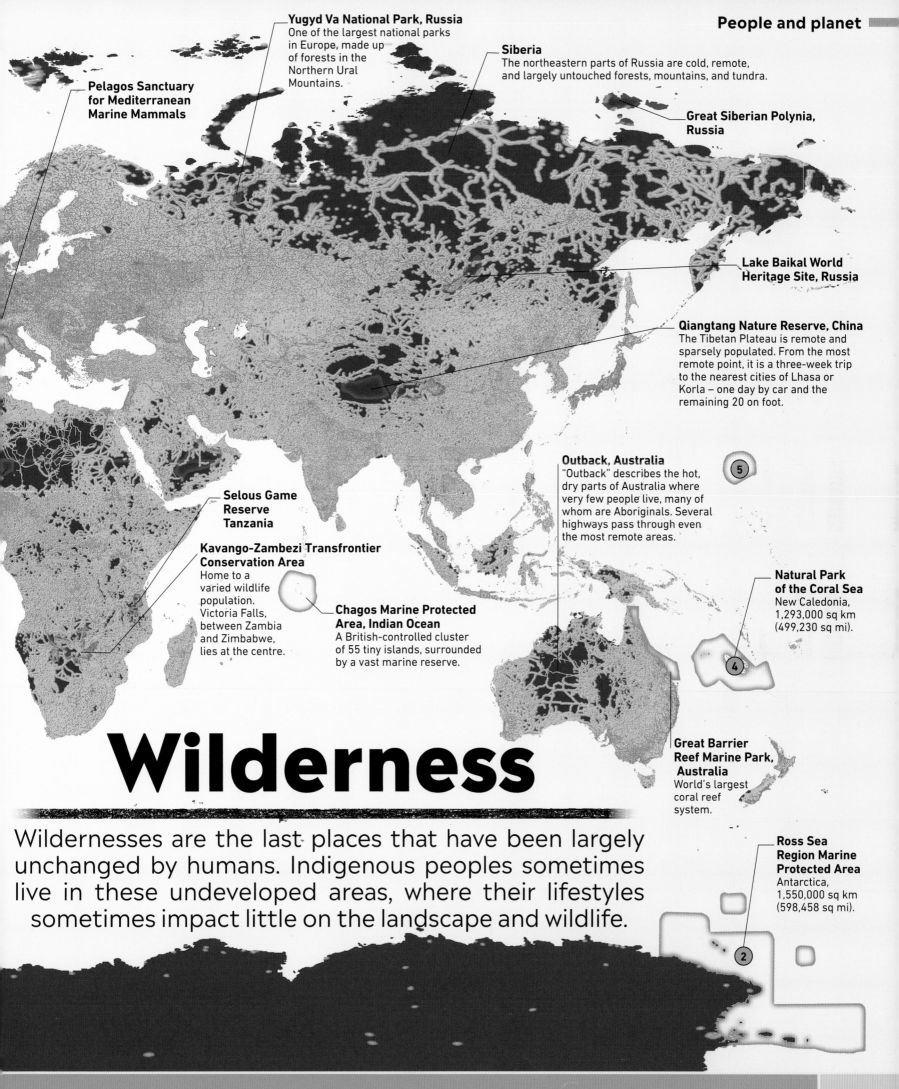

Yugyd Va National Park, Russia
One of the largest national parks in Europe, made up of forests in the Northern Ural Mountains.

Siberia
The northeastern parts of Russia are cold, remote, and largely untouched forests, mountains, and tundra.

Great Siberian Polynia, Russia

Pelagos Sanctuary for Mediterranean Marine Mammals

Lake Baikal World Heritage Site, Russia

Qiangtang Nature Reserve, China
The Tibetan Plateau is remote and sparsely populated. From the most remote point, it is a three-week trip to the nearest cities of Lhasa or Korla – one day by car and the remaining 20 on foot.

Selous Game Reserve Tanzania

Outback, Australia
"Outback" describes the hot, dry parts of Australia where very few people live, many of whom are Aboriginals. Several highways pass through even the most remote areas.

Kavango-Zambezi Transfrontier Conservation Area
Home to a varied wildlife population. Victoria Falls, between Zambia and Zimbabwe, lies at the centre.

Chagos Marine Protected Area, Indian Ocean
A British-controlled cluster of 55 tiny islands, surrounded by a vast marine reserve.

Natural Park of the Coral Sea
New Caledonia, 1,293,000 sq km (499,230 sq mi).

Great Barrier Reef Marine Park, Australia
World's largest coral reef system.

Ross Sea Region Marine Protected Area
Antarctica, 1,550,000 sq km (598,458 sq mi).

Wilderness

Wildernesses are the last places that have been largely unchanged by humans. Indigenous peoples sometimes live in these undeveloped areas, where their lifestyles sometimes impact little on the landscape and wildlife.

Engineering and technology

Reaching for the sky
The Burj Khalifa, the world's tallest building, can be seen in the distance in this view of fog-bound Dubai, largest city in the United Arab Emirates.

Introduction

Engineering and technology enable humans to achieve amazing feats. We build skyscrapers that reach towards the clouds, bridges that span great canyons, and tunnels that pierce mountains and travel under the sea. Our computer networks and transport systems keep people and places connected. We can even explore other planets.

World in motion

Transport has shrunk our world. Thanks to jet airliners, motorways, and high-speed rail routes, we can go on long-distance journeys that would have been unthinkable just a few decades ago. This transport revolution began with the invention of the railway at the start of the 19th century, and it has continued at speed ever since.

Train collects electricity from power cables suspended above the track.

High-speed electric locomotive
Launched in 1999, the Velaro is now in service in Germany, Spain, France, the UK, China, Russia, Belgium, Turkey, and the Netherlands. It is powered by electricity and can reach speeds of more than 350 kph (218 mph).

Shrinking technology

Few, if any, areas of technology have advanced faster than computing. ENIAC, developed by the US Army in 1946, was the first general-purpose programmable electronic computer. ENIAC contained over 100,000 components. Since then, electronic components have become smaller and smaller. A modern laptop computer is controlled by a tiny microchip that may be etched with more than a billion components.

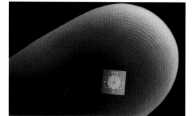

Modern marvel
This tiny computer, just 1 mm (0.04 in) square, is implanted into the eye to help people with the disease glaucoma.

Enormous ancestor
ENIAC weighed 30 tonnes and occupied an entire room. Operators programmed ENIAC by plugging and unplugging cables and adjusting switches.

FUGAKU WAS CROWNED THE WORLD'S FASTEST COMPUTER IN 2020, AND

Early steam engine
Puffing Billy is the world's oldest surviving steam locomotive. Built in 1813 to haul coal in northern England, it had a top speed of about 10 kph (6 mph).

Coal carried in the tender was burned to heat water in the boiler and produce steam to drive the wheels.

Bullet-shaped nose enables locomotive to cut through the air more easily, increasing speed.

Construction

A steel-and-concrete building revolution began in the late 19th century. Frames made of steel girders allowed taller structures to be built, and the invention of reinforced concrete – concrete with steel rods set into it – introduced an amazingly strong, durable new material. Together, steel and reinforced concrete gave birth to the modern skyscraper, changing the face of the world's cities.

- **Ancient concrete**
  The Romans were experts in building with concrete. It was used in the construction of the Colosseum and the Pantheon in Rome.

- **World's oldest skycraper city?**
  Shibam, in Yemen, has about 500 high-rise apartment buildings made of mud brick, most dating from the 16th century.

- **First steel-framed skyscraper**
  Completed in 1885, the innovative 10-storey Home Insurance Building in Chicago, USA, used a steel frame to support the walls.

- **Reinforced first**
  The first skyscraper built with reinforced concrete was the 15-storey Ingalls Building, in Cincinnati, USA, erected in 1903.

Manhattan, then and now
The Brooklyn Bridge spans New York's East River. The view across to Manhattan Island has changed dramatically since the bridge opened in 1883, and it now bristles with skyscrapers.

Infrastructure

The built and engineered systems that we rely on every day – from sewers and telecommunication networks to power lines, railways, and roads – are collectively known as infrastructure. Without such systems, our modern way of life would be impossible.

- **First telephone exchange**
  The first commercial exchange to connect callers was built in New Haven, Connecticut, USA, in 1878.

- **Intercity railway**
  Opened in 1830, the Manchester to Liverpool route in England was the first intercity railway.

Ulm–Stuttgart autobahn, 1950
Germany was a pioneer of the freeway, or autobahn, in the 1930s. Cars did not clog the roads until much later!

IN **2019**,
HARTSFIELD-JACKSON,
ATLANTA, AVERAGED
2,569 FLIGHTS
PER DAY

Top 10 busiest passenger airports 2019

Around 9.1 billion air passengers passed through the world's top 100 airports in 2019. The world's busiest airport, Hartsfield-Jackson International in Atlanta, Georgia, USA, averaged 275,000 passengers per day in 2019, and handled over 904,301 flights during the year. The industry declined drastically in 2020, however, when COVID-19 brought the world to a standstill.

RANK	AIRPORT	PASSENGERS PER YEAR
1	Hartsfield–Jackson Atlanta International, USA	110,531,300
2	Beijing Capital International, China	100,011,438
3	Los Angeles International, USA	88,068,013
4	Dubai International, Dubai	86,396,757
5	Tokyo International, Japan	85,505,054
6	O'Hare International, Chicago, USA	84,649,115
7	London Heathrow, United Kingdom	80,888,305
8	Shanghai Pudong International, China	76,153,455
9	Paris Charles de Gaulle, France	76,150,009
10	Dallas Fort Worth International, USA	75,066,956

Air traffic

Air-traffic controllers have a tough job ensuring safe routes, takeoffs, and landings for the thousands of planes that crisscross our skies each day. This map shows nearly 6,000 routes carrying scheduled commercial traffic.

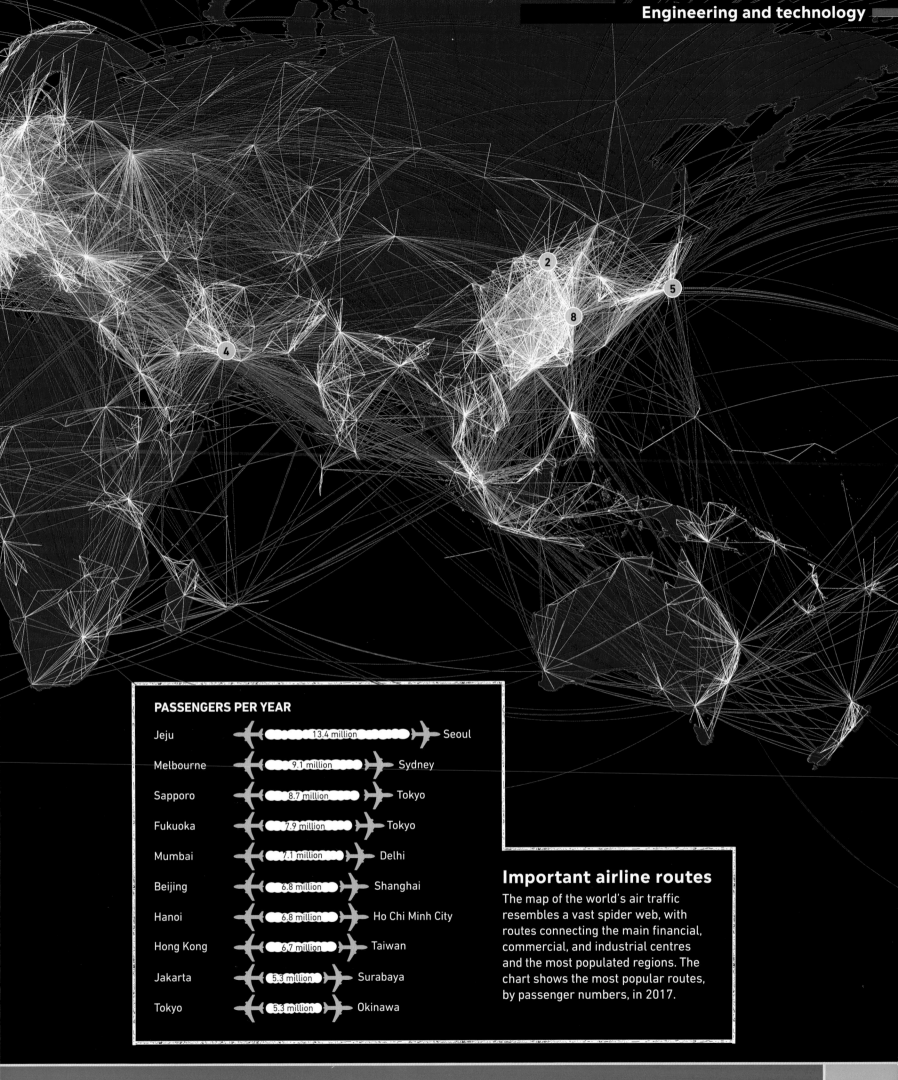

PASSENGERS PER YEAR

Jeju	13.4 million	Seoul
Melbourne	9.1 million	Sydney
Sapporo	8.7 million	Tokyo
Fukuoka	7.9 million	Tokyo
Mumbai	7.1 million	Delhi
Beijing	6.8 million	Shanghai
Hanoi	6.8 million	Ho Chi Minh City
Hong Kong	6.7 million	Taiwan
Jakarta	5.3 million	Surabaya
Tokyo	5.3 million	Okinawa

Important airline routes

The map of the world's air traffic resembles a vast spider web, with routes connecting the main financial, commercial, and industrial centres and the most populated regions. The chart shows the most popular routes, by passenger numbers, in 2017.

IN 2019. IT IS PREDICTED THAT THERE WILL BE 51.71 MILLION IN 2030.

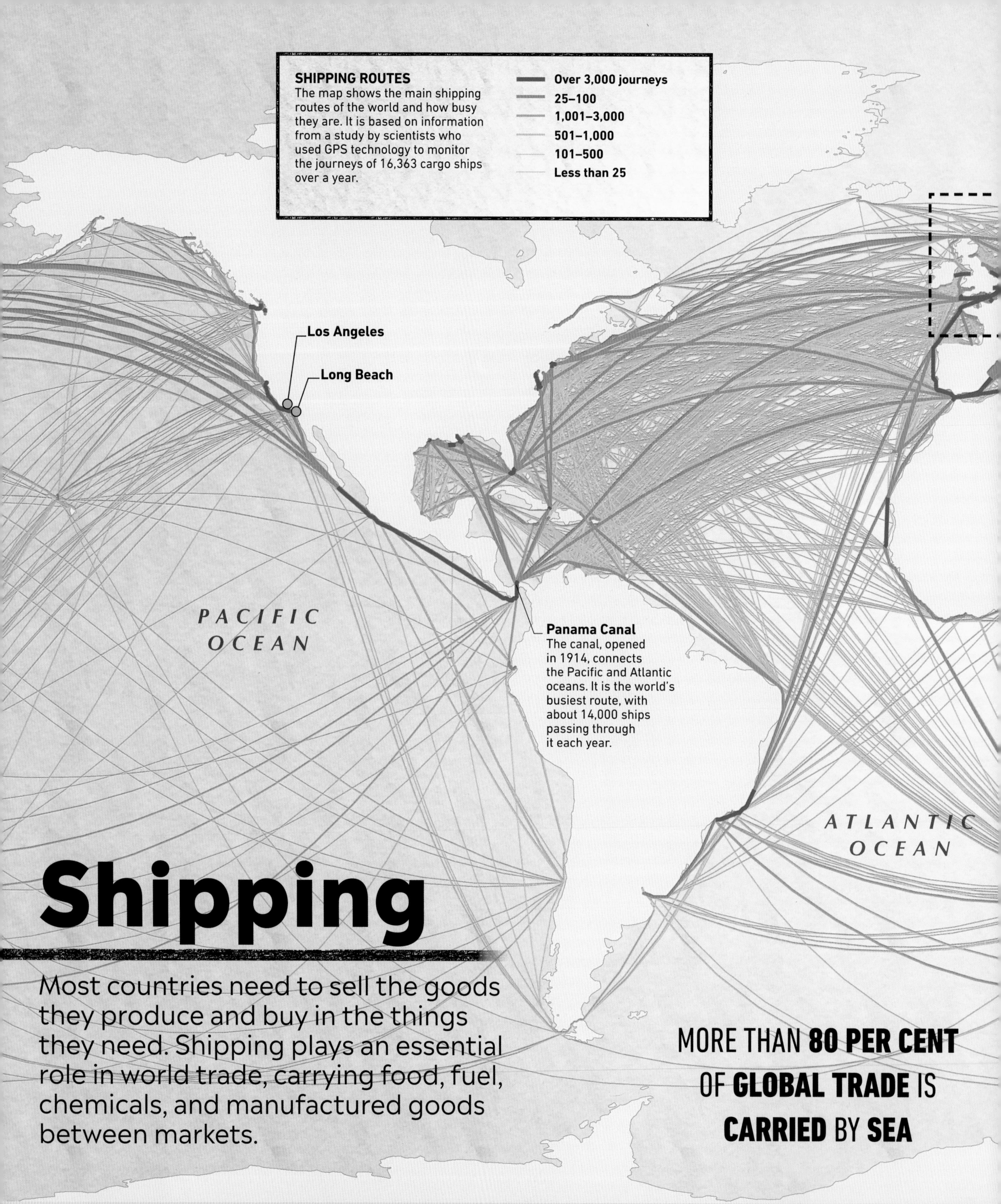
SHIPPING ROUTES
The map shows the main shipping routes of the world and how busy they are. It is based on information from a study by scientists who used GPS technology to monitor the journeys of 16,363 cargo ships over a year.
Over 3,000 journeys
25–100
1,001–3,000
501–1,000
101–500
Less than 25
Los Angeles
Long Beach
PACIFIC OCEAN
Panama Canal
The canal, opened in 1914, connects the Pacific and Atlantic oceans. It is the world's busiest route, with about 14,000 ships passing through it each year.
ATLANTIC OCEAN

Shipping

Most countries need to sell the goods they produce and buy in the things they need. Shipping plays an essential role in world trade, carrying food, fuel, chemicals, and manufactured goods between markets.

MORE THAN **80 PER CENT** OF **GLOBAL TRADE** IS **CARRIED** BY **SEA**

MOVING CARGO BY SHIP IS ABOUT TWICE AS ENERGY EFFICIENT

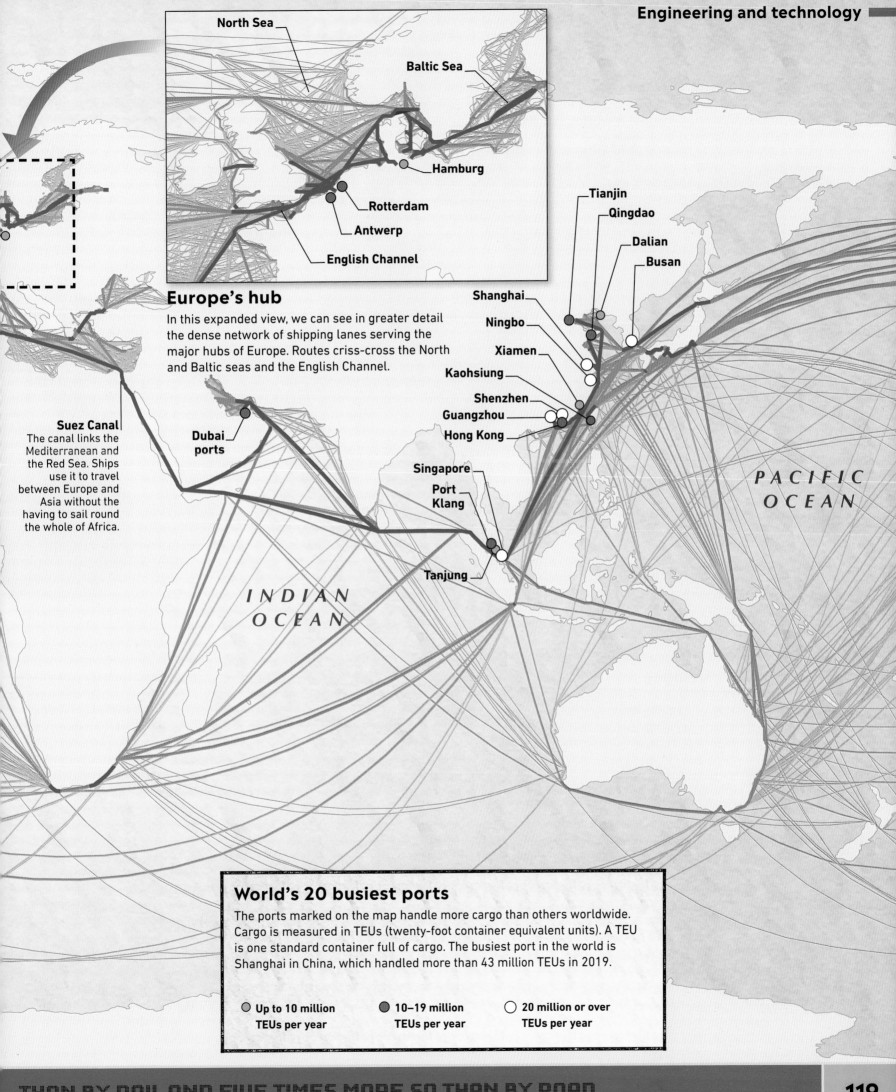

North Sea

Baltic Sea

Hamburg

Rotterdam

Antwerp

English Channel

Europe's hub

In this expanded view, we can see in greater detail the dense network of shipping lanes serving the major hubs of Europe. Routes criss-cross the North and Baltic seas and the English Channel.

Tianjin

Qingdao

Dalian

Busan

Shanghai

Ningbo

Xiamen

Kaohsiung

Shenzhen

Guangzhou

Hong Kong

Suez Canal

The canal links the Mediterranean and the Red Sea. Ships use it to travel between Europe and Asia without the having to sail round the whole of Africa.

Dubai ports

Singapore

Port Klang

Tanjung

PACIFIC OCEAN

INDIAN OCEAN

World's 20 busiest ports

The ports marked on the map handle more cargo than others worldwide. Cargo is measured in TEUs (twenty-foot container equivalent units). A TEU is one standard container full of cargo. The busiest port in the world is Shanghai in China, which handled more than 43 million TEUs in 2019.

○ **Up to 10 million TEUs per year**

● **10–19 million TEUs per year**

○ **20 million or over TEUs per year**

Railways

In the early 19th century, railways began to change the world radically by opening up new opportunities for travel and trade. Today, with roads gridlocked by traffic, modern railways are making a comeback.

EN453 (France to Russia)
A trans-European train connecting Paris and Moscow over 3,315 km (2,060 miles).

The Canadian (Canada)
Spectacular 4,466-km (2,775-mile) route between Vancouver and Toronto, travelling through mountains, prairies, and lakeland.

California Zephyr (USA)
Follows the route of the first US transcontinental railway (completed in 1869) from San Francisco to Chicago.

Salta to Antofagasta (Chile to Argentina)
At 941 km (585 miles), this is the longest main line in South America.

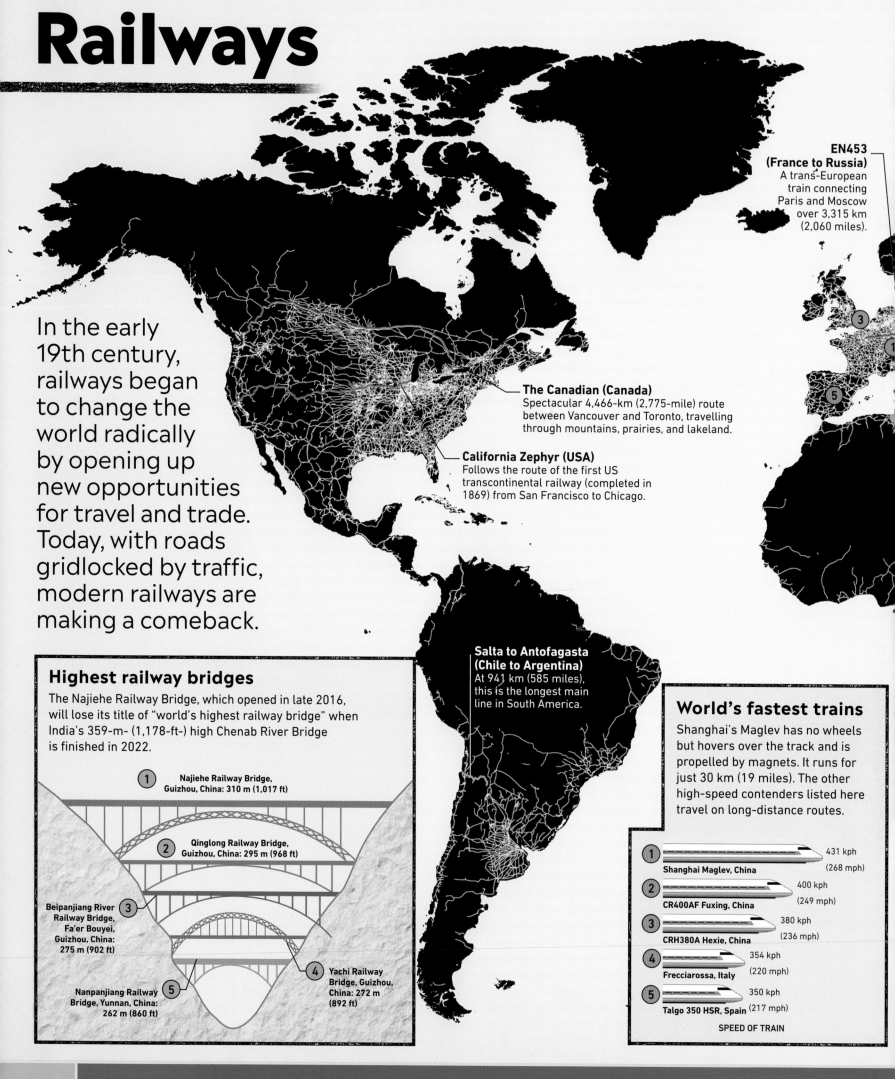

Highest railway bridges

The Najiehe Railway Bridge, which opened in late 2016, will lose its title of "world's highest railway bridge" when India's 359-m- (1,178-ft-) high Chenab River Bridge is finished in 2022.

1. Najiehe Railway Bridge, Guizhou, China: 310 m (1,017 ft)
2. Qinglong Railway Bridge, Guizhou, China: 295 m (968 ft)
3. Beipanjiang River Railway Bridge, Fa'er Bouyei, Guizhou, China: 275 m (902 ft)
4. Yachi Railway Bridge, Guizhou, China: 272 m (892 ft)
5. Nanpanjiang Railway Bridge, Yunnan, China: 262 m (860 ft)

World's fastest trains

Shanghai's Maglev has no wheels but hovers over the track and is propelled by magnets. It runs for just 30 km (19 miles). The other high-speed contenders listed here travel on long-distance routes.

1. Shanghai Maglev, China — 431 kph (268 mph)
2. CR400AF Fuxing, China — 400 kph (249 mph)
3. CRH380A Hexie, China — 380 kph (236 mph)
4. Frecciarossa, Italy — 354 kph (220 mph)
5. Talgo 350 HSR, Spain — 350 kph (217 mph)

SPEED OF TRAIN

Trans-Siberian Railway (Russia)
The world's longest rail journey passes through seven time zones as it runs 9,288 km (5,771 miles) from Moscow in the west to Vladivostock on the Pacific coast.

Guangzhou to Lhasa (China)
The Tanggula Pass section is the world's highest track, at 5,072 m (16,640 ft).

Alexandria to Aswan (Egypt)
Travelling via Cairo and Luxor, this line follows the Nile Valley, with its ancient pyramids and temples.

Dibrugarh to Kanyakumari (India)
Longest route in India, at 4,286 km (2,657 miles).

THE WORLD HAS
1 MILLION KM
(620,000 MILES)
OF RAILTRACK

Five longest railway tunnels

In 2016, the Gotthard Base Tunnel – a 57-km- (35-mile-) long tunnel that travels beneath the Swiss Alps – surpassed the Seikan Tunnel to become the world's longest railway tunnel.

Yulhyeon Tunnel, Gyeonggi South Korea: 4
50.3 km (31.3 miles)

Songshan Lake Tunnel, Dongguan, China: 5
38.8 km (24.1 miles)

Gotthard Base Tunnel, Swiss Alps, Switzerland: 1
57.1 km (35.5 miles)

Channel Tunnel, English Channel: 3
50.4 km (31.5 miles)

Seikan Tunnel, Tsugaru Strait, Japan: 2
53.8 km (33.5 miles)

Blue Train, South Africa
A luxurious train that runs from Cape Town to Pretoria through vineyards, mountains, and the arid landscape of the Karoo.

Indian Pacific (Australia)
This 4,352-km (2,704-mile) route, links Sydney on the east coast with Perth in the west.

Dempster Highway Extension

An ice road built on the frozen Mackenzie River and Arctic Ocean, it provides a winter route to the isolated community of Tuktoyaktuk.

Mountain roads and passes

① Trollstigen, Norway
This dramatic road's name means "Trolls' ladder". It has 11 hairpin bends, which wind up the steep mountainside.

② Stelvio Pass, Italy
One of the highest roads in the Alps, its 60 hairpin bends provide a challenge for both motorists and cyclists.

③ Khardung La, India
This famously high mountain pass in the Ladakh part of Kashmir was built in 1976 and opened to motor vehicles in 1988.

④ Semo La, Tibet, China
Possibly the highest vehicle-accessible pass in the world, it was reliably measured in 1999 at 5,565 m (18,258 ft).

⑤ Irohazaka Winding Road
Each of the 48 hairpin turns on this route in Japan is labelled with one of the 48 characters of the Japanese alphabet.

Bonn-Köln Autobahn

Built in 1932, it was the first road designed exclusively for cars, with separate carriageways and no intersections with other roads.

Tibbit to Contwoyto Winter Road

An ice road built over frozen lakes, it is open for about 10 weeks from late January each year.

Cabot Trail

Looping round the northern tip of Cape Breton Island, Nova Scotia, and named after 16th-century Italian explorer, John Cabot.

Route 66

A 3,940-km (2,448-mile) road that follows the historic route taken by migrants to California during the Great Depression.

Pacific Coast Highway

This world-famous route hugs the Californian coast from Orange County in the south to the forests of giant redwood trees in the north.

Natchez Trace Parkway

A route used by Native Americans and their animals for thousands of years before the modern road was built.

Darién Gap, Panama

A stretch of rainforest that breaks the Pan-American Highway's route.

Pan-American Highway

About 48,000 km (29,800 miles) long, it runs through 18 countries, from Alaska to the southern tip of Argentina.

Yungas Road, Bolivia

A single-track mountain road heavily used by lorries but with unprotected sheer drops of 600 m (1,970 ft). Up to 300 travellers are killed on the route every year.

World's busiest roads

① Ontario Highway 401, Canada
The busiest highway in North America – more than 440,000 vehicles pass through the Toronto section every day. It is also one of the widest in the world – some sections of the route have 18 lanes.

② Interstate 405, USA
Runs north from the city of Irvine in Orange County to San Fernando, a route that is known as the northern segment of the San Diego Freeway. This freeway is the busiest and most congested in the USA, carrying up to 379,000 vehicles a day.

HIGHWAY 401, ONTARIO, CANADA

Roads

The planet is now more accessible by road than it has ever been. There are about 104 million km (65 million miles) of roads on Earth, from multi-lane urban freeways to seasonal ice roads made from frozen lakes and seas.

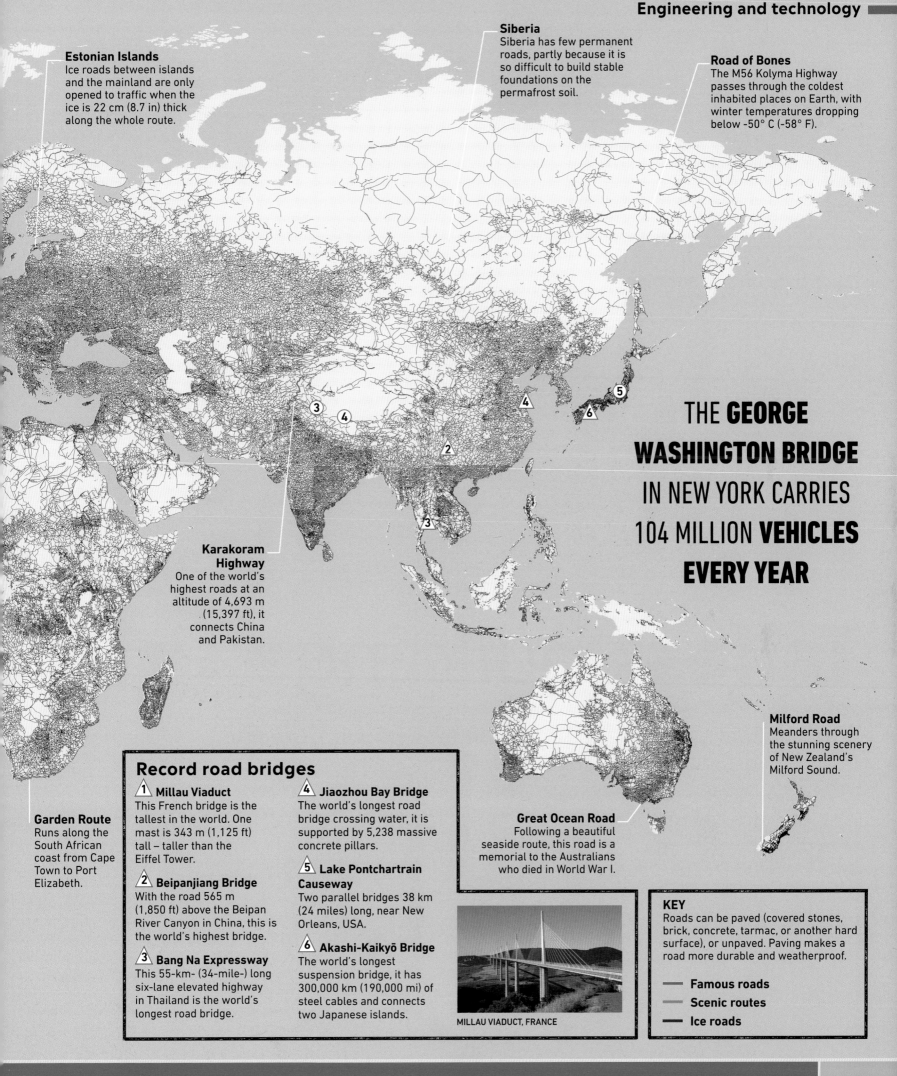

Estonian Islands
Ice roads between islands and the mainland are only opened to traffic when the ice is 22 cm (8.7 in) thick along the whole route.

Siberia
Siberia has few permanent roads, partly because it is so difficult to build stable foundations on the permafrost soil.

Road of Bones
The M56 Kolyma Highway passes through the coldest inhabited places on Earth, with winter temperatures dropping below -50° C (-58° F).

Karakoram Highway
One of the world's highest roads at an altitude of 4,693 m (15,397 ft), it connects China and Pakistan.

THE **GEORGE WASHINGTON BRIDGE** IN NEW YORK CARRIES 104 MILLION **VEHICLES EVERY YEAR**

Milford Road
Meanders through the stunning scenery of New Zealand's Milford Sound.

Garden Route
Runs along the South African coast from Cape Town to Port Elizabeth.

Great Ocean Road
Following a beautiful seaside route, this road is a memorial to the Australians who died in World War I.

Record road bridges

① Millau Viaduct
This French bridge is the tallest in the world. One mast is 343 m (1,125 ft) tall – taller than the Eiffel Tower.

② Beipanjiang Bridge
With the road 565 m (1,850 ft) above the Beipan River Canyon in China, this is the world's highest bridge.

③ Bang Na Expressway
This 55-km- (34-mile-) long six-lane elevated highway in Thailand is the world's longest road bridge.

④ Jiaozhou Bay Bridge
The world's longest road bridge crossing water, it is supported by 5,238 massive concrete pillars.

⑤ Lake Pontchartrain Causeway
Two parallel bridges 38 km (24 miles) long, near New Orleans, USA.

⑥ Akashi-Kaikyō Bridge
The world's longest suspension bridge, it has 300,000 km (190,000 mi) of steel cables and connects two Japanese islands.

MILLAU VIADUCT, FRANCE

KEY
Roads can be paved (covered stones, brick, concrete, tarmac, or another hard surface), or unpaved. Paving makes a road more durable and weatherproof.

— Famous roads
— Scenic routes
— Ice roads

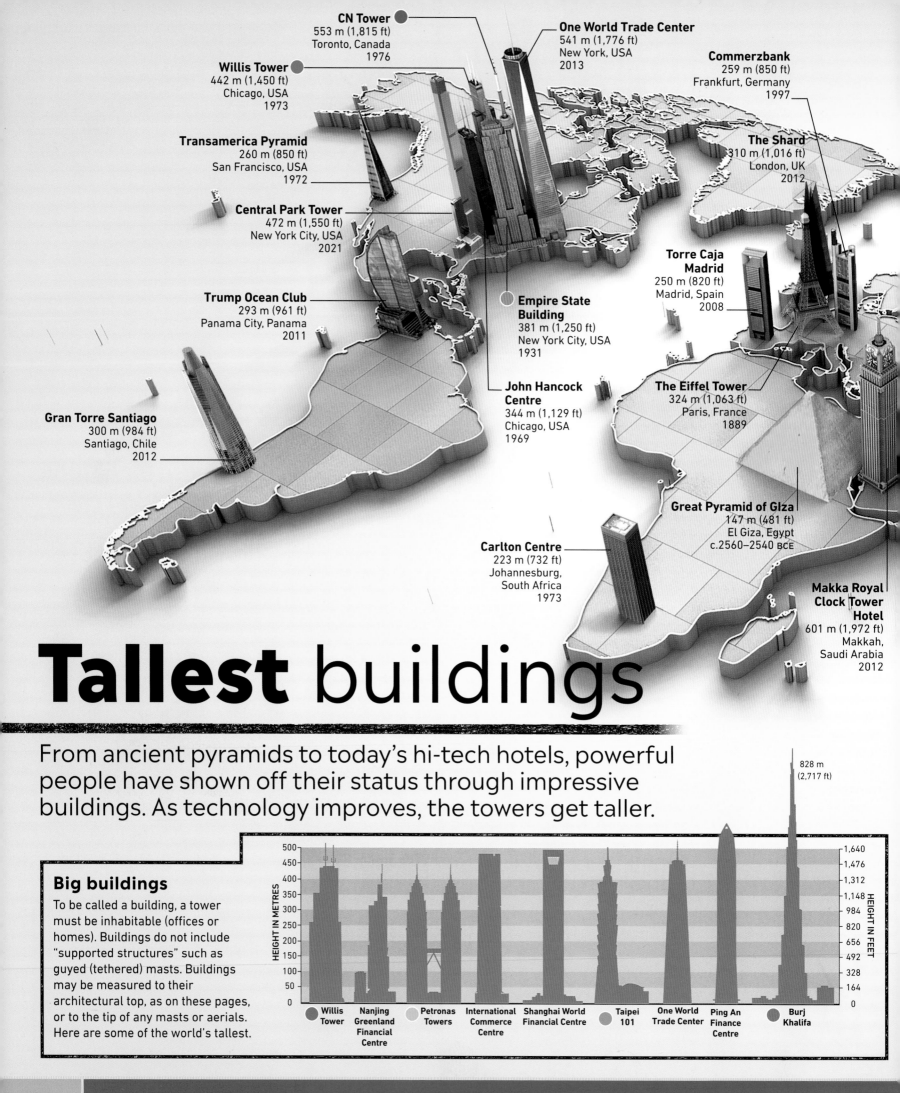

CN Tower
553 m (1,815 ft)
Toronto, Canada
1976

One World Trade Center
541 m (1,776 ft)
New York, USA
2013

Commerzbank
259 m (850 ft)
Frankfurt, Germany
1997

Willis Tower
442 m (1,450 ft)
Chicago, USA
1973

Transamerica Pyramid
260 m (850 ft)
San Francisco, USA
1972

The Shard
310 m (1,016 ft)
London, UK
2012

Central Park Tower
472 m (1,550 ft)
New York City, USA
2021

Empire State Building
381 m (1,250 ft)
New York City, USA
1931

Torre Caja Madrid
250 m (820 ft)
Madrid, Spain
2008

Trump Ocean Club
293 m (961 ft)
Panama City, Panama
2011

The Eiffel Tower
324 m (1,063 ft)
Paris, France
1889

John Hancock Centre
344 m (1,129 ft)
Chicago, USA
1969

Gran Torre Santiago
300 m (984 ft)
Santiago, Chile
2012

Great Pyramid of Giza
147 m (481 ft)
El Giza, Egypt
c.2560–2540 BCE

Carlton Centre
223 m (732 ft)
Johannesburg, South Africa
1973

Makka Royal Clock Tower Hotel
601 m (1,972 ft)
Makkah, Saudi Arabia
2012

Tallest buildings

From ancient pyramids to today's hi-tech hotels, powerful people have shown off their status through impressive buildings. As technology improves, the towers get taller.

Big buildings

To be called a building, a tower must be inhabitable (offices or homes). Buildings do not include "supported structures" such as guyed (tethered) masts. Buildings may be measured to their architectural top, as on these pages, or to the tip of any masts or aerials. Here are some of the world's tallest.

828 m (2,717 ft)

HEIGHT IN METRES

HEIGHT IN FEET

Willis Tower · Nanjing Greenland Financial Centre · Petronas Towers · International Commerce Centre · Shanghai World Financial Centre · Taipei 101 · One World Trade Center · Ping An Finance Centre · Burj Khalifa

NEW YORK'S CHRYSLER BUILDING WAS THE WORLD'S TALLEST FOR JUST

THE BURJ KHALIFA HAS **163** FLOORS LINKED BY **57** DOUBLE-DECKER LIFTS

Ostankino Tower
540 m (1,770 ft)
Moscow, Russia
1967

Mercury City Tower
339 m (1,112 ft)
Moscow, Russia
2012

**International
Commerce Centre**
484 m (1,588 ft)
Hong Kong
2010

Oriental Pearl Tower
468 m (1,535 ft)
Shanghai, China
1994

**Shanghai World
Financial Centre**
492 m (1,614 ft)
Shanghai, China
2008

Shanghai Tower
632 m (2,073 ft)
Shanghai, China
2014

**Tianjin CTF
Finance Centre**
530 m (1,739 ft)
Tianjin, China
2018

**Ping An Finance
Centre**
599 m (1,965 ft)
Shenzhe, China
2017

Milad Tower
435 m (1,427 ft)
Tehran. Iran
2007

Burj Khalifa
828 m (2,717 ft)
Dubai, UAE
2010

Tokyo Sky Tree
634 m (2,080 ft)
Tokyo, Japan
2011

Taipei 101
509 m (1,670 ft)
Taipei, Taiwan
2004

Busan Lotte Tower
510.2 m (1,674 ft)
Busan, South Korea
2015

Canton Tower
600 m (1,969 ft)
Guangzhou, China
2010

Petronas Towers
452 m (1,483 ft)
Kuala Lumpur,
Malaysia
1998

Q1
323 m (1,060 ft)
Gold Coast,
Australia
2005

Unsupported towers

Unlike buildings, these structures don't contain offices, homes, or shops. They are observation and communications towers.

Tokyo Sky Tree
This communications tower overtook the Canton Tower in 2011 to become the world's tallest.

Canton Tower
Canton is the former name of Guangzhou, where this tower was completed in 2010.

CN Tower
More than 2 million people visit this tower's glass-floored observation deck every year.

Ostankino Tower
This broadcasting tower was the world's first free-standing structure over 500 m (1,640 ft) tall.

Oriental Pearl Tower
There are 11 spheres in the design of this TV tower, which has 15 observation levels.

Record-breaking buildings

The record for the tallest building (a structure that must be inhabitable) is a fiercely contested prize. These five have all won it.

Burj Khalifa, 2010–present
This building has broken all records, including the tallest building and tallest unsupported structure.

Taipei 101, 2004–10
The world's tallest building until the Burj Khalifa was built, Taipei 101 has 101 floors above ground.

Petronas Towers, 1998–2004
These office blocks were the tallest buildings until 2004. They are still the tallest twin towers.

Willis Tower, 1973–98
Formerly known as the Sears Tower, this 108-storey skyscraper towers above Chicago.

Empire State Building, 1931–72
This was the first building in the world to have more than 100 storeys – it has 102. It was the tallest building for 40 years.

ONE YEAR, UNTIL THE EMPIRE STATE BUILDING WAS FINISHED IN 1931.

Internet connections

The Internet has revolutionized the way we live our lives. At the click of a mouse, we can instantly exchange news, ideas, and images with people on the other side of the world, and we can buy or sell goods without having to leave our homes.

The Internet in a minute

Today, there are more than three times as many computers, phones, and other devices connected to the Internet as there are people in the world. As a result, an incredible amount of Internet activity can occur in just one minute.

4.7 million videos viewed

4.1 million Google searches

59 million messages sent

347,222 stories viewed

764,000 hours of Netflix watched

US$1.1 million in online sales

THERE ARE 4.54 BILLION INTERNET USERS

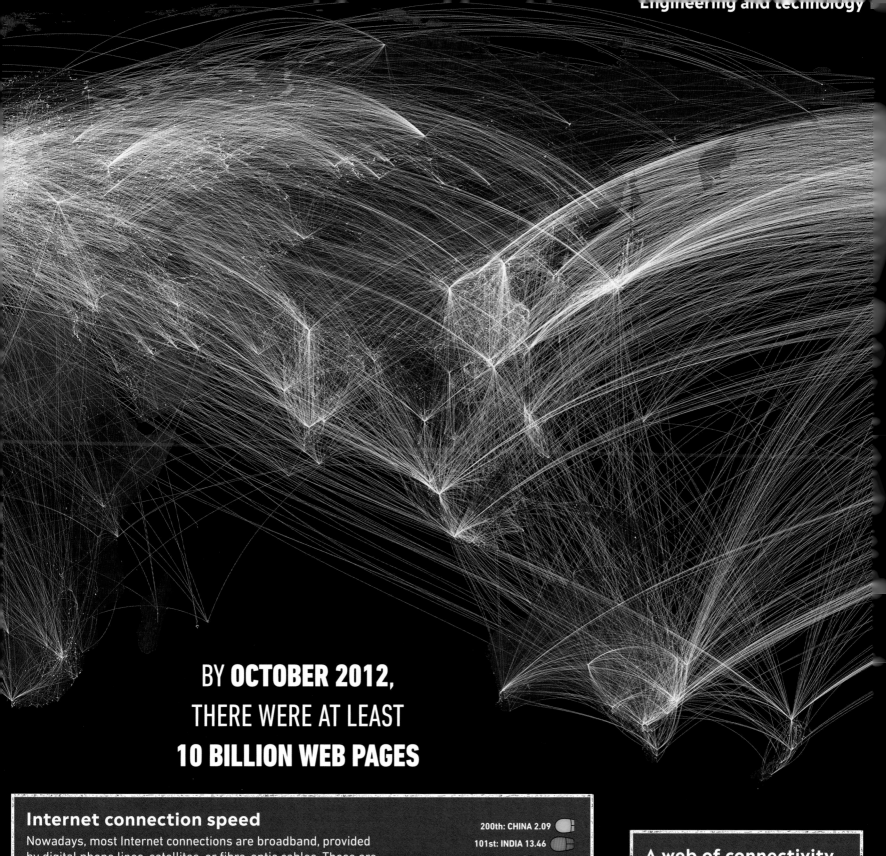

BY **OCTOBER 2012,**
THERE WERE AT LEAST
10 BILLION WEB PAGES

Internet connection speed

Nowadays, most Internet connections are broadband, provided by digital phone lines, satellites, or fibre-optic cables. These are much faster than the connections that used to be common, provided via ordinary phone lines and a modem. Following the huge rise of working from home due to the COVID-19 pandemic, Internet speed has never been more important. Here is a selection of the download speeds in different countries in 2020. Internet users in Liechtenstein had the world's fastest broadband, with an average peak download speed of just under 230 megabits per second.

200th: CHINA 2.09
101st: INDIA 13.46
76th: GREENLAND 18.65
47th: UNITED KINGDOM 37.82
20th: UNITED STATES 71.30
5th: LUXEMBOURG 118.05
4th: GIBRALTAR 183.1
3rd: ANDORRA 213.41
2nd: JERSEY 218.37
1st: LIECHTENSTEIN 229.98

PEAK CONNECTION SPEED (MEGABITS PER SECOND) AND WORLD RANKING

A web of connectivity

The map shows how the world's cities are connected by the Internet – the brighter the area, the more connections there are. Connections are not the same as users. Many people, for example, use a single connection in an Internet café.

——— Lines represent Internet connections between cities

Satellites and space junk

The first satellite, *Sputnik 1*, was launched by the Soviet Union in 1957. Since then, thousands of satellites and millions of other objects have accumulated around Earth, creating a serious hazard for space travel.

Geosynchronous ring

This ring-shaped concentration of satellites appears more than 35,700 km (22,200 miles) above Earth's equator. It exists because it is extremely useful for a satellite to "hover" above a point on Earth's turning surface.

High-speed danger

The pattern of spots shows the strikes collected during the entire NASA Space Shuttle program, from 1983–2002. The vast majority of space debris is less than 1 cm (0.5 in) across and includes specks of solid rocket fuel and flakes of paint. But even dust acts like tiny bullets at speeds of up to 42,000 kph (26,000 mph).

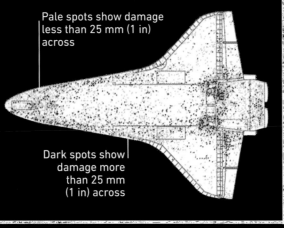

Pale spots show damage less than 25 mm (1 in) across

Dark spots show damage more than 25 mm (1 in) across

AT LEAST **10 MILLION** PIECES OF ARTIFICIAL DEBRIS ARE NOW IN **EARTH ORBIT**

Low Earth Orbit
This region is full of orbiting spacecraft, but also full of waste material ejected from spacecraft during missions and countless pieces of debris from collisions.

GPS (Global Positioning System) satellite
One of 31 forming a network, the GPS satellites orbit in one of six orbits. Each orbit is at a different angle to ensure they cover the entire surface of Earth. Someone on the ground is in contact with at least six of them at any one time.

How high are satellites?

Most objects launched into space are in Low Earth Orbit (LEO). At the lowest LEOs (160 km / 99 miles) objects circle Earth in 87 minutes at 28,100 kph (17,470 mph). Certain orbits are particularly useful. Image-taking satellites use polar Sun-synchronous orbits, which pass the equator at the same local time on every pass, so the shadows are the same.

Geosynchronous orbit
35,786 km (22,236 miles)
Satellites at this height orbit at the same speed as Earth turns, so they stay in the same spot over Earth's surface.

Hubble Space Telescope
555 km (345 miles)

Polar Sun-synchronous satellites
600–800 km (373–497 miles)

2,000 km (1,244 miles)

HIGH EARTH ORBIT ZONE

MEDIUM EARTH ORBIT ZONE

LOW EARTH ORBIT ZONE

GPS satellites
22,200 km (12,600 miles)
Objects orbit once every 12 hours, or twice a day.

International Space Station
410 km (255 miles)

SPACEWALK IN 1965, ORBITED FOR A MONTH AT 28,000 KPH (17,000 MPH).

12

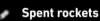

A FEW **COUNTRIES,** SUCH AS **LIECHTENSTEIN** AND **COSTA RICA,** HAVE **NO MILITARY FORCES**

UK
In 2010, the UK spent $56 billion on its armed forces, making it the world's fifth-biggest military spender.

USA
The USA spends almost $934 billion per year on its armed forces – more than the next seven-biggest spending countries added together.

France
France holds the world's third-largest nuclear arsenal, with 300 active warheads.

Israel
All Israeli men and women must serve for 2 to 3 years in their armed forces. Israel is the only country to make service for women compulsory.

KEY
The total amount of military expenditure by all the countries of the world in 2010 was $1.83 trillion, which is equivalent to $235 for every person on the planet – almost double what was spent per capita in 2001. The map shows the total number of military vehicles, hardware, and weapons held by selected major countries.

Up to 10 large warships (including aircraft carriers, cruisers, destroyers, frigates, and corvettes)

Up to 10 submarines

Up to 500 combat-capable aircraft

Up to 1,000 main battle tanks

Up to 500 nuclear warheads

Brazil
Brazil's armed forces are the largest in South America. The army takes an active role in education, health care, and the construction of roads and railways.

Egypt
All Egyptian men between 18 and 30 must serve in the army for 1 to 3 years.

Armed
forces

Almost all countries have a military – an organized force of soldiers and weapons that defends the country against threats from outside or within. Many countries believe that a large, well-equipped military will discourage others from attacking.

Sky-high warfare
Armed forces are increasingly using unmanned drones for surveillance or to launch missiles. Drones are controlled remotely from the ground, so air crew is not risked during missions.

THE USA HAS 4 PER CENT OF THE WORLD'S POPULATION BUT

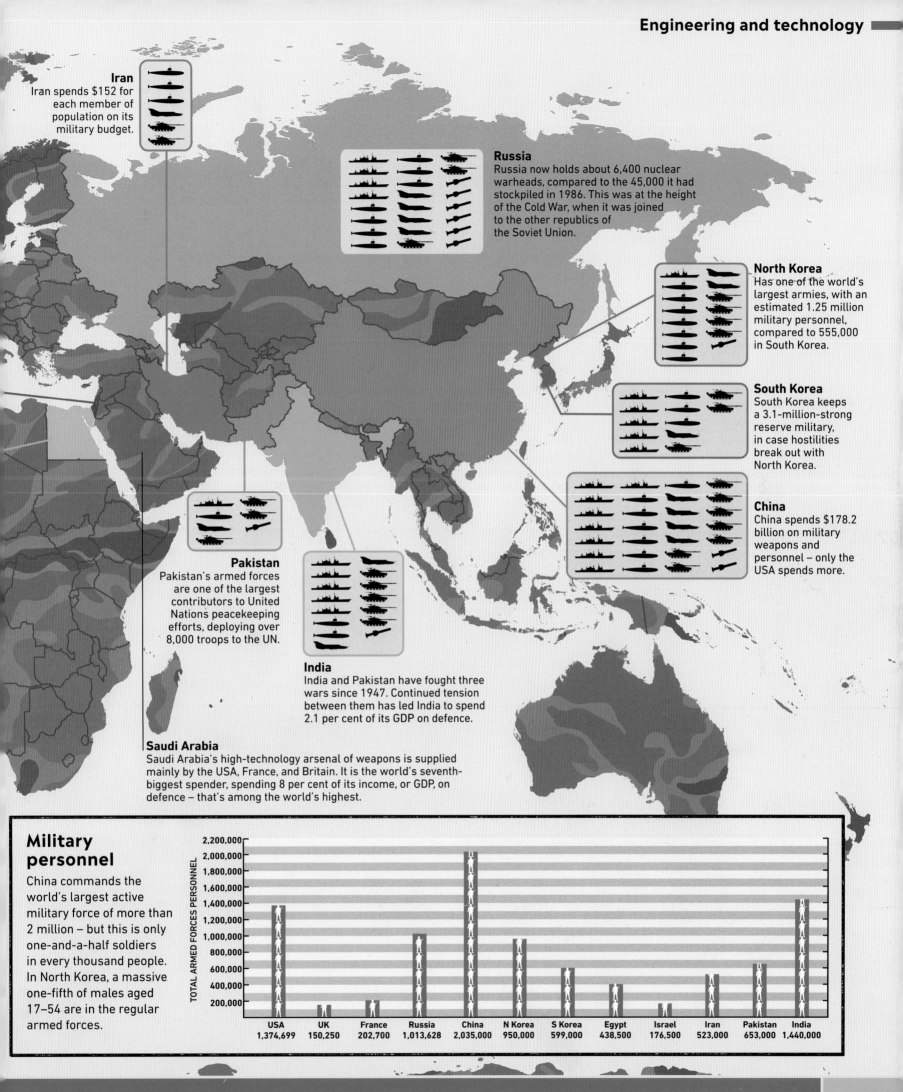

Iran
Iran spends $152 for each member of population on its military budget.

Russia
Russia now holds about 6,400 nuclear warheads, compared to the 45,000 it had stockpiled in 1986. This was at the height of the Cold War, when it was joined to the other republics of the Soviet Union.

North Korea
Has one of the world's largest armies, with an estimated 1.25 million military personnel, compared to 555,000 in South Korea.

South Korea
South Korea keeps a 3.1-million-strong reserve military, in case hostilities break out with North Korea.

China
China spends $178.2 billion on military weapons and personnel – only the USA spends more.

Pakistan
Pakistan's armed forces are one of the largest contributors to United Nations peacekeeping efforts, deploying over 8,000 troops to the UN.

India
India and Pakistan have fought three wars since 1947. Continued tension between them has led India to spend 2.1 per cent of its GDP on defence.

Saudi Arabia
Saudi Arabia's high-technology arsenal of weapons is supplied mainly by the USA, France, and Britain. It is the world's seventh-biggest spender, spending 8 per cent of its income, or GDP, on defence – that's among the world's highest.

Military personnel

China commands the world's largest active military force of more than 2 million – but this is only one-and-a-half soldiers in every thousand people. In North Korea, a massive one-fifth of males aged 17–54 are in the regular armed forces.

USA	UK	France	Russia	China	N Korea	S Korea	Egypt	Israel	Iran	Pakistan	India
1,374,699	150,250	202,700	1,013,628	2,035,000	950,000	599,000	438,500	176,500	523,000	653,000	1,440,000

TOTAL ARMED FORCES PERSONNEL

History

Easter Island statues
The giant statues, or *moai*, on this small Pacific island stand up to 10 m (33 ft) tall. They were carved with stone tools, mainly between 1250 and 1500, by the Polynesian people who settled the island.

Introduction

Human history is crammed full of incident, from civilizations rising and falling, as wars are fought and lost, to revolutions sweeping away the past to begin again. There has also been great architecture and many important innovations, from the first stone tools that enabled people to hunt animals to radio telescopes that can "see" into deep space.

The Great Sphinx
This statue at Giza, in Egypt, has a human head on a lion's body. It is thought to have been made around 4,500 years ago.

c.200,000 years ago
Modern humans
The *Homo sapiens* species (modern humans) evolves in east Africa.

c.2.4 million years ago
Earliest tools
The first stone tools are made by *Homo habilis*, an early human species.

c.100,000 years ago
Jewellery
Early people wear jewellery made from shell beads.

1227
Genghis Khan
At the death of its Mongol leader Genghis Khan, the Mongol Empire stretches across northern Asia.

1095–1272
The Crusades
Christian and Muslim armies fight nine wars to control Jerusalem.

1200
Holy Roman Empire
This "superpower" of the Middle Ages covers much of central Europe.

900
Khmer dominance, Asia
With their capital at Angkor, the Khmers rule over a large part of Southeast Asia.

1235
Battle of Kirina, Africa
Mandinka forces defeat the Sosso, leading to the birth of the Mali Empire.

1325
Templo Mayor, Mexico
Human sacrifices are made at this temple in the Aztec capital city of Tenochtitlan.

1300
Kanem Empire, Africa
Located north of Lake Chad, Kanem grow powerful and wealthy through its control of trade.

1350
Kingdom of Zimbabwe
The capital of this southern African kingdom is Great Zimbabwe, a stone-walled city.

1949
Chinese Revolution
Led by Mao Zedong, Chinese Communists take power after a long civil war.

1947
Indian independence
After a largely non-violent rebellion, India wins its independence from Britain.

1945–54
First Indochina War
Indochina (Vietnam, Cambodia, and Laos) wins independence from France.

1939–45
World War II
Allied forces (Britain, France, USA, USSR, and others) at war with Germany, Japan, and Italy.

1950–53
Korean War
Civil war: China and the USSR help North Korea, the United Nations helps South Korea.

1965
Indo-Pakistani War
Conflict between India and Pakistan over the disputed region of Kashmir.

1955–75
Vietnam War
Communist North Vietnam triumphs over South Vietnam, which is aided by US forces.

1969
Concorde
The world's first supersonic airliner, Concorde, flies for the first time.

2011
World's longest bridge, China
Completion of the 164.8-km- (102.4-mile-) long Danyang-Kunshan Grand Bridge.

2020
COVID-19
Outbreak of a newly discovered coronavirus causes a global pandemic, with up to 2.6 million deaths in the first year.

2011
"Arab Spring"
Revolution and protest sweep through Egypt, Libya, and other Arab countries.

c.90,000 years ago
Burial rites
People begin burying their
dead along with meaningful
objects such as beads.

c.3200 BCE
Pirámide Mayor, Peru
Built by the Norte Chico
civilization at Caral, the most
ancient city in the Americas.

1450 BCE
New Kingdom of Egypt
Egypt's empire stretches
north to Syria and south to
Nubia (modern Sudan).

490 BCE
First Persian Empire
Persia rules territory from the
edge of India to Egypt and
Greece, linking East with West.

265 BCE
Mauryan Empire, Asia
Under Ashoka, the Mauryan
Empire extends over almost
all of the Indian subcontinent.

c.40,000 years ago
First music and art
Music is played on simple
flutes, and figurines are
carved from stone.

c.2589–2500 BCE
Pyramids of Giza, Egypt
Vast tombs are built for the
Egyptian pharaohs Khufu,
Khafre, and Menkaure.

c.700 BCE
Olmec civilization
Mexico's Olmec culture reaches
its peak. It will influence the
later Mayan and Aztec cultures.

323 BCE
Macedonian Empire
King Alexander the Great of
Macedonia rules lands from
Greece to the edge of India.

264–146 BCE
Punic Wars
Three wars erupt between Rome
and Carthage, North Africa.
Rome emerges victorious.

750
Umayyad Caliphate
The second of four great
Islamic dynasties, with its
capital in Damascus (Syria).

650
Huari Empire, Peru
The highly organized Huari,
in Peru, conquer and control
much of the Andean region.

c.300 CE
Mayan culture, Central America
Established by 1000 BCE, Mayan
civilization is now at its height.
It will last until 1697 CE.

100 CE
Pyramid of the Sun, Mexico
One of two huge stepped
pyramids is built in the
city of Teotihuacán.

87 BCE
Han Dynasty, China
A time of prosperity in
China and an expansion of
territories ruled by China.

700
Tihuanaco, Peru/Bolivia
This strong state is centred
on a bustling city beside
Lake Titicaca in the Andes.

555
Byzantine power
Byzantine rule extends over
North Africa and the eastern
part of the old Roman Empire.

117 CE
Roman supremacy
Rome now controls much of
Europe, north Africa, and
the Middle East.

80 CE
Colosseum, Rome
Opening of the stadium in
Rome where gladiators
fought to the death.

214 BCE
Great Wall of China
Construction begins of this
vast defensive wall along
China's northern border.

Colosseum, Rome

1453
Fall of Constantinople
The capital of the Byzantine
Empire falls to invading
Muslim Ottoman forces.

1500
Songhai power, Africa
The Songhai control the Niger
Valley, west to Senegal and east
to Agades (modern Niger).

1532
Battle of Cajamarca, Peru
Spanish invaders defeat the Inca
forces of Atahualpa, leading to
300 years of Spanish rule.

1683
Battle of Vienna
Ottoman expansion finally
halts with a defeat by the
Holy Roman Empire.

1450
Machu Picchu, Peru
A secret hilltop city of the
Incas, who will dominate
northern South America.

1500
Ming Dynasty, China
After throwing out the Mongols,
China restores its culture and
expands its borders.

1519
Aztec rule, Mexico
The Aztecs now rule over
25 million people. In 1521, they
are conquered by the Spanish.

1642–51
English Civil War
Parliamentarians defeat
Royalists, leading to the
execution of King Charles I.

1690
Mughal Empire, India
Under Aurangzeb, the Islamic
Mughal Empire of India is at
its most powerful.

1922
Height of British Empire
Britain's empire now covers
more than 20 per cent of the
world's land area.

1914–18
World War I
Britain, France, the USA, and
other allies battle Germany,
Austria-Hungary, and Turkey.

1880–1902
Boer Wars, Africa
Two wars are fought between
Dutch Boer settlers in South
Africa and Britain.

1819–30
South American independence
Independence from Spain for
Colombia, Peru, Bolivia,
Ecuador, and Venezuela.

1789–99
French Revolution
Overthrow of the French
monarchy in a bloody revolution.
France becomes a republic.

1917
Russian Revolution
Revolt against rule by
Tsar Nicholas II; Russia
becomes Communist.

1912
Sinking of the *Titanic*
Over 1,500 people die when
this luxury liner hits an
iceberg and sinks.

1861–65
American Civil War
War between the southern
Confederate states and the
Union states of the north.

1799–1815
Napoleonic era
France, led by Napoleon
Bonaparte, is the dominant
military power in Europe.

1775–83
American Revolutionary War
With the help of France and
other countries, the USA wins
independence from Britain.

1980
Very Large Array
In New Mexico, USA, this
giant radio astronomy
observatory is completed.

Sydney Opera House
Opened in 1973, this arts venue
in Sydney, Australia, was
designed by Danish architect
Jørn Utzon.

1994
End of Apartheid
South Africa's official
segregation policy,
Apartheid, ends and
equality is reached for
Black South Africans.

1989–1991
End of Communist bloc
Communist regimes in
many countries of eastern
Europe are overthrown.

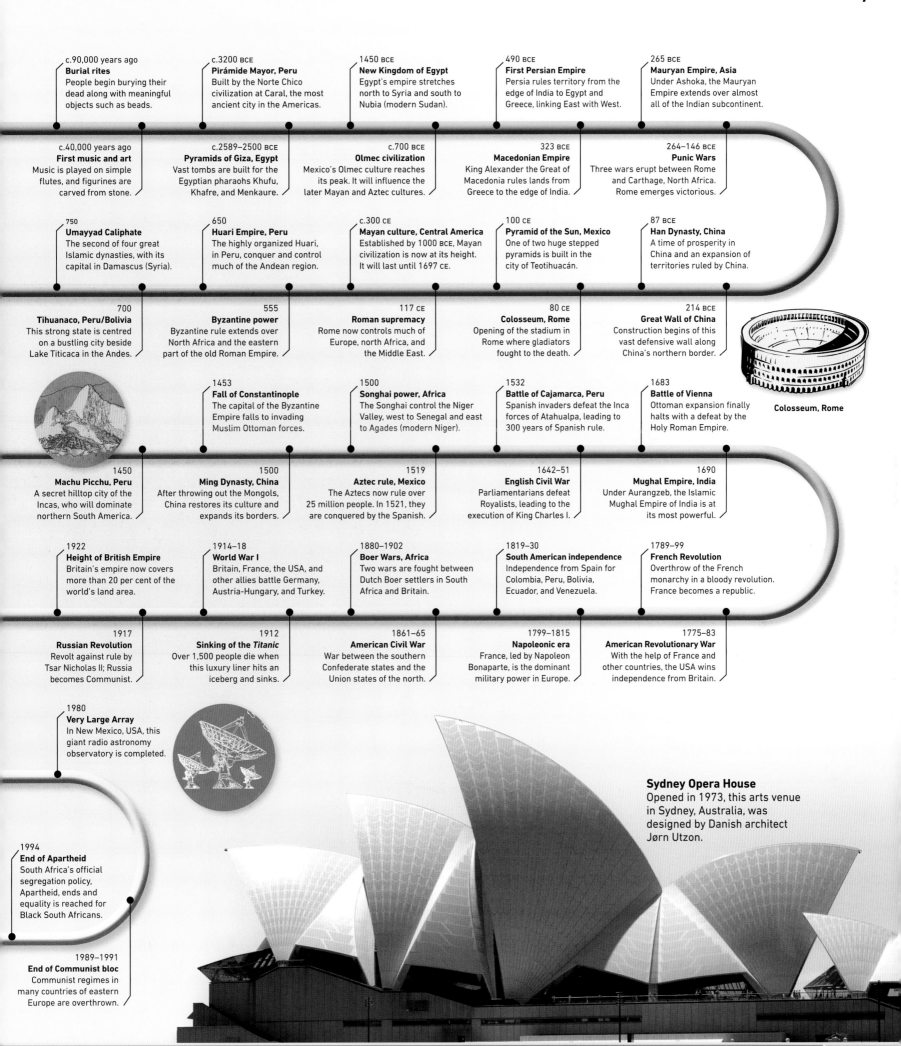

Australopithecus

Australopithecus hominins evolved about 4.2 million years ago in east Africa. Six species are known. One species, called *A. afarensis*, may be the ancestor of humans. Fossils show that it was up to 1.5 m (5 ft) tall and had a relatively small brain. Crucially, it could walk upright.

Paranthropus

The three *Paranthropus* species had a bony crest on top of the skull to anchor strong chewing muscles. *P. boisei* is nicknamed "nutcracker man" because of its massive jaws and cheek teeth.

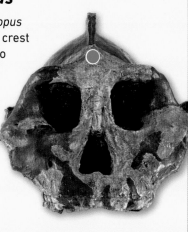

Neander Valley, Germany
A partial skeleton of *H. neanderthalensis* found in a cave here in 1856 was the first fossil to be identified as human remains.

Laetoli, Tanzania
Footprints of at least two *Australopithecus afarensis* individuals were discovered here preserved in volcanic ash.

Olduvai Gorge, Tanzania
Stone tools and fossils of *P. boisei* and *H. habilis* were found here.

South Africa
Finds include *Australopithecus*, *Paranthropus*, *H. habilis*, and *H. sapiens* fossils.

Fossil humans

Fossil discoveries have helped scientists to piece together the story of human evolution. Modern humans – *Homo sapiens* – and their ancestors are called hominins. *Sahelanthropus tchadensis*, the first hominin, was an apelike animal that appeared in Africa about 7 million years ago. Later hominin species left Africa and spread out around the world.

Ape-like
Australopithecus –

six species

4   million years ago   3

HOMO SAPIENS EVOLVED ABOUT 200,000 YEARS AGO. THE EARLIEST

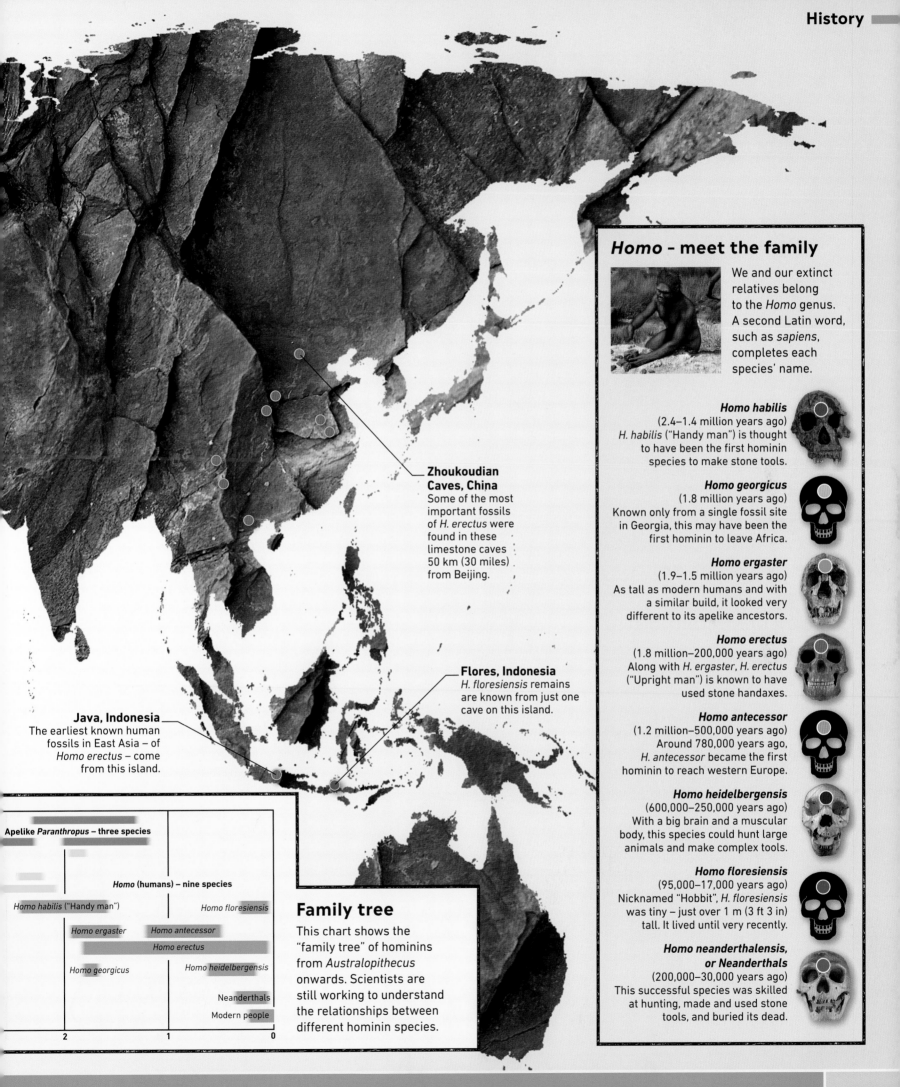

Zhoukoudian Caves, China
Some of the most important fossils of *H. erectus* were found in these limestone caves 50 km (30 miles) from Beijing.

Flores, Indonesia
H. floresiensis remains are known from just one cave on this island.

Java, Indonesia
The earliest known human fossils in East Asia – of *Homo erectus* – come from this island.

Homo – meet the family

We and our extinct relatives belong to the *Homo* genus. A second Latin word, such as *sapiens*, completes each species' name.

Homo habilis
(2.4–1.4 million years ago)
H. habilis ("Handy man") is thought to have been the first hominin species to make stone tools.

Homo georgicus
(1.8 million years ago)
Known only from a single fossil site in Georgia, this may have been the first hominin to leave Africa.

Homo ergaster
(1.9–1.5 million years ago)
As tall as modern humans and with a similar build, it looked very different to its apelike ancestors.

Homo erectus
(1.8 million–200,000 years ago)
Along with *H. ergaster*, *H. erectus* ("Upright man") is known to have used stone handaxes.

Homo antecessor
(1.2 million–500,000 years ago)
Around 780,000 years ago, *H. antecessor* became the first hominin to reach western Europe.

Homo heidelbergensis
(600,000–250,000 years ago)
With a big brain and a muscular body, this species could hunt large animals and make complex tools.

Homo floresiensis
(95,000–17,000 years ago)
Nicknamed "Hobbit", *H. floresiensis* was tiny – just over 1 m (3 ft 3 in) tall. It lived until very recently.

Homo neanderthalensis, or Neanderthals
(200,000–30,000 years ago)
This successful species was skilled at hunting, made and used stone tools, and buried its dead.

Apelike *Paranthropus* – three species

Homo (humans) – nine species

Homo habilis ("Handy man")   *Homo floresiensis*

Homo ergaster   *Homo antecessor*

Homo erectus

Homo georgicus   *Homo heidelbergensis*

Neanderthals

Modern people

2   1   0

Family tree

This chart shows the "family tree" of hominins from *Australopithecus* onwards. Scientists are still working to understand the relationships between different hominin species.

Prehistoric culture

Music, art, religion, and technology all began so long ago, we can't be certain of exactly when. There are clues to early culture, however, such as ritual burial sites, which archaeologists can date.

Earliest music

Music, like art, is far older than writing, since bone flutes and other musical instruments have been made and played for more than 40,000 years.

◆ Early instrument site

Antler flute, Hohle Fels, Germany, 43,000 years ago

First jewellery

People wore jewellery more than 100,000 years ago in sites as distant as Israel and South Africa.

◆ Early jewellery site

Shell beads, Balzi Rossi, Italy

East Wenatchee, Washington, USA

Walker, Minnesota, USA

Horseshoe Canyon paintings, Utah, USA

Cactus Hill, Virginia, USA

Clovis, New Mexico, USA

Salado, Texas, USA

Wicklow Pipes, Ireland

Shell bead necklace, Cro-Magnon, France

Lascaux Caves, France

Altamira and El Castillo caves, Spain. El Castillo features the oldest known paintings, made 40,800 years ago, possibly by Neanderthals

Lady of Brassempouy carving, France

Ivory horse figurine, Lourdes, France

Shell beads, Grotte des Pidgeons, Morocco

Algerian Sahara

Serra de Capivara paintings, Brazil

Cueva de las Manos paintings, Argentina

Cueva del Milodon, Chile

Changes in stone tools

2.4 million years ago
The earliest tools, called the Oldowan toolkit, were made by an early human species called "Handy Man", or *Homo habilis*, in Africa. Olduwan-style tools in Europe and Asia are much younger, made by later types of humans, including Neanderthals.

◉ Oldowan site

1.8 million years ago
The Acheulean toolkit of our later ancestors, such as *Homo erectus*, included a new invention – the hand axe, with a finely chiselled edge.

◉ Acheulian site

200,000 years ago
Mousterian tools spanned the Middle Stone Age (ended around 40,000 BCE) and included lots of specialized shapes for different jobs.

◉ Mousterian site

13,000 years ago
The earliest stone tools discovered in America are from the 13,000-year-old "Clovis" people.

◉ Clovis site

THE FIRST KNOWN SEWING NEEDLE DATES BACK ABOUT 25,000 YEARS

Flutes, Hohle Fels Cave, and Geissenklösterle, Germany

Bisovava, Russia

"Lion Man" bone carving, Germany

Sungir Graves, Russia

Carved ivory running lion, Czech Republic

Tata Plaque (mysterious object made by a Neanderthal 100,000 years ago), Hungary

Krapina, Croatia

Balzi Rossi caves, Italy

Tbilisi, Georgia

Pechka rock shelter, Armenia

Carved bone disc, Xiaogushan, China

Majuangou, China

Qafzeh, Israel

Shanidar Cave, Iraq

Kashafrud, Iran

Riwat, Pakistan

Bone flutes, Jiahu, China

Chauvet Cave, France

Shell beads, Skhūl, Israel

Gebelein, Egypt

Bhimbetka paintings, India

Bose, China

Gona, Ethiopia (world's oldest tools)

Isampur, India

Island of Socotra, Yemen

Konso-Gardula, Ethiopia

Omo, Ethiopia

Turkana, Kenya

Lokalalei, Kenya

Olduvai Gorge, Tanzania

Twin Rivers, Zambia

Inanke Cave, Zimbabwe

Sterkfontein, South Africa

Kakadu National Park, Australia

"Apollo 11" rock shelter, Namibia

Swartkrans, South Africa

Shell beads, Blombos Cave, South Africa

THE OLDEST KNOWN CLAY POTS WERE MADE IN CHINA ABOUT 20,000 YEARS AGO

Earliest burials

Our ancestors began burying their dead with significant objects, such as beads or other decorations, at least 100,000 years ago.

◆ Early burial site

Skull with shells, 25,000 years ago, Balzi Rossi, Italy

Earliest paintings

Humans have painted and carved rock surfaces since at least 40,000 years ago. Some paintings show people dancing and singing.

◆ Early painting site

Inanke Cave, Zimbabwe, 5,000–10,000 years ago

The first sculpture

The earliest known sculpture consists of figurines carved from stone and bone to look like humans and animals. Some date back up to 40,000 years.

◆ Site of artwork

"Lion Man", Germany, 40,000 years ago

IT WAS MADE OF BONE AND USED TO SEW TOGETHER ANIMAL HIDES.

BRITAIN

GERMANY

Rise and fall
This map shows the territories of each ancient empire at its peak. Some empires fell as dramatically as they rose, whereas others, such as the Roman Empire, declined gradually over centuries.

⬜ **New Kingdom of Egypt**
1550–1069 BCE
The Egyptian New Kingdom grew under Thutmose III, one of the first great generals in history. At its peak, Egypt ruled the southeast Mediterranean.

Stone head of Queen Meritaten of the 18th Dynasty of Egypt

Roman Empire in 117 CE

GAUL

Rome

IBERIA

GREECE

ASIA MINOR

MAURETANIA

MESOPOTAMIA

Babylon

PERSIA

First Persian Empire in 490 BCE

Pasargadae

Ancient empires

EGYPT

Thebes

Empires in retreat
The larger an empire grows, the more complex and expensive it becomes to rule. Roman Emperor Trajan seized Mesopotamia in 117 CE, but his successor Hadrian gave it up almost immediately, believing it not worth the expense.

In the ancient world, as civilizations grew, some had ambitions to become richer and more powerful by conquering or controlling their neighbours. The most successful conquerors created huge empires.

New Kingdom of Egypt in 1450 BCE

Civilizations of the Americas

The Olmec and Maya cultures spread, like the empires of Eurasia and Africa, as their communities merged and grew. Trade and cultural exchange, rather than violent conquest, was probably the main way their cultures expanded.

Olmec civilization
c.700 BCE

Mayan civilization
c.300 CE

Area of main map

AT ITS HEIGHT, THE HAN EMPIRE OF CHINA RULED 60 MILLION PEOPLE

Olmec civilization
1500–400 BCE
The first major culture in Central America, the Olmecs lived in what is now Mexico. They were expert farmers and traded all over the region. They developed one of the first writing systems in the Americas.

Olmec stone mask

First Persian Empire
550–336 BCE
Cyrus the Great and his army conquered huge swathes of central Asia and grabbed enormous wealth from the kingdoms they conquered. Cyrus's successor, Darius I, built cities, roads, and even a canal from the River Nile to the Red Sea.

Ornate Persian silver bowl

Empire of Alexander the Great
330–323 BCE
Alexander was a general from Macedon, a kingdom north of Greece. At its height, his empire covered most of the world known to Greeks. For centuries after his death, the Greek culture that he introduced continued to dominate the eastern Mediterranean and western Asia.

Coin showing Alexander the Great's head

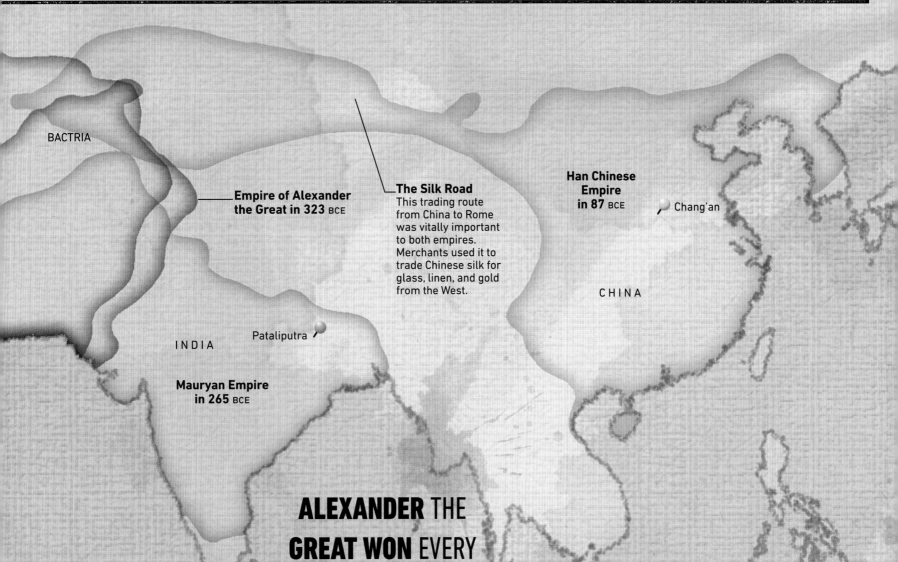

BACTRIA

Empire of Alexander the Great in 323 BCE

The Silk Road
This trading route from China to Rome was vitally important to both empires. Merchants used it to trade Chinese silk for glass, linen, and gold from the West.

Han Chinese Empire in 87 BCE

Chang'an

CHINA

INDIA

Pataliputra

Mauryan Empire in 265 BCE

ALEXANDER THE GREAT WON EVERY BATTLE HE FOUGHT

Mauryan Empire
321–185 BCE
Chandragupta Maurya was the first leader to conquer the whole Indian subcontinent. His son Ashoka became a Buddhist and ruled the empire peacefully for 42 years.

Mauryan figure

Han Empire
206–220 CE
The four centuries of Han rule are often called the Golden Age of Ancient China. It was an era of peace and prosperity in which China became a major world power.

Han pot

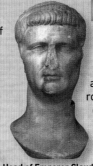

Roman Empire
27 BCE–476 CE
One of history's most influential civilizations, Rome controlled much of Europe, western Asia, and north Africa. Many roads, aqueducts, and canals built by the Romans are still in use today.

Head of Emperor Claudius

Mayan civilization
500–900 CE
One of the most advanced cultures of the ancient world, the Maya developed an accurate yearly calendar based on their sophisticated understanding of astronomy.

Mayan statuette

Ancient wonders

Ancient Greek travellers and authors such as Herodotus, Antipater, and Philo of Byzantium praised the architectural marvels of the age in their writings. The buildings and statues they described became known as the "Seven Wonders of the World". Today, we recognize many other amazing structures that architects, masons, and sculptors of the past built with relatively simple tools.

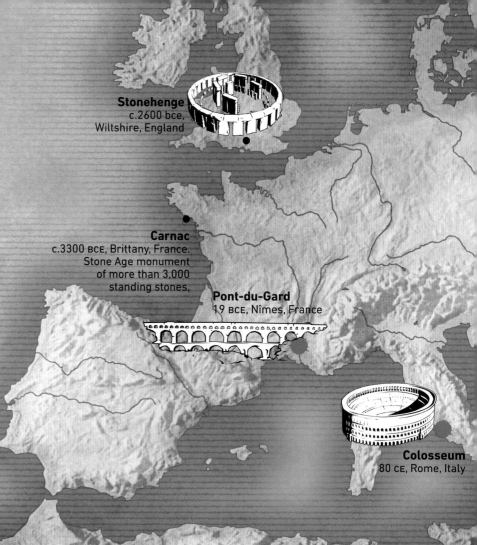

Stonehenge
c.2600 bce,
Wiltshire, England

Carnac
c.3300 BCE, Brittany, France.
Stone Age monument of more than 3,000 standing stones.

Pont-du-Gard
19 BCE, Nîmes, France

Colosseum
80 CE, Rome, Italy

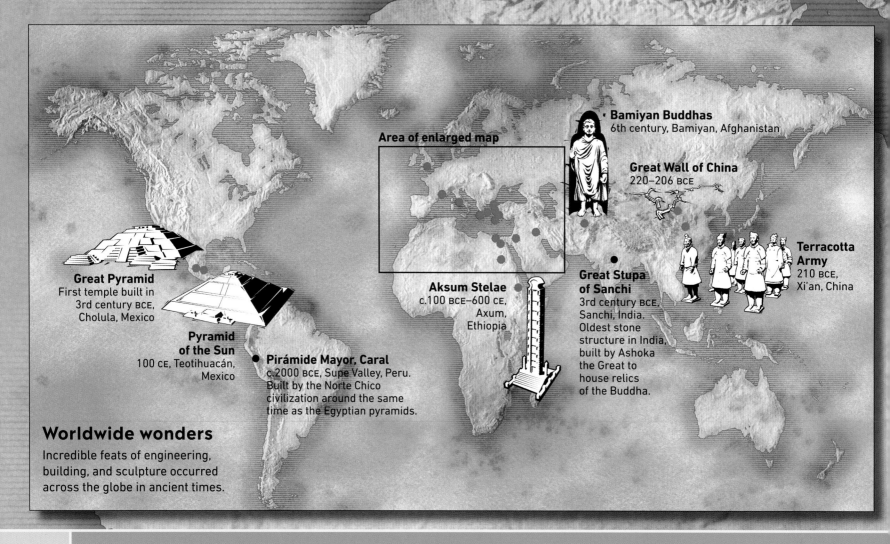

Bamiyan Buddhas
6th century, Bamiyan, Afghanistan

Great Wall of China
220–206 BCE

Area of enlarged map

Great Pyramid
First temple built in 3rd century BCE, Cholula, Mexico

Pyramid of the Sun
100 CE, Teotihuacán, Mexico

Pirámide Mayor, Caral
c.2000 BCE, Supe Valley, Peru. Built by the Norte Chico civilization around the same time as the Egyptian pyramids.

Aksum Stelae
c.100 BCE–600 CE, Axum, Ethiopia

Great Stupa of Sanchi
3rd century BCE, Sanchi, India. Oldest stone structure in India, built by Ashoka the Great to house relics of the Buddha.

Terracotta Army
210 BCE, Xi'an, China

Worldwide wonders
Incredible feats of engineering, building, and sculpture occurred across the globe in ancient times.

THE COLOSSEUM IN ROME COULD HOLD MORE THAN 50,000 SPECTATORS.

Seven Wonders of the World

Only the pyramids at Giza still stand. Earthquakes destroyed the Hanging Gardens, the Colossus, and the Pharos; flooding and fire ruined the Mausoleum and the Statue of Zeus. The Temple of Artemis was wrecked by the Goths.

 Pyramids of Giza
Built as tombs for the pharaohs Khufu, Khafre, and Menkaure.

 Hanging Gardens of Babylon
Nebuchadnezzar II built these lush, terraced gardens for his wife, Amytis.

 Mausoleum at Halicarnassus
Tomb of Persian governor Mausolus, famed for its size and lavish carvings.

 Temple of Artemis
Dedicated to the Greek goddess of hunting, chastity, and childbirth.

 Colossus of Rhodes
Vast bronze-and-iron statue, 32 m (105 ft) tall, of the Greek Sun-god Helios.

 Pharos of Alexandria
A fire at the top of this huge lighthouse was visible from 50 km (30 miles) away.

 Statue of Zeus in Olympia
The sculptor Phidias built this 13-m (43-ft) statue of the king of the gods.

Other ancient wonders

These wonders didn't make the Seven Wonders list, mainly because they were unknown to the Greeks. Some of them were built during later periods.

 Colosseum
Stadium where gladiators fought to the death.

 Hagia Sofia
Enormous, richly decorated church, later a mosque.

 Petra
A city hewn out of rock. Capital of the Nabataeans.

 Temples of Abu-Simbel
Two temples built to honour the pharaoh Rameses II.

 Pont-du-Gard
Roman aqueduct that carried water to Nîmes.

 Acropolis
Greek citadel that includes the Parthenon Temple.

 Great Pyramid
World's largest pyramid, now with a church on top.

 Pyramid of the Sun
Steep steps up the side led to a temple on the top.

 Stonehenge
Prehistoric monument with a circle of enormous stones.

 Bamiyan Buddhas
Huge statues chiselled into a cliff; destroyed in 2001.

 Great Wall of China
Once ran for 6,259 km (3,889 miles) along China's northern border.

 Terracotta Army
8,000 life-size warriors entombed with the first emperor of China.

 Aksum Stelae
A group of memorial obelisks carved from huge blocks of stone.

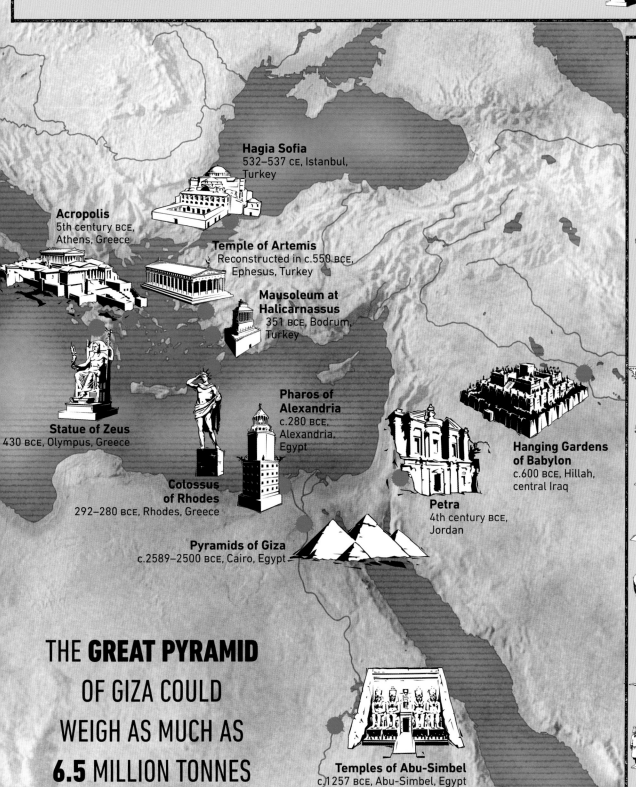

Hagia Sofia
532–537 CE, Istanbul, Turkey

Acropolis
5th century BCE, Athens, Greece

Temple of Artemis
Reconstructed in c.550 BCE, Ephesus, Turkey

Mausoleum at Halicarnassus
351 BCE, Bodrum, Turkey

Statue of Zeus
430 BCE, Olympus, Greece

Pharos of Alexandria
c.280 BCE, Alexandria, Egypt

Colossus of Rhodes
292–280 BCE, Rhodes, Greece

Hanging Gardens of Babylon
c.600 BCE, Hillah, central Iraq

Petra
4th century BCE, Jordan

Pyramids of Giza
c.2589–2500 BCE, Cairo, Egypt

Temples of Abu-Simbel
c.1257 BCE, Abu-Simbel, Egypt

THE **GREAT PYRAMID** OF GIZA COULD WEIGH AS MUCH AS **6.5** MILLION TONNES

THE ARENA COULD BE FLOODED TO STAGE MOCK SEA BATTLES.

Famous mummies

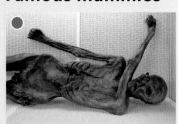

Ötzi the Iceman
Around 5,300 years ago, a traveller died when caught in a snowstorm in the Alps. His body became buried in the snow and then froze. In 1991, the corpse was discovered on top of a glacier.

Pharaoh Tutankhamun
The mummy of Tutankhamun was found in a tomb in the Valley of the Kings in 1922. It wore a gold mask and lay inside a nest of three gold cases. The tomb, which had been sealed for 3,200 years, contained statues, furniture, and jewellery.

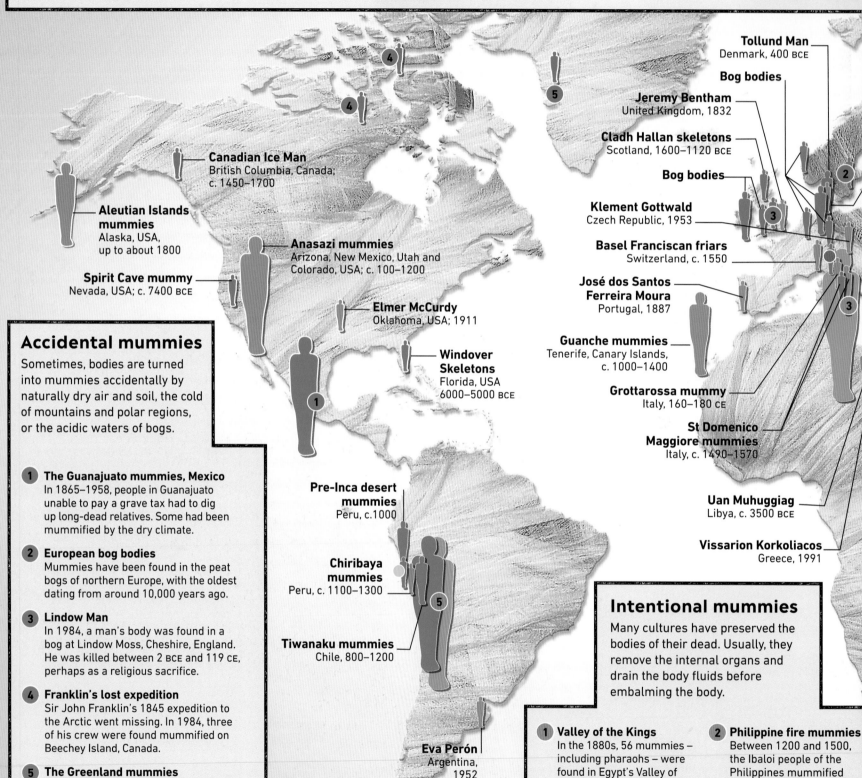

Tollund Man
Denmark, 400 BCE

Bog bodies

Jeremy Bentham
United Kingdom, 1832

Cladh Hallan skeletons
Scotland, 1600–1120 BCE

Bog bodies

Klement Gottwald
Czech Republic, 1953

Basel Franciscan friars
Switzerland, c. 1550

José dos Santos Ferreira Moura
Portugal, 1887

Guanche mummies
Tenerife, Canary Islands, c. 1000–1400

Grottarossa mummy
Italy, 160–180 CE

St Domenico Maggiore mummies
Italy, c. 1490–1570

Uan Muhuggiag
Libya, c. 3500 BCE

Vissarion Korkoliacos
Greece, 1991

Canadian Ice Man
British Columbia, Canada; c. 1450–1700

Aleutian Islands mummies
Alaska, USA, up to about 1800

Spirit Cave mummy
Nevada, USA; c. 7400 BCE

Anasazi mummies
Arizona, New Mexico, Utah and Colorado, USA; c. 100–1200

Elmer McCurdy
Oklahoma, USA; 1911

Windover Skeletons
Florida, USA 6000–5000 BCE

Pre-Inca desert mummies
Peru, c.1000

Chiribaya mummies
Peru, c. 1100–1300

Tiwanaku mummies
Chile, 800–1200

Eva Perón
Argentina, 1952

Accidental mummies

Sometimes, bodies are turned into mummies accidentally by naturally dry air and soil, the cold of mountains and polar regions, or the acidic waters of bogs.

1. The Guanajuato mummies, Mexico
In 1865–1958, people in Guanajuato unable to pay a grave tax had to dig up long-dead relatives. Some had been mummified by the dry climate.

2. European bog bodies
Mummies have been found in the peat bogs of northern Europe, with the oldest dating from around 10,000 years ago.

3. Lindow Man
In 1984, a man's body was found in a bog at Lindow Moss, Cheshire, England. He was killed between 2 BCE and 119 CE, perhaps as a religious sacrifice.

4. Franklin's lost expedition
Sir John Franklin's 1845 expedition to the Arctic went missing. In 1984, three of his crew were found mummified on Beechey Island, Canada.

5. The Greenland mummies
Eight mummified Inuit people who died in around 1475 were found on a cliff at Nuuk, Greenland, in 1972. Their bodies had freeze-dried.

Intentional mummies

Many cultures have preserved the bodies of their dead. Usually, they remove the internal organs and drain the body fluids before embalming the body.

1. Valley of the Kings
In the 1880s, 56 mummies – including pharaohs – were found in Egypt's Valley of the Kings. In 2019, a further 30 mummies were discovered in this area by Egyptian archaeologists.

2. Philippine fire mummies
Between 1200 and 1500, the Ibaloi people of the Philippines mummified their leaders by drying them over a fire then putting them in caves.

Juanita the Ice Maiden
In 1995, an Inca girl aged 11–15 was found on Mount Ampato, Peru. The discoverers named her Juanita, or the "Ice Maiden". She was sacrificed to the gods about 530 years ago. The cold had preserved her skin, organs, blood, and stomach contents.

James Hepburn, 4th Earl of Bothwell
Denmark, 1578

Charles Eugène de Croÿ
Estonia, 1702

Vladimir Lenin
Russia, 1924

Georgi Dimitrov
Bulgaria, 1949

Valley of the Golden Mummies Egypt, 332 BCE–395 CE

öbnitz Girl
land,
0 BCE

Maronite mummies
Lebanon, 1283

Chehrabad Salt Mine mummies Iran, 4th century BCE–4th century CE

Iufaa and family
Egypt, c.500 BCE

1

Saqqara mummies
Egypt, 640 BCE

Nubian mummies
Sudan, 250–1400

Tarim mummies
China, 1800–200 BCE

Siberian Ice Maiden
Russia, c. 400 BCE

Pazyryk ice mummies
Mongolia, c. 700–200 BCE

Mao Zedong
China, 1976

Xin Zhui
China, c. 150 BCE

Ho Chi Minh
Vietnam, 1969

Mummy monk "Luang Phor Daeng"
Thailand, c. 1985

Vu Khac Minh and Vu Khac Truong
Vietnam, c. 1600–1700

Chiang Kai-shek and Chiang Ching-kuo
Taiwan, 1975 and 1988

Buddhist self-mummified nun and monks
Taiwan, 1680–1830,

Fujiwara clan mummies
Japan, 1128–1189

Kim Il-Sung and Kim Jong-il
North Korea, 1994 and 2011

4

Korean mummies
South Korea, c. 1350–1500

2

Lost mummies of New Guinea
Papua New Guinea, up to 1950s

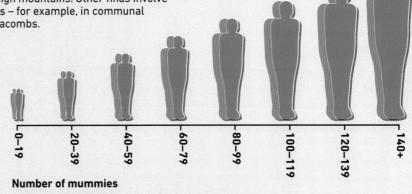

MUMMY DISCOVERIES WORLDWIDE
Some mummies are discovered singly, often in remote locations such as in peat bogs or on high mountains. Other finds involve larger numbers of mummies – for example, in communal graves, tombs, caves, or catacombs.

Accidental mummies

Intentional mummies

0–19 20–39 40–59 60–79 80–99 100–119 120–139 140+

Number of mummies

Mummies

Mummies – the preserved bodies of the dead – have been found the world over. Many were made deliberately, while others formed naturally. More recently, some countries have mummified their leaders.

3 **Mummies of Palermo**
In 1599, Christian monks in Palermo, Sicily, began to mummify their dead and stored them in catacombs. Later, rich people paid the monks to mummify their bodies.

4 **Self-mummified monks**
From 1680–1830, some Buddhist monks in Japan mummified themselves. They starved, drank special tea to make their body toxic to maggots, and then were sealed alive in a stone tomb.

5 **Chinchorro mummies**
The Chinchorro, who lived in what is now Chile and Peru, were the first people known to make mummies. Their oldest mummies date from as early as 5000 BCE.

THE PALERMO **CATACOMBS** CONTAIN AROUND **8,000** **MUMMIES**

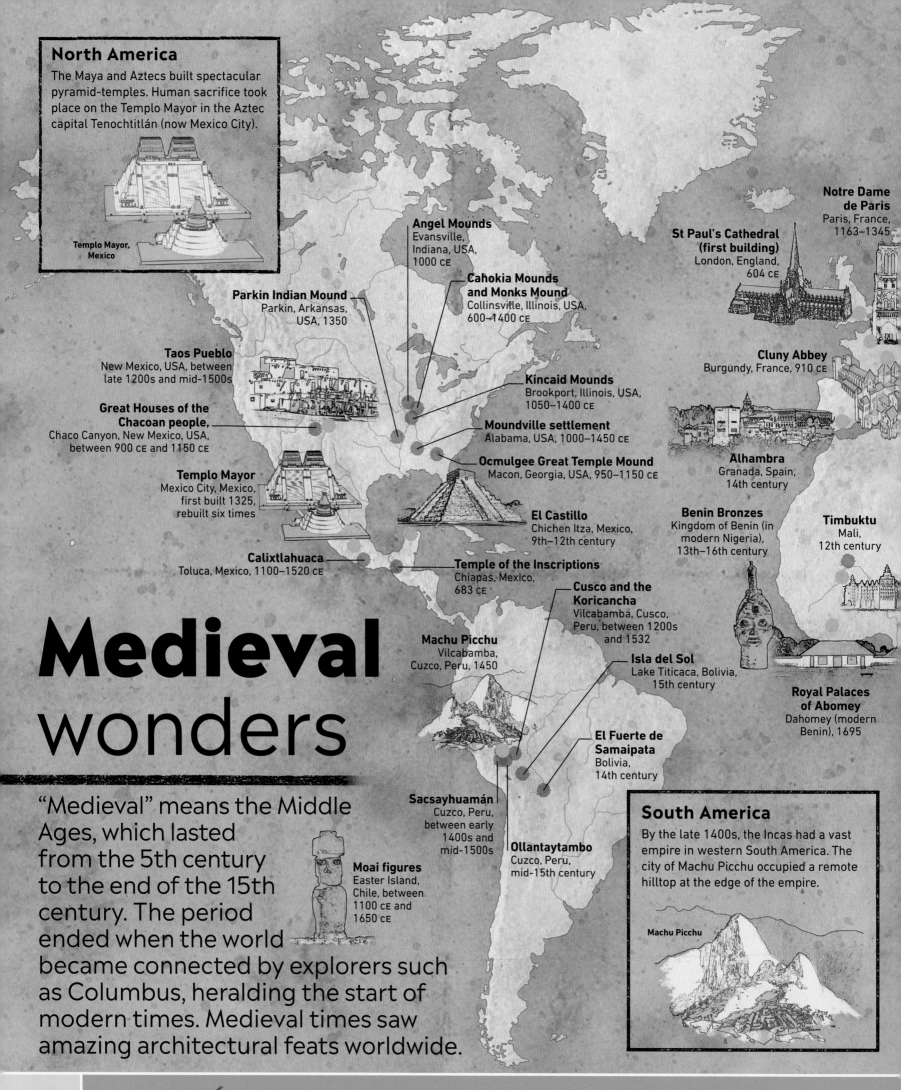

North America
The Maya and Aztecs built spectacular pyramid-temples. Human sacrifice took place on the Templo Mayor in the Aztec capital Tenochtitlán (now Mexico City).

Templo Mayor, Mexico

Angel Mounds
Evansville, Indiana, USA, 1000 CE

Cahokia Mounds and Monks Mound
Collinsville, Illinois, USA, 600–1400 CE

Parkin Indian Mound
Parkin, Arkansas, USA, 1350

Notre Dame de Paris
Paris, France, 1163–1345

St Paul's Cathedral (first building)
London, England, 604 CE

Taos Pueblo
New Mexico, USA, between late 1200s and mid-1500s

Kincaid Mounds
Brookport, Illinois, USA, 1050–1400 CE

Great Houses of the Chacoan people,
Chaco Canyon, New Mexico, USA, between 900 CE and 1150 CE

Moundville settlement
Alabama, USA, 1000–1450 CE

Cluny Abbey
Burgundy, France, 910 CE

Templo Mayor
Mexico City, Mexico, first built 1325, rebuilt six times

Ocmulgee Great Temple Mound
Macon, Georgia, USA, 950–1150 CE

Alhambra
Granada, Spain, 14th century

El Castillo
Chichen Itza, Mexico, 9th–12th century

Benin Bronzes
Kingdom of Benin (in modern Nigeria), 13th–16th century

Timbuktu
Mali, 12th century

Calixtlahuaca
Toluca, Mexico, 1100–1520 CE

Temple of the Inscriptions
Chiapas, Mexico, 683 CE

Cusco and the Koricancha
Vilcabamba, Cusco, Peru, between 1200s and 1532

Medieval wonders

Machu Picchu
Vilcabamba, Cuzco, Peru, 1450

Isla del Sol
Lake Titicaca, Bolivia, 15th century

Royal Palaces of Abomey
Dahomey (modern Benin), 1695

El Fuerte de Samaipata
Bolivia, 14th century

"Medieval" means the Middle Ages, which lasted from the 5th century to the end of the 15th century. The period ended when the world became connected by explorers such as Columbus, heralding the start of modern times. Medieval times saw amazing architectural feats worldwide.

Sacsayhuamán
Cuzco, Peru, between early 1400s and mid-1500s

Ollantaytambo
Cuzco, Peru, mid-15th century

South America
By the late 1400s, the Incas had a vast empire in western South America. The city of Machu Picchu occupied a remote hilltop at the edge of the empire.

Machu Picchu

Moai figures
Easter Island, Chile, between 1100 CE and 1650 CE

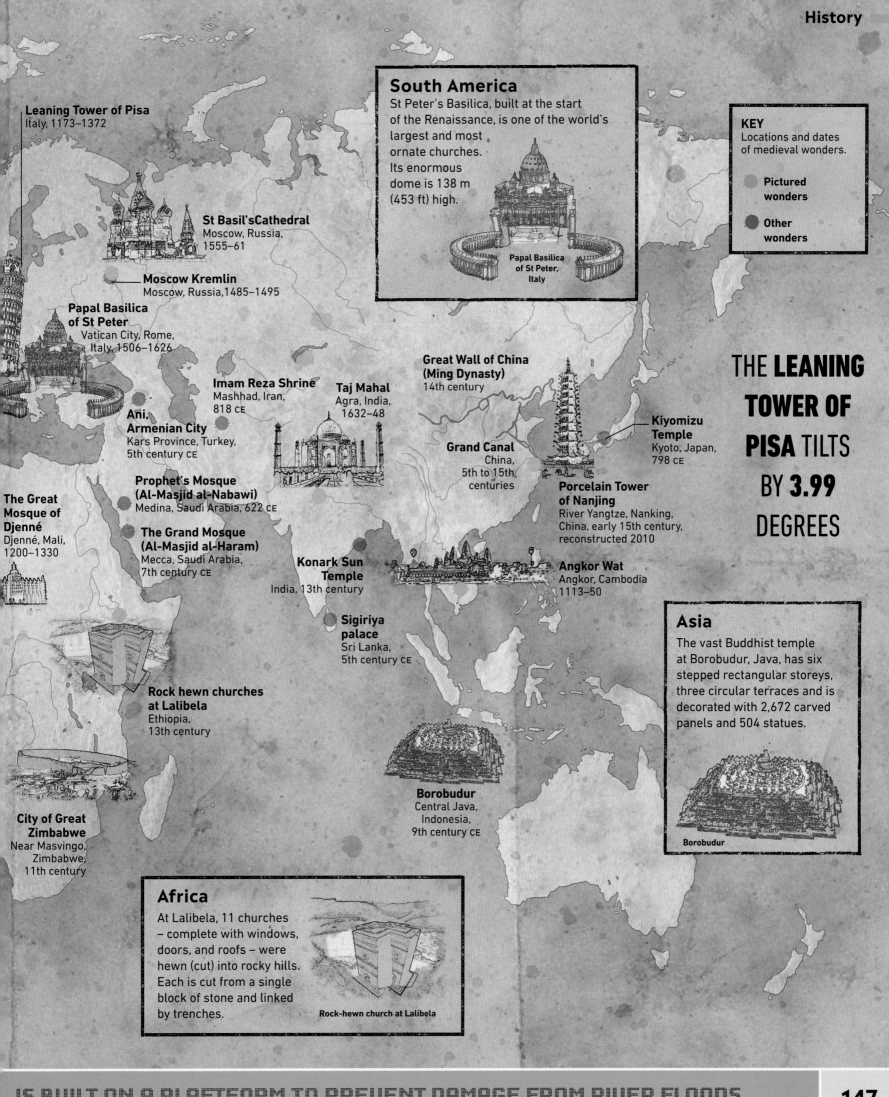

Leaning Tower of Pisa
Italy, 1173–1372

South America
St Peter's Basilica, built at the start of the Renaissance, is one of the world's largest and most ornate churches. Its enormous dome is 138 m (453 ft) high.

Papal Basilica of St Peter, Italy

KEY
Locations and dates of medieval wonders.

● **Pictured wonders**

● **Other wonders**

St Basil'sCathedral
Moscow, Russia, 1555–61

Moscow Kremlin
Moscow, Russia, 1485–1495

Papal Basilica of St Peter
Vatican City, Rome, Italy, 1506–1626

Imam Reza Shrine
Mashhad, Iran, 818 CE

Taj Mahal
Agra, India, 1632–48

Great Wall of China (Ming Dynasty)
14th century

Ani, Armenian City
Kars Province, Turkey, 5th century CE

Kiyomizu Temple
Kyoto, Japan, 798 CE

THE **LEANING TOWER OF PISA** TILTS BY **3.99** DEGREES

Grand Canal
China, 5th to 15th centuries

The Great Mosque of Djenné
Djenné, Mali, 1200–1330

Prophet's Mosque (Al-Masjid al-Nabawi)
Medina, Saudi Arabia, 622 CE

The Grand Mosque (Al-Masjid al-Haram)
Mecca, Saudi Arabia, 7th century CE

Konark Sun Temple
India, 13th century

Porcelain Tower of Nanjing
River Yangtze, Nanking, China, early 15th century, reconstructed 2010

Angkor Wat
Angkor, Cambodia 1113–50

Sigiriya palace
Sri Lanka, 5th century CE

Asia
The vast Buddhist temple at Borobudur, Java, has six stepped rectangular storeys, three circular terraces and is decorated with 2,672 carved panels and 504 statues.

Rock hewn churches at Lalibela
Ethiopia, 13th century

Borobudur
Central Java, Indonesia, 9th century CE

Borobudur

City of Great Zimbabwe
Near Masvingo, Zimbabwe, 11th century

Africa
At Lalibela, 11 churches – complete with windows, doors, and roofs – were hewn (cut) into rocky hills. Each is cut from a single block of stone and linked by trenches.

Rock-hewn church at Lalibela

Medieval empires

At times between 500 and 1500 CE, one power or another controlled vast parts of Europe and Asia, and spread Islam and Christianity across the world as they knew it. Little known to them, African rulers joined up large regions for the first time, while empires in the Americas grew in isolation from the rest of the world.

Ottoman battle helmet

Holy Roman Empire in 1200 CE

Frankfurt

Byzantine Empire in 555 CE

Ottoman Empire in 1683 CE

Istanbul

Constantinople

Damascus

Umayyad Caliphate in 750 CE

Songhai Empire in 1500 CE

Mali Empire in 1350 CE

Gao

Kanem Empire in 1300 CE

Koumbi Saleh

Njimi

Ka-ba (Kangaba)

Mali Empire
c. 1230–1600
A west African empire that became wealthy through trading gold and developing agriculture along the banks of the Niger.

Ancient Ghana
500s-1076
The kingdom of Ghana grew rich on gold mined from its valley and exported along the trans-Saharan trade routes. It was conquered by Berbers in 1076.

Kumasi

Asante Empire in 1750 CE

Asante Empire
1670–1902
A sophisticated and disciplined society. Clever strategies and adoption of western firearms helped bring about military expansion.

Asante trophy head

São Salvador (M'banza-Kongo)

Kingdom of Kongo in 1625 CE

Kingdom of Kongo
1390–1914
Ruled by a "manikongo" (king) and divided into six regions. The Atlantic slave trade weakened the empire, and eventually the Portuguese took control.

Ethiopian Empire
1137-1974
In around 1200, the ruling Zagew dynasty of this Christian empire carved churches straight into the rocky ground in the town of Lalibela.

Kingdom of Zimbabwe 1350 CE

Great Zimbabwe

Kingdom of Zimbabwe
1220–1450
Famous for its capital, Great Zimbabwe, where the elite lived in a stone enclosure. The rulers controlled gold mines and ivory and traded with the Middle East and China.

The Americas

Aztec Empire in 1519 CE

Huari Empire in 650 CE

Chimú culture in 1470 CE

Inca Empire in 1525 CE

Tihuanaco Empire in 700 CE

Eurasia and Africa

THE AZTECS SACRIFICED TENS OF THOUSANDS OF THEIR OWN

Mongol Empire in 1227 CE

Mongol Empire
1206–1368
Founded by Genghis Khan in 1206. Numerous violent conquests led to the largest continuous land empire in history.

Karakorum

Mongol horde helmet

AT ITS **PEAK**, THE **MONGOL EMPIRE** RULED OVER **100 MILLION** PEOPLE

Ming China in 1500 CE

Beijing

Ming China
1368–1644
Founded by Zhu Yuanzhang, the leader of an uprising that overthrew the Mongols. A socially stable era during which the Grand Canal and the Great Wall were rebuilt.

Mughal Empire in 1690 CE

Shahjahanabad (Old Delhi)

Mughal sword

Angkor

Khmer Empire in 900 CE

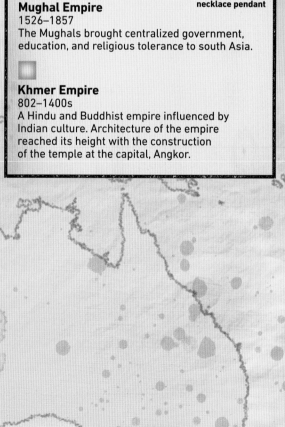

Holy Roman Empire
962–1806
One of the longest-lasting empires in history, this was a Christian state with no capital. In 1356 Frankfurt became the home of imperial elections.

Byzantine Empire
330–1453
Evolved from the Eastern Roman Empire. A Christian, Greek-speaking empire that preserved both Roman and Greek cultures.

Byzantine necklace pendant

Mughal Empire
1526–1857
The Mughals brought centralized government, education, and religious tolerance to south Asia.

Khmer Empire
802–1400s
A Hindu and Buddhist empire influenced by Indian culture. Architecture of the empire reached its height with the construction of the temple at the capital, Angkor.

Aztec Empire
1428–1521
From their capital built on artificial islands on a lake, the Aztecs, who called themselves Mexica, conquered most of modern-day Mexico.

Statue of Aztec god of death

Inca Empire
1438–1536
The largest empire of pre-Spanish Americas. Incas worshipped Inti, the Sun-god, and were skilled at building cities high up in the Andes mountains.

Songhai Empire
1375–1591
Rose up in the wake of the declining Mali Empire. The city of Timbuktu became a centre of Islamic learning.

Songhai coin

Chimú culture
c.850–1470
Skilled in pottery, textiles and metalwork. Territory covered coastal regions by the Andes mountains. Conquered by the rival Inca Empire in 1470.

Umayyad Caliphate
661–1031
The second of four great Muslim dynasties of the Arab caliphate, meaning "kingdom".

Kanem Empire
700–1387
One of the most powerful African empires. The main religion became Islam during the second dynasty under the rule of the Sayfawa.

Huari Empire
540–1100
The first of the New World powers to use large cities to run the empire and to live in, rather than just for religious ceremonies.

Huari wooden figure

Tihuanaco Empire
400–950
Began as a small town on the shores of Lake Titicaca on the border of Peru and Bolivia before rapidly expanding to the surrounding areas.

Ottoman Empire
1299–1922
Sometimes called the "Turkish Empire", a long-lasting Islamic state with the wealthy city of Constantinople (modern-day Istanbul) as its capital.

Castles

From castles and forts to walled cities, rulers and nations throughout history have tried to build impregnable structures to keep their enemies at bay and strengthen their grip on power.

KEY
Flags pinpoint some of the world's most impressive fortifications.

Selected castles, forts, citadels, and fortified cities

Fort Columbia, Washington, USA

Fort Union, New Mexico, USA

Castle of Santa Maria da Feira, Portugal

Castle of São Jorge, Portugal

Ribat of Monastir, Tunisia

Loropéni, Burkina Faso

Cape Coast Castle, Ghana

Elmina Castle, Ghana

Castillo San Felipe de Barajas, Colombia

Chan Chan ancient walled citadels, Peru

Fortifications of Valdivia, Chile

European castles

Most were fortified residences of nobles or monarchs; others were purely defensive.

Burghausen, Germany
Europe's longest castle complex, consisting of a main castle and inner courtyard protected by five outer courtyards.

Krak des Chevaliers, Syria This 12th-century crusader castle has an outer wall with 13 towers separated from the inner wall and keep by a moat.

Coastal prisons
These two castles on Ghana's coast have a dark history: they served as fortified links along the slave trade route during the 16th century.

Forts after the age of castles

Forts became vital military centres. Their low, thick, angled walls were able to deflect cannonballs.

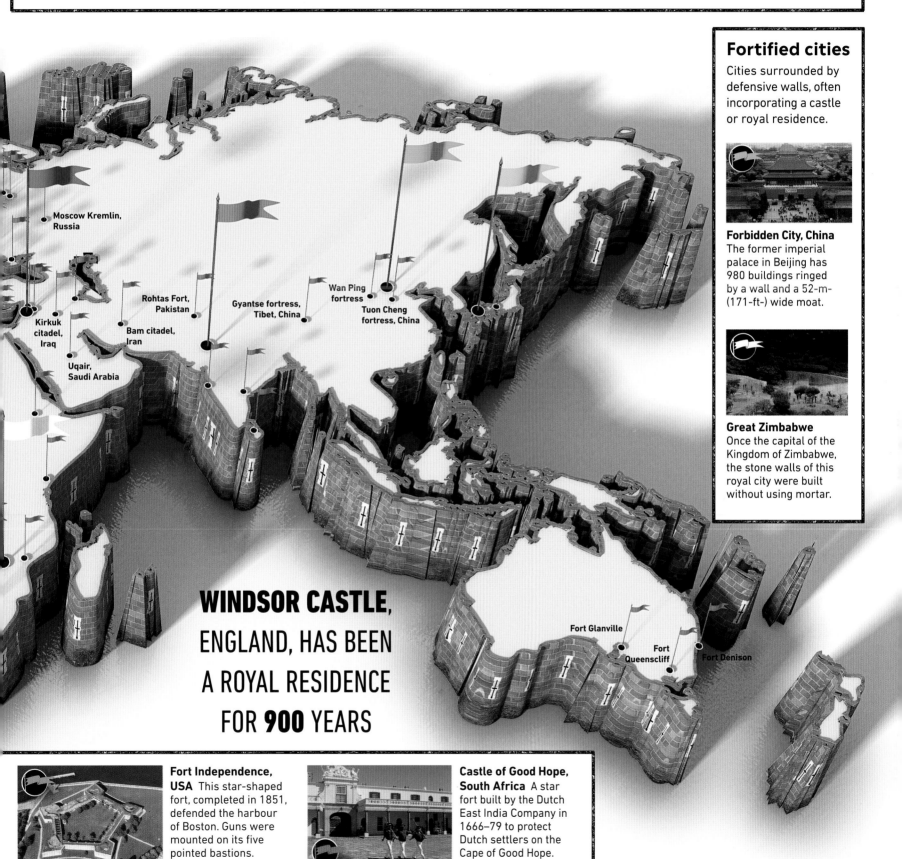

Asian castles

Castles in Asia reflect local building styles and look different to those in Europe, but they served the same purpose.

Himeji, Japan Built as a fort in 1333, Himeji was then rebuilt several times between the 14th and 17th centuries. It has 83 buildings protected by 26-m- (85-ft-) high walls and 3 moats, and is Japan's largest castle.

Mehrangarh Fort, India This fort, 122 m (400 ft) above the city of Jodhpur, hides several palaces within its walls. Built by the ruler Rao Jodha in 1459, it is entered through a series of seven gates.

Fortified cities

Cities surrounded by defensive walls, often incorporating a castle or royal residence.

Forbidden City, China The former imperial palace in Beijing has 980 buildings ringed by a wall and a 52-m- (171-ft-) wide moat.

Great Zimbabwe Once the capital of the Kingdom of Zimbabwe, the stone walls of this royal city were built without using mortar.

Moscow Kremlin, Russia

Kirkuk citadel, Iraq

Uqair, Saudi Arabia

Bam citadel, Iran

Rohtas Fort, Pakistan

Gyantse fortress, Tibet, China

Wan Ping fortress

Tuon Cheng fortress, China

Fort Glanville

Fort Queenscliff

Fort Denison

WINDSOR CASTLE, ENGLAND, HAS BEEN A ROYAL RESIDENCE FOR **900** YEARS

Fort Independence, USA This star-shaped fort, completed in 1851, defended the harbour of Boston. Guns were mounted on its five pointed bastions.

Castle of Good Hope, South Africa A star fort built by the Dutch East India Company in 1666–79 to protect Dutch settlers on the Cape of Good Hope.

PERIOD OF BATTLE

WWI and beyond
1914–

Modern revolutionary
1780–1914

Early modern
1500–1780

Medieval
500–1500

Ancient
Before 500 CE

Yorktown, 1781
French-American victory over the British led to independence for the USA.

Waterloo, 1815
Napoleon defeated by a coalition of European nations, marking an end to his domination of Europe.

Vienna, 1683
Holy Roman Empire's defeat of the Ottoman Empire halted the spread of Islam in Europe.

Antietam, 1862
Bloodiest single-day battle in American history, with 23,000 casualties.

Spanish Armada, 1588
English defeat of a vast Spanish fleet, causing the loss of 63 ships.

The Little Bighorn, 1876
Victory for the Lakota, Northern Cheyenne, and Arapaho peoples over the US Army led by General Custer.

Battle of France, 1940
German invasion and occupation of France during World War II.

The Alamo, 1836
Texan revolutionaries inflicted heavy losses on Mexican forces storming the Alamo Fort. Mexico won, but Texas gained independence the next year.

Algiers, 1957
Campaign of guerrilla warfare against French–Algerian authorities.

Gettysburg, 1863
Turning point of the US Civil War. Paved the way for a Union victory over the Confederate states.

Alcazar Quivir, 1578
Morocco and Ottoman Empire defeated the Portuguese Empire. Almost all Portuguese killed or imprisoned.

Military milestones

Changes in weapon technology have affected how battles are fought. As weapons get deadlier, the two sides in a battle grow further and further apart, until today, they sometimes don't meet or glimpse each other at all.

Bay of Pigs, 1961
CIA-trained force of Cuban exiles tried to invade Cuba and overthrow Communist leader Fidel Castro.

Carabobo, 1821
Victory for Simón Bolívar's Patriots over the Royalists, who supported Spanish rule. Led to Venezuela's independence.

(1) **Battle of Crécy, 1346**
A key battle in the Hundred Years' War between England and France. New long-range bows made close hand-to-hand combat, and the chivalry that went with it, a thing of the past.

Kirina, 1235
Mandinka forces beat the Sosso king and created the Mali Empire over west Africa.

Cajamarca, 1532
Defeat of the Inca Empire by Spanish conquistadors led to Spanish rule for the next three centuries.

(2) **The Somme, 1916**
The British and French attacked the German Army during World War I in what was the world's first use of tanks in battle. It was also one of the bloodiest military operations ever.

(3) **Battle of Britain, 1940**
Between Britain and Germany during World War II, this was the first major campaign fought entirely in the air.

Riachuelo, Paraguay River, 1865
A naval battle far upriver. Defeat for Paraguay by Brazil (allied with Argentina and Uruguay) during the ruinous Paraguayan War (1864–70).

(4) **Battle of the Coral Sea, 1942**
For the first time, ships in this sea battle never once sighted or directly fired on one another.

THE **OTTOMAN TURKS** TOOK CONSTANTINOPLE IN 1453 USING **CANNON** FOR THE **FIRST TIME** IN A MAJOR BATTLE

AFTER THE BLOODY BATTLE OF KALINGA, INDIAN EMPEROR ASHOKA

Sieges

Not strictly a battle, a siege is a military blockade of a city or fortress. The aim is to conquer the city by waiting for those inside to surrender. Sometimes, the side laying siege attacks to speed things up.

1 **Siege of Carthage 149–146 BCE**
One of the longest sieges in history. The Romans surrounded Carthage (in modern Tunisia) and waited 3 years for its surrender, then enslaved the Carthaginian population.

2 **Capture of Jerusalem, 1099**
During the Crusader wars between Christians and Muslims, the Muslim defenders of Jerusalem lost control when the Christians built two enormous siege engines (towers on wheels) and scaled the walls.

Austerlitz, 1805
With smaller forces, the French Empire crushed Russia and Austria. One of Napoleon's greatest victories.

Badger Mouth, 1211
Mongol ruler Genghis Khan's victory over the Jin Dynasty of China. One of history's bloodiest battles.

Huai-Hai, 1948
Final major fight in Chinese Civil War that led to the Communist takeover of China.

Actium, 31 BCE
Rome declared war on Antony and Cleopatra of Egypt. The Roman victory led to the beginning of the Roman Empire.

Thermopylae, 480 BCE
Vastly outnumbered Greek forces held the Persian Emperor Xerxes at bay for a vital 3 days.

Battle of Inchon, 1950
A clear victory for the United Nations against North Korean forces in the Korean War.

Stalingrad, 1942–43
Long siege of this Soviet city caused immense suffering on both sides and led eventually to crippling defeat for Nazi Germany.

Iwo Jima, 1945
The USA captured this island as a way of possibly invading Japan. Over 21,000 Japanese died.

Fall of Constantinople, 1453
After a 4-month siege, Byzantine Empire fell to the invading Ottoman Empire.

Battle of Phillora, 1965
One of the largest tank battles of the Indo-Pakistani War. Decisive victory for Indian Army.

Wuhan, 1938
Soviet and revolutionary Chinese forces totalling 1,100,000 troops and 200 aircraft failed to stop Japan capturing the city.

Omdurman, 1898
Small British and Egyptian forces massacred a huge, but ill-equipped, Sudanese Army.

El Alamein, 1942
Major tank battle of World War II. British-led victory over Axis Powers (Italy and Germany).

Dien Bien Phu, 1954
Viet Minh communist revolutionaries besieged and defeated the French to end the First Indochina War. The next year began another 20 years of fighting in Vietnam.

Isandlwana, 1879
Crushing victory for the Zulu nation over the British, despite relying mainly on spears and cowhide shields.

Kalinga, 262–261 BCE
The Mauryan Empire under Ashoka the Great fought the republic of Kalinga. At least 100,000 Kalingans were killed.

Surabaya, 1945
Heaviest battle of the Indonesian Revolution against the British and Dutch. Celebrated as Heroes' Day in Indonesia.

Coral Sea, 1942
World War II naval battle between Japan and the USA and Australia. The battle was the first time aircraft carriers engaged each other.

Battlegrounds

At one time, armies met in formation on a single field of battle and fought for one to several days. By the 20th century, long-range weapons had changed warfare. Battlefields in places became theatres of war the size of countries.

The last
empires

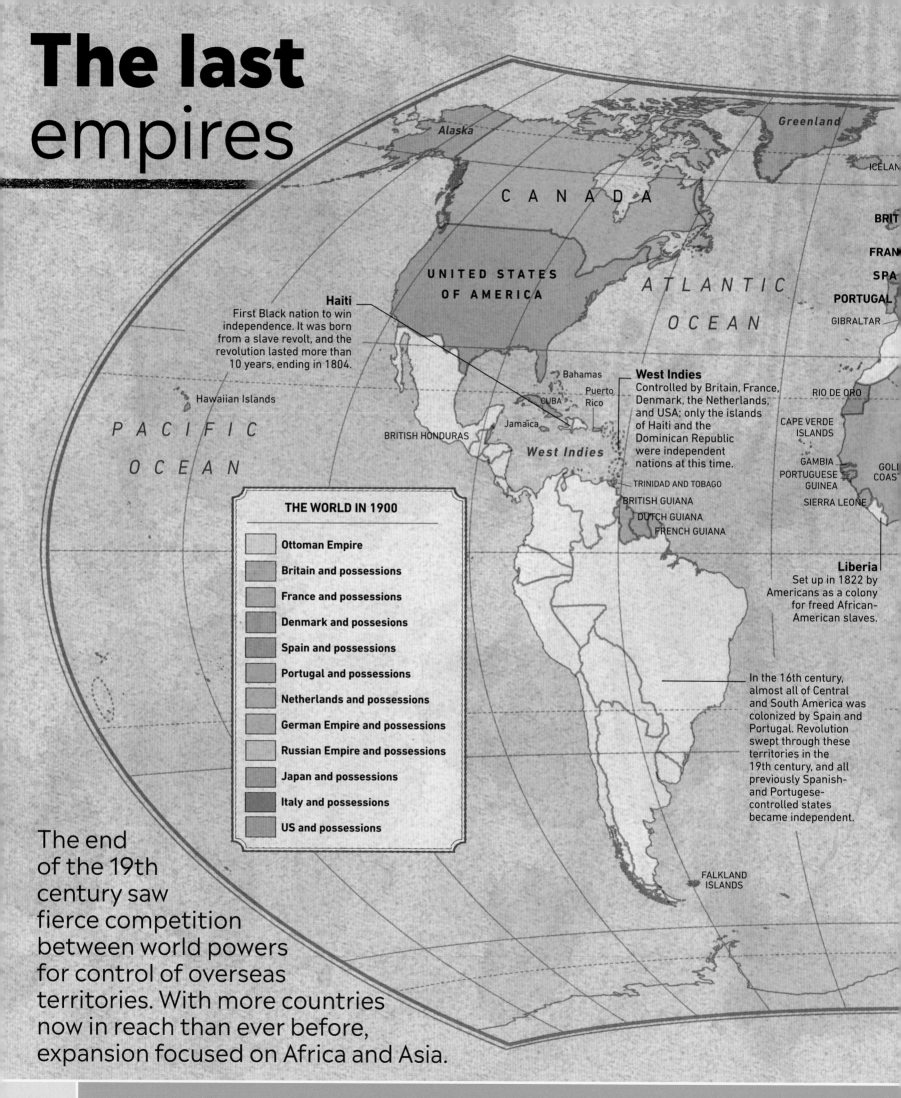

Alaska

Greenland

ICELAN

C A N A D A

BRIT

FRAN

SPA

UNITED STATES
OF AMERICA

ATLANTIC

OCEAN

PORTUGAL

GIBRALTAR

Haiti
First Black nation to win
independence. It was born
from a slave revolt, and the
revolution lasted more than
10 years, ending in 1804.

Bahamas

Puerto
Rico

CUBA

Jamaica

BRITISH HONDURAS

Hawaiian Islands

PACIFIC

OCEAN

West Indies

West Indies
Controlled by Britain, France,
Denmark, the Netherlands,
and USA; only the islands
of Haiti and the
Dominican Republic
were independent
nations at this time.

RIO DE ORO

CAPE VERDE
ISLANDS

GAMBIA
PORTUGUESE
GUINEA

GOL
COAS

SIERRA LEONE

TRINIDAD AND TOBAGO

BRITISH GUIANA

DUTCH GUIANA

FRENCH GUIANA

Liberia
Set up in 1822 by
Americans as a colony
for freed African-
American slaves.

THE WORLD IN 1900

- ☐ Ottoman Empire
- ☐ Britain and possessions
- ☐ France and possessions
- ☐ Denmark and possesions
- ☐ Spain and possessions
- ☐ Portugal and possessions
- ☐ Netherlands and possessions
- ☐ German Empire and possessions
- ☐ Russian Empire and possessions
- ☐ Japan and possessions
- ☐ Italy and possessions
- ☐ US and possessions

In the 16th century,
almost all of Central
and South America was
colonized by Spain and
Portugal. Revolution
swept through these
territories in the
19th century, and all
previously Spanish-
and Portugese-
controlled states
became independent.

FALKLAND
ISLANDS

The end
of the 19th
century saw
fierce competition
between world powers
for control of overseas
territories. With more countries
now in reach than ever before,
expansion focused on Africa and Asia.

AT ITS HEIGHT IN 1922, THE BRITISH EMPIRE CONTROLLED

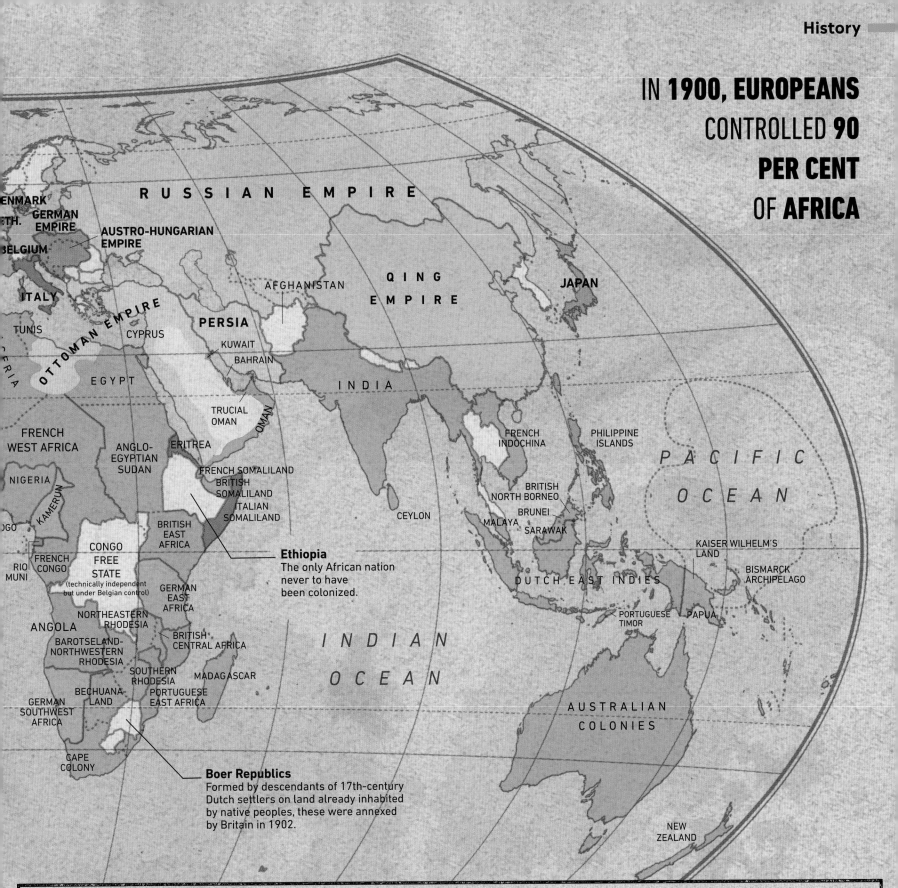

IN **1900**, EUROPEANS CONTROLLED **90** PER CENT OF **AFRICA**

DENMARK
NETH.
GERMAN EMPIRE
BELGIUM
AUSTRO-HUNGARIAN EMPIRE
ITALY
TUNIS
IBERIA
OTTOMAN EMPIRE
CYPRUS
EGYPT

RUSSIAN EMPIRE

AFGHANISTAN
PERSIA
KUWAIT
BAHRAIN

QING EMPIRE

JAPAN

INDIA

OMAN

TRUCIAL OMAN

FRENCH WEST AFRICA
ANGLO-EGYPTIAN SUDAN
NIGERIA
KAMERUN
OGO
FRENCH CONGO
RIO MUNI
CONGO FREE STATE
(technically independent but under Belgian control)
ANGOLA
BAROTSELAND-NORTHWESTERN RHODESIA
NORTHEASTERN RHODESIA
GERMAN EAST AFRICA
BRITISH CENTRAL AFRICA
SOUTHERN RHODESIA
GERMAN SOUTHWEST AFRICA
BECHUANA-LAND
MADAGASCAR
PORTUGUESE EAST AFRICA
CAPE COLONY

ERITREA
FRENCH SOMALILAND
BRITISH SOMALILAND
ITALIAN SOMALILAND
BRITISH EAST AFRICA

Ethiopia
The only African nation never to have been colonized.

CEYLON

FRENCH INDOCHINA

PHILIPPINE ISLANDS

BRITISH NORTH BORNEO
BRUNEI
MALAYA
SARAWAK

PACIFIC OCEAN

KAISER WILHELM'S LAND

BISMARCK ARCHIPELAGO

DUTCH EAST INDIES

PORTUGUESE TIMOR
PAPUA

INDIAN OCEAN

AUSTRALIAN COLONIES

NEW ZEALAND

Boer Republics
Formed by descendants of 17th-century Dutch settlers on land already inhabited by native peoples, these were annexed by Britain in 1902.

Scramble for Africa

The Atlantic slave trade, in which Africans were forcibly sold to people in the Americas, ended in the mid-19th century. European powers colonised Africa for economic, political, and religious reasons, scrambling to claim territory before their rivals.

- **1871:** Germany and Italy are both unified. No more territory available for expansion of empires in Europe.
- **1884–85:** Berlin Conference, where European powers decide rules on carving up Africa.
- **1900:** Only a handful of regions are still independent states. Britain rules 30 per cent of Africa's population.

The Great Game

In the 1830s, Britain feared Russia was planning on invading British-ruled India through controlling India's neighbour, Afghanistan. The "Great Game" was the rivalry for power in Asia between the British and Russian empires.

- **1839–42:** First Anglo-Afghan War. Terrible defeat at Kabul for the British.
- **1878–80:** Second Anglo-Afghan War. Russia is defeated and Britain withdraws but takes control of Afghanistan's foreign affairs.
- **1907:** Russia and Britain sign a peace treaty in the face of the German threat of expansion in the Middle East.

AT LEAST 1 MILLION PEOPLE DIED IN THE 1910 MEXICAN REVOLUTION

Collapse of Communist bloc
1989: East Germany, Poland, Slovakia, Hungary, Romania, Czech Republic, Slovenia, Croatia, Bosnia-Herzegovina, Montenegro, Kosovo, Albania, FYR Macedonia, Serbia, and Bulgaria

Norway
1905 (from Sweden)

Iceland
1944 (from Denmark)

England
1642–51

Ireland
1922 (from Britain)

Belgium
1830–31 (from Netherlands)

France
1789–99

Spain
1936–39

Portugal
1974

Tunisia
2011

Algeria
1954–62 (from France)

Thirteen colonies of North America
1776 (from Britain)

Cuba
1953–59

Mexico
1910–20

Haiti
1791–1804 (from France)

Ghana
1957 (from Britain)

Nicaragua
1979–90

Venezuela
1823 (from Spain)
1830 (from Gran Colombia)

Panama
1903 (from Colombia)

Equador
1822 (from Spain) and 1830 (from Gran Colombia)

Colombia
1819 (from Spain)

Peru
1824 (from Spain)

Angola
1961–75 (from Portugal)

Bolivia
1825 (from Spain)

Namibia
1968–88 (from South Africa)

Famous revolutionaries

Revolutionary leaders are driven by passionate ideals. They inspire people to rise up against governments. Such people are key in organizing effective group action against the authorities.

1 Che Guevara, 1928–67
Argentinian-born idealist – helped Fidel Castro overthrow Cuban dictator Fulgencio Batista. Now a global symbol of rebellion.

2 Kwame Nkrumah, 1909–72
Oversaw Ghana's independence from Britain. Ghana was the first in a wave of sub-Saharan African nations to break free of colonial rule.

3 Simón Bolivar, 1783–1830
Venezuelan politician and general who led Venezuela, Colombia, Ecuador, Peru, and Bolivia to independence. One of South America's most influential leaders.

4 Vladimir Lenin, 1870–1924
After being exiled to Siberia, Lenin returned to Russia to support and then lead the 1917 revolution.

5 Mao Zedong, 1893–1976
Founder of the People's Republic of China. Ruthless in bringing about modernization with the "Great Leap Forward" and enforced Communism with the "Cultural Revolution".

6 Mahatma Gandhi, 1869–1948
Devoted his life to bringing peace to India. Has inspired nonviolence and civil rights movements worldwide.

Revolutions and uprisings

Powerful nations that overpower other countries are often met with resistance from the people they conquer. In some cases, this can lead to revolutions. Sometimes a country's own government becomes so unpopular that a revolution occurs.

Internal uprising
Countries that have had internal revolutions

Uprising against an outside power
Countries achieving independence from a foreign ruling power through revolution

Countries with no involvement in the revolutions listed on these pages

Revolutions

People all over the world have risen up against oppressive rulers. Revolutions can be sudden or lengthy, bloody or peaceful, but have one thing in common: they are all an attempt to change the way a country is ruled.

Lithuania
1989 (from USSR)

Finland
1917 (from Russia)

Estonia
1989 (from USSR)

Latvia
1989 (from USSR)

Belarus
1989 (from USSR)

Ukraine
1989 (from USSR)

Moldova
1989 (from USSR)

Georgia
1989 (from USSR)

Armenia
1989 (from USSR)

Greece
1821–32 (from Ottoman Empire)

Libya
2011

Egypt
2011

Syria
From 2011

Eritrea
1961–91 (from Ethiopia)

South Sudan
2011 (from Sudan)

Democratic Republic of the Congo
1997

Rwanda
1961 (from Belgium)

South Africa
1994

Madagascar
1960 (from France)

Kenya (Mau Mau)
1952–60 (from Britain)

Somalia
1986–92

Yemen
2011

Iraq
2014–17

Iran
1979

Azerbaijan
1989 (from USSR)

Afghanistan
1996

Turkmenistan
1989 (from USSR)

Uzbekistan
1989 (from USSR)

Kazakhastan
1989 (from USSR)

Kyrgyzstan
1989 (from USSR)

Tajikistan
1989 (from USSR)

Russia
1917

4

5

India
1947 (from Britain)

6

Singapore
1965 (from Malaysia)

Indonesia
1945–49 (from the Netherlands)

Korea
1945 (from Japan)

Vietnam
1975 (Socialist Republic of Vietnam created after war between North and South Vietnam)

China
1949

Myanmar (Burma)
1962

Laos
1975 (from USSR)

Philippines
1896–98 (from Spain)

Cambodia
1979 (Khmer Rouge)

Papua New Guinea
1975 (from Australia)

East Timor
1975 (from Portugal) and 2002 (from Indonesia)

Collapse of Communism

The USSR was a Communist state that incorporated Russia and 14 other Soviet republics (some of the red areas on the map). The USSR also had great influence over several other European states that collectively were known as the "Communist bloc" (some of the yellow map areas). In 1989, revolution spread through all these states, and in 1991 the USSR was dissolved.

▼ **Fall of communism**
Indicates countries in which Communism collapsed in 1989–91

Arab Spring

The "Arab Spring" revolutions and protests swept through the Arab world in 2011. As the map shows, in some countries rulers were forced out, while in others there were failed uprisings. The Arab Spring was the first uprising where protestors used social media to coordinate their actions. Not all of the movements were successful, however; the uprising in Tunisia led to a number of improvements, but many of the other countries are still marked by unrest.

Arab Spring
Indicates countries involved in the Arab Spring

STRICKEN EUROPE AND INSPIRED THE 1789–99 FRENCH REVOLUTION.

Scapa Flow (1919)
After World War I, the German navy sank 52 of its own ships here, rather than surrender them to Britain.

SS Islander (1901)
Its cargo of gold, which some estimate is worth up to £500 million today, has never been found.

SS Sultana (1865)
This river steamer exploded in the Mississippi River with the loss of around 1,700 lives.

Medusa (1816)
When the Medusa sank, 147 crewmen built a life raft, but only 15 survived to be rescued.

HMS Agamemnon (1809)
A former command of Admiral Nelson, she struck an uncharted group of rocks in a bay off Uruguay.

Shipwrecks

The beds and shores of the world's seas, lakes, and rivers are littered with shipwrecks. Some are famous either for the huge loss of life they caused or the enormous value of their cargo.

Natural shipwrecks

Sailors battle constantly against the phenomenal forces of nature, and one of the most common causes of shipwrecks is bad weather. Storms and hurricanes batter ships and blow them off course, and fog, rain, or snow reduce visibility. Ice is another big risk. An iceberg can inflict fatal damage to a ship if it collides with one; while ice that builds up on the body of a ship can also cause it to become unstable and capsize.

Notorious wrecks

1 RMS *Titanic*
On 14 April 1912, this ship struck an iceberg and sank two hours and forty minutes later.
Death toll: 1,517

2 USS *Arizona*
Sunk in the opening minutes of the Japanese attack on the US Navy at Pearl Harbor in 1942.
Death toll: 1,177

3 RMS *Lusitania*
British liner sunk by a World War I German submarine in 1915.
Death toll: 1,200

4 *Bismarck*
German battleship, lost after battling the British Royal Navy in May 1941.
Death toll: 2,085

5 *Nuestra Señora de Atocha*
Spanish galleon, laden with treasure, caught in a hurricane in 1622.
Death toll: 260

6 *Wilhelm Gustloff*
German passenger ship torpedoed by a Russian submarine in 1945.
Death toll: approx. 9,100

7 HMS *Sussex*
Royal Navy ship lost in a storm off Gibraltar in 1694, carrying over 10 tonnes of gold coins.
Death toll: 500

8 MV *Doña Paz*
Passenger ferry that collided with an oil tanker off the Philippines in 1987.
Death toll: 4,375

9 HMS *Birkenhead*
British ship that sank after striking rocks at Danger Point in 1852.
Death toll: 460

10 *Batavia*
Dutch ship that sank off Australia in 1629, on its maiden voyage.
Death toll: wreck 40; later mutiny 233

Battle of Midway (1942)
US ships *Yorktown* and *Hammann* were lost here, along with four Japanese aircraft carriers and a cruiser, in one of World War II's fiercest naval battles.

Eduard Bohlen **(1909)**
Ran aground in fog and now lies 400 m (1,300 ft) inland, half-buried in huge sand dunes.

HMS *Pandora* (1791)
Sank while on a mission to find the HMS *Bounty* and her mutinous crew.

Man-made shipwrecks

Humans can be responsible for shipwrecks in many different ways. War is one of the main causes – missiles, mines, air attacks, and sabotage have all been used to destroy ships. Other factors can be bad design, shoddy construction, or poor maintenance and repairs; navigation errors that cause a ship to run aground or hit other traffic; and overloading cargo so that the vessel tips over.

Golden Gate Bridge
San Francisco, California, USA, 1937. World-famous steel bridge and longest suspension bridge in the world when built.

Boeing Everett Factory
Everett, Washington, USA, 1968. Aircraft assembly building and the largest building in the world.

Great Belt Fixed Link
Denmark, 1997. Connects islands of Zealand and Funen. Comprises two bridges and a railway tunnel.

Bell Rock Lighthouse
Inchcape, Scotland, 1810. Oldest surviving lighthouse at sea.

The Langeled Pipeline
2006. Undersea pipeline pumping Norwegian natural gas to Britain.

Hibbing Taconite Company Mine
Hibbing, Minnesota, USA, 1895. One of the world's largest iron ore mines.

London Sewage System
Late 19th century. Declared an engineering triumph for successfully diverting raw sewage away from the Thames.

Lockheed SR-71 Blackbird
Beale, California, USA, 1964. Fastest manned jet aircraft.

Channel Tunnel
Folkestone, UK – Calais, France, 1994. International undersea rail tunnel.

Guggenheim Museum
New York, USA, 1959. Architectural and design feat.

Graf Zeppelin

Guggenheim Museum
Bilbao, Spain, 1997. Important work of modern architecture.

Hoover Dam
Nevada/Arizona, USA, 1936. Largest concrete structure ever built at the time of construction.

Sagrada Familia
Barcelona, Spain, 1882–current. Huge church designed by Antoni Gaudí, considered a masterpiece, and still under construction.

WM Keck Observatory
Mauna Kea, Hawaii, USA, 1993 and 1996. Second-largest optical telescopes on Earth.

Concorde

Very Large Array
Socorro, New Mexico, USA, 1973–80. Astronomical observatory made up of 27 radio antennas arranged in a Y-shape.

Panama Canal
1914. 77 km (48 miles) long. Among the most difficult engineering projects in history.

Large Hadron Collider
Geneva, Switzerland, 1998–2008. Giant scientific instrument for testing particles.

Industrial wonders

The Industrial Revolution of the 18th and 19th centuries saw remarkable advances in technology and materials. This led to extraordinary design and engineering feats, the likes of which had never been seen before.

Itaipu Dam
Brazil/Paraguay, 1984. The second-largest dam in the world.

San Alfonso del Mar swimming pool
Algarrobo, Chile, 2006. 1 km (0.6 mile) long and 35 m (115 ft) deep. Second-largest swimming pool in the world.

Industrial pioneers

1 First transatlantic cable, Canada–Ireland, 1858
Cable that transported messages from one end to the other. The first of its kind to be laid across the Atlantic, meaning messages could be received in a matter of minutes.

2 Transcontinental Railroad, California–Nebraska, USA, 1869
Connected the east coast railways of the USA with the Pacific coast for the first time. Considered to be one of the greatest technological feats of the 19th century.

3 Home Insurance Building, Chicago, Illinois, USA, 1885
First ever steel-framed building, and first tall building to be supported by a fireproof metal frame. Although not very tall, the technology used made it the first "skyscraper".

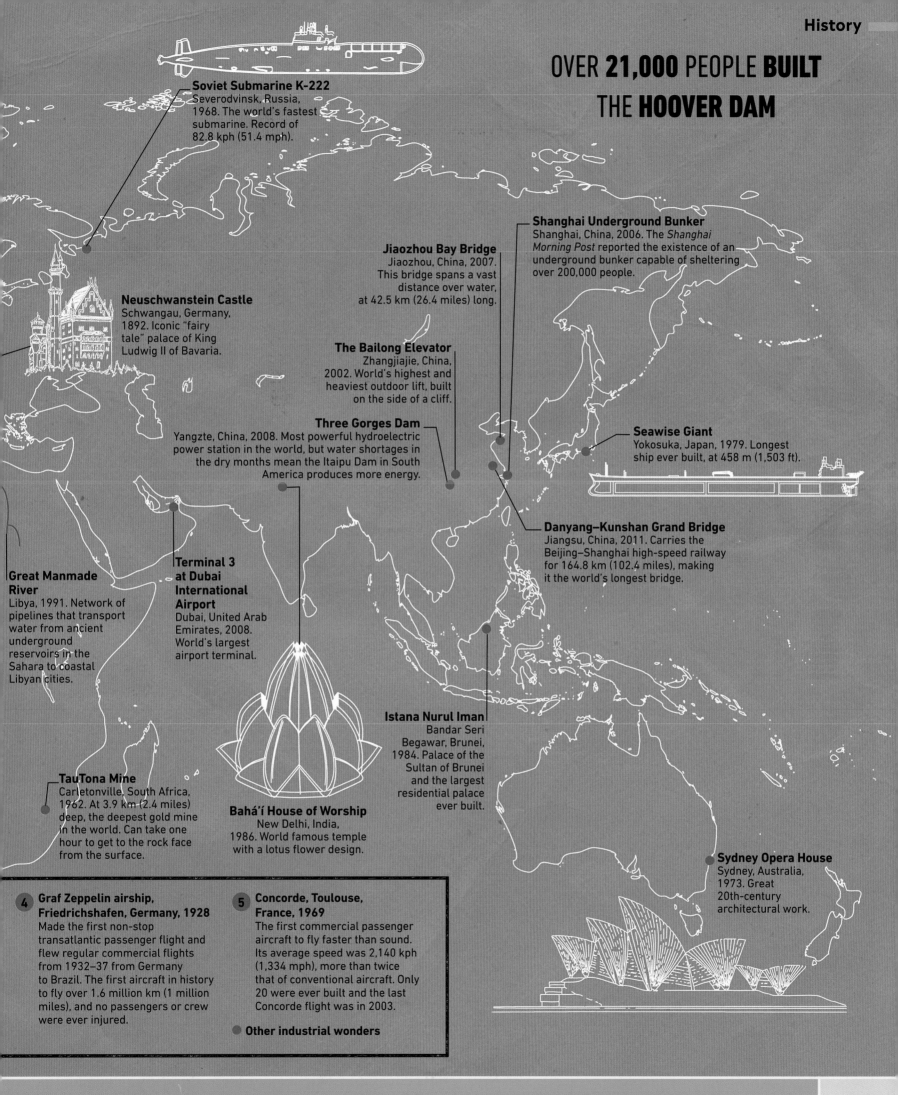

OVER **21,000** PEOPLE **BUILT** THE **HOOVER DAM**

Soviet Submarine K-222
Severodvinsk, Russia, 1968. The world's fastest submarine. Record of 82.8 kph (51.4 mph).

Neuschwanstein Castle
Schwangau, Germany, 1892. Iconic "fairy tale" palace of King Ludwig II of Bavaria.

Great Manmade River
Libya, 1991. Network of pipelines that transport water from ancient underground reservoirs in the Sahara to coastal Libyan cities.

Terminal 3 at Dubai International Airport
Dubai, United Arab Emirates, 2008. World's largest airport terminal.

TauTona Mine
Carletonville, South Africa, 1962. At 3.9 km (2.4 miles) deep, the deepest gold mine in the world. Can take one hour to get to the rock face from the surface.

Bahá'í House of Worship
New Delhi, India, 1986. World famous temple with a lotus flower design.

Jiaozhou Bay Bridge
Jiaozhou, China, 2007. This bridge spans a vast distance over water, at 42.5 km (26.4 miles) long.

The Bailong Elevator
Zhangjiajie, China, 2002. World's highest and heaviest outdoor lift, built on the side of a cliff.

Three Gorges Dam
Yangzte, China, 2008. Most powerful hydroelectric power station in the world, but water shortages in the dry months mean the Itaipu Dam in South America produces more energy.

Shanghai Underground Bunker
Shanghai, China, 2006. The *Shanghai Morning Post* reported the existence of an underground bunker capable of sheltering over 200,000 people.

Seawise Giant
Yokosuka, Japan, 1979. Longest ship ever built, at 458 m (1,503 ft).

Danyang–Kunshan Grand Bridge
Jiangsu, China, 2011. Carries the Beijing–Shanghai high-speed railway for 164.8 km (102.4 miles), making it the world's longest bridge.

Istana Nurul Iman
Bandar Seri Begawan, Brunei, 1984. Palace of the Sultan of Brunei and the largest residential palace ever built.

Sydney Opera House
Sydney, Australia, 1973. Great 20th-century architectural work.

4 **Graf Zeppelin airship, Friedrichshafen, Germany, 1928**
Made the first non-stop transatlantic passenger flight and flew regular commercial flights from 1932–37 from Germany to Brazil. The first aircraft in history to fly over 1.6 million km (1 million miles), and no passengers or crew were ever injured.

5 **Concorde, Toulouse, France, 1969**
The first commercial passenger aircraft to fly faster than sound. Its average speed was 2,140 kph (1,334 mph), more than twice that of conventional aircraft. Only 20 were ever built and the last Concorde flight was in 2003.

● **Other industrial wonders**

Culture

Holi Festival, Jodhpur, India
During the Hindu spring festival of Holi – known as the Festival of Colours – people throw pigments and coloured water over each other.

Introduction

The word "culture" is a broad idea, and includes the values, beliefs, and behaviour of a society, or group of people. Culture includes many things, including customs, language, religion, music, art, food, and clothing. Some points of culture are traditional, having survived virtually unchanged for centuries. Others are short-lived, such as fashion styles and trends in pop music.

Modern culture

Today's culture is fast moving and ever-changing, thanks in part to the instant communication offered by the Internet. But long before the Internet, the migration of people around the world began introducing people to cultures different from their own. Global broadcasting then accelerated this effect in the 20th century. The cultural contact often creates a fusion (uniting) of different cultural styles, especially in the fields of music, fashion, and cooking.

Live performances
Huge crowds watch singers, such as Beyoncé (right), perform live, just as they have always done. But today the "live" audience can number many millions, with most following remotely via Internet-based platforms like YouTube or Spotify.

Stadium spectators
For many sports fans, being part of a passionate, noisy, banner-waving stadium crowd makes them feel an important part of the event.

Headdress, called a *kiritam*, varies in size and design, according to the character being portrayed.

Hand gestures (known as *mudra*) are the dancer's main way of telling the story.

Noble-hearted characters always have green faces; dark red signifies a treacherous nature.

Kathakali dancer
Indian kathakali dancers enact stories from two epic poems, the *Ramayana* and the *Mahabarata*. Dealing with the constant struggle between good and evil, dances end with the destruction of a demon.

Heroes always wear red jackets

Dancer's skirt is made up of many layers of white cotton.

DRAGON DANCES ARE TRADITIONAL PERFORMANCES IN CHINESE

Hours per week

Experts say that watching over 2 hours of TV per day (14 hours per week) can be bad for your health, yet in many countries, people watch twice that.

United States	Poland	Japan	Brazil	Russia	Italy	Spain	France	Germany	United Kingdom
31.5	30.8	30.5	29.6	28.9	28.9	27.2	26	26	24.7

HOURS PER PERSON PER WEEK

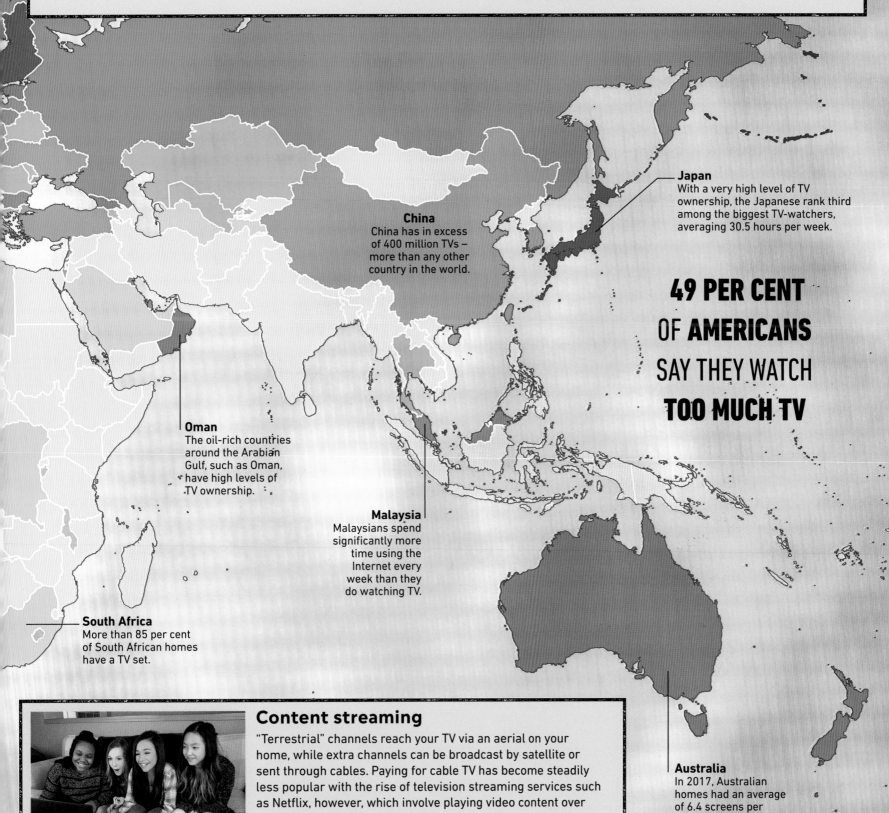

Japan
With a very high level of TV ownership, the Japanese rank third among the biggest TV-watchers, averaging 30.5 hours per week.

China
China has in excess of 400 million TVs – more than any other country in the world.

49 PER CENT OF AMERICANS SAY THEY WATCH TOO MUCH TV

Oman
The oil-rich countries around the Arabian Gulf, such as Oman, have high levels of TV ownership.

Malaysia
Malaysians spend significantly more time using the Internet every week than they do watching TV.

South Africa
More than 85 per cent of South African homes have a TV set.

Australia
In 2017, Australian homes had an average of 6.4 screens per household.

Content streaming

"Terrestrial" channels reach your TV via an aerial on your home, while extra channels can be broadcast by satellite or sent through cables. Paying for cable TV has become steadily less popular with the rise of television streaming services such as Netflix, however, which involve playing video content over an Internet connection. Since the content isn't live, viewers can choose exactly what they want to watch, and when. In 2020, the streaming subscription market grew by a massive 37 per cent.

REGULARLY WATCH TELEVISION WHILE EATING DINNER.

Americas

1 **Los Angeles Memorial Coliseum**
California, USA. Capacity 93,607; opened 1921

2 **Rose Bowl**
Pasadena, California, USA. Capacity 92,542; opened 1922

3 **Dodgers Stadium**
California, USA. Capacity 56,000; opened 1962

4 **Estadio Monumental "U"**
Lima, Peru. Capacity 80,093; opened 2000

5 **Bell Centre**
Montreal, Canada. Capacity 21,273; opened 1996

6 **Beaver Stadium**
Pennsylvania, USA. Capacity 106,572; opened 1960

7 **Madison Square Garden**
New York, USA. Capacity 22,292; opened 1968

8 **Arthur Ashe Stadium**
New York, USA. Capacity 23,200; opened 1997

9 **Ohio Stadium**
Ohio, USA. Capacity 102,329; opened 1922

10 **Neyland Stadium**
Tennessee, USA. Capacity 102,455; opened 1921

11 **Sanford Stadium**
Georgia, USA. Capacity 92,746; opened 1929

12 **Bryant–Denny Stadium**
Alabama, USA. Capacity 101,821; opened 1929

13 **Tiger Stadium**
Louisiana, USA. Capacity 92,542; opened 1924

14 **Darrell K. Royal – Texas Memorial Stadium** Texas, USA. Capacity 100,119; opened 1924

Michigan Stadium
Ann Arbor, Michigan, USA. Capacity 114,804; opened 1926. Nicknamed "The Big House", this is the largest stadium in the USA. It is home to the Michigan Wolverines American football team.

Camp Nou
Barcelona, Spain. Capacity 99,354; opened 1957. The biggest stadium in Europe and the world's 12th largest.

KEY
The colours show capacity (numbers of spectators).

- 110,000 and above
- 100,000–109,999
- 90,000–99,999
- 80,000–89,999
- Fewer than 80,000

Estádio Azteca
Mexico City, Mexico. Capacity 87,523; opened 1961. This huge soccer stadium is the official home of the Mexican national team. The Azteca and the Estádio Maracanã are the only stadiums in the world to have hosted two FIFA World Cup soccer finals.

Estádio do Maracanã
Rio de Janeiro, Brazil. Capacity 82,238; opened 1950. Built for the 1950 football FIFA World Cup, the Maracanã was the world's biggest stadium at the time, with room for nearly 200,000 people. Capacity was greatly reduced in the 1990s after part of the stadium collapsed. It served as the venue for the opening and closing ceremonies of the 2016 Summer Olympics and Paralympics.

Stadiums

Stadiums and arenas are among the largest and most impressive buildings on the planet. They not only enable us to experience the thrills and drama of competition between the best sports players, teams, and athletes, but also host pop concerts and other shows.

Europe

15 **Millennium Stadium**
Cardiff, UK. Capacity 74,500; opened 1999

16 **Wembley Stadium**
London, UK. Capacity 90,000; opened 2007

17 **Allianz Arena**
Munich, Germany. Capacity 69,901; opened 2005

18 **Estádio Santiago Bernabéu**
Madrid, Spain. Capacity 85,454; opened 1947

THE LARGEST EVER "MEXICAN WAVE" INVOLVED 157,574 PEOPLE AT

THE RECORD FOR THE LOUDEST CROWD ROAR OF
142.2 DECIBELS WAS SET AT ARROWHEAD STADIUM, KANSAS CITY, USA, DURING AN AMERICAN FOOTBALL GAME IN 2014

Rungrado May Day Stadium
Pyongyang, North Korea.
Capacity 150,000; built 1989.
Said to look like a magnolia
blossom, the stadium is used
for sport and military parades.

Record crowd sizes

Crowds were even larger before the
modern safety-conscious era, and
standing and overcrowding were
common. The largest-ever crowds
at sports events are below.

Football: 199,854. Maracanã Stadium,
Brazil. Brazil vs Uruguay,
World Cup Final, July 1950.

Wrestling: 190,000. May Day Stadium,
North Korea. Pro-Wrestling event,
April 1995.

Football: 149,415 (plus 20,000
without tickets). Hampden Park, Scotland.
Scotland vs England, 1937.

Football: 135,000. Estádio da Luz,
Portugal. Benfica vs Porto,
January 1987.

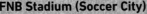

FNB Stadium (Soccer City)
Johannesburg, South Africa.
Capacity 94,736; opened 1989.
Nicknamed "The Calabash" because it looks
like the African pot of the same name, the FNB
is the largest stadium in Africa. The stadium
played host to the 2010 FIFA World Cup.

Melbourne Cricket Ground
Victoria, Australia.
Capacity 100,018; opened 1854.
This stadium holds the record
for the highest floodlight towers
of any sporting venue. It is
known to locals as "The G".

Asia

19 Azadi Stadium
Tehran, Iran. Capacity
100,000; opened 1971

20 Salt Lake Stadium
Kolkata, India. Capacity
120,000; built 1984

**21 Lumpinee
Boxing Stadium**
Bangkok, Thailand. Capacity
9,500; opened 1956

**22 Beijing National
Stadium ("Bird's Nest")**
China. Capacity: 80,000;
opened 2008

**23 Gwangmyeong
Velodrome**
South Korea.
Capacity 30,000;
opened 2006

Michigan International Speedway
Brooklyn, Michigan, USA

Chicagoland Speedway
Joliet, Illinois, USA

Indianapolis Motor Speedway
Speedway, Indiana, USA

Iowa Speedway
Newton, Iowa, USA

Bristol Motor Speedway
Bristol, Tennessee, USA

Kansas Speedway
Kansas City, Kansas, USA

Las Vegas Speedway
Las Vegas, Nevada, USA

Auto Club Speedway
Fontana, California, USA

Kentucky Speedway
Sparta, Kentucky, USA

Circuit of the Americas
Austin, Texas, USA

Atlanta Motor Speedway
Hampton, Georgia, USA

Autódromo Hermanos Rodríguez Mexico City,

Circuit Gilles Villeneuve Montreal, Québec, Canada

Dover International Speedway
Dover, Delaware, USA

Charlotte Motor Speedway
Concord, North Carolina

Darlington Raceway
Darlington, South Carolina, USA

Daytona International Speedway
Daytona Beach, Florida, USA

Homestead–Miami Speedway
Homestead, Florida, USA

Autódromo José Carlos Pace
São Paulo, Brazil

Red Bull Ring
Spielberg bei Knittelfeld, Austria

Circuit Zandvoort
Zandvoort, Netherlands

Circuit de Spa-Francorchamps
Spa, Belgium

Silverstone Circuit
Silverstone, UK

Circuit de la Sarthe
Le Mans, France

Circuit Paul Ricard
Le Castellet, France

Algarve International Circuit
Portimão, Portugal

Circuit de Catalunya
Montmeló, Spain

Circuit de Monaco
Monte Carlo, Monaco

Autodromo Nazionale Monza
Monza, Italy

Autodromo Internazionale Enzo e Dino Ferrari
Imola, Italy

Great champions

F1 is the pinnacle of "open-wheel" racing and the winner each season is called the world champion. NASCAR remains the top stock-car competition.

Dale Earnhardt Snr. Nationality: US
Killed while racing at Daytona in 2001, Earnhardt had already won seven NASCAR titles.

Motor racing

With engines roaring, race cars provide a thrilling spectator sport as they hurtle down the track, weave through chicanes, and hug hairpin bends. The highly tuned Formula 1 cars draw big crowds in many countries. In the United States, stock-car racing is more popular.

NASCAR Sprint Cup

The Sprint Cup Series is the world's premier stock-car racing competition. It involves 36 races over 10 months. As in F1, points awarded throughout the series decide the winner.

Michael Schumacher
Nationality: German
Seven-time F1 World Champion with 91 Grand Prix wins. He suffered a severe skiing accident in 2013 and has been receiving treatment ever since.

Ayrton Senna
Nationality: Brazilian
Three-time F1 World Champion. Fifth-most-successful driver of all time in terms of F1 race wins (41). Died in an accident at the 1994 San Marino Grand Prix.

Lewis Hamilton
Nationality: British
Jointly tied with Shumacher for the most World Championship titles, and holds the record outright for the most ever F1 wins.

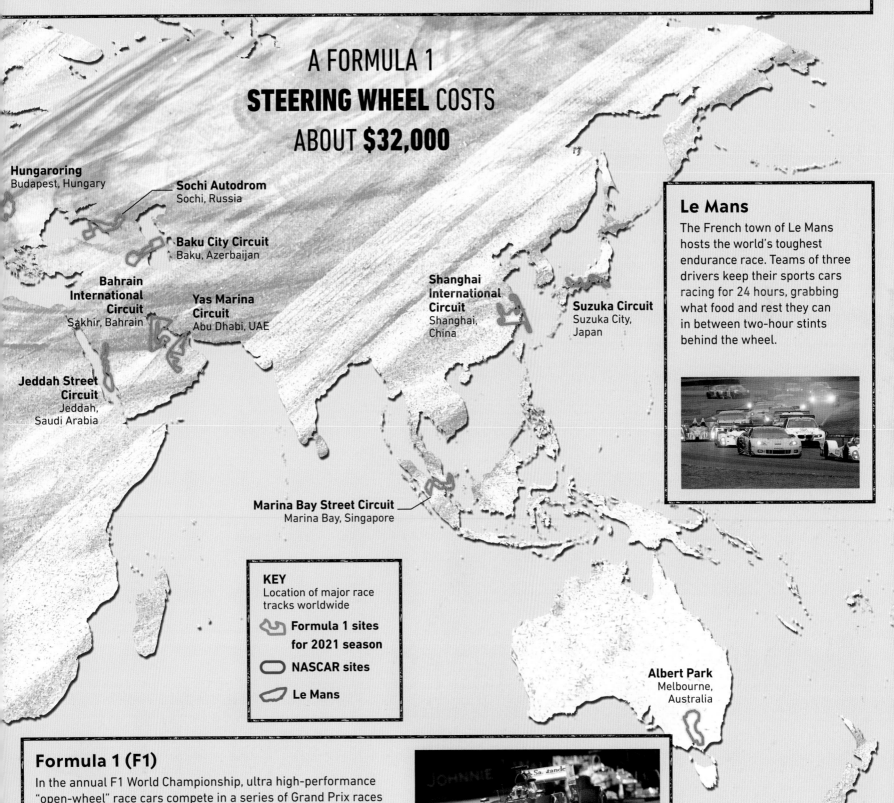

A FORMULA 1
STEERING WHEEL COSTS
ABOUT $32,000

Hungaroring
Budapest, Hungary

Sochi Autodrom
Sochi, Russia

Baku City Circuit
Baku, Azerbaijan

Bahrain International Circuit
Sakhir, Bahrain

Yas Marina Circuit
Abu Dhabi, UAE

Shanghai International Circuit
Shanghai, China

Suzuka Circuit
Suzuka City, Japan

Jeddah Street Circuit
Jeddah, Saudi Arabia

Le Mans

The French town of Le Mans hosts the world's toughest endurance race. Teams of three drivers keep their sports cars racing for 24 hours, grabbing what food and rest they can in between two-hour stints behind the wheel.

Marina Bay Street Circuit
Marina Bay, Singapore

KEY
Location of major race tracks worldwide

⌁ **Formula 1 sites for 2021 season**

◯ **NASCAR sites**

⬠ **Le Mans**

Albert Park
Melbourne, Australia

Formula 1 (F1)

In the annual F1 World Championship, ultra high-performance "open-wheel" race cars compete in a series of Grand Prix races worldwide. Cars finishing in the top-10 positions in each race win points. At the season's end, trophies are awarded for the driver and manufacturer with the most points.

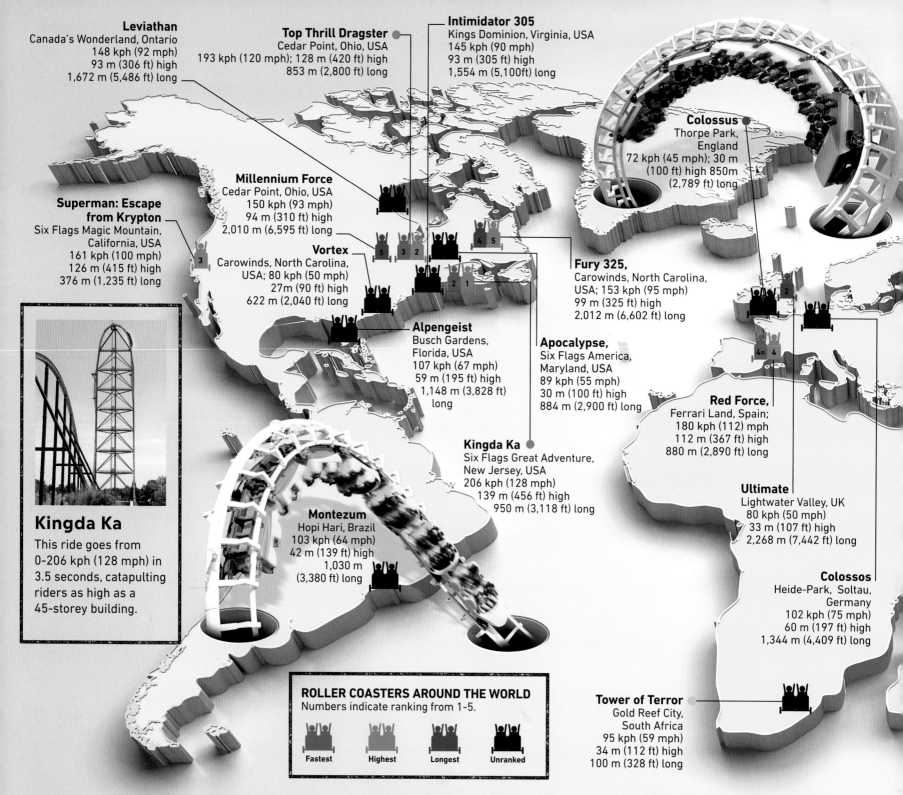

Leviathan
Canada's Wonderland, Ontario
148 kph (92 mph)
93 m (306 ft) high
1,672 m (5,486 ft) long

Top Thrill Dragster
Cedar Point, Ohio, USA
193 kph (120 mph); 128 m (420 ft) high
853 m (2,800 ft) long

Intimidator 305
Kings Dominion, Virginia, USA
145 kph (90 mph)
93 m (305 ft) high
1,554 m (5,100ft) long

Colossus
Thorpe Park,
England
72 kph (45 mph); 30 m
(100 ft) high 850m
(2,789 ft) long

Millennium Force
Cedar Point, Ohio, USA
150 kph (93 mph)
94 m (310 ft) high
2,010 m (6,595 ft) long

**Superman: Escape
from Krypton**
Six Flags Magic Mountain,
California, USA
161 kph (100 mph)
126 m (415 ft) high
376 m (1,235 ft) long

Vortex
Carowinds, North Carolina,
USA; 80 kph (50 mph)
27m (90 ft) high
622 m (2,040 ft) long

Fury 325,
Carowinds, North Carolina,
USA; 153 kph (95 mph)
99 m (325 ft) high
2,012 m (6,602 ft) long

Alpengeist
Busch Gardens,
Florida, USA
107 kph (67 mph)
59 m (195 ft) high
1,148 m (3,828 ft)
long

Apocalypse,
Six Flags America,
Maryland, USA
89 kph (55 mph)
30 m (100 ft) high
884 m (2,900 ft) long

Red Force,
Ferrari Land, Spain;
180 kph (112) mph
112 m (367 ft) high
880 m (2,890 ft) long

Kingda Ka
Six Flags Great Adventure,
New Jersey, USA
206 kph (128 mph)
139 m (456 ft) high
950 m (3,118 ft) long

Ultimate
Lightwater Valley, UK
80 kph (50 mph)
33 m (107 ft) high
2,268 m (7,442 ft) long

Montezum
Hopi Hari, Brazil
103 kph (64 mph)
42 m (139 ft) high
1,030 m
(3,380 ft) long

Colossos
Heide-Park, Soltau,
Germany
102 kph (75 mph)
60 m (197 ft) high
1,344 m (4,409 ft) long

Kingda Ka
This ride goes from
0–206 kph (128 mph) in
3.5 seconds, catapulting
riders as high as a
45-storey building.

ROLLER COASTERS AROUND THE WORLD
Numbers indicate ranking from 1–5.

Fastest Highest Longest Unranked

Tower of Terror
Gold Reef City,
South Africa
95 kph (59 mph)
34 m (112 ft) high
100 m (328 ft) long

Roller coasters

Breakneck speeds, hair-raising twists and
turns, stomach-churning drops – roller
coasters can satisfy even hardened thrill-
seekers. This map shows some of the
world's biggest and best coasters.

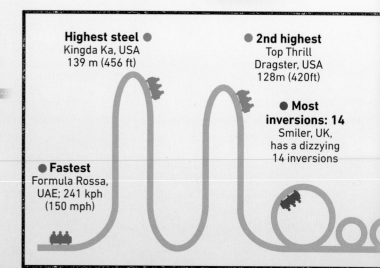

Highest steel ●
Kingda Ka, USA
139 m (456 ft)

● **2nd highest**
Top Thrill
Dragster, USA
128m (420ft)

● **Most
inversions: 14**
Smiler, UK,
has a dizzying
14 inversions

● **Fastest**
Formula Rossa,
UAE; 241 kph
(150 mph)

Flying roller coasters

These coasters – such as Manta at SeaWorld, Florida, USA (right) – make you feel as though you are flying. The cars run on the underside of the track. Riders start in a seated position, but as the ride starts they are rotated to face the ground.

Steel Dragon 2000
Nagashima Spa Land, Japan
153 kph (95 mph)
97 m (318 ft) high
2,437 m (8,133 ft) long

Formula Rossa
Ferrari World, UAE
241 kph (150 mph)
52 m (171 ft) high
2,070 m (6,791 ft) long

Do-Dodonpa
Fuji-Q Highland, Japan
172 kph (107 mph); 52 m (171 ft) high;
1,189 m (3,901 ft) long

Dinoconda
China Dinosaurs Park, China
128 kph (80 mph); 76 m (249 ft) high
1,058 m (3,471 ft) long

Ten Inversion Roller Coaster
Chimelong Paradise, China
72 kph (45 mph); 30 m (100 ft) high 850 m (2,789 ft) long

Fujiyama
Fuji-Q Highland, Japan
130 kph (81 mph)
70 m (260 ft) high
2,045 m (6,709 ft) long

Takabisha
Fuji-Q Highland, Japan
100 kph (62 mph)
43 m (141 ft) high
1,000 m (3,281 ft) long

29 KPH
(18 MPH): SPEED OF THE WORLD'S OLDEST COASTER, LEAP THE DIPS

4-D roller coasters

Fourth-dimension (4-D) coasters, such as China's Dinoconda, give theme parks an extra level of thrills. The seats on a 4-D coaster can rotate forwards or backwards, so as the riders hurtle along the track they also spin in a full circle. Eejanaika (below) is a 4-D ride at Japan's Fuji-Q Highland theme park.

Roller coaster records

Opened in 1902, the world's oldest coaster is the wooden Leap-the-Dips, at Lakemont Park, Pennsylvania, USA. Since then, coasters have become taller, longer, faster – and scarier! Today's coasters are usually made of steel. Wood is less flexible than steel, so wooden coasters tend to be less complex and extreme than steel ones.

● **Steepest drop**
TMNT Shellraiser, USA 121.5 degrees

● **Highest G-force**
Tower of Terror, South Africa 6.3G

DC Rivals Hypercoaster
Warner Bros. Movie World, Queensland, Australia; 115 kph (71.5 mph)1,400 m (4,593 ft) long; 61.6 m (202 ft) high

National flags

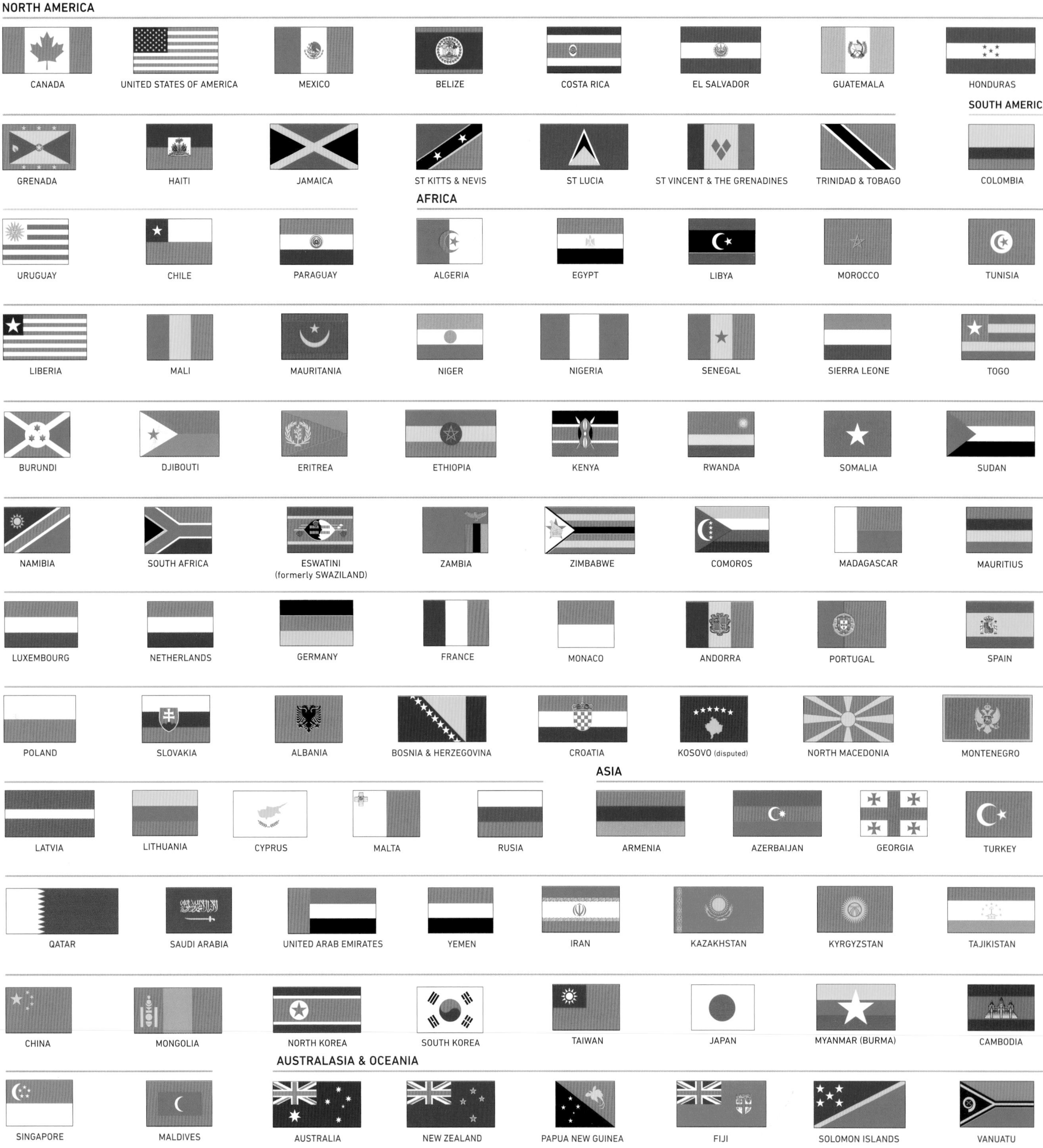
NORTH AMERICA
CANADA
UNITED STATES OF AMERICA
MEXICO
BELIZE
COSTA RICA
EL SALVADOR
GUATEMALA
HONDURAS
GRENADA
HAITI
JAMAICA
ST KITTS & NEVIS
ST LUCIA
ST VINCENT & THE GRENADINES
TRINIDAD & TOBAGO
SOUTH AMERICA
COLOMBIA
URUGUAY
CHILE
PARAGUAY
AFRICA
ALGERIA
EGYPT
LIBYA
MOROCCO
TUNISIA
LIBERIA
MALI
MAURITANIA
NIGER
NIGERIA
SENEGAL
SIERRA LEONE
TOGO
BURUNDI
DJIBOUTI
ERITREA
ETHIOPIA
KENYA
RWANDA
SOMALIA
SUDAN
NAMIBIA
SOUTH AFRICA
ESWATINI
(formerly SWAZILAND)
ZAMBIA
ZIMBABWE
COMOROS
MADAGASCAR
MAURITIUS
LUXEMBOURG
NETHERLANDS
GERMANY
FRANCE
MONACO
ANDORRA
PORTUGAL
SPAIN
POLAND
SLOVAKIA
ALBANIA
BOSNIA & HERZEGOVINA
CROATIA
KOSOVO (disputed)
NORTH MACEDONIA
MONTENEGRO
LATVIA
LITHUANIA
CYPRUS
MALTA
RUSIA
ASIA
ARMENIA
AZERBAIJAN
GEORGIA
TURKEY
QATAR
SAUDI ARABIA
UNITED ARAB EMIRATES
YEMEN
IRAN
KAZAKHSTAN
KYRGYZSTAN
TAJIKISTAN
CHINA
MONGOLIA
NORTH KOREA
SOUTH KOREA
TAIWAN
JAPAN
MYANMAR (BURMA)
CAMBODIA
SINGAPORE
MALDIVES
AUSTRALASIA & OCEANIA
AUSTRALIA
NEW ZEALAND
PAPUA NEW GUINEA
FIJI
SOLOMON ISLANDS
VANUATU

A SOVEREIGN STATE IS A COUNTRY INDEPENDENT OF OTHER STATES, AND

OF ALL THE FLAGS OF THE WORLD'S **195 SOVEREIGN STATES**, ONLY **NEPAL'S** HAS MORE THAN **FOUR SIDES**

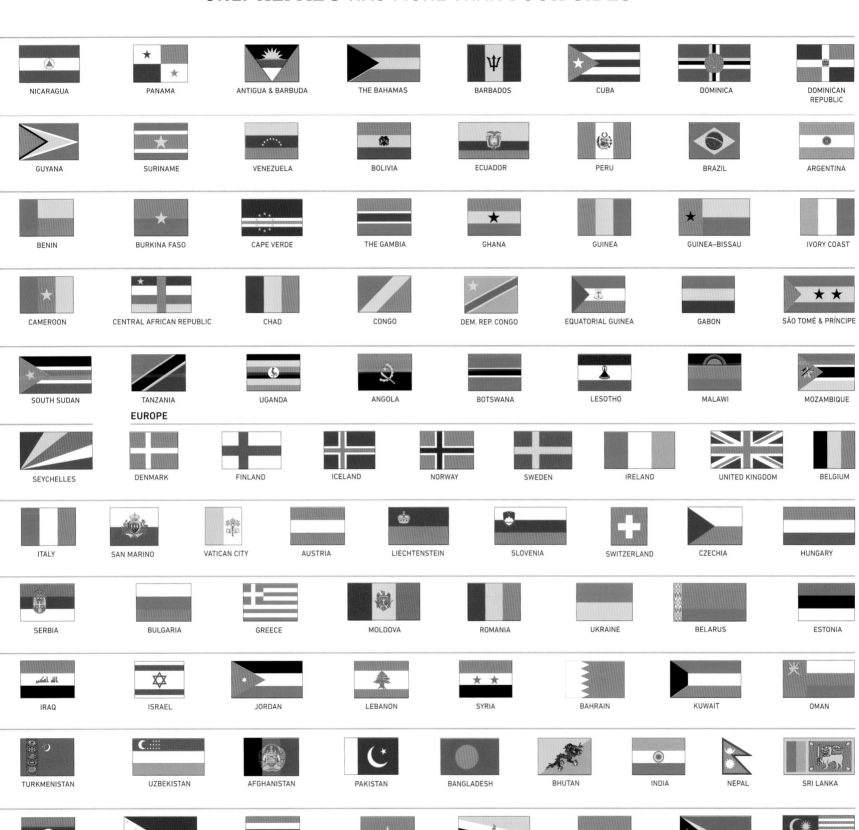

NICARAGUA · PANAMA · ANTIGUA & BARBUDA · THE BAHAMAS · BARBADOS · CUBA · DOMINICA · DOMINICAN REPUBLIC

GUYANA · SURINAME · VENEZUELA · BOLIVIA · ECUADOR · PERU · BRAZIL · ARGENTINA

BENIN · BURKINA FASO · CAPE VERDE · THE GAMBIA · GHANA · GUINEA · GUINEA–BISSAU · IVORY COAST

CAMEROON · CENTRAL AFRICAN REPUBLIC · CHAD · CONGO · DEM. REP. CONGO · EQUATORIAL GUINEA · GABON · SÃO TOMÉ & PRÍNCIPE

SOUTH SUDAN · TANZANIA · UGANDA · ANGOLA · BOTSWANA · LESOTHO · MALAWI · MOZAMBIQUE

EUROPE

SEYCHELLES · DENMARK · FINLAND · ICELAND · NORWAY · SWEDEN · IRELAND · UNITED KINGDOM · BELGIUM

ITALY · SAN MARINO · VATICAN CITY · AUSTRIA · LIECHTENSTEIN · SLOVENIA · SWITZERLAND · CZECHIA · HUNGARY

SERBIA · BULGARIA · GREECE · MOLDOVA · ROMANIA · UKRAINE · BELARUS · ESTONIA

IRAQ · ISRAEL · JORDAN · LEBANON · SYRIA · BAHRAIN · KUWAIT · OMAN

TURKMENISTAN · UZBEKISTAN · AFGHANISTAN · PAKISTAN · BANGLADESH · BHUTAN · INDIA · NEPAL · SRI LANKA

LAOS · PHILIPPINES · THAILAND · VIETNAM · BRUNEI · INDONESIA · EAST TIMOR · MALAYSIA

MARSHALL ISLANDS · MICRONESIA · NAURU · PALAU · KIRIBATI · TUVALU · TONGA · SAMOA

WITH ITS OWN GOVERNMENT SYSTEM AND A PERMANENT POPULATION.

Index

Acknowledgements

Dorling Kindersley would like to thank: Caitlin Doyle for proofreading, Helen Peters for indexing, Haisam Hussein, Anders Kjellberg, Peter Minister, Martin Sanders, and Surya Sarangi for illustration, Deeksha Miglani and Surbhi N. Kapoor for research, and David Roberts for cartographic assistance.

The publisher would like to thank the following for their kind permission to reproduce their photographs:

(Key: a-above; b-below/bottom; c-centre; f-far; l-left; r-right; t-top)

2 Andy Biggs: www.andybiggs.com (tc). Corbis: Alaska Stock (tr). 3 Corbis: Floris Leeuwenberg (ftr); SOPA / Pietro Canali (tl). Getty Images: Art Wolfe (tr). Sebastian Opitz: (tc). 4–5 Andy Biggs: www.andybiggs.com. 22 Getty Images: Mark Garlick (br). 23 Corbis: Charles & Josette Lenars (cr). 24–25 Robert J. Hijmans: Hijmans, R.J, S.E. Cameron, J.L. Parra, P.G. Jones and A. Jarvis, 2005. Very high resolution interpolated climate surfaces for global land areas. International Journal of Climatology 25: 1965–1978 (base-map data). 26–27 Robert J. Hijmans: Hijmans, R.J, S.E. Cameron, J.L. Parra, P.G. Jones and A. Jarvis, 2005. Very high resolution interpolated climate surfaces for global land areas. International Journal of Climatology 25: 1965–1978 (base-map data). 28–29 Adam Sparkes: Data of the tropical cyclones projected by Adam Sparkes. Base image: NASA Goddard Space Flight Center Image by Reto Stöckli (land surface, shallow water, clouds). Enhancements by Robert Simmon (ocean color, compositing, 3D globes, animation). Data and technical support: MODIS Land Group; MODIS Science Data Support Team; MODIS Atmosphere Group; MODIS Ocean Group Additional data: USGS EROS Data Center (topography); USGS Terrestrial Remote Sensing Flagstaff Field Center (Antarctica); Defense Meteorological Satellite Program (city lights). 29 NOAA: (tc). 30 Dorling Kindersley: Rough Guides (tl, tr). Shutterstock: Edwin van Wier (crb). 31 Dreamstime.com: (tc). PunchStock: Digital Vision / Peter Adams (tr). 35 NASA: Goddard Space Flight Center, image courtesy the NASA Scientific Visualization Studio, (bl). 36 Dorling Kindersley: Rough Guides / Tim Draper (bl). Dreamstime.com: Darryn Schneider (tr). 40–41 Corbis: Alaska Stock. 42 Alamy Images: Martin Strmiska (bl). Getty Images: Werner Van Steen (c). 43 NHPA / Photoshot: Ken Griffiths (cr). 45 Corbis: Science Faction / Louie Psihoyos (tr). Dorling Kindersley: Christian Williams (tc). 48 Alamy Images:

National Geographic Image Collection (bl). Dorling Kindersley: Courtesy of the Weymouth Sea Life Centre (bc). 49 Dreamstime.com: Francesco Pacienza (tr). 53 Corbis: Roger Tidman (bc). 55 Corbis: Paul Souders (ca). 56 Corbis: Minden Pictures / Mike Parry (cl); National Geographic Society / Ben Horton (tc). 60 Dorling Kindersley: Courtesy of the Natural History Museum, London (cra, c). Getty Images: Visuals Unlimited, Inc. / Alex Wild (cr). 61 Alamy Images: Premaphotos (tl). Corbis: Visuals Unlimited / Robert & Jean Pollock (tr). Getty Images: Mint Images / Frans Lanting (tc). Photoshot: Gerald Cubitt (br). 62–63 Dreamstime.com: Jezper. 62 Alamy Images: Tim Gainey (bc); John Glover (br). FLPA: Imagebroker / Ulrich Doering (cb). Getty Images: Shanna Baker (clb); Alessandra Sarti (bl). 64 Dorling Kindersley: Courtesy of Oxford University Museum of Natural History (clb). 64–65 Dr. Clinton N. Jenkins: Data: IUCN Red List of Threatened Species / www.iucnredlist.org / BirdLife International; Processing: Clinton Jenkins / SavingSpecies.org; Design & Render; Félix Pharand–Deschênes / Globaia.org. 66 Dorling Kindersley: Rough Guides (cl). 67 Corbis: Ocean (crb). Dorling Kindersley: Roger and Liz Charlwood (crb/New Caledonia). 72–73 Corbis: SOPA / Pietro Canali. 74–75 Getty Images: Doug Allan. 75 Corbis: Aurora Photos / Bridget Besaw (tl); Frank Lukasseck (ftl); Minden Pictures / Ch'ien Lee (tc); John Carnemolla (tr). 76–77 Center for International Earth Science Information Network (CIESIN): Columbia University; International Food Policy Research Institute (IFPRI); The World Bank; and Centro Internacional de Agricultura Tropical (CIAT). 84 Corbis: Dennis Kunkel Microscopy, Inc. / Visuals Unlimited (tc); Dr. Dennis Kunkel Microscopy / Visuals Unlimited (tr). 85 Dreamstime.com: Lukas Gojda (cr). 89 Dreamstime.com: Cammeraydave (tr). 90 Getty Images: AFP / Martin Bureau (br). James Leynse (bc). 91 Corbis: epa / Justin Lane (bl); Kim Kulish (cra); epa / Mario Guzman (br). Getty Images: AFP (cr); Bloomberg / Wei Leng Tay (br). 93 Dreamstime.com: Kheng Guan Toh (br). 101 Corbis: Peter Adams (bl). 105 Corbis: Shuli Hallak (bc). 107 Dreamstime.com: Milosluz (bc). 108–109 NASA: Goddard Space Flight Center Scientific Visualization Studio. 109 NASA: 1941 photo taken by Ulysses William O. Field; 2004 photo taken by Bruce F. Molnia. Courtesy of the Glacier Photograph Collection, National Snow and Ice Data Center / World Data Center for Glaciology. (bl). 110–111 UNEP–WCMC: Dataset derived using the Digital Chart of the World 1993 version and methods based

on the Australian National Wilderness Inventory (Lesslie, R. and Maslen, M. 1995. National Wilderness Inventory Handbook. 2nd edn, Australian Heritage Commission. Australian Government Publishing Service, Canberra) (base-map data). 112–113 Sebastian Opitz. 114–115 Dreamstime. com: Dmitry Mizintsev (c). 114 Corbis: (bc); Science Faction / Louie Psihoyos (br). 115 Corbis: Bettmann (crb); Cameron Davidson (br). Dorling Kindersley: Courtesy of The Science Museum, London (tc). Getty Images: Three Lions (bc). 116–117 Michael Markieta: www.spatialanalysis.ca. 118–119 Prof. Dr. Bernd Blasius: Journal of the Royal Society Interface, The complex network of global cargo ship movements, p1094, 2010 (base-map data). 122 Getty Images: Radius Images (bc). 126–127 Chris Harrison (base-map). 128–129 ESA. 128 NASA: Columbia Accident Investigation Report, (bc). 129 ESA: (cra). NASA: Image created by Reto Stockli with the help of Alan Nelson, under the leadership of Fritz Hasle (br). 130 Corbis: DoD (br). 132–133 Getty Images: Art Wolfe. 134 Corbis: Radius Images (bl); Getty Images: (cr). Dreamstime.com: Kawee Srital On (cb). 135 Corbis: Sodapix / Bernd Schuler (b). 136–137 Corbis: W. Cody. 137 Science Photo Library: MSF / Javier Trueba (crb). 138 akg-images: Oronoz (clb/Mousterian Tool). Dorling Kindersley: The American Museum of Natural History; Natural History Museum, London (cl, clb). Getty Images: AFP (tc); De Agostini (tr). 139 akg-images: Ulmer Museum (bc). Getty Images: De Agostini (crb). 141 Dorling Kindersley: Courtesy of the University Museum of Archaeology and Anthropology, Cambridge (tl); Ancient Art / Judith Miller (bc/Urn); Alan Hills and Barbara Winter / The Trustees of the British Museum (tc); Stephen Dodd / The Trustees of the British Museum (tr). Getty Images: De Agostini (bl). 144 Alamy Images: Ancient Art & Architecture Collection Ltd (tc). Getty Images: Copper Age (tl). Rex Features: (tr). 148 Dorling Kindersley: © The Board of Trustees of the Armouries (tr); The Wallace Collection, London (cb). 149 Dorling Kindersley: © The Board of Trustees of the Armouries (cla); Lennox Gallery Ltd / Judith Miller (cra); William Jamieson Tribal Art / Judith Miller (bl); Courtesy of the Royal Armories (tc); The Trustees of the British Museum (cb); Peter Wilson / CONACULTA–INAH– MEX. Authorized reproduction by the Instituto Nacional de Antropología e Historia (clb). 150 Corbis: Walter Geiersperger (cl); Robert Harding World Imagery / Michael Jenner (clb). 151 Alamy Images: Peter Titmuss (bc). Corbis: Design Pics / Keith Levit (cra). Dreamstime.com:

(bl). Getty Images: AFP (cr). 156 Corbis: Bettmann (cb, cra). Getty Images: (c). 157 Corbis: Bryan Denton (bl); Peter Turnley (cr). Getty Images: AFP (ca); (c); (clb). 159 Dreamstime.com: (bc). 162–163 Corbis: Floris Leeuwenberg. 164 Getty Images: Redferns / Tabatha Fireman (c). Dreamstime.com: Constantin Sava (bl). 165 Alamy Images: Hemis (br). Corbis: Godong / Julian Kumar (tr). Dreamstime. com: F9photos (cr); Teptong (crb). Getty Images: Philippe Lissac (tc). 172 Alamy Images: GL Archive (tr); The Art Archive (cb). Corbis: Bettmann (cl, cr); Oscar White (cla); The Gallery Collection (crb). Dorling Kindersley: Philip Keith Private Collection / Judith Miller (br). Getty Images: De Agostini (cra, cra/Gainsborough); Stringer / Powell (tc). 172–173 123RF.com. 173 Corbis: (cl, cr, cb); Contemporary African Art Collection Limited (clb). Getty Images: AFP (bc); (tl, tr); (cla). 174 Corbis: In Pictures / Barry Lewis (br). 175 Corbis: JAI / Michele Falzone (cra). Dorling Kindersley: Rough Guides (bc); Surya Sankash Sarangi (c). 176 Dorling Kindersley: Alex Robinson (br). 177 Corbis: Jose Fuste Raga (bc). 178–179 Dreamstime.com: Luminis (background image). 179 Dreamstime. com: Mathayward (bl). 180 Alamy Images: Aerial Archives (cl). Getty Images: (ca). 180–181 Getty Images: AFP (cb); (ca). 181 Corbis: Arcaid / John Gollings (br). Getty Images: (ca). 182 Corbis: GT Images / George Tiedemann (tr); Icon SMI / Jeff Vest (br). 182–183 Dreamstime.com: Eugenesergeev (tyre tracks on the map). 183 Getty Images: (tl, tc, cr, bc). Dreamstime.com: Marco Canoniero (tr). 184 Alamy Images: David Wall (tr). Dreamstime.com: Anthony Aneese Totah Jr (c). Getty Images: AFP (cl). 185 Alamy Images: G.P.Bowater (tr); Philip Sayer (tc). Getty Images: AFP (br)

All other images © Dorling Kindersley
For further information see: www.dkimages.com

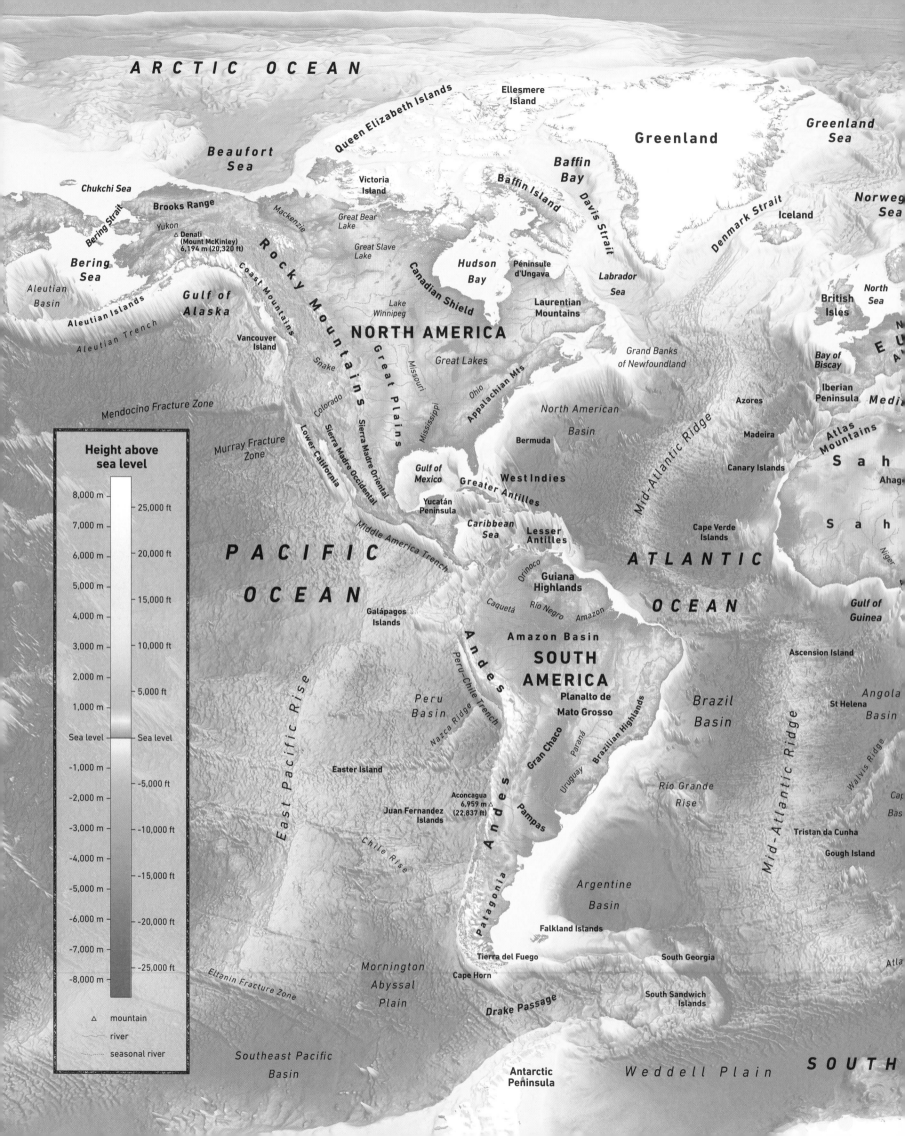

E
Van

Van Laan, Nancy

So say the little
monkeys

		DATE DUE	

Amanha—tomorrow, will it *ever* come?

They swing, WHEEEE, over here.
They swing, WHEEEE, over there.
They sing, "Amanha—tomorrow!"
as they jump and run.
JUMP, JABBA JABBA,
RUN, JABBA JABBA,
SLIDE, JABBA JABBA,
SCREECH, JABBA JABBA,
SHOUT, JABBA JABBA,
MUNCH, JABBA JABBA,
SWING, JABBA JABBA,
SING, JABBA JABBA.

But what do you think
they *do* the next day?
Do they build a warm nest?
Or do they eat and play?

Now each tired monkey
is wishing for a bed—
"We should have built a house,
just like we said!"

Night falls again
as the sun goes down,
and they huddle all together
when the rain starts to pound.

Comes the rain, PLINKA PLINKA.
Comes the wind, WOOYA WOOYA.
Comes the jaguar, GURR-YUH GURR-YUH.
Monkeys run, run, run!

JUMP, JABBA JABBA,
RUN, JABBA JABBA,
SLIDE, JABBA JABBA,
SCREECH, JABBA JABBA,
SHOUT, JABBA JABBA,
MUNCH, JABBA JABBA,
Tiny, tiny monkeys having fun!

They swing, WHEEEE, over here.
They swing, WHEEEE, over there.
They sing, "Jibba jibba jabba,"
as they jump and run.

But when two monkeys find
ripe bananas in a bunch,
all the tiny monkeys
stop and MUNCH MUNCH MUNCH.

Then one monkey says,
"Let's gather wood!"
"Yes! Yes!" howl the others.
"We really should."

With a leap and a shriek,
they pick, pick, pick,
a leaf or a twig
or a fat, fat stick.

JUMP, JABBA JABBA,
RUN, JABBA JABBA,
SLIDE, JABBA JABBA,
SCREECH, JABBA JABBA,
SHOUT, JABBA JABBA,
Tiny, tiny monkeys having fun!

They swing, WHEEEE, over here.
They swing, WHEEEE, over there.
They sing, "Jibba jibba jabba,"
as they jump and run.

But when the next day dawns,
and the sun comes out,
Tiny, tiny monkeys
screech and shout.

Comes the rain, PLINKA PLINKA.
Comes the wind, WOOYA WOOYA.
"EEEYI!" cry the monkeys.
"It's c-cold out here!"

Tiny, tiny monkeys,
soaked to the bone,
chatter to each other,
"L-let's b-build us a home!"

There's an OUCH over there.
There's an OUCH over here.
They cry, "Jabba jabba,"
as the rain draws near.

But the tiny, tiny monkeys
creep, creep, creep,
up thorny, thorny trees
where they try to sleep.

At the end of the day,
when it's time to rest,
most others go to
their warm, cozy nests.

Toucan snuggles deep
in a dry tree hole.
Armadillo burrows
underground like a mole.

JUMP, JABBA JABBA,
RUN, JABBA JABBA,
SLIDE, JABBA JABBA,
Tiny, tiny monkeys having fun!

Still they climb, UP–UP!
And they slide, DOWN–DOWN!
They sing, "Jibba jibba jabba,"
swinging round and round.

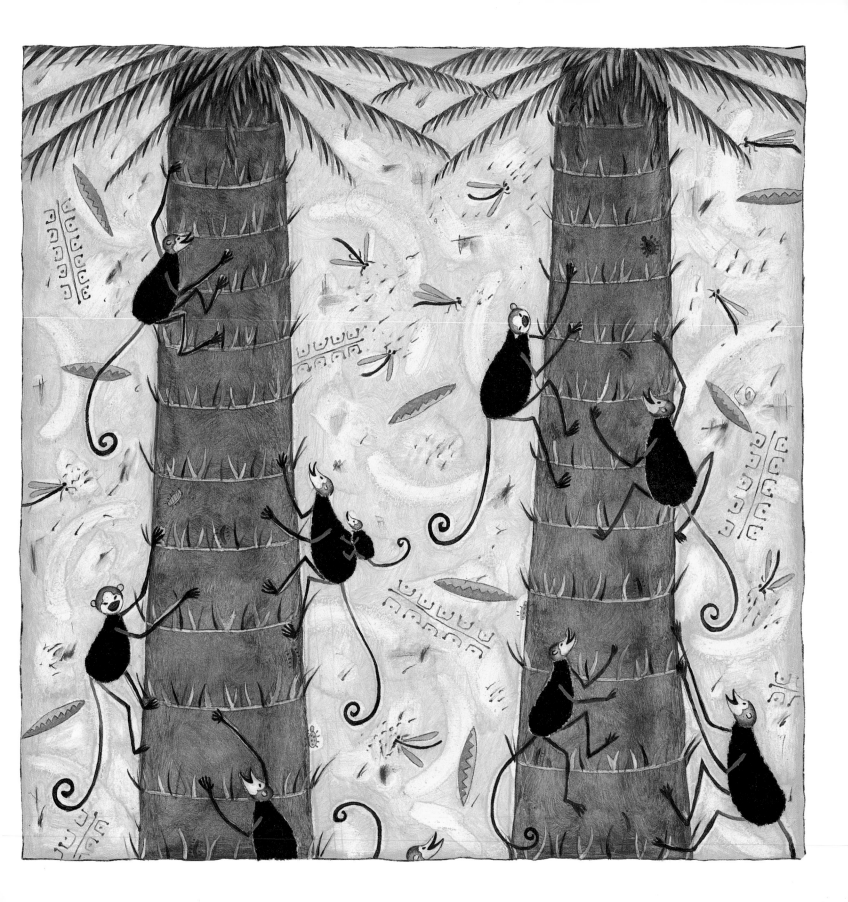

As they climb tall trees
full of sharp, sharp thorns,
their tiny black mouths
shriek, "OW OW OW!"

JUMP, JABBA JABBA,

RUN, JABBA JABBA,

Tiny, tiny monkeys having fun!

They swing, WHEEEE, over here.

They swing, WHEEEE, over there.

They sing, "Jibba jibba jabba,"

as they jump and run.

Near the deep black waters
of a dark, cool river,
tiny, tiny monkeys
jabber in the sun.

A Note About the Story

In Brazil, a huge country in South America, there are many rivers. Second in size to the Amazon is the Rio Negro, the Black River, which got its name from its dark waters, black as coal.

In the trees along its banks live tiny monkeys, which the Indians call "blackmouths." Their mouths are as dark as the waters of the river. These monkeys live in the tall palms which are full of sharp thorns. Unlike the birds, the monkeys do not make any type of permanent home. Even though the thorns must be very uncomfortable, they sleep on top of them each night. The Indians who live there created an amusing tale to explain why this is so.

For my sister, Julie, and her menagerie
—N. V. L.

For my son, Auden
—Y. H.

First Aladdin Paperbacks edition November 2001
Text copyright © 1998 by Nancy Van Laan
Illustrations copyright © 1998 by Yumi Heo

Aladdin Paperbacks
An imprint of Simon & Schuster Children's Publishing Division
1230 Avenue of the Americas
New York, NY 10020

Book design by Michael Nelson.
The text of this book is set in Kosmik.
The illustrations were rendered in pencil, oil, and collage.
Printed in Hong Kong
10 9 8 7 6 5 4 3 2 1

The Library of Congress has cataloged the hardcover edition as follows:
Van Laan, Nancy.
So say the little monkeys / by Nancy Van Laan ; illustrated by Yumi Heo.
p. cm.
"An Anne Schwartz Book"
Summary: A rhyming retelling of an Indian folktale from Brazil about
tiny, playful monkeys and why they have no place to call home.

ISBN 0-689-81038-5 (hc.)
[1. Indians of South America—Brazil—Folklore. 2. Monkeys—Brazil—Folklore.
3. Folklore—Brazil—Juvenile literature.]
I. Heo, Yumi, ill. II. Title.
F2519.3.F6V36   1998
398.2'098'0452982—dc20
[E]   95-17360
ISBN 0-689-84690-8 (Aladdin pbk.)

So Say The Little Monkeys

by **Nancy Van Laan**   pictures by **Yumi Heo**

An Anne Schwartz Book

Aladdin Paperbacks

NEW YORK   LONDON   TORONTO   SYDNEY   SINGAPORE

Foreword
by Anne, Countess of Rosse

Brought up in two beautiful houses enriched by rare collections, I was well schooled to observe and appreciate the nuances inherent in the English room. All of my own five houses have been totally different in style, date and size. I have been happy in all, but have never wanted to intrude upon or change the aura I loved. In each case I have tried to belong to the house rather than the house to me; to let it remain itself but to enhance it a little in its own way. I lean on a mélange of things I treasure and have never boasted of 'good taste'. Yet detail matters: flowers and a warm fire are as important as beautiful furniture. A room '*trop bien arrangée*' is fussy and unrestful. Only our beautiful Paine ballroom at Wormersley has had the helping hand of a decorator who, proudly, was none other than John Fowler to whom the English room owes so much.

What differentiates English rooms from those of other nations is that they are primarily rooms for living in, not only for looking at. They reflect immediately at all levels the personalities and whims of the people themselves in whose houses they are, their individual tastes (or no taste at all!) and their way of life. The ideal English room breathes welcome, ease and effortless imagination. We often mix superb period furniture, *objets d'art*, valuable paintings and tapestry with 'things we love'. Great-uncle Elmo's elephant-leg umbrella-stand looks quite happy next to an exquisite piece of early *cloisonné*. Family photographs do not necessarily ruin the balance of a Louis xv table and the little things made by one's children sit cheerfully on the chimney-piece.

When I inherited 18 Stafford Terrace, the charming Victorian house which inspired the founding of the Victorian Society, Cecil Beaton threw up his hands in horror. 'Can't she make just one room normal?' he shouted. 'But dear Anne has always loved clutter.' A certain amount of clutter is essential. Remember that it is very often raining in England so that life is frequently lived indoors. English rooms must radiate a calm and reticence forming a sympathetic background for occupation or work lasting for hours on end. Books should abound, needlework and always and ever a well-equipped writing table with a wastepaper basket to boot. Comfortable chairs, cushions and footstools will invite intimate tête-à-têtes and parties. In the dining room we strive to create an atmosphere that will be sympathetic and inspiring to lively conversation and laughter, whether for four or for twenty, with deliciously simple English food and flattering candlelight.

This most fascinating survey of the English room spreads its wings over the widest variety of styles, tastes and characters of the English people and their way of life. It transports us from the grandest and most ambitious of palaces and castles to architectural masterpieces of all dates and forms and even to humble terraced town houses and cottage rooms. Superbly illustrated by Derry Moore with his sensitive eye for shapes and colours, each example of the English room is here given generous appreciation and understanding by Michael Pick, so that the individuality and immense variety of the rooms is apparent and welcoming to all in this enchanting book.

Introduction

THIS is neither a history of the English house nor of English decoration, both of which have been more fully described by others. It is a survey of that most elusive concept now so often misrepresented and misunderstood by decorators and their clients: the 'English Room'. No slur is cast on the rooms of Scotland, Wales or Ireland. To consider all the variations and nuances of style contained in those countries would require a far larger book and would deviate from our central theme of investigating the essential English qualities captured in the photographs. Inevitably, certain aspects of the history of architectural and decorative styles are discussed as various rooms are scrutinized and dissected to uncover different qualities, all reflecting national characteristics. These are indeed varied and often highly eccentric. A mid-nineteenth-century American view of the English by Ralph Waldo Emerson in *English Traits* (1856) is still applicable to the style of our most English-looking rooms: 'Every one of the islanders is an island himself, safe, tranquil, incommunicable.' In this book Emerson describes the very stuff of which England was – and still is – made: an assertive, inventive and rich nation, one slow to change, but remarkably receptive to outside ideas and influences, which are assessed and then utilized to the advantage of its people.

Since Emerson wrote his appraisal we can see the development of another trend in English life, that of a distaste for sudden change and upheaval. Many of the rooms pictured here reveal a blending of all these characteristics in an interpretation of old styles. This disinclination to be 'up to date' was already manifest in 1934 when Evelyn Waugh wrote *A Handful of Dust*. The owner of a Victorian mansion in a medieval style reacted in horror to his wife's modernization of one room, and his lady friend 'stirred the mouldings of fleurs-de-lis that littered the floor, fragments of tarnished gilding and dusty stencil-work. "You know, Brenda's been a wonderful friend to me. I wouldn't say anything against her . . . but ever since I came here I've been wondering whether she really understands this beautiful place and all it means to you."' Every room in this book has an individual quality which is the personal response of an Englishman to his surroundings; each reflects both the country's heritage and the capacity of its people to assimilate outside influences in a unique way.

For nearly two centuries there has been an acknowledged export of an English style to America. The world of the late nineteenth century, described by Henry James and Edith Wharton, was one which first experienced the lucrative beginnings of an export trade in English antiques to America, whilst England imported heiresses to bolster the fortunes of its noble families. This two-way traffic slowly spread an aura of exclusive 'chic' to the very concept of a room decorated in the English manner, so much so that even in France the possession of English antiques, or of rooms pretending to be 'English', is now a status symbol. Once French rooms were universally more 'chic' than English in the illustrated journals devoted to decoration; now French antique furniture is no longer the most sought

Opposite The Red Drawing Room, Alnwick Castle

after, and the enormous rise in the value of English antique furniture over the past five years is the conclusive measure of this. Record prices have been paid, usually by non-English buyers. Never has the 'English room' been more in demand, and the desired look is no longer simply that of the seventeenth or eighteenth centuries, but also of the late nineteenth century and more lavish Edwardian periods.

No-one doubts the existence of an English style of decoration, but the definition of such a style varies with every attempt at explanation. Why does a room look specifically English rather than French, Italian, German or American? Furniture alone does not give the look of an English room, and nor is the use of chintz a yardstick for measuring 'Englishness', as many contemporary decorators would seem to believe. There must be certain qualities apart from the furniture which contribute to an English look, and these include the choice of fabrics, carpets, decorative objects and paintings, as well as fittings. Whatever the architectural style of a room the effect can be made 'English'. In the history of post-Renaissance English architecture only the Perpendicular and 'Tudor' styles can claim to be truly English in origin, for all other styles derive ultimately from foreign sources; the English look must therefore emerge not from specific architectural references but by mastering a diverse range of styles and foreign influences. The ability to create this look is an inborn trait which may be developed but not acquired, and an examination of the illustrations in this book will reveal what is an instinctive decorative skill. Most of the rooms are not the work of professional decorators creating a setting entirely from their own resources; they are rooms that have evolved to fulfil the needs of the owners.

In his 1955 series of BBC Reith lectures, 'The Englishness of English Art', Professor Sir Nikolaus Pevsner gave the personal view of an academic observer. His German background gave him a clearer and more detached perspective as he pointed to 'those features in our national character which inspire in our art its essential Englishness'. His lectures affirmed the English genius for the assimilation of apparently contradictory beliefs and ideas as well as of decorative styles from abroad, all of which are fused into something essentially English. With an incisive Germanic erudition he separated influences and new inventions, ranging from 'the immense international influence of Palladianism, the Picturesque garden, Robert Adam and Wedgwood, to the equally all-embracing influence of English iron construction, to the great art of landscape painting in the early nineteenth century and its influence in France, and to William Morris, the so-called Domestic Revival of the late Victorian decades, and the idea of a garden city'. He arrived at the conclusion that, 'What English character gained of tolerance and fair play, she lost of that fanaticism or at least that intensity which alone can bring forth the very greatest in art.'

In the creation of English rooms, an often transient but no less demanding branch of the arts, we must often disagree with Pevsner, for examples such as the work of Adam and Chippendale at Nostell Priory (pages 46–9) are manifestations of English genius ranking as the very greatest. Pevsner himself recognized that most subtle of English achievements, the use of light as a decorative medium. He admired the early-nineteenth-century house of Sir John Soane in Lincoln's Inn, London, in which the Monk's Parlour relied on sources of light that were concealed from the visitor's eyes by the architectural structure of the room.

The subtlety of English light is perhaps the greatest dictator of English tastes: from the high clear skies of late spring and early autumn, to the soft twilight of damp winter days and the golden aura of a fine summer, our eyes are accustomed to changing shades and depths of colour. The Elizabethans were the first to embrace this wonderfully varied English quality, and the size of the windows at Wollaton Hall in Nottinghamshire, Longleat House in Wiltshire, or Hardwick Hall in Derbyshire, reflect not merely the settled state of the country, becoming peaceful and progressive, nor the wealth of the owner, but also the feeling of being a civilized human being living in ordered surroundings. The rooms at Hardwick are not particularly remarkable for their size (the halls of earlier castles and houses were just as large), it is the construction which is of importance. The foremost reason is summed up by the old jingle, 'Hardwick Hall, More glass than wall.' Built by the formidable Bess of Hardwick between 1591 and 1597 the house was an affirmation of her position in society, and her initials were carved in the commanding heights of the decorative stone parapets. She could afford the expensive glass, and she could also afford to rely on the unfiltered light of the Derbyshire Peak District as the principal decorative element in her house. No need to fortify windows or fill the interior with particularly sumptuous or expensive decoration, her powerful status is seen rather in the revolutionary form of the architecture. Apart from tapestries, decorative plaster and woodwork, the furniture was mainly simple and sturdy with great patches of colour coming from various wall-hangings. The forms of the windows and fireplaces already show an awareness of the architecture of both France and, primarily, developments in Renaissance Italy, but although such influence is undeniably present it is still true to say that Hardwick represents a truly English style – and of the 375 workmen recorded as working on the house not even one had a discernibly foreign name. When Britain was at the zenith of her imperial and industrial might in the nineteenth century this style was revived for its apparently true English roots. It gave a spurious ambiance of antiquity to acquired fortunes, and seemed to assert that Victorian men were equally as cultured and worldly as the dashing adventurers of the Elizabethan era.

When revived by architects such as Anthony Salvin the style became known as 'Jacobethan', and although the huge windows were reintroduced, as for example at Alnwick Castle (pages 8 and 72–3), they were not leaded but formed of sheets of plate glass. The strong light they permitted was now subtly filtered by blinds and heavy drapes in deference to more decorative interiors. The extreme reaction aroused by the Modern Movement and such houses as The Homewood (pages 116–17) often centred on the immense quantity of glass used as walling and the consequently very strong light in small rooms. The modern 'picture window' may be a novelty of the years after the First World War as far as using one sheet of glass is concerned, but windows using leaded glass covered just as large an area when Sir Francis Bacon was writing his *Essay on Building* at the turn of the sixteenth century. He was actually advancing the complaints of the twentieth-century house dweller: 'you should have sometimes faire Houses, so full of Glasse, that one cannot tell, where to become to be out of the sunne or cold'; even then Englishmen were wary of new developments in architecture.

For centuries the English lived for the most part in gloomy and uncomfortable surroundings, cooking and heating by means of open fireplaces and only putting a premium on comfort by the end of the sixteenth century. The large number of houses that survive from the seventeenth century show how firmly established the search for comfort had become by then. The Romans had introduced a form of central heating to England but this was ignored for almost fifteen hundred years, and even Robert Adam in the eighteenth century relied on open fireplaces to provide heat, for his study of Roman decoration and architecture was more aesthetic than scientific. He did attempt a form of central heating in at least three buildings, including Kedleston Hall (pages 38–9) and Newby Hall (pages 44–5.) From the time of the Normans in the eleventh century, the fireplace came to be moved from an open place in the middle of a large hall to a convenient construction made of masonry against a wall, connecting to a flue and chimney. Four centuries later they were simple constructions such as that in an Oxfordshire country house illustrated on pages 16–17. The slow development of the fireplace forms a barometer of taste in reaching the sophistication of a carved marble chimney-piece in the eighteenth century, as seen in many of the interiors illustrated in this book. Even today there is something peculiarly English about an open fireplace. Clean and efficient stoves were established components of continental rooms by the eighteenth century, particularly in northern Europe. They remained rare in England, where a general taste for central heating only became well established in the 1960s.

A fireplace is by its very nature a dominating fixture in any room and has often held the portrait of the house-owner above it, so that one feels at the very heart of the house. The Library at Hatfield House (opposite) has a Venetian mosaic of Robert Cecil sunk into the wall above the fireplace that forms part of the decoration of the chimney-piece. The size of the fireplace dictates not merely the decoration of a wall but also the scale of its decoration and often that of the whole room. The positioning of the furniture will also stem from the various properties of the fireplace and the chimney decoration, determining size, composition and style. Given that other walls will hold doors and windows it can be appreciated how limiting a fireplace can be on the decoration of a room, particularly in winter when the fire is needed. It is fascinating that such a form of heating with all its attendant draughts and discomforts should have survived in England for nine hundred years. Even a Modern Movement house such as The Homewood retains a fireplace and in the smooth monolith of the grey-black Levanto marble wall a flickering bank of flames mocks the expanse of plate-glass windows and the hot-air ducts beneath (page 117).

An appreciation of the subtleties of English light, the craving for a visible warming flame in the hearth; these are dominant factors in the decoration of English rooms and few decorators or their clients now fully appreciate either. They can learn from Robert Adam's Marble Hall at Kedleston Hall (pages 38–9), where firelight will bring the cold alabaster to life, or from Mrs Syrie Maugham's rooms at Upper Grosvenor Street, dispelling all hint of the foggy atmosphere of 1930s London with Venetian colours and a fireplace glowing in the Bathroom (pages 110–13). The love of warmth and light and a longing for their incorporation into an English setting are part and parcel of the decoration of English rooms. Ultimately a room's success or failure can be judged on the quality of colours, materials and objects, and the manner in which all these are handled. This is a subjective process, but, as Mrs Nancy Lancaster has so rightly reminded us, the decoration of a room should be blended in as delicious a manner as a well-mixed salad.

Opposite The Library, Hatfield House

Few decorative schemes can match the apparently effortless brilliance of the Library at Nostell Priory (page 46), an English triumph of blended tastes if ever there was one. It seems unnecessary to have to understand the motives of either a decorator or an owner (or both), one's own initial reaction should settle the matter of whether it appeals or not. But an understanding of the planning behind a room may turn dislike into a degree of appreciation, even if dislike is rarely overcome. In this book the photographer's skill has often changed near-geese into swans, because he has known the elements to emphasize – some rooms, like some people, are not photogenic.

When Erasmus visited Britain in the 1490s he wrote with distaste: 'The floors are commonly clay, strewed with rushes, so renewed that the substratum may be unmolested for twenty years, with an ancient collection of beer, grease, fragments, bones, spittle and everything that is nasty.' Because of the difficulty of keeping any floor particularly clean until the early nineteenth century, the objective was to conduct life on surfaces well away from the floor. Furniture had high legs and was built for sitting up, and the decoration of rooms was scaled around such comparatively high furniture; for even in the houses of the very rich the floor could never be kept as clean as it is today. By the 1980s, however, the pertinent observer Quentin Crisp was noting a very different social phenomenon: 'It is always possible for anyone to judge the financial status of his host by the distance of the table tops and chair seats from the floor. The higher the income bracket, the lower the furniture. In Miss Deterding's house all horizontal surfaces were well below the knee' (*How to Become a Virgin*, 1981). His remarks reflect a complete revolution in decoration and domestic arrangements.

Much of our decoration today is undoubtedly a form of nostalgia for the past, and in particular for the apparent comfort of the Edwardian era. The look and atmosphere of the English Edwardian country house, with overtones of royal visits, is a style of decoration attempted so often as to elicit a groan and a yawn. It is as though the spirit of one of Lady Londonderry's housemaids has insinuated itself into the hearts of some of the most crusty of Englishmen and most sensible of Englishwomen, all longing to be part of Edwardian England: 'It was after one of these Royal visits [by King Edward VII] that [the then] Lady Londonderry had dressed early and, happening to go down into the drawing room before dinner discovered one of the house-maids with a duster in her hand sitting on all the chairs in the room by turns. With great intuition she immediately guessed the reason for this curious behaviour. "That is the chair His Majesty sat in," she said, pointing: "now have a good sit in it."' (The Marchioness of Londonderry, *Retrospect*, 1938).

There are many stilted re-creations of would-be Edwardian rooms. Few have bothered to sort out the more appealing elements and adapt them to our own day. Successful interpretations are often almost subconscious and result in such delightful interiors as those of Lady Rupert Nevill at Horsted Place, Sussex (page 56), or the Duchess of Beaufort (pages 128–9). This form of nostalgia is fostered by some decorators and appears to have succeeded the desire for an eighteenth-century room. (That look was popular for the first sixty years of this century, but the finest English antique furniture of that date has become so expensive that only the serious or status-seeking collector will buy it.) But it also has its roots in both the Shell Guides of the 1930s and then the social upheaval of the Second World War and after, when such publications as *The Saturday Book* were creating a nostalgic image of a fast-changing and vanishing Britain in a series of beautifully produced and illustrated articles and photo-essays that continued through the 1950s and 1960s. The nostalgia extended to surveys of English arts and crafts and a glimpse of idyllic country life, all cats and singing kettles. Even if the editors of *The Saturday Book* admitted as early as 1946 that cottages of the type illustrated in this book were already virtually extinct (pages 30–1), the pressures of wartime life had sharpened ideas and feelings in crisis and clarified nostalgic thoughts only half-felt in peacetime. 'We have a tendency to mourn the disappearance of places we have never seen, or of which we know nothing,' wrote James Pope-Hennessey in *History Under Fire* (1941).

Through the whole of English decorative history run very rich veins of individuality and eccentricity, veins we can trace through the writings of so-called 'social observers'. The Victorian diarist Augustus Hare is an invaluable source of lively gossip and anecdotes. He was related to many of the oldest families of England, however distantly, and made the best possible use of his contacts. He was almost a professional guest, travelling around Europe and Great Britain recording anecdotes and descriptions of domestic surroundings in town and country, published in six volumes between 1896 and 1900 in *The Story of My Life*. The Frenchman Louis Simond was a similarly fascinating and highly critical observer of the English, visiting Britain to investigate agricultural and industrial progress just after the Napoleonic wars, when England presented a rich variety of widely differing lifestyles, housing and industries to his sharp eyes. His impressions were published as *Voyages en Angleterre pendant les années 1810 et 1811*, in 1817. Both men described the eccentricities of their hosts with a certain astonished admiration. I, for one, feel great sympathy for Lady Harriet Wentworth, visited in January 1881 by Augustus Hare. He found her in the precincts of what he termed her 'great Italian Palace' at Stainsborough, Yorkshire, 'Wentworth Castle': 'I do so hate the thraldom of civilization,' she told him, and he went on, 'Her stately rooms have no charm for her, and though they are so immense, she declares that she cannot breathe in them, and she lives entirely, and has all her meals in the conservatory with a damp, warm, marshy climate from which she does not scruple to emerge into the bitter winds of the Yorkshire Wolds (for the conservatory does not join the house) with nothing extra on.' And indeed, what is an English room without at least some hint of an English garden and the countryside to breathe life into it?

An Oxfordshire Country House

THE COUNTRYSIDE is full of houses such as this, houses which have evolved naturally and are still enjoyed as comfortable and beautiful homes. Given the ancient architectural features of this sixteenth-century country house it would be difficult not to create an interesting atmosphere, although not easy to acquire from scratch the furnishings we see here.

The powerful arch of the Dining Room fireplace (opposite) dominates the scene and is the centre of attraction when lit – a room within a room. Apart from the fire-irons and implements the area is enlivened by the marble bust placed in the brick recess: in the light of the flames it creates an uncanny effect. Unusually, the brick surround leading to the chimney has been whitened and this is a clever way of diminishing the otherwise overpowering effect of the great size of the fireplace. The trestle table is seventeenth century. There is an Italian feeling of warmth and colour which is generally absent from English houses of this period and is in part attributable to the three busts of varying origin on display, and to the paintings in their gilt frames. The needlework of the chairbacks and the carpet is of course in characteristic English taste, as is the blue and white Chinese garden seat. The incongruous juxtaposition of all these objects is part of the character of this house.

The extraordinary triangular window in the Study (above) is thankfully left uncurtained and emphasized by a stark modern sculpture. It is the main source of light for a sensual painting, completely dominating one wall in spite of the heavy beams and door. Through the open door the eye is led on to another large canvas, and the warmth of fleshy bodies lends the room a vitality and interest quite remote from the hard white walls and tough beams. Whether the paintings are correct in scale, date or subject matter for the house is of total irrelevance. The owners have utilized their possessions and surroundings originally and to the best advantage, and have created a fascinating atmosphere.

Loseley House
The Surrey House of James More-Molyneux Esq.

The Great Hall forms the heart of this Elizabethan house built in 1562 by Sir William More, at a carefully recorded cost of £1,640 19s 7d. He was adviser to Queen Elizabeth I, but the house is not comparable in scale or design to such a building as Hatfield House (pages 20–3). There is no grandeur, but a sense of domesticity which has acquired a mellow charm. The Hall reflects warmth and hospitality and still holds the appeal it undoubtedly had on the three occasions when Queen Elizabeth visited it. It was probably also the scene for the anxious calculations of the enormous cost of entertaining the Queen and her retinue.

A large square-bayed oriel window lights the far end of the room, and other windows high above the panelling keep the room bright. Although a large fireplace (not visible in the picture) is the main feature, the room is completely dominated by the canvas depicting Sir More Molyneux and his family. They have gazed down on the scene since 1739 and the house was then already antiquated, not just old-fashioned. But the room is full of charm

and pleasant things and it is not surprising to find it still loved and used. A comfortable mixture of sofas, antique chairs of various periods and mellow panelling is a background for the paintings. That of Sir More and his family is so enormous that the room's size is immediately diminished to less overpowering proportions. The colours give warmth to the uncurtained windows and stonework, and this is also reflected by the panelling; that on the wall below Sir More's portrait is thought to have come from Henry VIII's Nonsuch Palace, built at Ewell in Surrey for Catherine Parr. It was demolished in the late seventeenth century, and the decorated panels to either side of the chimney-piece are also thought to have come from there. The room therefore contains elements reminding us of episodes in English history and portraits by Kneller and Lely (among others) conjure up the spirits of generations of the family. The room is as comfortable now as it has even been since first built more than 400 years ago, gaining in charm as the room mellows with age.

Sissinghurst Castle
The Kent House of the Hon. Nigel Nicolson Esq.

WHEN Vita Sackville-West and her husband Sir Harold Nicolson bought Sissinghurst Castle in Kent in 1930 there were only four ruined buildings standing, fragments of the original Elizabethan mansion. The two new owners created the beautiful gardens, the focal point of the setting.

The arrangement of the buildings allowed for each of the four members of the family to live quite separately, giving the privacy essential to both authors. Miss Sackville-West's Sitting Room, situated on the first floor of the tower where she could 'see without being seen', is an intensely personal and private room: no family chatter echoes here. Plain wooden bookshelves, simple curtains, buff papered walls: in these surroundings Vita wrote her many books, her weekly gardening articles for the *Observer*, and the vast number of letters she sent regularly – even daily – to her friends, husband and sons. The strong Tudor arch and octagonal table with great lion paws dominate the scene, although the low divan is clearly of the inter-war years and reflects the 'studio' look of much contemporary decoration. Over the well-used brick fireplace are stepped shelves more typical of southern Germany or Austria, but which did occur in England; the turquoise ornaments are part of Vita's large collection of coloured glass, and provide a brilliant splash of colour. Paintings are positioned without any formal arrangement, or concern for scale. Books line the walls and little alcove, and follow the octagonal shape of the turret: they include her own and her husband's works, source books for her biographies, as well as books on travel, literature and, of course, gardening. It is a practical living room, without pretension or self-consciousness. The couch and carpet are shabby and worn, they are there for comfort not effect and possess a charm that only age can create.

Hatfield House
The Hertfordshire House of the Marquess of Salisbury

HATFIELD HOUSE has been the seat of the Salisbury branch of the Cecil family since the present house was built by Robert Cecil between 1607 and 1611. It was his reward from James I, for whom Cecil had secured the succession to the English throne from the dying Queen Elizabeth I. Cecil became High Treasurer and principal adviser to the King, and set about rebuilding Hatfield to make it a worthy reflection of his status. Apart from the substitution of plate glass for the leaded lights and the screening in of the colonnade on the façade, the look of the house has remained relatively unaltered for centuries.

Only the Great Hall (page 22) survived the construction of the new building. Cecil supervised the details of planning and construction with the architect Robert Lyminge to advise him, and it is a curious building revealing something of the new owner's aspirations. The 'E' shape is said to commemorate Elizabeth I. Cecil was clearly gifted in many ways and the building reflects the taste of an Elizabethan Renaissance man, interested in the arts as well as affairs of state. There are strange anachronisms in the design which incorporates a Long and North Gallery and a Great Hall of enormous size, filled with Italianate Renaissance detail carved into the English oak panels and beams. Cecil must have conceived these rooms as a reflection of his new status as first Earl of Salisbury, and no doubt envisaged meetings of great state importance occurring there; but he died in 1612, having spent over £38,000 on the house and only eight nights there.

The Grand Staircase (opposite) is one of the less overpowering pieces of design in the house, and is historically important as one of the earliest free-standing English wooden examples to survive – that at Knole is earlier still, but less sophisticated. The carved newel posts become alternately figures or heraldic beasts above the arcaded balustrade. Rather crude strapwork decorates the plaster under the stairs. On the walls are some of the paintings admired by Samuel Pepys on a visit in 1662. The house and gardens (designed by Salisbury in collaboration with John Tradescant) did not excite the admiration of everyone. As a contemporary verse pithily put it:

Here lies, thrown for worms to eat
Little bossive Robin that was so great
Not Robin Goodfellow, nor Robin Hood
But Robin the encloser of Hatfield Wood.

It might seem impossible for a house such as Hatfield to disappear given the history of the family and site, but a period of neglect under the sixth Earl (1713–80) saw Hatfield fall into decay.

According to Augustus Hare: 'He died a death as horrible as his life. His is the phantom coach which arrives and drives up the stair-case and disappears. Lord Salisbury heard it the other night when he was in his dressing room, and dressed again, thinking it was visitors, and went down, but it was no-one.' Luckily the sixth Earl's son James had a political career and no doubt kept up the house as a firm symbol of his family's ancestry.

In 1835 the same Earl's widow was incinerated in the West Wing, having suffered an accident with candles in her bedroom. 'It would have been impossible to identify her ashes for burial but for a ruby which the present Lady Salisbury wears in a ring,' wrote Augustus Hare on 14 December 1872. Danger to guests was also present in other forms: 'In the drawing room, over the chimney-piece is a huge statue of James I in bronze. It is not fixed, but supported by its own weight. A ball was once given in that room. In the midst of the dancing someone observed that the bronze statue was slowly nodding its head, and gave the alarm. The stampede was frightful. All the guests fled down the long gallery.'

Still the house survived and came to be of great importance again as the third Marquess involved himself in politics: he was three times Prime Minister to Queen Victoria and was the first to combine this office with that of Foreign Minister. It is from this period that the Library dates. The third Marquess was interested in scientific experiments, and had a room equipped with apparatus; he introduced electricity to the house, and even had a rudimentary telephone system installed in the Library (pages 13 and 23). This room has a look of sober politics, the books, leather upholstery and dark woodwork are all evocative of the House of Lords. The room is also a splendidly restful evocation of the flamboyant Renaissance style of the house. We can see how the carved pilasters are separated by the various colours of the book spines. Below are simple neo-Classical pilasters, while above on the gallery are neo-Renaissance details, along with a modern construction for the cast-iron balustrade. The detailing is a slimmer, more delicate version of that found on the Grand Staircase. The furniture is a mixture of contemporary cabinets with Regency and Sheraton chairs and settees, and the worn old leather gives a warmth to the room which is lacking in the white and gilt ceiling. This is English neo-Renaissance, as much as the Italian decoration at Alnwick (page 72–3), and the well-worn upholstery exudes a comfort that is lacking in Alnwick's more formal setting. It is nevertheless a distinguished room, redolent of tobacco smoke and the discussion of politics, in a Hatfield tradition nearly 400 years old.

Hatfield House

Opposite The Great Hall *Above* The Library

Nymans
The Sussex House of Anne, Countess of Rosse

THE SPIRIT of the famous gardens begun by Ludwig Messel in the 1890s has entered this house, so that both are fused into a tranquil expression of English country-house living. This is not his house. His undistinguished late-nineteenth-century villa had replaced an eighteenth-century farmhouse which stood on still earlier foundations, but the present house was built by Lady Rosse's parents, Colonel Leonard and Mrs Maud Messel, in the 1920s. One whole wing, including the Hall and Library, was destroyed by fire in 1947 and remains as just a shell. The remaining wing, the home of the present Countess of Rosse, has the comfortable look of a Cotswolds manor house built of stone in the late-sixteenth or early-seventeenth-century style. The effect was undoubtedly more Oxbridge College than Surrey Stockbroker when new; and that this taste for late English Gothic should still be manifest in the 1920s says little for the contemporary architecture and much for the strength of English traditions. Time has mellowed the stone and the ruined wing gives a spurious additional quality of age, particularly

as creeping plants encircle the empty oriel windows and finger the sharp outlines with a green embrace. Rhododendrons, camellias and magnolias are famous ingredients of the gardens laid out with the aid of such experts as Gertrude Jekyll; and inside flowers everywhere give a sense of warmth and colour to the robust architecture. In vases, pots, or as patterns on fabrics they insinuate the garden's spirit into the whole house.

In the Countess's Oriel Bedroom (opposite) is a comfortable mixture of modern and antique English furniture, mainly of the late eighteenth century, softening the uncompromising lines of the window, chimney-piece and recesses. The draped dressing-table is a particularly charming and feminine touch amongst such austerity, but chintz curtains, a yellow-covered easy chair, the brocade bed-cover formed from an eighteenth-century Italian clerical fabric, and a tray-table all lend warmth to the room, whilst the elegant cheval glass gives light and sparkle to a corner. Pleasing touches are added by items of family memorabilia, like the walking

Nymans

Opposite Mrs Messel's Bedroom *Above* The Dining Room

---

stick hung over the fireplace with *moiré* ribbon: it is a Linley heirloom from the eighteenth century.

The seventeenth-century furnishings of Mrs Messel's Bedroom (opposite) create the romantic surroundings that are so much a part of inter-war decoration, as in Hollywood's evocation of Manderley in Daphne du Maurier's *Rebecca*. Part of the charm lies in understatement: no use of dominant colour, but soft hydrangeas, the marquetry of the William and Mary chest-on-stand, the tapestry on the wall and in the fire screen, all reflect the garden, as does the great oak bed with posts as strong as young trees and a counterpane as soft and inviting as an English bowling green. The soft pinks and reds of the carpets glow against the mellow woods and light walls, welcoming the visitor to a restful night's sleep.

Comfort and hospitality are captured in the Library (page 25), which houses an outstanding collection of books on flowers. The muted colours of covers and chintz curtains are enlivened by the books' spines, and flowers are arranged to suggest the informal life of the country. Lady Rosse worked the needlepoint cushions. Although the room has old English furniture, it is distinctly twentieth century in appearance, the past being a pleasant background.

Bygone ages are more strongly suggested in the Dining Room (above), once the maids' sewing room, where a mixture of furniture of different periods subtly suggests the natural development of a long-established English house. A simple seventeenth-century oak dresser base blends with an early-nineteenth-century looking-glass with a well-decorated giltwood frame. The blue and white porcelain, some Delftware, some eighteenth-century English and some oriental, is arranged with an eye for proportion and effect, and graceful Regency chairs cluster around a simple early table. This fusion of styles is as English as the gardens which are the dominant presence throughout the house.

Weston Hall
The Northamptonshire House of Sir Sacheverell Sitwell

WHEN Sacheverell Sitwell went to live in this seventeenth-century house in early 1928 he found a timeless atmosphere conducive to reflection and writing. The faded grey stone of the exterior was surrounded by lush gardens and fine old trees, amongst which the later Gothick decorations to the façades gain a comfortable softness of outline. Weston Hall was left to Sir George Sitwell by his aunt Harriet, Lady Hanmer, but was intended for his son Sacheverell. Sir George was typically difficult about handing over the house outright, and teased with his ideas for it, saying 'I don't intend to do much here; just a sheet of water and a line of statues'. The house was to be administered by trustees. Its simplicity was appreciated by Sir Sacheverell, who always used a bedroom as his study: 'Too fine a view from a window would also be an impediment to writing. There should not be, and in any case there

are not, too many flowers. The room, it is true, is much too small, but I am used to it . . . having spent some four to five hours every day, during seven to eight months of every year, in this room, writing. From quarter or half-past nine to half-past twelve, and again from five o'clock to seven. Every weekday, on Christmas Day, Easter, Whitsun, all public holidays, and *always on Sunday* which works out at about seven years on end here "in solitary" in this room, working and looking out of the window' (*For Want of the Golden City*, 1973).

Ordered calm is steeped throughout the rooms and the objects in them. In the Justice Room (above) is nothing to disturb the eye or alarm the senses. Against a soft background of pale lilac walls and white woodwork is ranged an unusual pair of black lacquer cabinets on stands: they hint at trade with the Orient and the British

love for 'japanned' or lacquered furniture and objects. Together with the elaborate frames of the mirrors they form the major components in a scheme linking various types and styles of furniture. Birds, stuffed and under a glass dome, or painted and set in lacquered frames, remind one of exotic and local climes. Bronzes and mirrors give movement and light to the eighteenth- and early-nineteenth-century English furniture and a decorative floral border applied to the walls links objects and colours. The room has an unusual mixture of objects; and the red glass in the door is typically unexpected. The furnishings are all unlikely pieces to accompany one another, yet combine to give elegance to a peaceful interior.

The Library (above) has a vibrant quality which is in contrast to the soothing furnishings, which include an early-eighteenth-century walnut armchair and a sensible library drum-table laden with books. The sparkle comes from the delicate portrait of Dame Edith Sitwell by Pavel Tchelitchew, painted in 1929. The colours of the painting are reflected in the room; but in spite of the rather intrusive turquoise lamps and the book spines, it is the portrait that holds a magnetic power. One of six paintings of Dame Edith by Tchelitchew, it lay behind a cupboard in her Paris flat throughout the war years until retrieved by her secretary Elizabeth Salter in 1959. Dame Edith gave the startling opinion that her relationship with Tchelitchew was 'exactly like the relationship between Vittoria Colonna and Michelangelo'. It was certainly one of considerable emotional torment, and to the artist she had the 'green-gold hair and most beautiful nose any woman ever had'. The painting has a strength and strange beauty quite in sympathy with the atmosphere and decoration of this ancient house.

Two Traditional English Cottages

NOSTALGIA is an English passion. There has been no era in our history when we have not looked back to another age for either inspiration or comforting glimpses of what we imagine our own age should be. These two cottage interiors charm by their evocation of a cosy, bygone era. They are comfortable homes that have so far escaped the tide of gentrification. Can they really still exist? In many such cottages forests of paper with artless designs in peculiar combinations cover the walls. On broad swathes of nylon, flowers become geometric shapes and are pinned down by the polystyrene comfort of a three-piece suite angled at the household gods of TV and electric or gas 'log' fire. These rooms represent an England as traditional as Anne Hathaway's Cottage, with simple, centuries-old decoration for comfort. The former inhabitants of the 'gentrified' cottage are now in neat modern bungalows.

Already in 1946 *The Saturday Book* was accurately recording immediate post-war changes with contrasting photographs of a Somerset cottage and Queen Anne's bedroom at Warwick Castle, captioned 'This, and the parlour ... are socially and respectively rare and common. Yet the cottage hearth has qualities, domestic and aesthetic, as rare as the castle chimney piece, and still rarer in point of survival.'

Both the cottages illustrated here rely on the open coal fire for warmth and decoration. Britain, as Aneurin Bevan once pointed out, is secure in being an island built on coal. Take away the fireplaces here and there is no heart left to either house. These rooms are unself-conscious arrays of trivial furniture and decoration. The Gloucestershire cottage (above) has a fireplace blacked in a manner which even the proudest Northern housewife, as so

vividly described in Richard Hoggart's *Uses of Literacy* (1957), would gloat over. This is a fully working survivor of the millions of ranges once found throughout Britain. They heated the living room, provided cooking facilities with hot-plates and oven, even heated water through a boiler built in behind the grate. Other countries had enclosed stoves, but D. H. Lawrence's mining heroes could bath in their tin tubs in front of a hot coal fire. The range dominates the whole room, although the framed photograph of the soldier has such a magnetic poignancy in its association of simple English cottage life with service in the British Empire overseas that the eye is drawn automatically to it. China, glasses and a 'Royal Memento' are all essential elements of the cosy atmosphere.

This also applies to the Dorset cottage (above) with its equally welcoming fire set in a brick grate framed by a wooden mantelpiece. The whole decoration of the room is built up around this glowing hearth. A mirror sparkles above, Staffordshire pottery dogs and knick-knacks are peculiarly English in their odd shapes. Niches to either side contain books and useful pieces of furniture – including a TV set. The snug Victorian chair might have sat there for decades, for the room is timeless and so planned for comfort that there is no reason for change.

In neither room is there anything strident or flashy, nor is there anything to indicate a change from Ralph Waldo Emerson's view of 1856 when he wrote: 'The stability of England is the security of the world.' These rooms afford a tranquil welcome and pretend to be nothing other than cosy.

Chatsworth
The Derbyshire Seat of the Dukes of Devonshire

Unlike many palatial houses Chatsworth is more welcoming than most and this is partly due to the quirky floor-plan and adaptation of spaces to their present use; it is also due to the way the house visibly displays changes in taste and ownership. The present Duke's ancestress Bess of Hardwick would have approved of the decision by William Cavendish, fourth Earl of Devonshire, to demolish her house of the 1550s and build his own in 1686. This house has a distinctive English baroque style both inside and out, and although the four elevations of the exterior were not planned at the same time and were designed by different hands, they have achieved some coherence. However, successive generations have spent much time and money trying to impose a sensible floor-plan on the muddle created inside. The Entrance Hall was thus once a kitchen; and the staircase, which leads up to the inconveniently positioned State Rooms on the second floor, has been replaced three times in an effort to generate the right effect – the present version

was built in 1912. The architecture of Chatsworth appealed to Louis Simond in 1811, but not the interior. He found the tapestries in bad taste, and the pictures even worse: 'It is truly inconceivable how someone with the cultured taste of the Duchess of Devonshire could put up with such decoration.'

Much has changed since then. The Lower Library (opposite), by Crace, is a pleasant light room furnished with pieces in maplewood, particularly popular in the 1840s. It is full of clutter and useful desks and writing surfaces. Unobtrusive bookcases are banded by Italianate painted decoration.

The walls of the Yellow Drawing Room (above) are hung with a silk fabric from India. A finely carved chimney-piece of white statuary marble has heads of putti which pout into the room, and a gilt overmantel glitters above. A portrait by Tintoretto looks down on to a comfortable country-house jumble of objects, and light reflects off the sparkling Waterford lustres on the chimney-piece.

Honington Hall
The Warwickshire House of Sir John Wiggin Bart

EIGHTEENTH-CENTURY plasterwork reached sublime heights of craftsmanship and here we see fine detailing, as good as at Ditchley or anywhere. Hall, Saloon and Boudoir are decorated with plasterwork that approaches an English rococo style, all to be found in a red brick stone-dressed Carolingian house of modest design. Even more remarkable is the fact that it seems to be of entirely English craftsmanship with no Italians involved: it was carried out in the mid-eighteenth century for the owner Joseph Townsend by either Charles Stanley or Thomas Roberts under the guidance of a local craftsman, William Jones. It is remarkable that they could have produced such wonderful work.

The floor of the Hall is now smothered by a beautiful carpet, a distraction from the lightness of the scheme which relies on the black and white decoration of the floor for a definite contrast. This is also true of the club fender, which obscures the fine proportions of the chimney-piece. There is a charming intimacy about this room that embraces so much fine decoration.

Ditchley Park
An Oxfordshire House Decorated by William Kent

IN THIS COUNTRY HOUSE of the early 1720s James Gibbs created an austere Palladian exterior, thankfully enlivened with the elaborate interiors devised by William Kent and Henry Flitcroft. English plasterwork reached perfection during this period in a manner unlike that of previous centuries. The English Baroque was given a freshness by such Italian master plasterers as Artari and Bagutti. Gibbs employed both, and one of them may have produced the design and work for the Saloon (above) with its warm yellow curtains and walls of sienna marble colouring, admirable in contrast to the stark white of ceiling and wall decoration. In this English variation of an Italian style we can see a unifying element in the detailing of the dado and ceiling decoration, contrived to unite a bold scheme that embraces an asymmetrically placed chimney-piece, elaborate plaster relief, framing surrounds, putti, mirror and pilasters. They are all linked one to another in a manner seen off and on for the next 200 years as successive generations played with this unifying technique. It can

be seen again in Sir Mervyn Macartney's work of 1890 at 167 Queen's Gate (pages 96–7).

Here the sophisticated plasterwork should be seen with the views of the grounds through the large windows, so that artifice and Nature are linked in a peculiarly English manner. It is also to be set in the context of the adjoining Great Hall and famous White Drawing Room with its Kent door and picture surrounds. When Mrs Nancy Lancaster owned the house (as Mrs Ronald Tree) the White Drawing Room was given an imaginative touch by the use of fine antique furniture: a large coromandel lacquer screen, massive gilt and marble-topped tables, sofas and a Lely portrait of Charles II gave it a distinguished air. In the spirit of her business partner John Fowler, she did not repaint the rooms, but had them stripped to reveal the glowing original colours beneath. This tangerine-like pigment was probably mixed into the plaster in the Italian manner to give the solid depth of colour we still see, but her furnishings have mainly gone.

Houghton Hall
The Norfolk House of the Marquess of Cholmondeley

HOUGHTON is a delicious triumph of architectural genius, both inside and out. This is rare. Colen Campbell's designs for the house appeared in his huge compendium of elevations and plans, *Vitruvius Britannicus*, in 1725, but Campbell did not complete the building. Instead Sir Robert Walpole, Prime Minister 1721–42, employed Thomas Ripley to execute Campbell's designs, with certain alterations and modifications. He created a building admired since completion, not least by Catherine the Great, who bought most of Walpole's fine collection of Old Masters from his profligate grandson. The collaboration of William Kent, Vasari and Michael Rysbrack on various rooms has left us a vision of the antique which surpasses that of the English Renaissance. Nancy Lancaster said that Houghton taught her 'the most': Kent's apple-green velvet-hung bed 'brings to mind a waterfall'.

William Kent was responsible for the decoration of the State Rooms. Above the fireplace in the Stone Hall (opposite) is a deep relief by Rysbrack in the neo-Classical manner, as are the reliefs on the walls and over the door. Although the influence of Palladio lies heavily on Campbell, Kent's interpretation of his ideas is handled with ease and ingenuity, and he evokes more the spirit of the Venetian or Roman Renaissance, rather than the later, more academic copy-book 'antique' of Robert Adam. For what softens Kent's inventive interpretation of Italianate styles in this forty-foot cube is a judicious mixture of fine furniture and textiles. The giltwood arm and side chairs have curvaceous legs terminating in strong claws and the show-wood is decorated with shell motifs. Covered with the original green velvet, this suite glows against the rich colours of the carpet covering the stone floor.

The Marble Parlour (above) is just as strongly Italianate in feeling. Kent's handling of the columns, pilasters and plasterwork is as masterful as Rysbrack's carving of 'The Sacrifice of Bacchus' over the fireplace. If the carrara marble seems frigid, this mood is soon dispelled by the twelve giltwood chairs blazing with Genoese velvet, and by the Venetian references in their decoration.

Kedleston Hall
The Derbyshire House of the Viscount Scarsdale

AT KEDLESTON, DERBYSHIRE, Robert Adam was presented by Sir Nathaniel Curzon with an unsatisfactory building begun by James Paine. It seems that as a result Adam must have gained a reputation for correcting or modifying the mistakes of others, for he was also called in to complete what Paine had begun at Nostell Priory (pages 46–9). As at Syon House (pages 40–3) and elsewhere, Adam used Joseph Rose Jr to execute his plasterwork. He began work on the house in 1760, finishing the Marble Hall in 1763.

Adam undoubtedly knew of William Kent's Marble Hall at Holkham, Norfolk, completed by 1759, but at Kedleston the scale is lighter and more intimate, and the detail more refined. The ceiling is left light and airy with a graceful design of Roman motifs, while at Holkham the heavy ceiling is only made possible because the floor is sunk into the basement storey to give the room an impressive height. Far from being a basilica like Kent's Hall, the Hall at Kedleston is based on the idea of a Roman atrium and the columns are firmly set into the floor and do not seek to overpower the visitor by means of great plinths. The alabaster is local. The room is entered under a form of screen created by free-standing columns, but at the other end of the room Paine's original building forced Adam to set the columns flanking the door against the wall, thus reducing the effect of all the columns appearing to support the roof, and detracting from his probable original intention.

To either side of the room are disposed benches and fine marble chimney-pieces surmounted by painted roundels of classical scenes, with a surround of gilt plasterwork figures in relief. The steel fire-grates are said to be by Adam, and the firelight must have created a wonderful effect in the evening of a cold day, sparkling off the reflective cold surfaces of columns and floor. Dr Johnson mentioned the house in his *Diary*: 'The large room with the pillars would do for the Judges to sit in at Assizes ... the pillars are very large and massy, they take up too much room, they were better away.' As so often when discussing aesthetic matters, he was wrong.

Syon House
The Middlesex House of the Duke and Duchess
of Northumberland

THERE is so much work by Robert Adam for us to see, and even more by his imitators, that we tend to take it too much for granted. Some of his finest achievements are arguably those in which he was amending the work of others or reconstructing interiors within an existing framework; and Syon is just such a case. Adam had finished his work at Alnwick (page 72) for the former Sir Hugh Smithson, created the first Duke of Northumberland, and had high hopes of being given a free hand at Syon. But the Duke had other ideas and Adam was not allowed to rebuild the elevations of the house, so that the curious Tudor facades with their large inserted sash windows give no hint of the interior decoration and are more picturesque than beautiful. Nevertheless Adam looked back with some satisfaction on his work there: 'I endeavoured to render it a noble and elegant habitation,' he wrote, 'not unworthy of a proprietor who possessed not only wealth to execute a great design, but skill to judge of its merit.' Whereas at nearby Osterley Park Adam was able to proclaim his bold interior remodelling with a brilliantly conceived neo-Classical portico, at Syon in 1762 he had to use the Entrance Hall (pages 42–3) and not a portico to heighten aesthetic anticipation for the progression of splendours inside the house.

He achieved this by creating his own idea of a 'Roman room' using the area taken up by the refectory in the original Tudor convent. The Hall is on a lower level than the other rooms, and was devoid of all colour save for the black and white flags of the floor and a bronze copy of the 'Dying Gaul' which stands at the end of the room leading by means of a few steps under Doric columns to the Ante-Room. In Adam's own words: 'The inequality of the levels has been managed in such a manner as to increase and add to the movement, so that an apparent defect has been converted into a real beauty.' The Hall is top-lit by small windows beneath the cornice, in turn given elaborate surrounds. The plasterwork of the ceiling is one of Adam's boldest and heaviest designs. Doric columns rise from the floor to half-way up the wall and a rich entablature is echoed in the deeply coffered ceiling of the apse or half-domed alcove framing a copy of the Apollo Belvedere. This room is one of Adam's most underestimated achievements in

which every disadvantage of location and scale was brilliantly brushed aside. The walls have now been given colour, so that the Ante-Room (opposite) is no longer the extreme contrast it once was.

Here we see the twelve *antico-verde* columns dredged from the Tiber and brought from Rome by the first Duke in 1765, according to an old story. Adam has created the richest possible setting for these beautiful columns, in which only the form of the doors and chimney-piece serve as reminders that this is all in England. In fact wartime damage revealed them to be scagliola, and the story of their dredging was therefore probably that of an Italian dealer selling them to a gullible client. For all his research into Roman architecture Adam only incorporated a form of central heating into a few buildings (including Newby Hall, pages 44–5), and this was not one of them. He studied in Italy with Clérisseau, admired and examined the buildings of the early Renaissance and even rediscovered the colouring of Roman buildings. All this is apparent in the Ante-Room, where the proportions, compositions and colours provide perfect background material for the columns. Here is the 'picturesque antique', Adam's main preoccupation, as his drawings of the ruins of Spalato and his aquaintance with Piranesi reveal.

In the Ante-Room the fine plasterwork smothering walls and ceiling in intricate pattern is all the work of the English master-craftsman Joseph Rose Jr. Gilt anthemions blaze against the blue painted entablature. Gilt statues stand aloft crowning the columns given Ionic bases and capitals by Adam. The scagliola floor is a richly coloured counterpart to the design of the ceiling, an idea carried out with even greater intricacy in the Dining Room next door. Lest there be any doubt about the Roman inspiration, panels of gilt plaster trophies glow on the walls. Yet this room was used by servants waiting 'out of livery'!

As an expression of English style, Syon is no more typical than any of the other grand houses built as an exercise in flaunting the owner's power and forming a lavish display of his 'taste'. It is typical in its idiosyncrasy and in its reflection of a boldness of vision on the part of both owner and architect, allied to consummate craftsmanship and a great capacity for adaptation.

Syon House

The Entrance Hall

Newby Hall
The Yorkshire House of R.E.J. Compton Esq.

THE SCULPTURE gallery at Newby Hall, Yorkshire, is one of Robert Adam's more unusual and interesting exercises in re-creating a room in the Roman style, built around a domed rotunda. The designs are dated 1772 and 1776, and the gallery reveals him to be a master technician in the handling of a complex variety of apsidal and recessed wall constructions. His patron was one William Weddell, a rich connoisseur who liked to enjoy his collection of fine works of art in the distant wilds of Yorkshire, a landscape far removed from that of the Rome he visited in 1765. His death in a cold water bath 'occurred with tragic suddenness on April 30, 1792, at the age of 68 years'.

Weddell was planning to compile a catalogue of his collection when he died so suddenly, but left no notes. We know that the great bath was originally installed in a Roman *thermae*. It is a remarkable piece of hollowed-out white and purple *pavonazetto* marble, holding 214 gallons of water. The Barberini 'Venus' is also known about. It was found by an Englishman in the cellar of the Barberini Palace and sold to Weddell, who made a down-payment and then agreed to pay an annuity until his death (the amounts involved are not known). The Frenchman Louis Simond writing in 1810–11 found the gallery stupendous and the marbles true antiques, not just the fakes so often made for rich men on a Grand Tour and passed off as rare objects, such as, for example, the scagliola columns at Syon (page 40).

There is no English reticence in the background to the marble delights. The original oil lamps stand on their carved wall brackets. The effect can be little different to that achieved in Roman times and Adam even installed a version of under-floor heating, the vents clearly visible beneath some of the statues. Some of the bases are antique marble ones, and some were designed by Adam himself. He would also have liked a marble floor, but was thwarted in this by his patron, who decided on an oak floor. Since money was clearly no object, this single detraction from the total 'Roman' effect must be regretted.

Nostell Priory
The Yorkshire House of Lord St Oswald

JAMES PAINE was employed by Sir Rowland Winn, fourth Baronet, as the original architect of Nostell Priory in 1733, but it was left to Robert Adam to embellish his work. Paine was almost as prolific a designer as Adam, and the Victoria and Albert Museum, London, contains two fat volumes of his detailed designs for decoration; but his work has solid worthiness that lacks dash. Nor were his buildings as practical to live in as they were attractive on paper, so that in 1765 the fifth Baronet asked Adam to rectify the design and remodel, much as Adam was asked to follow Paine at Kedleston (pages 38–9) and to make sense of the old buildings of Osterley and Syon (pages 40–3). But his work at Nostell was scarcely appreciated until our day, and even now it is the craftsmanship of Chippendale that arouses our greatest interest.

When Augustus Hare visited the house in January 1881 he noted in his diary: 'We went to see Nostell, a very grand but little known house of the Winns', full of splendid things, glorious tapestries, china, Chippendale furniture, but most remarkable of all, a doll's house of the last century. . . .' There is no mention of Adam, let alone Paine, and it is an interesting reflection on late-nineteenth-century taste that Chippendale should be mentioned.

The finest room in the house is in fact a collaboration of both Chippendale and Adam, for the Library (opposite) is as English a room as one might expect to find. Adam employed Joseph Rose Jr to execute the fine plasterwork and he was assisted by Thomas Perritt in creating the light ceiling that is such an excellent foil for the solid colours of the woods used below. For all their delicacy the decoration of entablature and ceiling is no more sugary in colouring than that used by Josiah Wedgwood in the decoration of porcelain. The design of the carved and pedimented bookcases is a manifestation of the restraint found in much of the finest English cabinet-making and an echo of Adam's own researches into Roman styles and motifs. The leather spines of the books give an unexpected dimension to the room, creating a form of rhythm along the wall and giving it subtle depth. The Roman forms of the

Nostell Priory

Above The State Bedroom *Opposite* The Dining Room

chairs, evident in such details as their lyre-backs, and the imperial scale and decoration of Chippendale's desk give a solid nobility to the whole scheme, one that is as durable as the presence of the painting of the room and its instigator suggests.

The Dining Room (opposite) shows evidence of Paine's work in the more florid design of chimney-piece, overmantel decoration and ceiling plasterwork. The Adam details in the form of great swirls of strictly delineated Roman pattern to either side of the chimney-piece cannot be said to add to Paine's scheme, but the overall effect is very comfortable with a long set of capacious side chairs upholstered in figured velvet ranged around the gleaming mahogany table.

In the chintz-hung State Bedroom (above), the *chinoiserie* decoration and furniture set against hand-painted wallpaper were all provided by Chippendale. This room is completely English in the way it is handled, but one is nevertheless surprised at how well all the varied elements of decoration blend together. England was famous for chintz in the mid-eighteenth century (page 57), indeed a list of processes long since vanished achieved effects at which we can now only guess, for they have perished or lost their finish. Here the windows and bed are hung with a fabric that is at odds with the *chinoiserie* decoration of the furniture and wallpaper, yet it is all pulled together by the beautiful yet grotesque looking-glass.

Downstairs is now made comfortable with a flaming yellow colour scheme in the former Breakfast Room (page 47) full of pictures, eighteenth- and early-nineteenth-century furniture and full-blown festoon curtains to cut out the Yorkshire weather. After a fire at Nostell in 1980 David Mlinaric advised on the restoration, and in this room he re-used a Paine chimney-piece (originally in an upstairs bedroom) in an overall reinterpretation of the mid-eighteenth century. The room is more in the spirit of Paine than Adam; but more than that it is an indication of how varied the interior of an English house can be, as successive owners and decorators stamp their taste into the fabric.

Royal Lodge
The Windsor House of Her Majesty Queen Elizabeth the Queen Mother

Aᴌᴛʜᴏᴜɢʜ this house has only existed in its present form for little more than fifty years, it has an atmosphere of age and a strange beauty that is essentially English. Because of royal ownership the house has experienced momentous events, yet it possesses the spirit of a family house and has witnessed all the joys, griefs, anxieties and expectations that any home will contain. It also breathes the English country air of Windsor Great Park and is full of flowers and plants from the surrounding informal gardens designed by King George vi and Queen Elizabeth.

The portrait of the Prince Regent, later George iv, above the arched Gothick chimney-piece in the Saloon reminds us that this is part of the *cottage orné* built for the Prince Regent by John Nash and Sir Jeffry Wyatville, almost all of which was broken up on his death in 1830. It was a favourite retreat of his. Flanked by wings at either end, the Saloon (these pages) is now the main room in the house as reconstructed for the Duke and Duchess of York after the worst of the recession was over in 1931–2.

Around the fireplace is a conventionally comfortable arrangement of damask-covered chairs and sofas. The decoration might have been undertaken at any time since 1920 and has a timeless quality. Useful tables are crowded with objects, plants, flowers and books, and the huge size of the room is made an advantage by the arrangement of further sitting areas and the placing of desks near the windows. The light Regency decoration in the Gothick manner is a pleasant background for the chandeliers and large tapestry, which in turn provides a sense of scale for this huge room. The Italianate look of the giltwood and damask-covered chairs round the heavy table is emphasized by the height of the altar candlesticks, now converted into electric lamps. By placing such large pieces against one wall all the other smaller arrangements fall into place, and are unified by the enormous oriental carpet spread across the floor. The writing-table and desk provide useful working areas beneath the Gothick windows. For all the grandeur of the room the atmosphere remains that of a much-loved family house.

A Country *Cottage Orné* in the Gothick Manner

WHAT could be more joyous than this modern interpretation of a Gothick *cottage orné*, a form of idyllic country architecture which gained impetus at the turn of the eighteenth century. The use of the Gothick style has never ceased to form an element of delightful eccentricity in an English building, and few examples have achieved the warmth and friendliness seen here. This small house has more in common with Batty Langley's Gothick designs of 1742 than the later enthusiasm for Plantagenet England evident in the 1840s publication of Joseph Nash's *Mansions of England in the Olden Times*; but the date of the building is actually closer to Nash's time, and the white-painted Gothick hall chair (actually in the Drawing Room, above and opposite) is a near contemporary of the fine oriel window behind. Warm colours make the interior of this house glow with a welcoming embrace that is far removed from any lingering ecclesiastical feelings initially suggested by the form of the Gothick windows. The owner has filled the interior with a wealth of unusual English porcelain and pottery which forms the main decoration, for the elegant English antique furniture is very restrained in comparison with this abundant pattern and colour, particularly effective in autumn and winter.

In the spring and summer the English garden blooms outside and the seasons are reflected as an integral part of the decoration. The Drawing Room's large Gothick window (above) is left undraped, revealing the view to advantage, and the garden fruits decorating the plates together with the china pigs on the table give a countrified Beatrix Potter look. The amusing low table is almost an Indian version of English Gothick with its hint of Islamic influence. Over the marble-topped side cabinet (opposite) is a good Regency looking-glass with a *verre eglomisé* panel unusually painted with fruit. The frame's Gothick-style cluster columns are naturally perfect for the house. The *tôle* tray and oil lamp are simple decorative touches, but the main feature of the room is without doubt the collection of Wemyss pottery.

A Country *Cottage Orné*

Opposite The Dining Room *Above* The Garden Room

In the room with the garden door (above) are mustard yellow decorations and a window seat for maximum enjoyment of the garden. The plates give green blobs of colour, and are a satisfying reminder of the kitchen; the Gothick style of the house is continued in the decoration of the cornice.

The Dining Room (opposite) has similar decoration, more obviously picked out. It is full of delightful details, such as the fine collection of Staffordshire pottery hens over the fireplace. With the mahogany sideboard of about 1800 is a set of eighteenth-century French provincial chairs, and the informal mixture of styles and periods is again peculiarly English and countrified.

Before the recent redecoration Cecil Beaton visited the house and wrote of his rain-drenched stay: 'I, however, was content to bask in the summery atmosphere of his pretty 1800 Gothic house with roses in Victorian vases, on china and on chintz. The house is like the home of an old aunt or of the girl in *Spectre de la Rose*!' Bolder designs and colours now reflect the mood of the 1980s.

Horsted Place
The Sussex House of Lady Rupert Nevill

THE CHINTZ CURTAINS and loose covers seen in this room are so much a part of English decoration that we tend to take them for granted. The word 'chintz' came into the English language as Britain expanded her interests over the globe and is first recorded in use around 1614; it derives from the Hindi word *chint*, referring to Indian calico cloth painted over with a design. What followed was a great technological achievement, for the British thought to combine the European technique of using wooden blocks to print on cloth with the Indian technique of dyeing the cotton with a process that fixed the colour. By the 1670s dye-fast cloth was being produced using several colours in one pattern. During the first half of the eighteenth century British products were considered the best, despite heavy competition from abroad. After the introduction of copper-plate stamping in the middle of the century production increased without any fall in quality, and competition was effectively eliminated. The early designs often depicted scenes with figures or architectural devices; the flowery designs we associate with chintz came into common use in the late eighteenth century, when they were firmly established as favourite patterns for all types of rooms. Chintz rather than silk-hung rooms such as that at Chatsworth were now in the height of fashion (page 33). With the introduction of roller printing after 1815 chintz rushed off the machines to fill an insatiable demand, and the British textile industry boomed as much from this as from the use of any other type of fabric.

The style of the hangings in the Drawing Room at Horsted Place are particularly appropriate in a house that was designed by Samuel Dawkes and built in 1851 by George Myers, formerly Augustus Pugin's builder. Dawkes was as interested in the Gothic revival as any of Pugin's followers and he created a great mausoleum of a house with loving care paid to all the fine details of staircase and chimney-pieces. When Lady Rupert Nevill moved into the house in the mid-1960s she whitened all the stained woodwork and set about creating an interior full of light and warmth. It is now more a reflection of the Edwardian period than of the rather oppressive and earnest Gothic revival, and the house has clearly benefited both from her sensitive treatment and from the advice of Martin Battersby and Carl Toms. (Battersby's wallpaper in the Gallery is particularly striking and was designed and printed in his own workshop.) The Drawing Room could so easily be dominated by the great chimney-piece of Caen stone, with its deeply recessed carving leading to a fairly small grate. However, Colefax & Fowler chintz and wall-coverings immediately lighten the whole appearance of the room and the gilding applied to such details as the dividing arch and the ceiling decoration give an extra lift. Adding sparkle to the collection of antique and modern furniture (most of which came from the Regency house previously inhabited by the family) is a mirror between two windows that sprinkles light over the collections of enamels and paintings.

'I had forgotten what a bright, sparkling kind of room it was, bright with an Edwardian brightness of chintz and cut-glass and shiny furniture and silk lampshades and long windows filled with the greenness of lawns outside' (*All My Sins Remembered*, 1965): the second Viscount Churchill was describing his parents' house in the Midlands, but the atmosphere in Lady Rupert's Drawing Room is the same. For this is an interior that is not dead or stilted, it is a comfortable twentieth-century room that makes no demands on its occupants other than to relax.

Highclere Castle
The Hampshire House of the Earl of Carnarvon

MANY nineteenth-century country houses were not unlike the great London railway stations from which owners and guests set out to enjoy the delights of country sports and entertainments. St Pancras Station, London, is not far removed from the style of Highclere, nor are the Houses of Parliament – and not surprisingly, since the same architects worked there. The Entrance Hall (above) is particularly chilly in its Perpendicular style and extends a forbidding welcome, not softened by the galleried Hall beyond (opposite). Sir Charles Barry reconstructed the house in 1838 for the third Earl of Carnarvon, the third scheme to be submitted to the Earl. The interiors shown here were executed later, after about 1860, by Thomas Allom and (possibly) Gilbert Scott.

There is undoubtedly a cool beauty to the house. The coloured marbles to floor and columns in the Entrance Hall are as lively as the fluting, arching and vaulting that supports the roof. The bright carpet is delightfully out of place in this setting, and is a desperate attempt to lend domesticity to the cold surroundings and conjure up a warm welcome in this expression of noble antiquity.

The galleried Hall is another impressive space in which sofas and chairs invite a repose hard to achieve in surroundings like these. Rich colours, a portrait of the present Earl in uniform, a high screen and an oriental carpet strike a human note, but the room is impossible to decorate in any really comfortable manner. It was undoubtedly perfect for pre-sporting activities, gatherings and for tea after a meet, but it has no other function. Law courts, Parliament, banks, railway stations: the architecture is redolent of all these and suitable for them. Barry himself was happiest designing such buildings as the Travellers' and Reform Clubs, and these are also suggested here. The owner and his guests no doubt felt at home in all these buildings, moving from one to the other with ease, and the style of Highclere shows the world with which they were familiar, staffed by many servants, warmed by huge fires, and full of chattering voices. Devoid of all this the great Halls seem still and empty, a reminder of past lives.

Calke Abbey
The Derbyshire House of Henry Harpur-Crewe Esq.

So much has been made of the fact that this elephantine house has slumbered undisturbed for decades in its hollow amongst the Derbyshire hills that it comes as no surprise to find it little more than a huge attic full of the most marvellous delights – all as fascinating as only someone else's debris can be. Partly early seventeenth century, the house was later remodelled from 1793 to 1811. The Harpur-Crewe family have lived here for generations, and with engaging eccentricity they have squirrelled away a hoard of unconsidered trifles. Certain bedrooms have remained untouched, and are crammed to bursting point with relics of former collections accumulated by deceased members of the family, who nearly all had an intense passion for collecting. There is also a touch of a good horror film to the whole house, a feeling heightened by the decoration of Hall and Bird Lobby; both reflect a style which Evelyn Waugh described as owing 'more to the taxidermist than the sculptor or painter' (*Officers and Gentlemen*, 1955).

In the Entrance Hall (above) a wooden letter-box awaits the correspondence of long dead members of the family or guests; forlornly neglected on the hall table, it survives the era of large house parties and a necessary habit of regular letter-writing. Hard hall chairs stand waiting for the messenger, dripping with rain from his journey. Horns stab the air in mute fury and in the small Bird Lobby (page 64) – now the Breakfast Room – a table laid ready for a meal is surrounded by the unblinking glares of slaughtered animals: no convivial company is suggested by their accusing glass eyes. There is no escape from the game hunter, nor from his trophies.

Amongst the elegant pilasters and brass-nailed doors of an adjoining (remodelled) Saloon of 1841 (opposite), Harpur-Crewe ancestors look down from above. The gorgeous velvets of the chairs are now shrouded in slip-covers and the piano is as mute as the cases of 'things'. This room was conceived in its present form by the local architect Stevens of Derby, who does not seem to have known quite what to do with the space at his disposal, so that the present furnishings are as good a solution as any and reflect the late-

61

Calke Abbey

Above 'Collection of Egyptian Curiosities' *Opposite* The Drawing Room
Page 64 The Breakfast Room

nineteenth-century desire for sociable arrangements and rather too much furniture.

Throughout the whole house is remarkable evidence of collecting passions that only become understandable in the context of the isolated position of the house and a lust to fill empty hours and days with constructive activity. The marvellous 'Collection of Egyptian Curiosities' (above) is surely a reminder of a happy escape on a Nile Cruise from the chill and ice of a Derbyshire winter; parts of a Georgian state bed still in the chest in which they were sent from London during the 1780s hint at further delights in store. It is for such remarkable items as these that the house has achieved fame, but there is more here than that.

The appearance of the Drawing Room (opposite) is a perfect example of mid-Victorian taste, as though a time-machine is in action. Decorated by Tatham and Bailey, the room dates from 1733 with later decoration of about 1810 and the furniture is now arranged in informal groupings to stimulate conversation. It is as it was arranged in 1868. Baggy chintz covers protect the fabric of the chairs beneath, glass domes fend dust off intricate arrangements of unusual objects, and light glints from the wide gilt frames on the paintings. The room is asleep. The heavy damask curtains allow enough light in to shine in the great pier-glasses of the 1840s. 'It was a room whose furnishings should have been completed by the sound of sweet silly voices, the crackle of a fire and the tinkle of a piano and the smell of freshly made tea. But all was still, airless and silent' (Stella Gibbons, *Bassett*, 1934).

Thirty years or so ago it was still possible to find less imposing versions of such a room surviving in the suburbs of most of our large industrial cities. The villas have gone now and the contents dispersed so that this house is, on a large scale, a reflection of that particularly comfortable taste, with no pretensions to grandeur, which once formed the backbone of most English decoration.

Thorp Perrow
The Yorkshire House of Sir John Ropner

WHAT would an English country house be without a good cloakroom? Everyone loves solid Edwardian fittings – a mahogany lavatory seat, heavy porcelain and shiny brass handles. The basin should have a good marble surround and sensible plate-glass mirror with a decent brass light-fitting above. Something like a club, but better. In this 1903 ground-floor Lavatory (above) is an added luxury in the abundant and unnecessary tiles and a good-sized bearskin in which Monsieur Hulot would surely ensnare his spurs. There are useful old sticks, boots, coats and capes – just in case. Also a wonderful collection of odd photographs: insignificant scenes presumably of enormous sentimental value to someone dead for at least thirty years. Best of all are the trophies, bagged by Sir Leonard Ropner, the father of the present owner. The Ropners were a family of shipowners and entrepreneurs, who bought this early-nineteenth-century house in 1897. Although the game was all shot in the 1920s and 1930s – in Kenya, Scotland and North America – it epitomizes the *style coloniale* that was so beloved of the Edwardians.

As the second Viscount Churchill wrote of Barleythorpe, his Uncle Hugh Lowther's house in the Midlands: 'It was an incredible house, bristling with claws and teeth, smelling of taxidermy. A rhinoceros with a huge stumpy nose and eyes like bicycle lamps glared down from the top of the stair. . . . As a child I approved of Barleythorpe, and so did the rest of the children, because everything in it *was* something. Coffee tables were not just tables, they were sawn-off legs of elephants. Inkstands were the hooves of favourite horses and even paper-knives had fur handles' (*All My Sins Remembered*, 1965). That sort of house is evoked here, and this form of decoration is no longer possible now that so few of the victims' descendants survive.

Callaly Castle
The Northumberland House of Major Simon Browne

VARIOUS BRANCHES of the Clavering family have lived in this house since it first rose on its site, and when it came to the present owner's grandfather in 1877 there were already 650 years of family history connected with Callaly, parts of which date from the fourteenth century. The present building is mainly of the late seventeenth century, but there are eighteenth- and nineteenth-century additions seen here.

The remarkable confection of the Drawing Room (above) plasterwork, fretted balustrade, pillars and chimney-piece dates from 1757. The plasterwork is of Italian craftsmanship, handled delicately and with restraint; its medallions depict a mixed group of poets and philosophers, among them Pope and Newton. Galleries in a room can give the occupants an uncanny sensation that they are being watched, and this is no exception. The brittle outlines of the *chinoiserie* design in the open fret of the balustrade are in sharp contrast to the plasterwork, and lend a feeling of light and fantasy to what is in any case an ethereal setting, given vibrance by the cut-

glass chandeliers and table-lustres on walls and furniture. The tables are of good mahogany in the manner of Chippendale's Chinese-Gothick designs, with fine Italian scagliola tops.

The products of the Industrial Revolution held evident appeal for Major Alexander Henry Browne, who purchased the house in 1877. The glass-roofed and stone-walled Hall (opposite) was once an external courtyard, but was made into a museum for his large collection of objects, most of which were sold to the British Museum at the end of the century. The ironwork is all rather reminiscent of an early continental department store, although the Victorian spiral staircase was actually made by the Glaswegian ironmasters Walter Macfarlane & Co. Sheaves of unused lances fan over the stone. Long dead animals are remembered as their mounted heads stare out accusingly at humans below. In the depths lurks another surprise in the shape of a horse's head. Of marble, it was dug up at Ephesus in 1841 and reflects yet another aspect of the taste for collecting apparent in this remarkable building.

An Early-Nineteenth-Century Interior
Holland Park, London

T HESE INTERIORS form a pleasing pastiche of an early-ninteenth-century English town house. Just as Linley Sambourne's house (page 82–5) reflects the refined aesthetic taste of the latter decades of the century, so this is a microcosm of English taste as it evolved up to around 1840. It belongs to an architect, an enthusiastic supporter of the Victorian Society, but is neither a sterile nor academic exercise in re-creating a period. It is a functional twentieth-century adaptation of the furnishing and decorating styles of the early nineteenth century.

The Sitting Room (page 71) is built around the white marble chimney-piece of a design often seen in England with slight variations until the 1860s. Above it is another typical sight, a single sheet of mirror glass formed into an overmantel reflecting light into the room. The gasolier embellished with cut glass decoration is exceptional and a reminder that gas-lighting has been with us for a long time – Brighton Pavilion's 'dragon' chandelier was already a gasolier in the 1820s. The furniture reflects the decoration that emerged as an English version of continental 'Empire', given impetus by the works of such designers as Thomas Hope, George Smith and George Tatham, and made by cabinet-makers catering for the new taste in decoration. The massive lion end-supports of the sofa remind us of the contemporary fashion for archaeological excavations arising from Napoleon's Egyptian campaigns, while the design of the chairs derives from French influences of the time. But this room is no slavish copy. Apart from the lamps, the room is brought into the twentieth century by the leopard-skin rug over the sofa, a touch of softness which disposes of what could be a stiffly formal setting. Well-draped windows provide light, and the room is given warmth by the appealing colour scheme dictated by the fine carpet and reflected in the decoration of the wall, cornice and ceiling rose. The exact colouring of earlier periods is irrelevant to the effect here created.

With the striped papered Drawing Room (opposite) we are on more dangerous ground, for the 'tented room' look of many Regency or Empire rooms has been so often misapplied that it now invites an immediate criticism of modish over-indulgence, and is aptly termed 'Vogue Regency'. However, this blue stripe is a fine and pretty variation – it was the cheapest Sanderson design on sale (4s 6d) when the owner decorated the room in 1960. The surfaces of the room are broken by a white picture rail and cornice and are given interesting lighting by means of two suspended lamps acting as up-lighters. Although the ceiling is architecturally 'tented' there is no more contrivance than this; 'tented' rooms hung with fabric were another result of the Napoleonic campaigns in southern Europe and were more commonly seen abroad. The Empire and Regency are here further suggested by a fine pair of bookcases topped with busts; a pleasing jumble of pictures surrounds the centrally positioned overmantel. The brightness of walls and ceiling is allowed to make maximum impact by the use of softer, duller tones for the upholstery and furniture, and, since this does not exactly copy 1820s decoration, a period is again suggested rather than austerely re-created.

In the Muniment Room (page 70) is reflection of a more European style of decoration, emerging from a preoccupation with Ancient Greece and the Roman Empire. It might just as well be the room of a cultured German of the period around 1820 to about 1840, with a warm reddish colour lending a background to the gilt anthemion border, mahogany cabinet and marble busts. If the wall-lights seem over-grand for a room of small scale, they are eye-catching additions to the array of framed objects and reveal an eccentricity in arrangement which characterizes so much English decoration.

An Early-Nineteenth-Century Interior

Above The Muniment Room *Opposite* The Sitting Room

Alnwick Castle
The Northumberland House of the
Duke and Duchess of Northumberland

Amongst the many great architects of reconstruction during the mid-nineteenth century, the name of Anthony Salvin is not high on the list of favourites. This is possibly because of his predilection for the Jacobethan style, and his playful use of distinctive elements of the architectural details stemming from the English and Italian Renaissance. He was capable of fascinating and impressive work on a huge scale as at Thoresby Hall, Nottinghamshire, and Harlaxton Manor, Lincolnshire: the interiors of both are widely different and full of unexpected delights. Here at Alnwick for the Duke of Northumberland he was in a more serious mood as he 'restored' what was basically a twelfth-century castle, with later additions and subtractions by Adam, to a full semblance of a great medieval fortress. He was neither a James Wyatt nor a William Burges and this is no Windsor, Belvoir or Cardiff Castle, but what it lacks in style it gains in a subtle handling of a complex variety of shapes and masses. Where other castles have romantic terraces and suggest *Romeo and Juliet* rather than *Ivanhoe*, this is much more to the taste of Sir Walter Scott. It stands determinedly square and forbidding on the borders of England and Scotland. It has a keep, armoury and Guard Chamber to assert the long history of the Percy family's occupation of the place back to Norman times, with a dungeon for good measure. The Frenchman Louis Simond visited Alnwick in 1810, and commented on the stone figures carved to resemble defending soldiers then set on the battlements. His senses set on edge by this, he toured the dungeons and lower regions of the Castle in some trepidation: 'We saw a crenellated iron wheel with chains and trembled at the sight of this object of torture and on questioning our guide in a sort of fright, he then reassured us that this served to ring the dining bell.'

Above ground the setting is a great Italianate Palazzo. Beautiful as much of the furniture is, it is to the paintings that we look for a continuation of this flavour. Titian, Van Dyck, even Canaletto and Meissen porcelain are somehow not what one expects or hopes to see (Canaletto actually painted a view of Alnwick itself, which still hangs in the Red Drawing Room). This is an eclectic Ducal mixture which is certainly grand in its content and very English, for the various decorative styles and elements are made to work together – but only just.

On 4 November 1887 Augustus Hare found a sad party at Alnwick. 'The actual Duchess did not appear till dinner, when she was wheeled into the room in a chair, very sweet and attractive looking, but very fragile. [She died in 1890.] The Duke [6th] looks wiry, refined, rather bored, and some people would find him alarming. Lord and Lady Percy seem to be two of the most silent people in the world – she pretty still in spite of her ten children. . . .

The charming Duchess Eleanor showed me the rooms – the magnificent rooms, which owe their glory to her husband, Duke Algernon, who, when remonstrated with for thus changing a medieval fortress, said, "Would you wish us only to sit on benches upon a floor strewn with rushes?" He purchased the whole of the Cammuccini collection at Rome, because of his great wish to have one single picture which they would not sell separately. The magnificent decorations of the rooms are by Canina, but the most lasting attraction of the castle is the library, with the really splendid collection of books formed by Duke Algernon.'

The Library (opposite) is a pleasantly lit room of wonderful proportions. The reds of wall- and floor-coverings are a soft but lively contrast to the woodwork of the shelves and the spines of the many volumes housed there. To break the great height of the room with a gallery was no great invention, but it is handled with a delicacy of feeling for the light structure and the elegant brass of the balustrade railing. The large chimney-piece is not allowed to dominate the room. White marble is inset with panels of mustard yellow and topped by mirror-glass, so that light is reflected above the fire. The room now contains enough comfortable chairs and tables to fulfil the needs of the most energetic scholar, while also making a comfortable drawing room. Above all floats the coffered plaster ceiling with richly gilt decoration. It gives the room warmth and interest, echoing the comfortable clutter of the English country house down below.

In the Red Drawing Room (page 8) we can see more clearly the Renaissance detailing and are struck particularly by the finely detailed woodwork. As at Thoresby, the doors are well constructed and heavily carved and to either side of the door runs a beautifully inlaid wooden dado. Again, a remarkably intricate plaster ceiling is highly decorated, and the delicate frieze was painted in Rome for the house; its pattern was often to be seen in Renaissance Italy. A team of Italian craftsmen was actually brought over to work at Alnwick. The damask-lined walls look rich and warm, but the room is furnished with a selection of well-made to indifferent pieces of furniture in eighteenth-century styles that fail to excite any great reaction – not even the chandelier. The room is full of light, for Salvin put in great plate-glass windows wherever he could so that we should not dismiss the room without taking into account the views which are a major (and here unseen) part of the decoration of all country houses. It is a room which demands people to make it work, to gather around the great carved, white marble chimney-piece and laugh. Such undeniably formal, semi-royal decoration is hard to live with today without the visitors and parties described by Augustus Hare.

Flintham Hall
The Nottinghamshire House of Myles Thoroton Hildyard Esq.

THIS is a mid-nineteenth-century evocation of the Italianate Renaissance, as rural as that of 167 Queen's Gate is urban (pages 96–7). Here the allure is in a suggestion of warm southern skies, as the vegetation of the conservatory (above) seems to spill into the whole room. The idea of a conservatory gained impetus from Thomas Paxton's designs for both the Duke of Devonshire's glasshouse at Chatsworth and the Crystal Palace for the Great Exhibition held in Hyde Park in 1851. The English are devoted to their gardens; a conservatory made it possible to enjoy plants inside the house out of season. Cheap coal for fuelling hot-water pipes made it practical and exploration overseas meant that new and interesting forms of plant-life were imported. But, even if conservatories were heated and orchids nurtured through the winter months, Victorian standards rarely ran to piping central heating through houses. In 1853 the owner of Flintham, Mr Thomas Blackborne Thoroton Hildyard, and a local architect added this conservatory to his ancestral home. With its little fountain it makes an idyllic picture that could be of St John's Wood in the days of Alma-Tadema; both the fountain and the putto (a former gas bracket) are relics of the Great Exhibition. The windows and door form a neo-Renaissance screen of stout columns and rounded arches, but the furniture inside the Library (opposite) is a reminder that this is England of the nineteenth century. A large fire should blaze in the grate of what looks like a carved oak altar-piece but is in fact a chimney-piece; designed by a Mr McQuoid, it was manufactured by Holland & Sons and exhibited as a supreme piece of design at the Great Exhibition. It sold for £500. The design of central columns, arches and niches holding bronze statuettes is nicely echoed in the windows at the end of the room. The arrangement of the furniture (also supplied by Holland & Sons) and objects can have altered little since the room was originally planned. The same areas for reading, conversation, games or writing would have been appropriate in the mid-nineteenth century and there is no reason to change them now.

Holker Hall
The Cumbria House of Mr and Mrs Hugh Cavendish

HOLKER HALL is a pleasant rambling building set on the edge of the Lake District next to Morecambe Bay. The first house on the site is thought to have been built in 1604, and some eighteenth-century rebuilding is evident in the older surviving portions. In March 1871 the west wing was destroyed by fire and almost immediately rebuilt by the architects Paley & Austin of Lancaster in a style best described as neo-Elizabethan. It contains a series of beautifully proportioned rooms lit by enormous windows and given a wealth of detailed plaster and oak woodwork; the Billiard Room (opposite) is typical of the general style. The linenfold panelling of the dado and doors shows both the high quality of the craftsmanship and the pleasing nature of the architects' designs.

This is distinctively a man's room. At this time women generally retired to Drawing and Sitting Rooms, while the men had Billiard and Smoking Rooms in which to discuss business and other matters. A solid leather-covered chair, a high-backed deep-buttoned settle (above), the great legs of the table all befit the scene of such a leisurely game as billiards. The game derives from one called 'Pall Mall', a forms of bowls from which the London street got its name in the early eighteenth century, but it was not played on a large table until the nineteenth century. By 1907 an oval table was even being marketed! This one is of oak and the usual single piece of slate to form an absolutely flat surface, and was carved nearby. Like the light-fittings in the rest of the house, the lighting above it was installed in 1911. Elsewhere fittings were designed to be unobtrusive – in the Library the switches were hidden behind dummy books – but this room has a very different purpose and the light beams down upon the green baize. The early-eighteenth-century hunting scenes around the walls proclaim this room to be the preserve of the country gentleman.

Madresfield Court
The Worcestershire House of Mona, Countess of Beauchamp

THE intrepid Augustus Hare, long-suffering guest of so many house parties, was at Madresfield on 21 December 1892, 'a moated house with a lovely view of the Malvern hills, and full of precious collections of every kind – old books, old music, old miniatures, ivories, enamels etc. There is a Chapel, where Lady Mary Lygon watches over the musical part of the services, aided by a footman who sings splendidly and plays five instruments as well!'

The house that he saw had been largely rebuilt between 1863 and 1888 by the architect Philip Charles Hardwick for the fifth and sixth Earls of Beauchamp. Hardwick was responsible for several neo-Tudor buildings, mainly in London, and at Madresfield his use of English Renaissance idioms turned a moated brick house of true Elizabethan origins into this Victorian mansion. It has lost the intimate spirit of the original, evoking instead something much grander. Often visited by Evelyn Waugh, the inspiration for *Brideshead Revisited*, he wrote much of his novel *Black Mischief* here.

Augustus Hare would not have seen the Dining Room (oppo-

site), created from two existing rooms in around 1900 by the seventh Earl, Liberal Leader of the House of Lords. Rising through two stories, its scale re-creates a Dickensian spirit of 'Merrie England' and establishes an aristocratic medieval style much as Sir Jeffry Wyatville's work had done a century earlier. A good collection of oak furniture and old portraits is dominated by the massively beamed roof, all lit by huge windows of Gothick design. The contrast with Hardwick's rooms is intriguing: this is a more luxurious, less rigidly handled exercise in pseudo-medievalism.

The galleried Hall (page 2) has a timeless English appearance and houses a well-mixed collection of furniture: there is a long oak refectory table with its cargo of porcelain, lamps, flowers and objects, and a pretty early-twentieth-century sofa with French curves. In one corner a case full of books gives a splash of colour. Newel posts along the gallery are surmounted by heraldic beasts in the same way as earlier examples at Hatfield (page 20) and Knole.

The soft colours used everywhere are seen again in Hardwick's

Madresfield Court

Opposite The Drawing Room *Above* The Victorian Bedroom

panelled Drawing Room (opposite), where warm greens reflect the gardens and landscapes seen through the windows. A leather screen lends more colour to the decorative scheme. In a dark corner a boullework cabinet adds lustre and an elegant low table between the sofas reflects the light of a cut-glass chandelier. There is no corner without an interesting object and the triumph of the room is in containing such a huge array of apparently unconnected objects all in harmony with one another.

Upstairs is a Victorian Bedroom (above) calculated to induce insomnia in the nervous. An ebonized wardrobe built like a small cottage and a bed with ends fit for a grave menace the occupant with a plethora of serious carving. Oak table and chairs reflect an early phase of nineteenth-century antique collecting, when oak was prized and faked from old church materials.

The oriental lacquer and panelling of the other Bedroom (page 79) take us into the period of domestic *style Ritz*. The rose brocade, painted sky of the ceiling and rococo scrolls on the walls are typical of the new look in comfortable decoration which began to gain ground in the 1890s. The wardrobe is a trifle casual: no fitted dressing room here, but the effect of luxury is as evident as in Vita Sackville-West's description of the doctor's wife staying at Chevron in *The Edwardians* (1930): 'The dressing-table, the washstand, the writing table with its appointments, the vast four-poster on which some unseen hand had already laid out her clothes, the drawn curtains, the brightly burning fire, the muslin cushions, the couch with a chinchilla rug lying folded across it – all these things led Theresa from transport to transport. She lingered for a long time over the writing table, fingering all its details. There was a printed card, gilt-edged, which said:

POST ARRIVES 8 AM, 4 PM,
POST LEAVES 6 PM, SUNDAYS,
POST ARRIVES 8 AM, LEAVES 5 PM
LUNCHEON 1.30.   DINNER 8.30.'

18 Stafford Terrace, Kensington
The Former London House of Anne, Countess of Rosse

I T IS DUE to both Lady Rosse and her mother, Mrs Maud Messel, that this monument to one man's taste still survives; it has remained virtually unchanged since Linley Sambourne, chief political cartoonist of *Punch* and maternal grandfather of Lady Rosse, lived there from 1870 to 1910. To say that the house is typical of the period would be a mistake, for it contains a highly individual collection of furniture, objects, paintings and drawings. Many of the latter are Sambourne's own cartoons, but Walter Crane, Sir John Tenniel, Myles Birket Foster and Kate Greenaway are among those friends whose work is also represented. The building itself may be conventional, but the arrangement of the interior is not.

At the entrance a large doormat proclaims SALVE to all who pass. The downstairs rooms appear somewhat gloomy and it takes time to appreciate the subtle effects of light. There are so many objects, patterns and colours that one might give up too easily. But the house repays exploration. The influence of William Morris is certainly to be found – if only in the patterns on the original wall-coverings and textile hangings – but the decoration steers far away from Morris's entirely English concept of translating nature into a unified decorative scheme. Here the background may reflect Morris, but the furnishings of the main rooms do not. A small room on the ground floor (opposite) contains fine late-eighteenth-century English furniture, yet the bold oriental carpets and Morris-pattern curtains do not appear to clash with these Linley heirlooms.

Even as a town house, the English love of the countryside and foreign places permeates the atmosphere. In *The Lesser Arts* (Collected Works, Vol. XXII), Morris gives a description of the English landscape that is equally applicable to contemporary attitudes in decoration: 'Not much space for swelling into hugeness; . . . no great wastes overwhelming in their dreariness, no great solitudes of forests, no terrible untrodden mountain walls; all is measured, mingled, varied, gliding easily one thing into another, little rivers, little plains, . . . little hills, little mountains . . . neither prison, nor palace, but a decent home.'

18 Stafford Terrace, Kensington

Above and opposite The Drawing Room

In the first-floor Drawing Room (opposite and above) extending from one side of this terraced house to the other, we are faced with such a plethora of objects that one might be forgiven for wincing. It is quite remarkable that this particular interior has survived a complete revolution both in decorating tastes and in society; for the maintenance of such a room demands constant staff and attention, rare commodities today. The scale of the great 'boullework' clock on the wall is balanced by the two vases with chrysanthemum decoration on the commode beneath. To either side are mahogany cabinets giving a balance and variety to the wall, and marble chimney-pieces. Having achieved this balance, the wall is smothered with pictures jostling into a patchwork of light and colour. Sculpture and porcelain are added, the latter in a way that now seems to us peculiarly suggestive of the Arts and Crafts movement, running characteristically along a projecting cornice at picture rail height. The upholstered furniture is typically solid and occupies a considerable amount of space, as was usual at the time.

Comfort was as important as display, and both are united throughout the house, no more so than in the Bedroom (page 83). The elaborately moulded chimney-piece is typical of English decoration of the period 1880–1910 and is a type found in many interiors influenced by the Arts and Crafts movement. Very often a mirror panel was set into the centre of the top section, but here decoration is provided by Chinese pots and miniatures of Michelangelo's figures from the Medici tombs. In front stands a fan inscribed with artists' signatures, including those of Sir John Everett Millais, William Frith, George Watts and Alma-Tadema. Sambourne is depicted with his pipe in the photograph above the chest-of-drawers to the right, his drawing board propped against the easel in the Drawing Room. The early electric light-fittings with adjustable height mechanism over the dressing table are also worthy of note as a practical invention.

As the founder of the Victorian Society Lady Rosse most certainly appreciates the products and taste of that age.

Elveden Hall
The Suffolk House of the Earl of Iveagh

REMARKABLE as these pastiche 'Indian' interiors are, it is doubly surprising to find them inside an undistinguished Italianate red brick and stone country house of the late nineteenth century. The Brighton Pavilion is one thing, exotic inside and out, with the lure of the sea at hand, but Elveden is set amongst the cold Suffolk landscape, with clumps of conifers around: its only attraction originally was the shooting possibilities for the Maharajah Duleep Singh, who arrived here in 1863, and for the first Earl of Iveagh, who acquired the 5555 acres from the Maharajah's son in 1894. Since first seeing the name under a group photograph of a shoot in *'Chips': The Diaries of Sir Henry Channon* (1967), the life led at Elveden had intrigued me. Why, having given Kenwood to the nation and owning other houses, did Lord Iveagh choose to keep up this enormous house? Channon's brief comments for 8 January 1935 give no explanation, but the real reason must surely have been the shooting and the house's proximity to Sandringham: 'There was a fog on my return, and I arrived back at Elveden late, cold and hungry. Our guests were all still up but all fifty servants had gone to bed, and I could get nothing to eat. In spite of that, of all the Iveagh houses I like Elveden best. I love its calm, its luxurious Edwardian atmosphere. For a fortnight now I have slept in the King's bed, which both Edward VII and George V have used.' Quite clearly this house was not merely loved, but well cared for, having fifty servants as late as 1935. Even though largely asleep since the last war it has been preserved and the contents maintained until their sale in May 1984, For example, until their auction over 200 assorted oriental carpets were examined, cleaned and moth-proofed every year – a month's work for two men and a remarkable survival of an Edwardian feat.

Pastiche 'Indian rooms' form the true heart of Elveden. Much as he enjoyed the shooting opportunities in Suffolk, the Maharajah longed for home, and the rooms in his original house (opposite) were carefully constructed by John Norton after examples in Lahore and Delhi. Originally the ceiling was inlaid with mirror (which still remains) and bright colours were applied to parts of the decoration. Broad swoops of off-white paint have swept this away, and Edwardian chintz, eighteenth-century furniture, nineteenth-century fakes and china pots gave the rooms their colour and interest. But the atmosphere of this wing has remained that of war-time. Signs caution: 'Save Electricity', 'Not to Be Opened During Blackout'; others point the way to offices. The occupation by RAF and USAF forces has given a permanent feeling of tension to the wing.

The Indian Hall (pages 88–9) is in the centre of the house, joining the Maharajah's original house with a replica and so creating a huge new house for the Iveaghs. If Duleep Singh's building had not existed it is unlikely that the 'Indian' style would have been used here. It is a mad jumble of Islamic and Indian architectural motifs, unrelated to time or culture, but made into a great folly of a room. Imagine a room embracing Romanesque, Perpendicular, Palladian and Gothic elements and one has an idea of the confusion of styles. The Indian Hall is a welcoming room, full of light and interest, in strong contrast to the Singh wing which has not been lived in since the war. Furniture seems superfluous, for nothing can match the proportions or the profusion of styles hewn out of marble by Italian craftsmen (to add a final bizarre touch). The dome above is lit at night by a galaxy of electric bulbs hidden in the cornice at the base. Pity the electrician up there on his padded ladder! If Sir Caspar Prudon Clarke had been active in the era of the super cinema he might have become really famous; he assisted the architects William and Clyde Young (father and son) in their work here with his knowledge of Islamic and Indian stylistic details. When Augustus Hare visited on 14 November 1895 he noted: 'floated here in the luxurious saloon carriage of a private train . . . much of his [Duleep Singh's] decoration remains and the delicate white stucco work has a pretty effect when mingled with groups of tall palms and flowering plants. Otherwise the house is almost appallingly luxurious, such masses of orchids, electric light everywhere etc. However a set-off the other way is an electric piano which goes on pounding away by itself with a pertinacity which is painfully distracting. In the evenings singing men and dancing women are brought down from London and are supposed to entertain the Royal guest [the Duke of York, later King George V].'

No amount of heat could warm this great room and how cold it was to dance in can be imagined. The floor is said to be sprung with railway buffers (although there is no record of dancing elephants). In the 'new' wing are glorious Edwardian rooms of Ritz style and decoration. We also find the second Lady Iveagh turning a gloomy cavern of a north-facing room into a glamorous bedroom, completed for her in around 1930 by Betty Joel; with black carpet and silvered walls and door it contained a giant's version of her Savoy Hotel furniture in dark hardwoods lined with camphor. This is a house to remember.

Elveden Hall

The Indian Hall

Sledmere House
The Humberside House of
Sir Tatton Sykes Bart

Around this house stretches a park by Capability Brown and within is one of the grandest neo-Roman rooms in England. The long Library (page 92) fully rivals that of Adam at Luton Hoo and was initially remarkable for the barrel-vaulted decorated ceiling running one hundred and fifty feet across the house, the carpets echoing the design above. All in the best Adam tradition, but the surprise lay in the fact that it was all conceived by Joseph Rose Jr, working independently of Adam and exhibiting capabilities all of his own. This was in 1794, when the third generation of the Sykes family to live at Sledmere received a baronetcy. Successive generations have also loved the house; so that when it was badly damaged by fire in 1911 it was soon the subject of a superb restoration programme under the supervision of Sir Mark Sykes, sixth Baronet. The present Library is a reconstruction of the original by the local firm of Brierley – as the fashionable firms of Lenygon and Morant, White Allom and Trollopes were all at work re-creating such interiors it is interesting to find a local firm being given the chance to perform a fairly sophisticated project. They did not overprettify or elaborate, in fact the substitution of a parquet floor in the Library exactly repeating the pattern of the burnt carpets is a practical idea giving the room an even more neo-Classical look – even if it looks more Russian than English.

Compared to this, the principal guest Bedroom (page 93), is comfortable and luxurious, two factors high on an Edwardian's list of priorities. Warm rugs, the armchair, the sofa with its French lines and the paintings by Luca Giordano and Abraham Breughel all combine to give us this impression. The bed is a pretty version of late-eighteenth-century taste, with extravagant chintz swags and inserts enlivening the monochrome drapery; and in the corner an Empire cheval-glass reflects a superb, gilt Adam overmantel.

English interest in the Middle East is also reflected in this house, an interest that had existed on both a religious and commercial level for many centuries before Byron added romance to a vision of the Orient. In the late nineteenth century enthusiasm was expressed in the use of Moorish motifs in, for example, the tiled room at Leighton House, London, rooms for William Burges round the corner in Melbury Road, even at Cardiff Castle for the Marquess of Bute. The Smoking Room at Sledmere (opposite) was added for Sir Mark Sykes, who was a distinguished soldier and diplomat with a direct interest in the Middle East – he helped draw up the Sykes–Picot Palestine Agreement of 1916. T. E. Lawrence made this typically incisive comment about the Smoking Room's creator: 'the imaginative advocate of unconvincing world movements, Mark Sykes: also a bundle of prejudices, intuitions, half-sciences. . . . He saw the odd in everything and missed the even' (*Seven Pillars of Wisdom*, 1935).

The room was originally planned as a Turkish Bathroom, but the First World War prevented the export of a large number of the specially commissioned tiles from Turkey and the bath was not completed. Apart from the early-nineteenth-century chairs in one corner, the main decoration is Islamic in concept, based on the Sultan's rooms in the Valedih Mosque in Istanbul and re-created by the designer of this room, David Ohanessian, with considerable skill. The light-fitting is a particularly fine piece of decoration, in its own way as good as anything at the Brighton Pavilion. In the corner broods a bronze bust of Sir Mark himself, by Bryant Baker; it is an incongruous touch in the midst of this hectic Orientalism. This was by no means the last 'Moorish' room to be constructed in England. In the late 1920s White Allom created a mosaic-filled Moorish court for Sir Julien Cahn in Leicestershire. Like so much decoration appealing to the English, oriental motifs suggest a warmth and light quite alien to a damp northern climate.

Sledmere House

Opposite The Library *Above* Bedroom

The House of Mrs Pandora Astor
The Boltons, London

NOSTALGIC DECORATION is an inherent characteristic of many English houses that extends far beyond any reinterpretation of historic styles. Certain forms reappear in decoration, but are usually given an up-to-date twist that brings them out of the category of purely 'period' decoration – Syrie Maugham's interiors are an example. Here Mrs Pandora Astor set out rather to recapture an 'atmosphere', a loose evocation of past centuries.

There is more than a whiff of decay in this recent exercise in creating an opulent interior of a dead epoch. It is too casual to be a 'goût Rothschild' and too informal to be stagy, although Mrs Astor has acknowledged the influence of Visconti's last film *The Innocents*. Fabrics billow round the huge early Victorian town-house windows and envelop a table like a vast birthday-cake, in a manner

that a late-nineteenth-century German handbook on lavish entertaining 'At Home' would have recommended. Chairs are shrouded less with old-fashioned case-covers such as at Calke Abbey (page 60), but more with covers like dust sheets that give the semblance of a Russian country house sighing through the heat of an interminable summer. This is a setting in which things are about to happen. The air of expectancy will be fulfilled by parties of people basking in the welcome of a house designed to entertain. Up the walls spin plates thrown by an invisible juggler, continental chandeliers flash with light, throwing lustre on to the French curves of the fireplace, the gilt and the brocade. Yet it is all part of a masque. The bare stripped boards are those of a set. No fine parquet, no soft Wilton. This is unashamed fantasy garnished with nostalgia.

The Estonian Legation
167 Queen's Gate, Kensington, London

THIS large town house by Sir Mervyn Macartney was completed in 1890 and is the culmination of many influences in English architecture and decoration. Apart from new furnishings, it has remained virtually unchanged since it was finished and so gives us a complete picture of late-Victorian progressive architecture. Macartney was a pupil of Norman Shaw and a keen student of English architecture, cycling all over Britain with his sketchbook: he was an enthusiastic practitioner of revivalist new styles – such as the 'Wrenaissance'. Every detail of the house at Queen's Gate is a reference to some existing building in England, but it would take an eagle eye and keen intelligence to attribute each one. The house externally reflects forms used in English Renaissance architecture. The original owner, Mr Davidson, was a successful sugar merchant and a Governor of the Bank of Mauritius. Macartney obviously saw his client as a modern version of a Renaissance merchant prince, and inside the house his constant references to the English Renaissance style and to Adam assert this in their associations with new money and status.

Two neo-Classical columns, great chunks of alabaster, inspired the central theme of the architectural and interior design which Macartney plotted throughout the building. That theme begins with the Portland stone columns of the portico, is carried through the marble-floored Entrance Hall to the pillared screen dividing Hall and stairwell, and is then continued up through the stairwell and balustrades to the very top of the five-storied house. The large L-shaped Drawing Room is divided by the transluscent columns of alabaster, a form of screen with surrounding cladding and pilasters of the same material. This is a clear reference to the work of Adam (an Adam fanlight is also inserted in the top of the French windows to the right of the fireplace). A fine panelled dado runs all round the room, uniting the high marble chimney-pieces with the mullioned and leaded windows and the elaborately pedimented doorcases. Throughout the house decorations by William Morris, lavish plasterwork, possibly by Hasley Ricardo, light-fittings by Benson and tiles by William de Morgan, all give away the true period of the house and indicate the taste and interests of both owner and architect.

Sir Mervyn was Surveyor of St Paul's Cathedral on his death, by which time the house had ceased to belong to Davidson's widow and had become the residence and offices of the Estonian Legation and Consul General. It was last decorated in 1935 by Hamptons, a large and worthy, if unexciting, firm of decorators. The 1930s Bohemian cut-glass chandeliers glitter above a mixture of French, Baltic and Russian furniture, whilst Mrs Davidson's original Collard and Collard grand piano encased in rosewood stands in the same position it has occupied for almost a century. Hamptons' 'diplomatic' Drawing Room of the 1930s is essentially English in its timelessness, and was designed to be in keeping with the architecture and decoration of the rest of the house. Many of the servants' bells in the basement still have the names of the members of the Davidson family above them, and the old speaking tube running through four stories is in working order. One hundred and sixty-seven Queen's Gate has survived intact the post-war political disputes that have left occupied the country the Legation represents.

The London House of
Bernard Nevill Esq.

When Sir Cecil Beaton enthused over the Edwardian era he managed to create a surprisingly frothy parody of the real thing in his drawings of the sets and costumes for *My Fair Lady*. He undoubtedly captured something of the English nostalgia for a 'golden age', just as these rooms do. The Bedroom (pages 100–1) is a confection of over-indulgence that can only arouse our open-mouthed admiration. Elsewhere glass vases, pictures and objects all jostle gently up to the wall surrounding the fireplace in a manner that would even have seemed excessive to our grandparents.

'She did not know that she was walking into a perfect specimen of an Edwardian drawing-room, which at once reflected and embraced, like a mirror and a crystal in one, the happy thoughtless-ness of an era gone forever. Yet so it was. No period is so lost as the Edwardian. The state of society that made it possible is more dead than the pre-historic ferns pressed into streaks of coal; that exquisite silliness summed up in the word "Dolly" can never return.' When Stella Gibbons wrote this in her novel *Bassett* in 1934 the Edwardian era was little more than twenty years dead, and many houses remained unchanged in their decoration. Rooms such as these would have been quite familiar if slightly emptier of objects. Certainly the tiled Kitchen (above) with sensible furniture would have been familiar for longer, and is in a style still to be found in many houses, re-created in preference to plastic and steel. Copper pans and a knife-cleaning machine add to the Edwardian illusion.

In the Bedroom we find the fragility of lace evoking a unique sense of luxury. Apart from the money needed to create or maintain such a room in London in the smoggy years of the Edwardian era, such intricacy of design ceased to be fashionable except for evening dresses. As at Nymans (page 24), the dressing-table is given a fragile trousseau of lace and ribbon trimmings, a form of altar to the owner's beauty. The sprigged paper, curvaceous picture frame and furniture of a more conventional English bedroom are in stark contrast to the unabashed hedo-nism of the bed-covering, as full blown as the roses on the table.

The London House of Bernard Nevill Esq.

The Bedroom

The Chelsea House of
Felix Hope-Nicholson Esq.

THESE ROOMS evoke the England of the cultured upper-middle classes at the height of Britain's Imperial power during the decades before the First World War. Henry James's characters would have felt at home in rooms like these – one can imagine them setting out from here on an expedition to an antique shop, as in *The Golden Bowl* (1904). Or in the paintings of James Tissot this might be the muted, unostentatious background, showing an essentially English restraint that was vanishing by the 1930s.

In the Studio (opposite) is an eclectic array of furniture and objects, unified by a mellow background of dark floorboards, panelled dado and doors. The warm olive green of the ceiling is relieved by a touch of gilt and a terracotta stripe. Even the heavy chandeliers fail to obtrude. When the furniture was bought it was undoubtedly inexpensive and acquired for the interest or beauty of each object. When William Morris wrote 'have nothing in your house, which is not beautiful', the reverberations extended to anyone with aesthetic sensibilities, and rooms like these might have been found in any number of houses from about 1870 to the 1930s. A Dutch marquetry bureau glows beneath a painting of the Orientalist school. The early-eighteenth-century gate-leg table in the centre is surrounded by ladder-back chairs of country origin. Flowers were very much a part of the decorative ideas of the 1880s, and chrysanthemums and asters like those William de Morgan used in tile decoration add a dash of colour on the table.

In the Dining Room (above) the English late-eighteenth-century mahogany table is conveniently made to collapse so that the ends can be used as elliptically-shaped side tables. A set of Regency chairs with an unusual form of sabre leg in the front is placed around the room, which is liberally hung with prints and oil-paintings. The small convex mirror over the door is a version of larger types popular in Regency and William IV dining rooms. They reflect the whole room in miniature and are often said to have been used by butlers and servants who, while busy with dishes on the side table, could survey the main table and so calculate the needs of the diners.

Shaw's Corner
The Hertfordshire House of Mr and Mrs George Bernard Shaw

IT IS SAID that the Shaws bought the house, originally the New Rectory, because they had seen a gravestone in the village churchyard bearing the following inscription:

BORN MARCH 5 1825
DIED FEBRUARY 13 1895
Her time was Short.

Cecil Roberts narrates that soon after his arrival, G.B.S. announced in the village pub: 'I've decided to take a house in the village for my mistress,' and Charlotte Shaw wondered why no-one called on them for over a year. Whatever the truth of these stories, Shaw did live from 1906 to 1950 in this unpretentious red brick house vaguely following the Arts and Crafts style at its most simple, and all the rooms on the ground floor look almost exactly the same as during his lifetime. Quite what one should expect Shaw's home to look like is debatable, but this house is not dissimilar from that of many University dons of the same vintage. It has an academic look with a peculiarly English restraint that suggests a self-depriving celery-and-sandals existence of the utmost hedonism. In the Drawing Room (above) this is partly due to the absence of any curtains to soften the uncompromising off-white and white decoration – Mrs Shaw was no Syrie Maugham. In fact there are some pleasant pieces of furniture scattered around the room, if one can ignore the grotesque and shabby armchairs that nuzzle up to the fire like decrepit bulldogs. The other chairs are late-eighteenth century and like the secretaire and bureau are perfectly respectable antiques, no doubt acquired because they were relatively inexpensive as well as pretty. The busts on the bureau are both by Rodin, the larger of Shaw and the smaller of Balzac; Rodin himself by Prince Paul Troubetskoy sits on a gate-leg table on the left side of the deep bay window. The room is extremely light with fine woodland views, but it is not welcoming and looks uncomfortable:

now a museum, it lacks the human touch that transforms a furnished house into an inviting home.

The Dining Room (above) has more well-made and nicely proportioned English antique furniture, but is dominated by the fireplace, a masterpiece of ill-conceived Arts and Crafts design on which we can see some of the more unexpected manifestations of Shaw's socialist musings and lion-chasing. Ibsen, on the far right, was returned from the framers the day before Shaw died in this very room. To think of the flamboyant G.B.S. entertaining here is to stretch the imagination, although T. E. Lawrence would have been at ease on his visits. Some of the furniture may have come from Shaw's London house, but the curious clash of surroundings and objects, together with a complete disregard for proportion and colour, is a notable achievement which must be partly explained by the presence of Lenin in pride of place amongst the photographs on the mantelpiece. Such a disregard for surroundings is not uncommon amongst academics; but this was the home of a witty playwright. He was termed a man of the world, meeting and conversing with the greatest men of his day. Perhaps a lack of visual sense, and the minimal thought apparently given to the decoration of the rooms, is not surprising from one who could write to *The Times* on 28 August 1937 about 'the joyful news that Hitler is now under the thumb of Stalin whose interest in peace is overwhelming. And everyone except myself', he went on, 'is frightened out of his or her wits. Why? Am I mad? If not, why? Why? Why?' He was to be answered a couple of days later by another correspondent, who asked: 'Who is frightened out of his wits? Who? Who? Who?' (Robert Kee, *1939*, 1984).

What a curious figure Shaw was, lumbering around this frigid house in his old tweeds, choosing to work in a revolving summer house in the garden connected with the world by a telephone – adjusted for out-going calls only.

Clouds Hill
The Dorset Retreat of Lawrence of Arabia

S ET AMONGST the wooded slopes of the West Country in the neighbourhood of Wool, this simple building looks no more than the quiet cottage of a farm-worker of the 1900s when seen from the outside. Thomas Hardy was living locally when T. E. Lawrence found the place and rented it in 1923. He had some family connections with the area, members of his father's family lived nearby, but the intention was to make a retreat for himself, as an eventual place of retirement. At the time, Lawrence was in the ranks of the Royal Tank Corps, having failed to find any worthwhile work or satisfactory use for his talents after his dramatic career in the First World War. As both house and interior were gradually repaired and decorated to Lawrence's taste, the present arrangement emerged. Since 1935 little has changed, apart from the removal of some 1,250 books that formed his library. The absence of books gives an excessively spartan air to an already stark interior, and serves to highlight Lawrence's own frugal habits. He demanded little in the way of material possessions and everything in the interior is simple, well made and utilitarian.

The decoration of the house is dictated not simply by Lawrence's near poverty nor just a desire for simplicity but also by his love of great quantities of exposed woodwork. In the main Living Room (opposite and page 108) we seem to be in a comfortable attic with beams and rafters supporting a plank roof. A note of warmth and colour comes from the fireplace of red brick, but this looks slightly sinister as the arrangement of candlesticks suggests an altar. In this room is his gramophone, his only luxurious possession. Having sold his gold dagger he could afford some records and this gramophone, with its fibre needles, sophisticated soundbox and dusting graphite. The horn now strikes an out-dated note. The room has a 'cultish' feeling to it. Light filters in from a skylight and a low window with seats and wooden shutters to either side. It is hard to imagine the great 'T.E.' entertaining soldier friends here on stuffed olives, salted almonds and baked beans with his own blend of china tea. But then it is equally odd to imagine the chocolates

Clouds Hill

Opposite The Living Room *Above* The Study Room

from Gunters', the peach-fed ham or *pâté de foie gras* sent to him at Christmas by Mrs George Bernard Shaw. She also gave Lawrence a huge quantity of good recordings of classical music, as Lawrence earned only three shillings a day in the ranks.

If the feeling of an English cottage is sought it is soon dispelled by the extraordinary Bedroom (page 107), one of such eccentricity that even a monk might shiver. The high bunk-bed is the top of a sensible built-in chest of drawers. Lawrence was of course a small man (5ft 5in.) and his neat figure must be imagined in this peculiar foil-lined room: the foil kept it cool in summer and warm in winter, theoretically. The glass covers reflect another eccentric habit, eating cheese in his Bedroom. His eccentric lifestyle also meant that the house only gained a chemical lavatory for visits by his mother – Lawrence preferred to use the bushes.

The Study Room (above) lined with shelves and photographs is more practical and welcoming. There is undoubtedly a fetishistic quality to the leather 'reading-couch' and the fine cubist armchair, resembling a flying jacket with fine square-shaped and fleece cushions, but this is a practical room designed for cosy evenings.

At Oxford 'T.E.' had been something of a Pre-Raphaelite aesthete, and the more robust writings of William Morris with its socialist musings appealed to him. On his death on 19 May 1935 Lawrence's collection of books still included sixteen by Morris, and in his later years he even evinced some enthusiasm for Lenin. A particular favourite among Morris's work (according to Vyvyan Richards) was *The Roots of the Mountains* (Collected Works), a story of Nordic-Arcadian life in which communities live in 'halls' and everyone is fighting the Huns. Clouds Hill must owe its cultish, Nordic atmosphere to this, and Lawrence's interest in Morris must also explain his purchase of fourteenth-century house timbers for possible future use and his winter trek in the snow to a 'Morris house' at Chipping Camden, where he enthused over 'the large living room with the old open chapel roof'. These youthful experiences undoubtedly explain the decoration of Clouds Hill.

The Former London House of Margaret, Duchess of Argyll
Upper Grosvenor Street, Mayfair

THIS Georgian terraced house was one of the first to be constructed on the Grosvenor Estate. The rooms shown here were all decorated by Mrs Syrie Maugham for the mother of the Duchess of Argyll, Mrs George Whigham, in 1936. Her scheme is superimposed on earlier decoration for a previous inhabitant by the royal decorators, White Allom, masters of 'Millionaires Georgian'. Syrie Maugham decorated both this house and the Duchess's first house in Regent's Park at the same time. Upper Grosvenor Street is really more the Duchess's house than her mother's, for it was closed during most of the war and the Duchess lived in it for the next thirty-five years or so. It is impossible to look at these rooms and not see her elegant figure there, for these are rooms created as a background for sophisticated living.

It is in a suggestion of warmth and light that is alien to Britain and more suggestive of southern climates that Mrs Maugham's triumph as a decorator is to be found. Apart from the Venetian mirrors and cut-glass chandeliers of the Drawing Room, the theme was fully evident in the Bedroom (opposite and above), which, with the Bathroom (pages 112–13) and connecting Dressing Room, occupied the whole of the second floor. The Bedroom's rich effect of simple light colours, from cream to white, dusty pink to pale blue, was not merely a subtle background for the inhabitants; it blatantly proclaimed expensive luxury in the middle of a grimy city. The interiors did not reflect their London surroundings although they were fully in the English tradition of decoration.

The bed was of film-set proportions, the design in the neo-Greek style of Robsjohn-Gibbings. The draperies round the *chinoiserie* decoration softened the hard, painted surfaces of the walls. Decorative pilasters were inlaid with sparkling panels of mirror and gave unexpected dimensions. On the Maugham tables were her glass lamps: most of the furniture was originally supplied from her shop. The built-in cupboards (probably by White Allom) held shoes. The chimney-piece was the focal point, undiminished by the well-draped bay window flanked by late Regency furniture. All the

The Former London House of Margaret, Duchess of Argyll

Above and opposite The Bathroom

fabrics were faithfully replaced as they became worn.

Just as the silks and satins were part of Mrs Maugham's epoch, so innovative bathroom design was a feature of decoration at the time. For Mrs Whigham she constructed a fantastic room with various parts mirrored, giving a unique and magical look. The fittings were the most modern American ones of the period, showing how remarkably up to date Mrs Maugham was. Yet she never lost track of the style of the house and on one side of the room there is a 1930s chromed fireplace with a pair of upholstered chairs and a stool between them: what arrangement could be more English?

Some of the work in this house echoes that of her friend, the pioneering Elsie de Wolfe, Lady Mendl, but Mrs Maugham showed more ingenuity in handling some unpromising rooms with style. The Duchess recalls her formidable methods: objects would be rejected, but return again and again. She says that her mother preferred and chose Mrs Maugham because their tastes were similar. Neither had a reverence for strict application of stylistic periods and details. Both liked an elegant mixture of comfortable objects and furniture. Syrie Maugham, Mrs Whigham and the Duchess 'hated mahogany'. Mr Whigham was not too keen on Mrs Maugham; he chose the sober pine-panelled library.

In 1941 Peter Quennell captioned a Cecil Beaton photograph of Syrie Maugham's work thus: 'with off-white upholstery went pickled oak side tables and baroque accessories denuded of the paintwork they demanded and deserved. Such an interior was smart, chilly, entirely impractical, and for many reasons, including the gullibility of the rich and the ingenuity of fashionable interior decorators, extraordinarily expensive.' How wrong Mr Quennell was. This house was loved for over four decades and maintained with great care. It was welcoming and had a shimmering quality encapsulated in the Bathroom. This room was turned down by the Victoria and Albert Museum, London, when the Duchess left the house in 1978. We can see here Mrs Maugham's genius in going towards an excess that is firmly held in check.

The Brighton Flat
of the Late Martin Battersby

THIS ROOM in Brighton was intended to display an interesting collection of items from the 1920s and 1930s. Martin Battersby was most famous as a *trompe-l'oeil* artist, although he had also been active as a set-designer for the stage. His diverse work is to be found in private New York elevators, in fine apartments and in the houses of the rich or famous (such as Lady Diana Cooper, page 120). In his own tiny flat Battersby created a glittering jewel-box that shows his great enthusiasm for the styles of the 1920s. By lining the walls with a cunning paper of silvery-gold, Klimt-like design he suggests the ground colouring of a Japanese screen, and therefore by implication echoes the work of the French genius in lacquer, Jean Dunand. One vase by Dunand can be seen in each window; they date from the mid-1920s, and Dunand also worked on the rare bronze-framed lacquer cabinet by Eugen Printz that stands between the windows. Above a Neilz vase hangs a Bakst ballet design evoking the heyday of the Ballets Russes in the 1920s. French

chairs of earlier in that decade show the curious blending of French Louis XVI forms with German and Austrian pre-First World War decorative details. The rather hard appearance of the *moiré* and silk furnishing fabrics suggests a brittle 'chic' and contrasts with the exuberant display cabinet. To one side is a marble-topped wrought-iron side table not unlike those by Edgar Brandt.

A Chinese coromandel lacquer screen is an echo of the 'Chinese craze' of the 1920s for lacquerwork and *chinoiserie* decoration; it becomes an amusing backdrop for a good Ruhlmann table of burr amboyna and ivory holding a collection of miscellaneous objects – including cigarette cases of Paul Brandt and Fabergé with a typical and slightly kitsch lamp by the Parisian Roland.

With such a plethora of valuable objects displayed in this manner there is an air of being in a rather good shop, particularly as the floor is devoid of the coverings necessary to give a softer look to the often severe outlines.

The Homewood
The Surrey House of Patrick Gwynne Esq.

WHEN Margot Beste-Chetwynde asked Professor Silenius for a new house in Evelyn Waugh's *Decline and Fall* (1928), it was 'something clean and square' that she had in mind. She should have been given this house. Designed in 1937 by the present owner Mr Patrick Gwynne, then in partnership with Wells Coates, it was built for the former's parents and is one of the few twentieth-century domestic buildings to be protected by a Preservation Order. For sheer excellence of congenial design and construction it is probably unrivalled. The sprung maple floor of the Living Room (opposite) has a golden warmth of its own and was designed for dancing; 'Cocktails and laughter, and what comes after, Nobody knows,' wrote Noel Coward. The natural successor, High Tech, seems a vulgar sham compared to the materials used here.

White leather is used to pad the doors to the Living Room, which are surrounded by an aluminium frame set in a wall of grey-tinted mirror (above). An elegantly curved staircase is constructed of the artificial stone mixture known as 'Terrazzo' with an ebonized liner-style hand-rail. The well is lit from below by a ground-glass panel in the floor, casting light up to the antique Bristol-glass chandelier. This was found by Mr Gwynne's father and incorporated as a daring Le Corbusier touch reminiscent of the effects achieved in the apartment of Carlos de Béstigui in Paris.

The Living Room is divided by a black-grey wall of Levanto marble in which a fire blazes. This wall is continued with a folding screen, and beyond is the Dining Room and a terrace with staircases to both roof and garden. Much of the furniture was designed by Mr Gwynne, including the glass-topped table; the reclining chairs are early examples by Bruno Matthsson. The right-hand wall is veneered in rosewood and contains tambour-fronted cupboards.

This large area is all on the first-floor level, apart from the kitchen all the service areas are below. The views over the grounds from the Living Room are therefore unimpeded and show the gardens off. The panorama changes with the seasons and is part of the decoration of the room, like a large Japanese screen.

The Belgravia House of
Mr and Mrs Hugh Clifford-Wing

WHEN Mr and Mrs Clifford-Wing moved into this Georgian town house in 1955 they found a light sunny house with a good parquet floor in the first-floor Drawing Room, good proportions, and little else. As the owner is a professional decorator who began his career with the old-established London firm of Trollopes in the 1930s, he has been able to exploit the potential of the house to full advantage. Experience of the great years of decorating for a variety of clients, including palaces and yachts, was brought to bear on a conventional interior and every last detail has been used to effect. The owner's wife has converted a room at the turn of the stairs between ground and first floor into a charming garden room with a small terrace beyond; and the basement now includes an Office and Studio, as well as retaining the Kitchen.

In the master Bedroom light colours are an unashamed reflection of fashionable taste in the 1930s and 1940s. The soft pinkish background is muralled with pale blue and grey scenes by Peter Stebbing, who has done similar work in Greek villas for several of Mr Clifford-Wing's clients. This decoration is in a style reminiscent of 'Chinese' painting exported to England in the eighteenth century, and is also seen in the Bathroom next door. Here solid old fittings are the chief ingredients in the room's success. Chintz curtains, a covered stool, a close-fitted carpet: all proclaim the room to be as English as the charmingly antiquated taps and lavatory cistern with domed porcelain lid. Warm towels stand ready at the foot of the splendidly deep old-fashioned bath, near the no-nonsense set of scales in the window. The charm of such a room depends on its mixture of functional and luxurious touches: so the substantial eighteenth-century tall-boy on the other side of the room contrasts with the generous chintz curtains and electric wall-heater. It all creates the feeling of a comfortable and practical bathroom, on a less imposing scale but in the same spirit of fun as that of Syrie Maugham in the Duchess of Argyll's house (page 113).

A Knightsbridge Town House

A stone's throw from Harrods, this house has all the brittle chic of a sophisticated London house, but differs from Mr Clifford-Wing's house of similar size and layout (opposite) by its use of striking pieces of furniture. The owner spent some time as an assistant to John Fowler, who gave advice on the decoration of this terraced house. Its clean lines and light colours reflect the less hectic decorative styles of the 1950s and early 1960s, before the invasion of bright colours, patterns, glass and chrome.

One end of the cool off-white and grey first-floor Drawing Room is dominated by a glistening 1930s grand piano of unusual design, and the other is filled with comfortable seating arrangements. A considerable amount of the room's charm lies in its airy quality, epitomized by the painted and decorated chairs – some are eighteenth century. A solid and architectural bookcase is built up against one wall (facing the fireplace) and is painted in sympathy with walls and woodwork; a clock, two covered, urn-shaped vases known as cassolettes, and plates are ranged along the shelf. An orange tree stands on a 'cloud-table'. This table forms an unusual link between the elements of eighteenth-century decoration in the room and the last introduction of an unusual style in the 1940s. It was a style evolved in Scandinavia in the late 1930s, picked up by French designers after the Second World War and brought to prominence in England after the festival of Britain in 1951. It was around that time that this table was purchased by the owner, then an Oxford undergraduate, an original having been used by Jean Royère in a scheme in Paris in 1946. As with the emergence of *art déco* as a collector's style, the products of the 1950s are now enjoying a new vogue; few examples, however, are of as high quality as this cloud-table. Other notable features of the room are the simple French furniture and needlepoint rugs, both elements of John Fowler's style in the 1950s and also seen in Mrs Lancaster's flat in Avery Row (pages 124–7). Elaborately draped curtains give a final touch of colour and grandeur to a sophisticated scheme that is a triumph of subtle understatement.

The London House of Lady Diana Cooper, Little Venice

LADY DIANA COOPER's three volumes of autobiography have decorative end-papers reproducing *trompe-l'oeil* panels painted for her by Martin Battersby to hang in her former house in Chantilly. It was there that she and her husband lived after he ceased to be Ambassador to France, and the panels are painted with mementoes and vignettes of her life. They now hang at the dining end of the L-shaped Drawing Room (these pages) in her London house, a quiet building in the solid neo-Classical manner of the early decades of the nineteenth century.

In the 1930s Lady Diana was one of the few enthusiasts of both the Regency and Empire styles. Her previous London house reflected this taste, but her residence at the British Embassy in Paris no doubt gave her a surfeit of the style. This house accommodates the mementoes of a long and eventful life.

With English ingenuity the downstairs Cloakroom (page 123) is given a highly personal mixture of decorative elements. Amongst the solid fittings is a galaxy of pictures and photographs, many depicting members of the Royal Family. No need to dig out albums or clutter the place with frames, for the photographs can be viewed and scrutinized at leisure. A potentially dull room is given immediate interest and a very individual style.

The Hall (page 122) of her present house is left to rely on its fine architectural proportions and stone-flagged floor, while the Drawing Room has achieved the English style that comes from a judicious mixture of French and English taste, of periods and of decorative styles. In the Hall a welcoming array of glasses forms a self-service alternative to a butler's pantry, and above is a portrait of Lady Diana by Ambrose McEvoy. In the Drawing Room comfortable sofas and armchairs are devoid of strict formality, screens break the firm lines of the proportions of the room and painted chairs give light and movement. For the room has a vivacity that reflects the owner, while the colours echo the gardens outside. It has a countrified look that marks it as English, an effect that stems from Lady Diana's instinctive handling of the decoration.

The London House of Lady Diana Cooper

Above The Hall *Opposite* The Cloakroom

The Former London House
of Mrs Nancy Lancaster, Avery Row, Mayfair

DITCHLEY PARK by Gibbs and Kent (page 35), Kelmarsh and Haseley Court are all fine eighteenth-century houses once lived in by the Virginian-born Mrs Lancaster, owner of Colefax & Fowler from 1944 to 1960. These rooms 'above the shop' were hers until 1980, and now form part of the premises of Colefax & Fowler itself. The yellow Drawing Room (opposite) is now empty of her furniture and reveals the colours she used to create its sumptuous effect, a decorative technique she also used in the decoration of her country houses.

This Drawing and Dining Room was once part of Sir Jeffry Wyatville's offices, leased to him in 1821. It was probably used by his draughtsmen and is 16 feet wide and 46 feet long with three large and deep windows overlooking a small garden to the side of the old Bath Club. Completely hidden from the street, Mrs Lancaster turned the room into a perpetually sunny living room and achieved an English look of countrified sophistication in the city. This look was also a speciality of her partner and collaborator John Fowler: his decoration of another unusual building nearby for the elegant Mrs Jack Dennis achieved a similar effect of light and space. Both appeared to be large houses at a time when the 'London house' was shrinking in size.

A description of the room a few years after its completion sums up what was then considered a great achievement: 'Yellow rather than cream! Thus the walls are a semi-gloss Pekin yellow, the ceiling is painted in three tones of subtle beige; the cornice and high skirting-board are *trompe-l'oeil* simulating sienna marble. The curtains are in two shades of golden yellow taffeta and shantung and hang from gilded wooden rods with brown and yellow cords. Sofas and armchairs are covered in deep citrus yellow shantung with heavy fringes to match. And, marigold yellow cushions. The gilt chairs are covered in a special chintz copied from an 1840 design. The yellow background of the magnificent Ukrainian rug before the fireplace sets the theme' (*House and Garden Book of Interiors*, 1962). The use of colour shows an ingenuity typical of John Fowler, an expert in this field. The assembly of various objects achieves a rare harmony, a look of having grown slowly rather than just being acquired. This is very English. Pieces of mirror around the doors, the bookcases, lamps, gilt wall-lights and a blackamoor stool are all inventive touches achieving a balance and symmetry, in keeping with the scale of the room.

The Former London House of Mrs Nancy Lancaster

Above The Bathroom *Opposite* The Bedroom

The quiet little Bedroom (opposite) is a complete contrast, with cool off-white and bluish-grey giving a slightly French flavour to the overall effect. A surprisingly jazzy lacquered early-eighteenth-century bureau-bookcase lends a sparkle to the room, and the simple Bathroom beyond (above) contains old engravings depicting bulbs. Mrs Lancaster has said that she likes a mixture of styles and objects appropriate to a room, together with a sense of scale: 'As in a salad the ingredients should "marry well" – although I am probably better at rooms than salads.'

The Dower House, Badminton
The Former House of the Duke and Duchess of Beaufort

DOMINATED by a beautiful English chimney-piece, this Drawing Room epitomizes the look so often sought by decorators in their attempts to create an 'English' room and so rarely achieved. The sienna and white statuary marble chimney-piece sits in the centre of the room, a carved panel depicting a classical scene – a favourite device of the late eighteenth century. Above it is an array of postcards which reduces the extreme formality of a beautiful portrait to a more domestic scale; this is a room to be lived in rather than just looked at. Amusing needlework bell-pulls give a sense of scale to either side of the chimney-piece. For chilly days a stack of logs stands ready to give a good blaze in the grate, and the club fender has a welcoming look.

The room is also a study and library, so wall space for pictures is restricted. The solution has been overcome by the use of an easel and a stand, and the paintings are given a setting that is dignified and yet does not detract from the subject matter. The chintz upholstery plays a prominent part in the decoration. Although not much is used, the eye is drawn to it, and the flowery pattern is so peculiarly English that it stamps the room with its rosy personality. Chintz-covered sofa and chairs sit on an old carpet, and fringes to both table draperies and covers are echoed in the details on the curtains, in turn suspended from a mahogany pole over the arched French windows. Other furniture in the room includes a useful pedestal desk and low tables made from eighteenth-century mahogany trays on modern stands. Flowers, plants and lamps made from old vases inject fresh colours into this pleasing English room.

The London House
of Stephen Long Esq.

THE ENGLISH are a nation of collectors. At Calke Abbey (pages 60–4) successive generations left accumulations of carefully hoarded clutter. Old ladies die pinioned beneath heaps of preserved copies of the *Daily Beast* that have collapsed into the walkways that remain of their rooms. Recently a fleet of lorries removed the accumulated junk of a lifetime from a modest house in the North of England: everything had been kept, including canned food decades old. Such clutter takes control by its sheer volume. Fortunately, the owner of this room has an eye for colour and juxtaposition of objects that is savagely keen; in spite of the extraordinary number of objects in the room he has maintained perfect control – just.

A warm yellow background creates a glowing effect, heightened by the boldly patterned carpet with its crowns and Tudor roses that hint at a royal provenance. Generously large curtains are echoed in the swags and bows of the ribbons above the portraits, adding to the lush feeling of almost suffocating hospitality. On bookcase and table are a selection of black busts, porcelain and objects of some

interest and importance to their owner as 'household gods', irrespective of their value. (The 'Delft' ginger jars are in reality only painted old tobacco pots.) Their arrangement is a work of art, beside which a David Hicks 'tablescape' would be reduced to the level of a Boots countertop. A dozen early-nineteenth-century Davenport botanical dessert plates are ranged above the desk; over the fireplace hangs a triple portrait of Charles I (a contemporary copy of the famous Van Dyck); and below that is a collection of red pottery, some from the Isleworth factory of Shore & Goulding and some from Bohemia; all jostle for space and attention in a manner that most people would find overpowering. It defies any personality but that of the owner – and why not? It is fully in the tradition of creating one's own surroundings in one's own way, much as Mole loved his own little house in Kenneth Grahame's *The Wind in the Willows*. Calke Abbey, the interior of a country cottage, this London house: all are equally an expression of the English spirit of individuality.

Two Interiors Designed by David Hicks Esq.

Dᴀᴠɪᴅ Hɪᴄᴋs's look is Syrie Maugham in hell. Where she conjured soft curves and pastel shades with a wave of a braceletted wrist, Mr Hicks takes a straight line to vibrant colour. No detail has escaped his scrutiny, from bathrooms to letter-boxes he has pronounced a verdict, with succinct explanation he has reduced everything to bare essentials. From Totnes to Tokyo his name is synonymous with Good Taste. His first books in the 1960s showed him to be a ruthless dictator, so that when the 'tablescapes' at his last country house, Britwell Salome, were sold, the plans for reconstruction in less aesthetic hands went with them. ('Table-scapes' are arrangements of objects on a table, a decorative feature devised and much used by David Hicks.) He has a clear style and a distinctive panache visible in every room and where he treads carpets take on geometric patterns.

In his own red-hued London Bedroom (opposite) are many historical references: covered vases, a bust, canopied bed and severely Louis xvɪ chimney-piece. The mirror and lighting keep any tendency towards a mere period pastiche firmly in check, but Mr Hicks has himself described his flat as 'an atmosphere in antiquity'. Originally a cornice ran along the top of the 1930s cupboards, but this was removed and the cupboards were re-decorated to produce what Hicks describes as a 'dramatic and unexpected support for the urns' (*Living with Design*, 1979). Symmetry and order are plainly part of the decorative scheme. The aggressive geometric carpet and gilt table are unusual components in a bedroom, and this one is very much Hicks 'decorated' – as is the Drawing Room in his present country house (above).

Shades of pink, mustard, brown and white are the main colours here and the combination could be fatal. But Mr Hicks skates on thin ice with all the confidence we expect of the English tradition and continues to take the prizes for practical backgrounds that form undemanding interiors for life today.

A Country House
Decorated by David Mlinaric Esq.

THESE ROOMS in a country house reflect an approach to interior design and decoration that now seems slightly *démodé*, emerging as it did during the mid-1960s. Muted backgrounds, patches of colouring in textiles, a few pieces of carefully chosen furniture, all these are framed by stripped floorboards. Parallel to this approach was the look inspired by 'Habitat' shops, with simple modern furniture and one carefully positioned 'antique'. Both forms of decoration suffer the disadvantage of being in such good taste that they become bland. Handled by David Mlinaric, a prominent initiator and master of a sophisticated development of these styles, the results achieve subtlety and distinction, as seen here.

The owner is an antique dealer, and Mr Mlinaric has combined some good antique furniture and porcelain to create a look of understated elegance. Both rooms are dominated by pleasantly simple fireplaces and built-in cupboards, which have been painted inside and filled with a colourful array of Chinese export porcelain and metal objects. The cupboards are thus made into a feature, the

doors hanging open to reveal the contents. A loose evocation of the eighteenth century is there, a period explored by Mr Mlinaric in his justly famous restoration work for the National Trust.

The Dining Room (opposite) has light fresh colours and a pretty landscape in the overmantel is part of the comfortable countrified atmosphere. A late-eighteenth-century mahogany breakfast table is surrounded by curvaceous decorated chairs in the style of the early part of that century.

In the Sitting Room (above) an unusual standing oil lamp has been electrified and placed next to an early-nineteenth-century Anglo-Indian chair. The boldly patterned carpet and brass table conjure up the idea of the British Empire and travel abroad, as so often expressed in English country houses.

This is all so typically English that one looks for the discordant note, an ugly souvenir or some grotesque object. They are naturally not there – and this is the difference between a decorator's carefully styled room and one evolved by the owner himself.

Charleston Manor
The Former Sussex House of
Vanessa Bell

THERE is something about these rooms which suggests both the best and the worst of English decoration, and it is irresistible as well as slightly repellent. There is certainly a naïve quality, a schoolroom exultation in the joy of vivid effects, bold strokes and lush patterns. But it is a very knowing naïvety. The colours are more subtle than those of the fairground or the decorated barge, the forms and patterns being more delicate than our almost extinct 'folk-art'. It reflects a painter's urge to colour everything in sight.

Charleston Manor is an eighteenth-century farmhouse nestling in beautiful Sussex downland, and was the home of the painters Vanessa Bell and Duncan Grant. Between 1919 and 1939 it was used by them mainly as a 'holiday' house (although in those days that meant all the summer months), but every year Vanessa became more reluctant to leave it and lived there permanently after the Second World War. When she moved to Charleston in 1916 it required an immense amount of work to make it habitable, although such a rambling house could never be made really convenient or even particularly warm – it had no piped water or electricity. Comfort was low on the list of priorities. With the highly developed visual sense of a painter, Mrs Bell gradually added pattern and colour to the low-ceilinged, generously proportioned rooms, using a warm but neutral background of grey distemper to throw the colours out. She devised exuberant geometrical motifs to decorate and link together fireplaces, doors, overmantels, walls and furniture. The rooms were not furnished all at once, instead odd and often unusual pieces of furniture appeared over the years. This is an artist's home: and by the 1940s when Vanessa Bell, Duncan Grant and their daughter Angelica were all painting the smell of paint was everywhere.

Charleston was a meeting place for some of the Bloomsbury set. John Maynard Keynes, Lytton Strachey, David Garnett and Vanessa's sister Virginia Woolf were all frequent visitors – 'Very plain living and high thinking,' was Vita Sackville-West's comment on lunch there. Taken piece by piece the decoration of the rooms has little impact, but it is all done in the confident and individual style that is characteristic of Bloomsbury taste. In Raymond Mortimer and Dorothy Todd's *The New Interior Decoration* of 1929 it is amazing to find Grant's painted decoration of a Cambridge don's rooms featured amongst the austere lines of Le Corbusier and the Bauhaus. Todd summed up the look as something uniquely British in an essay *The Modern Interior* published in the same year: 'a compromise characteristic of the British temperament is being effected which does not break too ruthlessly with the time-hallowed domesticity of London. The Englishman will be allowed to remain in his castle and not be turned violently into his steam-ship or electric yacht.'

There is nothing in Charleston to suggest the twentieth century of Cubism or Expressionism, or even the new forms of design. The peculiar Englishness of such rooms as these is emphasized by Dorothy Todd: '. . . such as Mr Duncan Grant, Mrs Clive Bell, Mr Douglas Davidson, Mr Alan Walton and Mr McKnight Kauffer have produced a style of decoration suitable for the eighteenth-century houses which are still such a delicious feature of British civilization. But they will never think of copying a Louis XV sofa or a Beauvais tapestry. They rather seek to discover and isolate what was ultimately essential in the eighteenth century and re-invigorate that spirit with the oxygen of today.'

At Charleston the results of this approach are quite unique. In front of the Dining Room fireplace (opposite) is an enormous table made bright by the application of a blobby form of decoration. An Italian painted side table gives a dash of exoticism as does the construction of the lampshade, like some antique Roman pot on display. The arrangement of a few objects in the Sitting Room (pages 138–9) is reflected in Vanessa's still-life of them, set against a wall freely decorated with a design resembling a feathery Paisley pattern. Grant's mural above the fireplace is surprisingly moving both in its directness and because of the oddity of finding such a subject in this house. And there is much here that is odd: Grant and Bell even painted the feathers of the white chickens in the yard, as well as the woodwork, furniture and paintings.

The appeal of this Bloomsbury-decoration was short-lived, for the British are quickly bored of intellectual snobbery and there was a great deal involved here: 'On my first afternoon I proudly hung a reproduction of Van Gogh's "Sun-flowers" over the fire and set up a screen, painted by Roger Fry with a Provençal landscape, which I had bought inexpensively when the Omega workshops were sold up. I displayed also a poster by McKnight Kauffer and Rhyme Sheets from the Poetry Bookshop, and, most painful to recall, a porcelain figure of Polly Peachum which stood between black tapers on the chimney-piece . . . but it was not until Sebastian, idly turning the page of Clive Bell's *Art*, read: "Does anyone feel the same kind of emotion for a butterfly or a flower that he feels for a cathedral or a picture?" "Yes, *I* do!" that my eyes were opened' (Evelyn Waugh, *Brideshead Revisited*, 1945).

Charleston Manor

The Sitting Room

Brief Notes on some Designers and Architects mentioned in the Text

ROBERT ADAM (1728–91)   Together with his brother James (1732–94), he created a light neo-Classical style of architecture and interior decoration. Trained by his architect father in Edinburgh, then in Rome where he was in contact with Clérisseau and Piranesi, Adam made an extensive study of Roman decoration and colouring. The result of his researches and training is to be seen in the decoration of Kedleston Hall (pages 38–9), Syon House (pages 40–3) and Nostell Priory (pages 46–9). At Nostell the furniture by Chippendale is a particularly successful example of the Adam style. Adam also designed in the Gothick manner at Alnwick (pages 72–3), but his reputation rests on virtuoso adaptions of Roman styles and motifs for a remarkable variety of buildings and interiors in town and country.

GIOVANNI BAGUTTI (1681–c.1730)   Italian master plasterer whose elaborate work can be seen at Ditchley Park (page 35).

SIR CHARLES BARRY (1795–1860)   Architect of the Palace of Westminster in a revival of the English Perpendicular style. He also practised in the more domestic surroundings of Highclere (pages 58–9) and Toddington and his versatility extended to neo-Renaissance architecture as seen in the Travellers' and Reform Clubs in London.

MARTIN BATTERSBY (1919–82)   *Trompe-l'oeil* painter, decorator, textile and stage designer. He was an early exponent of the *Art nouveau* revival and the author of books on this and on decoration in the 1920s and 1930s.

WILLIAM ARTHUR SMITH BENSON (1854–1928)   Metalworker, architect and designer. A collaborator of William Morris who encouraged his work, Benson produced a range of designs through his own factory for Morris & Co.

LANCELOT 'CAPABILITY' BROWN (1716–83)   Exponent of 'natural' landscaping of parklands and gardens.

WILLIAM BURGES (1827–81)   Architect and designer in a lavish interpretation of a medieval Gothic style. Cardiff Castle is a triumph of his romantic medievalism.

THOMAS CHIPPENDALE (1718–79)   The son of a Yorkshire carpenter, he became a successful businessman in charge of large workshops supplying all the necessities of house furnishing and decoration. His three editions of *The Gentleman and Cabinet Maker's Director* (first edition, 1754) show a wide variety of designs in Gothick, *chinoiserie* and a light Rococo, but some of his finest work was done under Adam's influence at Nostell (pages 46–9), a masterful display of marquetry and carving in the neo-Classical style. His son Thomas (1749–1822) worked with him and, after his death, carried on the family business.

HUGH CLIFFORD-WING (born 1914)   Decorator who began his career with the old-established firm of Trollopes in the early 1930s. His diverse range of styles was undoubtedly a result of the extensive training and experience acquired in such a huge firm and his work has included the royal palaces in Athens and Nepal, yachts, castles, Greek villas and houses in Norway as well as offices and houses in England.

WELLS COATES (1895–1958)   Architect and designer. He was in partnership with Patrick Gwynne from 1935 to 1938 (when 'The Homewood', illustrated on pages 116–17, was completed). An exponent of the most recent designing techniques and of modern design and architecture, Coates was interested in simple mass-housing experiments, but remains most famous for his work at the BBC headquarters at Broadcasting House, and the Lawn Road Flats in Hampstead, London.

COLEFAX & FOWLER   Founded by Lady Colefax in collaboration with the London dealers Stair and Andrew in 1934, joined by John Fowler in 1938, and acquired by Nancy Lancaster in 1950, this London firm of decorators has come to symbolize a uniquely English form of decoration based on the distinctive styles of its influential owners.

JEAN DUNAND (1877–1942)   Swiss-born metal craftsman who worked in France, he made an extensive study of the use of lacquer and enamel. His vases, panels and furniture are particularly prized by collectors of the products of the 1920s and 1930s.

PETER CARL FABERGÉ (1846–1920)   Working in Russia, this master goldsmith and jeweller had extensive workshops supplying luxuriously elegant jewellery, jewelled enamelled objects and carved hardstone pieces to his shop. His Easter eggs for the Czarina were a particularly triumphant blend of metalwork, enamelling and jewellery.

JOHN FOWLER (1906–77)   One of the most influential decorators of the twentieth century, he had an extensive knowledge of English decoration throughout the centuries, and his use of textiles, furniture and colour could achieve spectacular effects in a modern idiom based upon this knowledge. A partner of Sybil Colefax and Nancy Lancaster, Fowler produced a wide variety of work ranging from fresh interpretations of eighteenth-century ideas to completely faithful reconstructions of historic interiors for the National Trust.

PATRICK GWYNNE (born 1913)   In partnership with Wells Coates from 1935 to 1938, he is one of the finest architects and designers to practice in the style of the Modern Movement in England. He has created a relatively small number of buildings since 1938, but all share a remarkably high level of excellence in design and choice of material. Houses for the late Lawrence Harvey in London and California showed his adaptability to surroundings and climate. His restaurant buildings in Hyde Park and the interior of a recently reconstructed flat on Green Park reveal an elegant ingenuity that is rare in modern architecture.

THOMAS HOPE (1796–1831)   Of independent means, Hope was a patron of the arts and an enthusiastic researcher of antique Greek and Egyptian decoration, producing designs for furniture in these styles. He published his influential *Household Furniture and Decoration* in 1807.

BETTY JOEL   Active as a designer and decorator in London during the 1920s, 1930s and 1940s, her vast business included a suburban furniture factory and showrooms at Hyde Park Corner which displayed the latest designs in textiles and furnishings.

WILLIAM KENT (1685–1748)   Architect, designer and decorator. Drawing on Italian styles and influenced by Inigo Jones, he created a unique style that fused all the elements of a lavish Italianate architecture with an English restraint. The resulting triumph of his work can be seen at Houghton (pages 36–7), where the choice of subtle colour and fine woods is set against lush plasterwork and fine carving, with a sprinkling of gilding lending highlights to the massive quality of his work.

MRS NANCY LANCASTER   The American-born former owner of Colefax & Fowler, she has collaborated with Stephen Boudin of Jansen (the Parisian decorators) and John Fowler on the creation of fine interiors in her own houses (including Avery Row, pages 124–7 and Ditchley, page 35). She is generally acclaimed as possessing a unique sense of colour and scale.

BATTY LANGLEY (1695–1751)   Designer and author. His first designs for furniture were in the Palladian manner, but his greatest success was his book *Gothic Architecture improved by rules and proportions in many grand designs of columns, doors, windows.* This was a 1747 reissue of *Ancient Architecture Restored and Improved* (1742) and was the beginning of the revival of the style soon to be known as Gothick.

SIR MERVYN MACARTNEY (1853–1932)   Editor of the *Architectural Journal* and an encylopaedic mine of information on all English architectural styles and details, he was a pupil of Norman Shaw and became part of the generation of architects who created new buildings using a reinterpretation of essentially English vernacular styles. He had many links with members of the Arts and Crafts movement.

KARL BRUNO MATTHSSON (born 1907)   Swedish designer of furniture, especially famous for bentwood designs.

SYRIE MAUGHAM (1879–1953)   Wife of Somerset Maugham, she was generally thought of as the creator of the all-white room. In fact, the range of styles and colours which she mastered show that she had a remarkable eye for colour and balance. Although shapes and styles might be 'antique', furnishings were handled in the most modern way and her upholstery was much admired by John Fowler. She created a look of effortless elegance.

WILLIAM DE MORGAN (1839–1917)   Ceramic designer. An associate of William Morris, he produced plates, vases and especially tiles with patterns derived from a variety of sources – Chinese, Persian, Gothic and Greek pottery.

WILLIAM MORRIS (1834–96)   Dissatisfied with mid-Victorian industrially-produced decorative furnishings and furniture, Morris set out to produce new designs. Wallpapers, textiles and furniture were designed by him, often inspired by the simplicity of sixteenth and early-seventeenth-century designs. His own factory, Morris & Co., produced the goods, but Morris was never happy with industrialization and indulged in impractical socialist musings whilst living well from the profits of his enterprises.

JOHN NASH (1752–1835)   Architect. Trained with Sir Robert Taylor and then became a speculative builder before he was employed by the Prince Regent from 1798. He developed Regent Street from 1811 and the Regent's Park area in a stuccoed neo-Classical style. The Royal Pavilion, Brighton, was rebuilt by him (1815–23), he worked at Royal Lodge, Windsor, and began the reconstruction of Buckingham House (1821) which was still unfinished when George IV died in 1830.

OMEGA WORKSHOPS   Founded by Roger Fry in 1913 with the aim of improving design. Furniture and textiles were designed by such artists as Vanessa Bell and Duncan Grant. The workshops closed in 1920.

AUGUSTUS WELBY NORTHMORE PUGIN (1812–52)   Architect and designer in the neo-Gothic manner, and influential enthusiast for the Gothic revival in England. His work at the Houses of Parliament (1836–37) was preceded by his *Gothic Furniture in the Style of the Fifteenth Century* (1835).

TERENCE ROBSJOHN-GIBBINGS (died 1976)   Worked with Lord Duveen's brother in selling antiques and then became a designer and decorator in the late 1930s, specializing in a modern interpretation of antique Greek interiors and furniture. He also produced designs for elegantly simple modern furniture which could be mass produced.

ANTHONY SALVIN (1799–1881)   Architect and designer. From Gothick to Jacobethan Salvin brought a robust touch to his buildings, often extraordinarily elaborate as at Harlaxton in Lincolnshire, or quietly domestic as at Thoresby Hall in Nottinghamshire. Salvin could also create a more chilling form of architecture as in his 'Normanesque' style at Alnwick (pages 72–3). His interiors are all well proportioned and generally pleasingly inventive.

RICHARD NORMAN SHAW (1831–1912)   Architect. Shaw was one of the most influential architects of the nineteenth century. After attending the Architectural School of the Royal Academy, he trained with G.E. Street, so that his early buildings reflect the style of the Gothic revival. His use of the 'Queen Anne' vernacular marked a new departure in nineteenth-century architecture, and his links with and inspiration of the Arts and Crafts Movement were connected with his study of earlier English styles. His eclectic taste embraced sixteenth-century styles of manorial building and even the neo-Baroque of his last years, as seen in the Piccadilly Hotel, London (1905–8). Just as the 'Wrenaissance' of his earlier years inspired such architects as Sir Mervyn Macartney (167 Queen's Gate), so his neo-Baroque had a profound influence on British building for the next thirty years. He is also credited with the first garden suburb of Bedford Park, London (1877).

SIR JEFFREY WYATVILLE (1760–1840)   Architect of the remodelling of Windsor Castle under George IV (1824–8). He was a nephew of James Wyatt (1747–1813) who was one of the most fashionable architects of his time and a master of the neo-Classical style as well as the romantic Gothick as seen in his designs for Fonthill Abbey. Wyatville added to his name in accordance with early-nineteenth-century pretensions to an ancient lineage and Norman connections, and practised in his architecture a romantic sham medievalism.

Acknowledgements

The authors and publishers would like to express their gratitude to Her Majesty Queen Elizabeth The Queen Mother for graciously permitting the inclusion of the Saloon at Royal Lodge, and to the many other owners of the rooms depicted in this book: Mrs Pandora Astor; Margaret, Duchess of Argyll; The Duke and Duchess of Beaufort; Mona, Countess of Beauchamp; Major Simon Browne; The Earl of Carnarvon; Mr and Mrs Hugh Cavendish; The Marquess of Chomondeley; Mr and Mrs Hugh Clifford-Wing; Lady Diana Cooper; The Ditchley Foundation; The Estonian Legation; R.E.J. Compton Esq. (Newby Hall is open to the public daily from 1 April to 1 October); The Greater London Council (for 18 Stafford Terrace); Patrick Gwynne Esq.; Henry Harpur-Crewe Esq.; David Hicks Esq.; Myles Thoroton Hildyard Esq.; Felix Hope-Nicolson Esq.; The Earl of Iveagh; Mrs Knowles; Mrs Nancy Lancaster; Stephen Long Esq.; The National Trust (for Clouds Hill, Shaw's Corner and Nostell Priory – properties of the National Trust); Bernard Nevill Esq.; Lady Rupert Nevill; The Hon. Nigel Nicolson Esq.; The Duke and Duchess of Northumberland; Sir John Ropner; Anne, Countess of Rosse; Lord St Oswald; The Marquess of Salisbury; Viscount Scarsdale; Sir Sacheverell Sitwell; Sir Tatton Sykes Bart; Sir John Wiggin Bart. Especial thanks are due to *Architectural Digest* for permission to reproduce several photographs included here.

Derry Moore wishes to thank particularly Gervase Jackson-Stops for his advice and the following who also gave valuable assistance: Alec Cobbe Esq., Peter Fleetwood-Hesketh Esq., Sir William Dugdale Bart, Ian Grant, Jane Heyworth, Henry Potts, Gavin Stamp and Mrs West de Wend-Fenton. Michael Pick wishes to thank the members of his family and friends who have provided generous hospitality during the preparation of the book and especially Nigel Logan Esq. in whose Casa Cordillera, Tangier, much of this book was written. He would also like to thank Sarah Bevan for her excellent advice and comments. Both are honoured by the appreciative Foreword by Anne, Countess of Rosse, a notable champion of the English room in all its varieties. They would like to thank all those who allowed their houses to be viewed for the purposes of this book.

Index